THE NATIONAL HISTORY OF FRANCE

EDITED BY

FR. FUNCK-BRENTANO

WITH AN INTRODUCTION BY J. E. C. BODLEY

THE THIRD REPUBLIC

THE NATIONAL HISTORY OF FRANCE

THE THIRD REPUBLIC

BY

RAYMOND RECOULY

TRANSLATED FROM THE FRENCH BY
E. F. BUCKLEY

LONDON
WILLIAM HEINEMANN LTD.

First published 1928

Printed in Great Britain by R. Clay & Sons, Ltd., Bungay, Suffolk.

CONTENTS

CONTENTS

CHAPTER I

THE COLLAPSE OF A THRONE

The news of the disaster. Fall of the Second Empire. Impotence of the legislative body. At the Hôtel de Ville. The new Government. A significant incident. Peace impossible. Bismarck and Jules Favre. The diplomatic and military situation.

O N Saturday the 3rd of September, 1870, the day after the capitulation of Sedan, the news of the disaster began to percolate from various sources into Paris, and the catastrophe, which was as terrible as it was unexpected, created an atmosphere of dejection and amazement which soon developed into frenzy.

The News of the Disaster.

It is true that for some weeks defeat had followed defeat with ever-increasing rapidity. After Reichshofen came Spicheren, followed by Borny, Gravelotte and Saint-Privat. At each encounter with the Germans the French army had been beaten. But these defeats were by no means regarded as irrevocable. On the contrary, it was well known that on two or three occasions, and particularly at Saint-Privat, they might and, if Napoleon's generals had only faced the enemy's fire, certainly would have been turned to victories.

Bazaine was in command of a strong army in the neighbourhood of Metz, the best fortified stronghold in France. Another army, under MacMahon, was stationed at Châlons.

And now, of these two armies, the one entrusted with the vital task of protecting Paris had suddenly been wiped out, swallowed up in a disaster unprecedented in the annals of French military history.

MacMahon and his whole army had been obliged to surrender unconditionally! The Emperor was a prisoner! These were the two pieces of news that fell like a thunderbolt on the capital.

B

No dynasty, least of all that of Napoleon, who was first and foremost a military leader, could possibly survive so terrible **Fall of the** a blow.
Second When a Government falls, its collapse is almost **Empire.** always due not so much to the strength of its enemies as to the weakness and lack of spirit of those entrusted with its defence. Never was a revolution carried out with such ease and simplicity as the revolution of the 4th of September. For the Imperial Government had literally no defenders. The throne suddenly became isolated and collapsed of its own accord, leaving the Emperor in the hands of the enemy, whilst the Empress unhesitatingly chose the path of exile. No one either in the Government or in the circle of the Imperial family contemplated resistance for a single moment, for they were one and all convinced that it would be perfectly useless.

The Imperial power had been laid low in the dust. Who could be found to seize it?

The legislative body, consisting of the elected representatives of the nation, at first seemed destined for the task. But swift **Impotence of** action was imperative, and in moments of crisis **the Legislative** parliamentary bodies are notoriously slow to **Body.** move. They listen to speeches and appoint commissions which discuss and hesitate, wasting time over questions of procedure and private disputes. Meanwhile events move rapidly, and when an effort is made to keep pace with them it is too late.

On the evening of the 3rd of September, as soon as the capitulation of Sedan was known, General de Palikao announced the news in the Palais Bourbon in carefully veiled terms. A short night session was held which was adjourned without having reached a decision.

In the early afternoon of September the 4th the House met again, when Jules Favre brought forward a motion announcing the fall of the Government, and declaring that Napoleon and his dynasty had ceased to reign. Thiers words the motion differently, substituting " vacancy of the throne " for " fall of the Government "; but it amounts to much the same. Whilst the deputies were debating and hesitating, a mob of insurgents, which swelled every minute, had collected before the Palais.

2

THE COLLAPSE OF A THRONE

It was a typical Paris Sunday on a glorious summer day. The fevered mob demanded immediate decisions—the fall of the Government, the establishment of the Republic. Growing impatient at the delay within, they forced the gates of the Palais without much difficulty, and burst into the council chamber. In vain did the leaders of the Left, Gambetta, Jules Favre, Picard, Crémieux, exhort the demonstrators to be calm, and endeavour to make them respect the precincts of Parliament and obtain a legal decision. The crowd grew more and more excited, and most of the deputies, especially the representatives of the Centre and the Right, left the hall. Whereupon President Schneider adjourned the House. The establishment of the Republic was not proclaimed by the legislative body, which had become impotent and too slow to move. In keeping with revolutionary and Jacobin tradition, it was to be proclaimed at the Hôtel de Ville.

It was thither that, cheek by jowl with the insurgents, the leaders of the parties of the Left, the future members of the Government, hastened with all speed—Gambetta, Jules Ferry, Jules Favre, Jules Simon, Crémieux, Pelletan, Ernest Picard.

At the Hôtel de Ville.

Meanwhile the Palace of the Tuileries, from which the Empress had already fled, had, like the Palais Bourbon and the Hôtel de Ville, been occupied by the mob. The foot-guards, under the command of General Mellinet, who had been entrusted with its defence, retired without a shot having been fired, thanks to the coolness and determination of Victorien Sardou, at that time quite a young man, who has described this incident with characteristic animation.

As soon as they reached the Hôtel de Ville, the deputies, afraid of being again forestalled, hastily drew up a list of members of the new Government. It included all the deputies for the Seine district together with those elected in Paris who had chosen to represent a Department. They decided to elect General Trochu President, and endow him with full powers for securing the defence of the realm.

While this list was being hastily drawn up, Henri Rochefort, who was also a deputy for Paris, but whom his colleagues had forgotten, swooped down on them like a whirlwind. His constituents had not been so forgetful, but had hastened to set him free from his detention at Saint-Pélagie. The members of the new Government received him with little enthusiasm, but, by closing their ranks a little, managed to make room for him. Trochu in particular showed considerable hesitation in taking a seat beside him. But, as somebody philosophically remarked, " It is better to have him with us than against us ! "

The new Government, though it was exclusively composed of deputies, was formed independently of the parliamentary Assembly, which from that moment could do **The New Government.** nothing but sink into oblivion. And it did indeed disappear. For from that night the legislative body and the Senate ceased to exist. But whilst the Government came into being at the Hôtel de Ville, the revolutionaries had collected in a neighbouring hall and were also occupied in drawing up a list, including the names of Blanqui, Pyat, Delescluze and Flourens, all of whom were destined to be leaders of the Commune.

This was extremely significant and ominous for the future.

Thus the Government for National Defence appeared from the first to be but a hasty compromise between different and even conflicting tendencies, between the spirit of Parliament and that of the Commune of Paris, between the provinces and the capital. By virtue of some of its members—Trochu, for instance, who was an extremely devout Breton Catholic—it was moderate, extremely moderate, whilst others, like Henri Rochefort, who, as a matter of fact, soon deserted it, were extremists. Thiers, though promising his support, refused to join it, which gave cause for some anxiety. Founded on compromise, it could not fail to possess all the inconveniences and weaknesses of its origin.

An incident which took place immediately after its inception affords the best proof of this. A crowd of workmen who happened to be in the Hôtel de Ville raised a **A Significant Incident.** violent demand for the red flag. They had already hoisted one over the building. Gambetta with considerable difficulty substituted the *tricolore* of '92 and '93. Whereupon a voice from the crowd shouted :

" That is a bastard flag. They are the Bourbon colours ! "

Another added :
" It is a filthy flag ! "
Whereupon a voice from the crowd replied :
" Well, we will wash it ! "

.   .   .   .

As a river springs from its source, so do revolutions derive the characteristics and original qualities which irrevocably determine their fate from the circumstances out of which they arise.

The Revolution of the 4th of September—and this is one of its essential features—was made by the people of Paris, by the gutter. As in the case of the great Revolution, as well as in 1830 and 1848, it was Paris which once more set everything in motion, imposed its own solution, and presented the provinces with the accomplished fact. As soon as the flood was let loose, professional politicians and parliamentary leaders at once tried to stem the tide, to dam it and if possible guide it. But this was by no means easy. These leaders of the Opposition, who suddenly found themselves members of the new Government, felt and continued to feel themselves weighed down by terrible responsibilities. The very charge with which they were entrusted made them incline towards prudence and moderation. Now it is characteristic of revolutions to rush immediately to extremes. Between them and the section of the military forces which raised them to power a gulf is immediately fixed which cannot fail to grow ever wider and wider.

Take, for instance, the Russian Revolution of 1917. This also came into being in the gutter, springing from a sudden alliance between the socialist insurgents and the regiments stationed in the capital, which one after the other went over to the side of the rioters. Members of Parliament, and of the Duma, tried, as in 1870, to direct the movement. They seized the reins of government, or rather imagined they had seized them. For the real power lay not in their hands but outside, in the Soviet, the Council of Workmen and Soldiers, which was immediately formed and was in reality the true master. So true is this, that the Revolution had hardly been accomplished before the Duma disappeared of its own accord. The Soviet alone remained, and dictated its decrees to the Ministers.

Kerensky was its creature and obeyed without a murmur. It pushed the Government towards an ever more extreme policy, which relaxed all military and social discipline, disorganised the country, destroyed the army, and prepared the way for the Bolshevist *coup d'état*.

Owing to the very fact that it was formed at the Hôtel de Ville, the Government of the 4th of September embraced all **Nature of** the traditions and habits of the Revolution. It **the New** was inevitably in favour of continuing the war **Government.** and of prolonging the struggle to the bitter end. A Government formed at the Palais Bourbon, with Thiers at its head, would possibly have decided to put a stop to a war which was not only useless but in any case almost hopelessly lost, and it would have hastened to sign a peace, the terms of which could only become more disastrous the longer it was delayed. Thiers was in favour of making peace at once, and on rational grounds alone he was obviously right.

But the Government of the Hôtel de Ville had no alternative but immediately to prosecute the war to the bitter end, con-script the masses, etc.—all echoes of the Revolution. Owing to its very origin, moreover, this Government was morally bound not to leave the capital even when it was on the point of being besieged.

Both from the military and political standpoint it could not have made a worse mistake than to remain in Paris during the siege. For by so doing it cut itself off from the rest of the country, severed its communications with the provinces, and thus paved the way for that complete isolation which culminated in the Commune. But as for the members of the Government themselves, the idea of leaving the capital never even entered their heads. Gambetta, who alone had any clear conception of the exigencies of the military situation, was in favour of trans-ferring the Government to the provinces, whither he himself repaired after a while. But no one heeded his advice for a moment.

Thus the new Government was established, and, allowing itself to be shut up in Paris, was content to dispatch to the provinces an extremely feeble delegation, consisting of two lifeless old men, with whom it was ultimately able to keep in touch only at intervals. Even in the capital itself its authority was by no means unquestioned. The more advanced elements in the population—those from which the revolutions of the metropolis have always recruited their principal adherents— were already beginning to organise opposition, and were destined to become more and more formidable.

Before proceeding to form any resolutions which might be big with fate in regard to the continuation of the war, domestic policy and the elections, it was incumbent on the Government to examine the situation with all possible speed. This is what sailors call " taking their bearings."

The Prussians would have nothing to do with a peace which was either honourable for France or acceptable to her new **Peace Impossible.** rulers. Both revolutionary and Jacobin in its origin, and therefore reminiscent of '93, the Government of National Defence, as its name implies, had become an established fact. On the 7th of September, three days after the Republic had been proclaimed, Jules Favre, the Minister for Foreign Affairs, addressed the following circular note to the diplomatic representatives :

" The King of Prussia has declared that he is waging war not against France, but against the Imperial dynasty. . . . *We refuse to surrender one inch of our territory or a single stone of our fortresses.*"

But, from the very beginning of the war, Bismarck had made it quite plain that he would demand Strasbourg and Metz.

These two points of view were absolutely irreconcilable. It seemed impossible to effect a compromise. Nevertheless, Jules Favre had two secret interviews with Bismarck at the Château de Ferrières (the 18th and 20th of September).

Nobody could have been less fit to negotiate with the Chancellor than Jules Favre. It is impossible to imagine a more **Bismarck and Jules Favre.** striking contrast than that presented by the characters and temperaments of these two men.

The German, realistic and dry, accustomed only to reckoning with force and facts, and capable of forming a very shrewd judgment of both men and situations at a glance, was a terrible adversary to negotiate with. He was unequalled in his ability to defeat his opponent by hurling the clinching argument at him like a hammer-stroke at the opportune moment. The Frenchman—a lawyer and nothing more (which is little enough when it is a matter not of convincing a court but of disputing with an adversary who not only knows what he wants but wants it with all his might)—was impressionable, incapable of concealing his emotions, and even on occasion went to the length of shedding tears. But what could be worse than a statesman who bursts into sobs at the slightest provocation?

When he inquired what the conditions of an armistice would be, Bismarck immediately presented them to him in writing— the occupation of Strasbourg, of the Vosges fortresses, of one of the forts commanding Paris, and the exclusion of Alsace and Lorraine from voting for the National Assembly.

As the meeting at Ferrières ended in smoke, there was but one alternative left—to fight.

What were the conditions under which the struggle was undertaken?

The Diplomatic and Military Situation. The Government had to make a rapid survey of its diplomatic and military resources.

From the diplomatic point of view the situation could not have been worse. It was decided to send Thiers on a mission to the various capitals, without, however, entertaining any false hopes of his success.

England, where the Liberals under Gladstone were in power, did not regard the defeat of France with altogether unfavourable eyes. Instinctively opportunist and with neither the will nor the desire to foresee the future, she displayed no sort of alarm at the possible consequences of the aggrandisement of Prussia. On the contrary, she regarded any such aggrandisement as likely to secure the balance of power in Europe—a consummation devoutly to be desired.

Austria, had she been free to act, might perhaps have come to the help of France, but she was handicapped in the first place by Hungary, which had become a State within the State, with distinct leanings towards Germany, but even more by Russia, where the Tsar had openly declared that if Austria mobilised he would immediately retaliate with a mobilisation of Russia.

Indeed, with regard to Russia, Bismarck had taken every

8

precaution. His policy here was the most carefully thought out and most successful of all his prolonged diplomatic efforts aiming at the isolation of France. No stone had been left unturned to bring Russia in on his side as soon as the decisive conflict was opened, and he had made admirable use of the situation in Poland, where the foolish and blundering diplomacy of Napoleon III had as usual heaped one mistake upon another.

As for Italy, her interests lay in one direction only—the achievement of national unity and the occupation of Rome, which Napoleon III, with characteristic inconsistency, insisted upon refusing her.

Thus France, with an implacable enemy at her throat, found herself isolated in Europe, without either allies or friends, as Thiers, in the course of a terrible mission amounting almost to martyrdom, found to his cost. Often enough he was received with fair words, but nobody had either the desire or the power to promise him the slightest assistance.

.   .   .   .

Such was the logical conclusion of eighteen years of Imperial government, which proved to be one of the most disastrous, *as far as foreign policy is concerned*, that France has ever had. The chief failing of this government and its policy can be summed up in a sentence—*it had no feeling for French interests*. In his confused imaginings and vapoury visions, supporting first the unity of Italy and then the unity of Germany, Napoleon III never seems for one moment to have inquired how such unity might affect the vital interests of France. He fought all the wars he should not have fought, but failed to engage in the only struggle upon which he should have entered without the smallest hesitation—war against Prussia after the battle of Sadowa.

.   .   .   .

From the military point of view the situation was no better. Only one army corps remained in action, the thirteenth, which after MacMahon's disaster had retreated by a circuitous route through Mézières. The rest consisted of mere fragments and remnants. It is true there was no shortage of men; it was the cadre, arms, organisation, and the high command, that is to say, the essentials of an army, that were lacking.

Only superficial minds could have been deceived by recollections of the great Revolution, when France, with raw recruits, held a coalition of enemies successfully at bay.

In the former case, her enemies, who were on very bad terms with each other, were extremely feeble in their attacks, and allowed the revolutionary forces time to consolidate and gain confidence in themselves and their leaders. Moreover, these troops possessed solid cadres of officers and non-commissioned officers belonging to the *ancien régime*.

Furthermore, as the art of war becomes perfected, and grows more scientific and complicated, it allows of less scope for scrap measures.

Under the Revolution, French territory was hardly invaded at all. In 1870 two formidable German armies were already beneath the walls of the capital.

. . . .

There was one redeeming feature, and one only—the fear, nay, the terror experienced by Bismarck at seeing the war prolonged. This was the one card still held by France. The prolongation of the war might allow time for diplomatic intervention against him, and Bismarck, who was well informed regarding the situation in Europe, was well aware of this. Germany's enterprise, both from the military and the political point of view, was entirely dependent on rapidity, lightning rapidity of action.

This was also the case in 1914.

Accordingly, if the Germans were to be driven to moderate their demands and consent to a reasonable peace, it was necessary to use every effort towards a prolongation of the war. The attainment of a definite object demanded the energetic prosecution of the means.

One man, who was a born leader, had a very clear perception of this—Gambetta. He did his best to rouse and galvanise the country, and to concentrate all its resources on war to the death. Unfortunately the nucleus of generals and officials capable of breathing his energy and political ideas into the military organisation was entirely lacking.

THE COLLAPSE OF A THRONE

BIBLIOGRAPHY.—*General Works.* The leading daily papers and weekly journals, especially *l'Illustration*, a most valuable document. De la Gorce, *Histoire du Second Empire* (1896–1905). E. Olivier, *l'Empire libéral* (1894–1902). G. Hanotaux, *Histoire de la France Contemporaine* (4 vols., 1903–8). A new edition containing fresh material is in course of publication. Zevort, *Histoire de la troisième République* (4 vols., 1896–1901). Larousse, *Histoire Contemporaine de la France* (1913). Lieutenant-Colonel Rousset, *Histoire de la troisième République* (1912). Zevaes, *Histoire de la troisième République* (1926).

Miscellaneous Works. Bismarck, *Pensées et souvenirs* (French translation, 3 vols., 1899). *Mémoires de Bismarck* (edited by Maurice Busch; 2 vols., 1899). *Mémoires du roi de Roumanie* (1905). J. Simon, *Le Gouvernement de la Défense Nationale* (1874). J. Favre, *Le Gouvernement de la Défense Nationale* (3 vols., 1873). Thiers, *Notes et Souvenirs* (1903). Daniel Halévy, *Le courrier de M. Thiers* (1921).

CHAPTER II

THE WAR IN PARIS AND THE PROVINCES. THE NATIONAL ASSEMBLY AND THE TREATY OF FRANKFORT

The siege of Paris. Trochu's plan. Excitement in the capital. The delegation to Tours. Fall of Metz. The armistice. The German Empire. Nature of German unity. The verdict of Foch. The elections. Peace above all. Thiers the leader of the Assembly. The treaty.

WHILST the German armies were investing the capital with a cordon of troops necessarily thin on account of the length of the front, resistance was being organised. Two army corps, one from Mézières and the other hastily composed of reservists, fugitive soldiers, gendarmes,

The Siege of Paris. guards, customs officers and police, constituted the fighting forces. The *garde mobile* and the *garde nationale* provided large numbers of men.

This army was one of quantity rather than quality, though it possessed many good elements. Its value depended upon the leaders entrusted with its command.

The latter, however, and first and foremost Trochu, had no confidence in it. It is essential to bear this in mind, for it explains everything. Professional soldiers, hidebound in their calling, they were convinced that no army worthy of the name could possibly be improvised in this way in a few weeks.

On the morning of the 19th, the day when the German armies had more or less completed the investment of Paris, a grave incident occurred which served to confirm this opinion. The Zouaves, who, under the command of Ducrot, were defending the Châtillon plateau, disbanded, and a troop of fugitives in great disorder reached the gates of the city.

This incident had the most disastrous consequences, for the

12

lack of confidence felt by the leaders in the troops hampered all subsequent operations. It was in vain that Trochu undertook, or rather pretended to undertake, the execution of his plan of campaign; in his heart of hearts *he never believed in the possibility of success.*

There is no recorded instance of a military leader who did not believe in success ever having achieved it.

What was this plan which quickly became an object of derision in Paris? It consisted in making a sortie with the **Trochu's** bulk of the besieged army in a westerly direction **Plan.** in order to join hands with the army of the Loire. When the latter won the victory of Coulmiers, which in other respects was exceedingly ephemeral, Trochu, on the pressing representations of Gambetta, modified his scheme and decided to strike to the south.

The capital mistake of making Paris the pivot of the national defence now at once becomes plain. The French armies were cut in half. In order to unite they were obliged to attack and to take the offensive against an enemy who had had time to entrench himself strongly. An offensive is extremely difficult, well-nigh impossible, with raw recruits, inadequately trained and indifferently officered.

Every one of these sorties eventually failed. There were one or two slight successes at first—Villejuif and the capture of the Redoute des Hautes-Bruyères (23rd of September), Le Bourget (28th to the 30th of October). But they were barren achievements.

The sortie from Champigny, which was the most important of all on account of the numbers engaged, developed into a regular battle (30th of November to the 3rd of December). Ducrot, who conducted it with great energy, found it impossible to break the resistance of the besiegers, and after three days' fighting and suffering appalling hardships in the bitter cold, he was obliged to retreat to the walls of the capital.

The Prussians, with their long-range guns, bombarded the quarters on the left bank of the river, counting on the terror thus produced, which they thought would drive the people to frenzy, so to depress the morale of their leaders as to lead to swift surrender.

13

Similar motives inspired them in 1918 in the Great War.

Whether in diplomacy or in war, the Teutonic spirit shows but little ingenuity of invention, and nearly always resorts to the same methods and processes.

Moreover, it would be a mistake to imagine that in the besieged city the Government was entirely concerned and pre-occupied with the problem of continuing the war. **Excitement in the Capital.** This was very far from being the case. Politics, the excitement in the capital, where all the passions which were destined to lead to the Commune were already fermenting, and the organisation of their forces gave the Government as much anxiety as the Prussians themselves.

There is a Russian proverb which says : " He who seizes the baton becomes a corporal." The men of the 4th of September had seized the baton and indeed held the reins of power, but it was, in Paris at all events, a weak and vacillating power. Regular elections alone could confirm such a Government and place it on a firm foundation.

The question of the elections was accordingly raised without delay. But how were they to be held in the middle of a campaign when two-thirds of the country had been invaded, the capital was in a state of siege, and the extremists were in possession of so much power? This was another result of the mistake made in shutting up the Government, the organ of the national defence, in Paris. From the military point of view the results were disastrous; politically they were equally disastrous.

Ineluctable necessity forced the Government to postpone the elections from week to week, and the discontent thus occasioned in certain quarters in Paris soon developed into exasperation. This discontent and exasperation were given practical expression in the riot of the 31st of October, when a crowd of insurgents forced their way into the Hôtel de Ville with shouts of " No armistice, the elections, the Commune ! " This 31st of October was a day of the greatest importance, for it heralded the serious events which were to take place a few months later. The whole Government were held prisoners. They escaped first by means of a bargaining and later by inaugurating a policy of repression.

14

THE WAR IN PARIS

Since Paris, owing to the original decision from which events followed upon each other with pitiless logic, had been made the centre of resistance, as soon as the capital had exhausted its resources and was obliged to capitulate, the war inevitably came to an end. In vain did Gambetta endeavour to struggle against this ineluctable necessity, in vain did he aspire to continue the struggle. His efforts were fruitless and resulted only in bitter conflict with the other members of the Government, which was ended by his resignation.

Gambetta, who at first had remained in Paris, was sent by the Government to Tours with full powers to organise the **The Delegation to Tours.** resistance. He went by balloon and undertook the direction of the war immediately on his arrival.

Gambetta was a typically Latin statesman, with all his qualities and all his faults. The son of a small Genoese tradesman, who had settled in the south of France, and French by adoption and inclination, he was sent as a young student to Paris by his family, who made the greatest sacrifices for his education. His letters to his father reveal an attractive and generous personality. His oratorical successes won him a reputation in the Quartier Latin, and his speech as counsel in the Bonin case established his fame. Elected a deputy for Paris in 1869, he was obviously the destined leader of republican France, and exerted all his energies towards the safeguarding of her territory. In his case impetuosity and spirit were tempered by good sense, clarity of judgment regarding men and things, and the art of inspiring devotion and affection in all who approached him.

Everywhere that his influence could be directly felt, without the intervention of third parties, in the political and administrative direction of the war, the results were remarkable. The sacred fire which burnt in his breast, his intelligence, and his art in the management of men, overcame almost every obstacle and succeeded in attaining apparently impossible results.

In the direction of military matters, it is true, he was obliged to work through his executive, and here he met with ill-will and mistrust on the part of many of the leaders, who regarded the game as lost.

15

Armies, or something at least resembling them, can be improvised from the most diverse elements, and be provided with more or less efficient material.

But when once these armies have been formed, it is necessary, if they are to be put in a fit state to accomplish their task, to allow them time to become acclimatised to war. But now the demands of strategy, owing once more to the mistake made in the beginning, did not allow of this, but imperiously demanded them to face the most formidable ordeal of being precipitately hurled into action and forced to take the offensive against seasoned and admirably disciplined troops.

Under the command of d'Aurelle de Paladines, the first army of the Loire crossed the river, and winning the victory of Coulmiers (9th November) recaptured Orleans from the Germans. Possibly a younger and more daring general would have turned this success to better account and marched forward.

D'Aurelle allowed the Germans time to recover, whilst the surrender of Metz, on the other hand, set free one of their most powerful armies, which hastened up by forced marches.

From that moment the issue of the war, as the situation everywhere proved, was a foregone conclusion. The French were beaten at Beaune-la-Rolande and Longwy. Orleans was again lost. The army of the Loire was cut in two, whilst the army of the west, under Chanzy, an energetic general, fell back on Le Mans, in the course of a memorable retreat, when the ground was disputed foot by foot and prodigies of valour performed, which nevertheless failed to change the result.

The army of the east under Bourbaki tried to move in the direction of Alsace and the Rhine in order to raise the blockade of Belfort, where Colonel Denfert-Rochereau was conducting a heroic defence, and thus threaten the enemy's lines of communication. Napoleon had made a somewhat similar attempt in 1814 when he tried to fall upon the Allies in the rear and thus wedge them in between his army and Paris.

But once again raw recruits, however brave, found it impossible to cope with a regular and well-disciplined army, especially when the latter also occupied good positions, prepared and strongly fortified beforehand. Bourbaki on his march towards Belfort came up against the enemy's lines at

16

Héricourt and found it impossible to break through. Caught between these lines and another German army under Manteuffel, who had hurried up in pursuit, he was in danger of being surrounded. By some unaccountable oversight, Jules Favre failed to include him in the terms of the armistice, and he had no alternative but to seek refuge in Switzerland.

In the north, which was only of minor importance, Faidherbe, with a small army, won a trifling victory at Bapaume, but in the end he was beaten at Saint-Quentin.

In short, the situation was everywhere the same. Similar causes inevitably produce the same results.

Meanwhile, what had happened at Metz, where Bazaine's defence was destined to have a direct influence on the result of the war?

Capitulation of Metz. As long as this great stronghold of Lorraine refused to capitulate, it held up one of the strongest of the German armies and prevented it from reaching the chief seat of war.

Unfortunately, the general in command was one of the worst military leaders to whom Napoleon III, an exceedingly bad judge of men, could possibly have confided so important a task.

The intellectual gifts of Bazaine were on a level with his moral character, which was low indeed. As a young man he had had a certain amount of push and go, but age had robbed him of the few gifts he possessed and made him coarse and heavy. His faults alone survived. His attitude at the time of the Mexican expedition, and his intrigues and machinations should have made him an object of suspicion. But they did nothing of the kind. He was made a Marshal and pushed to the top of the tree. For some unaccountable reason he enjoyed great popularity in the army, which only proves how suspect the popularity of a leader, whether civil or military, should be.

Bazaine did not possess even the most elementary knowledge of his profession. Feeling himself utterly incapable of commanding a large army, he abandoned all attempts to do so. His behaviour at Saint-Privat, where he might have won a brilliant victory, admits of no other explanation. He had but one idea—to retreat into the shadow of the fortress guns and wait.

c

17

Immediately after the capitulation of Sedan he gave up all thoughts of fighting or of saving his army and the country; his one idea was to negotiate. Thus he allowed himself to be drawn into equivocal political parleys with Bismarck which his conscience as a general and his duty as a Frenchman should have forbidden him. As soon as a soldier meddles in such matters he is lost.

Bismarck, who was perfectly clear as to his aims and had but one object—to gain time—afforded him some entertainment with this gossip. Day after day slipped by and rations grew low. Eventually there was but one alternative left— unconditional surrender, dishonourable surrender. And thus the whole of a great army, through the fault of its commanding officer, was obliged to capitulate together with its standards, its officers and its guns which it was only too anxious to use.

After Sedan, Metz : truly France deserved a better fate !

As soon as the capital, where all hope of deliverance had been abandoned and provisions were becoming more and more scarce, was obliged to capitulate, the war, whatever could be said or done to the contrary, was ended.

The Armistice.

The people, who were suffering from the cold and were already threatened with famine, incited by the revolutionary leaders, who every day grew bolder, insistently demanded a sortie, *a torrential sortie*, which would carry all before it. The sortie took place on the 19th of January and failed. After the repulse at Buzenval the revolutionaries grew bolder, and led by Flourens, whom they had set free from imprisonment at Mazas, made an attempt on Sunday, the 22nd of January, to seize the Hôtel de Ville. The National Guard, which had remained loyal to the Government, fired on the insurgents and, for the time being, saved the situation.

This disturbance, of which Bismarck was well informed, naturally had the result of making him harder than ever when negotiations for capitulation and an armistice were opened. Jules Favre presented himself before him at Versailles. The Prussian laid down all his conditions which had to be accepted— an indemnity of two hundred million francs, the disarmament of the line regiments and the fortifications, and the occupation

18

of all the forts. The armistice, concluded on the 28th of January, was binding for twenty-one days. This was the end.

Meanwhile an event of some considerable importance had taken place. On the 18th of January, in the *Galerie des Glaces* at Versailles, the German Empire had been proclaimed. All the confederated German princes had offered the imperial crown to William I, King of Prussia, and promised to regard him as their sovereign lord under the title of German Emperor—*Deutscher Kaiser*.

The German Empire.

The princes of southern Germany, Bavaria and Wurtemberg, had offered slight resistance. But Bismarck, who was not a man to have any scruples regarding means, soon got the better of them. As Frederick II remarked, King Chance once again came to his assistance. Throughout the war it had been consistently, both from the political and the military point of view, on the side of the Germans. Highly secret documents, found in a French castle, placed in their hands the proof of negotiations opened during the years preceding the war between the French Government and certain of the South German States. Bismarck immediately used them to bring pressure to bear on the recalcitrant princes, almost threatening them with blackmail. He informed them that if they did not immediately give way he would publish the documents proving their collusion with France.

Statesmen and diplomatists should make an invariable rule always to burn secret documents committed to their charge if, during a crisis, they are called upon to leave their homes. Neglect of this elementary precaution may cost their connections dear.

In 1914, during the first weeks of the war, a consul-general of the Allies in Beirut was guilty of a similar oversight in regard to papers proving his negotiations with certain well-known Syrians. The Turks seized them and the Syrians were immediately hanged.

And thus the German Empire was founded on the high tide of war and of victory in the palace of the kings of France at Versailles. The fruit of war and of victory, it owed its chief characteristics to this twofold origin. The war out of which it arose, as a river springs from its source, had been willed and planned

The Unification of Germany.

for many a long year, prepared for, hatched and won by Prussia, and consequently it sanctioned and once and for all secured Prussian hegemony over the rest of Germany. Bavaria, Wurtemberg, Baden, etc., etc., had no alternative but to bow their heads before the accomplished fact. Moreover, the physical and moral power which a Germany, united beneath the yoke of Prussia, derived from the victory was such that the people were even quicker than their rulers to congratulate themselves on the unification.

．　　．　　．　　．　　．　　．　　．

The efforts of the Government in Tours, which succeeded in prolonging the war a few months longer, did not fail to fill the Germans themselves with astonishment. Bismarck's *Memoirs* and Moltke's *Souvenirs* bear witness to this : " I hope very soon to be shooting hares at Creissau," the latter wrote to his brother in the early days of October. But the hunting party was postponed for several months, until the following year.

That France, robbed of the whole of her regular army, was able to struggle so long against the invader and keep him constantly on the alert was an unexpected and surprising phenomenon which Moltke and the military leaders found it impossible to explain. It modified and upset all their theories about war.

As a matter of fact the Germans, who are bad psychologists, never have had and never will have the smallest understanding of the spirit, character and temperament of the French people. Not only did they under-estimate their enemy, but, what was even more serious, they were unaware of one of his fundamental characteristics—elasticity and the capacity for recovery.

In 1870, from the moment they had beaten the French armies at Sedan, and afterwards at Metz, they regarded the war as ended. The resistance of the hastily organised troops, raised at a moment's notice by the Government in Tours, utterly disconcerted them. And it was for this reason that von der Goltz paid so striking a tribute to Gambetta.

Forty years later, in 1914, they were guilty of the same mistake. As soon as they had won the fight for the frontiers, they imagined that all was over. Von Kluck, in command of one of the chief German armies, rushed headlong forward, having but one aim and one object in view—to advance rapidly, pushing forward in more or less disorderly marches and neglecting on his right wing, *which was exceedingly vulnerable*, not only the garrison of Paris but also the new army which Joffre had raised there in the course of a few days.

Their General Headquarters made an even greater mistake. In order to silence the clamour of the German squirearchy, furious at seeing their property ravaged by the Russians in East Prussia, they despatched to this extremely unimportant theatre of war, almost on the eve of the great battle, two army corps which, if only they had been on the spot, might have made all the difference to the issue.

These mistakes, which were partly responsible for the French victory, were all founded upon the conviction that after the battles of the first few days France would be incapable of resistance.

Once again the psychology of the Germans was at fault.

The true nature of the war undertaken by the Government of the 4th of September, the spirit in which it was fought, the

The Verdict of Foch. mistakes made, and the inevitable result of these mistakes, defeat, has been clearly explained by one of the greatest soldiers of all time—Marshal Foch.

In his book *La Manœuvre pour la Bataille* he says : " What a different complexion the struggle might have assumed under a Government which, understanding the exigencies of a national war, had unanimously turned to the provincial armies, that is to say, the armies of France, and, separating the fate of Paris from that of the country, had realised that resistance was possible here where the sea for the supply of arms and corn, the soil for furnishing men, and all the resources of nature lay ready to hand, as well as plenty of room to fight and manœuvre in spite of the enemy.

" Faced by such a Government what could our adversaries have done except cross the Loire and, with an exhausted army, enter upon a campaign of methodical conquest of territory over a distance of 375 miles as far as our southern frontier, hoping that fortune would remain favourable as far as the

Pyrenees, which would perhaps have been asking too much of her.

" It is for this that Gambetta has won his place in history, for he understood that the central power of a State does not reside in the capital but in the whole nation with its resources of every description, and that while the former consisted of two million souls on the point of being surrounded, the latter was made up of thirty-six millions still free to manœuvre and attack, and upon this basis he organised the national war, the struggle to the death.

" Unfortunately, after having organised the national armies, he was unable to conduct a national war, and escape from the belief which bound up the fate of the country with that of the capital. To these armies, which he had raised as if by magic, he set as their foremost task the relief of Paris, and thus exhausted them by forcing them to attack a large, well-disciplined and victorious host, to conduct an offensive beyond their strength, and attempt to reach an immediate and final decision of which they were incapable across country (la Beauce) most unfavourable for young and untried troops.

" How different would have been a carefully planned scheme of national defence, aiming first and foremost at disputing inch by inch the territory which furnished supplies and ultimately at securing the deliverance of the country. The execution of such a scheme would at first have meant acting on the defensive, the only form of warfare possible for raw recruits, inasmuch as it exploits space, time and territory, and denies a decision by battle to an enemy who requires decisive victories in order to break resistance and thus conquer the country. In the end it would have meant an offensive conducted by seasoned troops whose confidence had been restored against an enemy dispersed over a necessarily extended front, exhausted by futile efforts, and, on account of the length of the lines of communication, suffering from a shortage of supplies. Such were the tactics that should have been practised.

" For this task, owing to lack of special knowledge, the great patriot, the efficient organiser, did not suffice. As with everything else, military institutions and conceptions only succeed when they are built upon a solid base—in this case a thorough acquaintance with the nature of war and of fighting forces. It is because he was familiar with both of these that Carnot, in his day, was able from the principle of conscription to give birth to victory."

THE NATIONAL ASSEMBLY AND THE TREATY OF FRANKFORT

As soon as the armistice was signed and the war ended, it became necessary to establish a *de jure* Government in place of the *de facto* system in existence, and to convoke the National Assembly. The elections were fixed for the 8th of February, 1871, and took place in an atmosphere of sad resignation. The separation between the capital and the provinces, foreshadowing the Commune, became more and more pronounced. Paris, still excited by a struggle in which she had been called upon to make heavy sacrifices and had lost and suffered much without gaining anything in return, was in favour of continuing it. She protested against any signature of peace.

The Elections.

A large majority in the provinces, however, declared themselves in favour of an immediate cessation of hostilities on any terms. The Prussians, under whose very eyes the elections were being held, were not deceived. They knew they could make almost any demands they chose. And thus Thiers, who was to conduct the negotiations, had his hands tied from the beginning.

In Paris an alliance, or what would to-day be called a cartel, was formed between the various groups of the Republican party. In addition to an insignificant number of moderates, the members of the coalition consisted of radicals, socialists and revolutionaries. The large towns, especially in the east and south-east, also elected Republicans. Most of the country districts, the "rural" districts as they were to be called a few weeks later, with a touch of disdain, instinctively searched for leaders. The Bonapartists, being entirely discredited, and left with no alternative, returned to their old allegiance, rallying round the Royalist personages whose local influence was still very great— lords of the manor who still lived on their estates, and the rich and moderately well-to-do bourgeois. It was in their favour too that the clergy, both bishops and priests, also exercised their influence, so that out of six hundred and thirty representatives, a bare third was Republican. In addition to some thirty Bonapartists, the remainder, about four hundred, was divided between the two branches of Royalists—the Orleanists and the Legitimists.

It would nevertheless be a mistake to suppose that the country, by voting in this way, gave its formal consent to a swift if not immediate re-establishment of the monarchy. This consent was far more apparent than real. The question that overshadowed all others was that of peace, and the Royalist candidates were openly in favour of peace, whilst the Republicans, on the contrary, were for war to the bitter end. The question as to what regime should be established was of quite secondary importance. Moreover, among the Royalists who were elected, large numbers were chosen, not in their capacity as Royalists, but because their local influence, their wealth and their reputation made them the natural holders of the office.

Peace above all.

Unless this important point is remembered, it would seem astonishing that the Royalist party, with such a huge majority, should not, in spite of the disagreement between its leaders, have succeeded in re-establishing the monarchy. But this would have been little short of miraculous, and history does not deal in miracles.

As plural candidature was not forbidden, a certain number of representatives, more particularly men of note, stood for several departments. Thiers was elected in twenty-six, Gambetta and Trochu in nine. This meant a kind of plebiscite in favour of certain leaders.

Hardly had the Assembly met at Bordeaux than all eyes were turned to Thiers. By a spontaneous and unanimous decision he was recognised as the natural leader. The great victor in the elections, he was destined to be the mouthpiece of the whole of France.

Thiers, the Leader of the Assembly.

Thiers at this time was seventy-three. His physical and mental energy, his powers of resistance, and his vivacity of spirit had remained intact, and age instead of diminishing had increased his power, strengthening his judgment, and making him less volatile and impressionable. He was like old wine which improves with age. His chief characteristic was rapidity

24

of thought, whilst his profound study of history, which, like a sort of mental gymnastic, had developed his mind, endowed him with a vast mass of knowledge, and made him capable of mastering with ease the most complex and varied questions— political, economic, financial and military.

When, during the last years of the Restoration, this young southerner arrived in Paris from his native town of Marseilles, after having completed his studies at Aix, he pushed his way in the capital like a man who has no time to lose but, conscious of his superiority, has made up his mind to reach the front rank with all possible speed. His energy, confidence and tact were phenomenal! Louis-Philippe, whose accession he helped to secure, was quick to commandeer his services, and the political and ministerial life offered him by the constitutional monarchy of July provided the field of activity of which he had always dreamed. This activity amounted on occasion to agitation, for Thiers was inclined to imagine that things were going very badly if he were not the leader, and he was not always a good leader. At moments of crisis he was lacking in balance and judgment, whilst his rivalry with Guizot helped to shake a throne which was already tottering and possessed no solid support.

Thiers and Guizot, as it has been aptly remarked, were the sort of men who would have played whist on a whale's back. When the whale dived both men were in the water and the country with them.

The accession of Napoleon III sent him back to his historical studies. In the last days of the Empire he became a member of the legislative body. From that time forward, and especially after Sadowa, he was continually prophesying disaster, but his utterances were as ineffective as those of Cassandra. His shrewdness, his vast political experience, his authority and good sense had all been matured by age. Nevertheless, when it came to negotiating with Bismarck, these qualities weighed but lightly in the balance. In order to cope with so terrible an adversary, greater realism and hardness were required; a younger man would perhaps also have been more suitable. At all events the cards he held were not good, though used with discretion they enabled him to play a safe game.

25

THE THIRD REPUBLIC

The negotiation of a treaty is like a battle, which, to use Marshal Foch's expression, is won by whatever remains over. The victory goes to the party which can hold out to the last minute, clinging, so to speak, like grim death to every branch.

In the parleys that took place, Bismarck seemed master of the situation, with the power to impose all his demands. As a matter of fact this was not altogether the case. His opponent could always retort : " You are asking impossibilities. I shall resign and go away, and leave you to get on as best you can ! "

The prolongation of the war had from every point of view, political, military and diplomatic, placed Germany in a very awkward position. The danger of foreign intervention was an ever-present possibility, either on the part of Austria or of England, whom Bismarck feared above all. Moreover, France having already lost so much, and being threatened with yet further losses, prolonged resistance would hardly cost her more.

But in order to play this card the determination to prolong resistance was imperative. Yet for some considerable time, if not from the very beginning, Thiers had believed this to be impossible. Gambetta, on the other hand, was more clear-sighted, though it must be acknowledged that a large majority in the country were of the same opinion as Thiers. They wanted peace at any price, which made the conduct of negotiations far from easy.

Bismarck, as was afterwards ascertained from a fairly reliable source, if he had felt there was any determination on the part of his adversary to continue the war, would **The Treaty.** perhaps eventually have consented to return Metz. As it was, Thiers only succeeded in obtaining Belfort.

Alsace-Lorraine, five milliard francs, which at that time seemed a colossal, impossible sum, the occupation of France until the whole amount had been paid—such was the price of peace ! It was impossible to imagine anything worse !

The preliminaries were signed at Versailles on the 20th of February and were ratified on the 1st of March by the National Assembly in Bordeaux. The treaty was concluded at Frankfort on the 10th of May, 1871.

THE WAR IN PARIS

BIBLIOGRAPHY.—See preceding chapter.
Great History of the War by German General Headquarters. *Der Deutsch-Französische Krieg* (5 vols., 1872–81). Von Moltke, *Gesch. Deutsch-Französischer Krieg* (1891). H. Welschinger, *La Guerre de 1870* (2 vols., 1910). A. Chuquet, *La Guerre 1870–71* (1895). E. Gay, *La Guerre en Province* (1908). von der Goltz, *Gambetta et ses Armées* (1877). Trochu, *Œuvres Posthumes : Le Siège de Paris* (1896). A. Ducrot, *La Défense de Paris* (4 vols., 1875–8). Faidherbe, *La Campagne du Nord* (1871). Chanzy, *La Campagne 1870–71* (1872). J. D'Arcay, *Notes Inédites sur M. Thiers* (1898). Ed. Simon, *L'Empereur Guillaume et son Règne* (1886). Falloux, *Mémoires d'un Royaliste* (1888). Ottokar Lorenz, *Kaiser Wilhelm und die Begründung des Reichs* (Jena, 1902). Marquis de Dampierre, *Cinq Années de vie Politique*.

CHAPTER III

THE COMMUNE AND ITS CONSEQUENCES

The causes of the Commune. The removal of the guns. A precedent. Thiers' decision. Jules Ferry at the Hôtel de Ville. The Government of the Commune. The officials of the Commune. The programme of the Commune. The acts of the Commune. Versailles *versus* Paris. Entry of the Versailles army. The excesses of the Communists. The fury of the struggle. Suppression of the Commune.

THE COMMUNE

AFTER war with the foreigner came civil war. Hardly had the former been terminated than the latter, a far more terrible struggle, broke out.

The Communist insurrection arose first and foremost from the destruction of equilibrium between Paris and the rest of **The Causes of** France, between the capital and the provinces, **the Commune.** which, in consequence of the war, had been completely isolated from each other. Thus they had developed along separate channels, and in the end were even more different, not to say opposed, to each other than they had been at first.

The Commune was the result of many diverse causes, both moral and material. The troubled waters were seething and all alive with fermentation.

At first there was the feeling of having been deceived and furious rage at the peace, which was one of the most grievous and humiliating that could possibly have been conceived—two provinces snatched from France and a huge indemnity. And now, to crown all, came the supreme humiliation—the entry of the Prussians into Paris, which Bismarck, with diabolical cruelty and perfidy, as though he had foreseen and desired the consequences which arose from it, had demanded from Thiers in exchange for the return of Belfort.

28

THE COMMUNE

So it was for this they had fought and endured all the sufferings and privations of a prolonged siege !

This peace, who had been responsible for it ? An assembly of the " rurals," who were enemies of the Republic, and enemies of Paris, of whose supremacy they were jealous and afraid, and of whom they were now more than ever suspicious since they had just installed the seat of Government at Versailles.

It was this bitter and discontented populace, inspired by what has been termed " siege madness," that was now bitten by the propaganda of the old revolutionary parties, the professional agitators and insurrectionaries—Blanqui, Delescluze, Pyat, Valles, etc., the propaganda of the Socialists and the members of the " International " recently founded by the Prussian Karl Marx.

Immediately after the Revolution of the 4th of September these diverse elements had tried to seize the reins of power; they renewed their attempts on the 31st of October, and on this occasion were within an ace of success.

Besides these moral causes there were all kinds of material causes—foolish measures passed by the Assembly, such as authorising the settlement within forty-eight hours of bills the payment of which had been postponed during the siege—this, as a certain journalist aptly remarked, meant " leaving the bailiffs in command "; the failure to deal with the question of rents; the rashness of the monarchist parties, who did not conceal their desire " to strangle the Hussy," that is to say, the Republic, thus arousing the fury of Paris, which was hotly Republican; and the affluence of foreigners of every nation, who had nothing to lose and everything to gain from a state of disorder. Of two of the chief leaders of the Commune, one, Cluseret, maintained he was an American citizen, and the other, Dombrowski, was a Pole.

Finally, and this was most serious of all, the whole of this mob was armed, all too terribly armed. They had rifles and guns in abundance. Arms had been distributed to all who wanted them, and almost to those who did not.

When once the war was over the most pressing duty was to call in these useless weapons, which would soon become dangerous; but this was no easy task. Bismarck proposed to

Jules Favre that the National Guard should be disarmed, and the latter afterwards bitterly regretted not having listened to this suggestion. Complete disarmament, however, could hardly have been carried out without the help of the Prussians, and this, for a French statesman, would have involved heavy responsibility.

. . . .

Peace was signed and the Government and the Assembly were installed at Versailles. Thiers, who apparently felt the necessity of maintaining some connection between the Government and the capital, took up his quarters at the Foreign Office, which he used as a *pied-à-terre*. The bond thus created was weak indeed and it was not long before it snapped.

The German army was about to make its entry into Paris. Hardly was the news made known than the National Guard, **The Removal of the Guns.** in order to prevent the guns which they regarded as *their property* from falling into the hands of the enemy, seized the two artillery parks of Passy and the Place Wagram and conveyed the guns to Montmartre.

A *Central Committee* of the National Guard was immediately formed which issued orders, seized the power and acted as though it were the Government.

These two incidents, the removal of the guns and the formation of a Central Committee, the nucleus of the future Commune, were both equally serious. They were the immediate result of the entry of the Prussians. Bismarck had been very clear-sighted when he had insisted on this entry.

Were these guns to be left in the hands of those who were denying the authority of the Government and were on the point of rebelling against it ? Thiers and his colleagues decided that all work, nay, that even life itself, was impossible as long as this sword of Damocles was hanging over their heads. The guns must be recaptured at all costs—a difficult task whose only hope of success lay in a surprise attack, carefully planned and vigorously executed. And yet both the preparation and the execution of the matter were equally badly handled.

Napoleon, with whose history no one was better acquainted than Thiers, had at the beginning of his career to surmount a similar obstacle. He too was called upon to seize some guns. The memoirs dictated at Saint Helena prove the determined spirit in which the seizure was conducted.

It was on the eve of the 13th Vendémiaire. The sections of Paris, which were playing a part similar to that of the Com-
A Precedent. mune, had rebelled against the Convention, which had at its disposal only a few unreliable troops. Menou, the general in command, was quite inefficient, and suffered a severe repulse.

The Convention immediately cashiered him and looked out for someone to take his place. Some officers and soldiers belonging to the Toulon army proposed Bonaparte, whom they had seen at work. In the midst of great commotion he was made second in command under Barras. Barras, Bonaparte's chief! History is full of such ironies.

As soon as he had received the appointment Bonaparte presented himself at the Tuileries to obtain the necessary particulars from Menou. The army consisted of barely 5000 men. There were forty guns in the park at Sablons in the charge of twenty-five men. We must now quote Napoleon's own words.

" It was an hour after midnight, and the general at once despatched Major Murat, together with three hundred horse, with all speed to Sablons, to fetch the artillery away and bring it to the Tuileries gardens. A moment afterwards it would have been too late. Murat reached Sablons at three o'clock and was met by a column belonging to Lepelletier's section which had just seized the park. But he was mounted and on level ground, and the Sectionaries, thinking that resistance would be useless, retired. At five o'clock in the morning the forty guns entered the Tuileries."

It was with these guns that Bonaparte fired on the insurgents the next day and dispersed them.

. . . .

General Vinoy was much more like Menou than like Bonaparte. His troops, sent out during the night, easily seized the guns. But when they had done so it was discovered that the means to remove them were lacking—they had merely forgotten the horses. And thus the soldiers stood with arms at the order all the morning. The whole effect of a surprise had been spoilt and the National Guard and the insurgents had time to pull themselves together. The general searched high and low for horses. Meanwhile a huge crowd had collected and surrounded the soldiers, who found themselves swamped and overwhelmed. The inevitable result followed. Some of the rank and file of the 88th, one of the regiments of Lecomte's brigade, whom the officers had ordered to fire on their assailants, came to terms with them. Lecomte and his staff were arrested.

The enterprise had failed utterly and the leaders very wisely decided to withdraw their troops.

Thiers, as he himself tells us, had spent the whole morning at the Foreign Office. Here he anxiously awaited news which grew worse from hour to hour. Soon it was not for the guns, of which he had already given up all hope, but for the soldiers that his gravest misgivings were aroused. At last a whole division, marching in orderly ranks, debouched from the Pont de la Concorde. On seeing them Thiers heaved a great sigh of relief.

Thiers, a profound student of history, had devoted much thought to the subject of revolutions.

Thiers' Decision. He had formulated a whole theory on the matter, which he explained of his own free will to his colleagues, and among others to Paul and Jules Cambon, who imparted it to the author of the present work.

In his opinion no insurrection could win the final victory, whatever its initial successes might have been, as long as there was in existence a Government determined to fight it, supported by troops that could be relied upon. The essential pre-requisite was not the capital, as Charles X and Louis-Philippe believed, but the army.

With the army it is always possible to win back the capital. But, on the other hand, when the army can no longer be relied upon, all is lost. Now, a body of troops left for too long in contact with revolutionaries runs the risk of disintegrating. It must be snatched from such contact and reorganised in order to be able to engage in a victorious struggle afterwards.

Thiers gave numerous examples of this—Charles V, Henry III, Mazarin, and lastly Louis-Philippe, who, in 1848, could quite

32

easily have vacated Paris with his troops and returned later on. This is what Windischgrätz actually did in Vienna in the same year and Radetzky at Milan.

Fortified by this doctrine, Thiers decided to retire to Versailles with the forces and the Government.

Meanwhile, Jules Ferry, Prefect of the Seine, together with his brother Charles, remained at the Hôtel de Ville. They were **Jules Ferry at** joined by the two young Cambons, and subsisted **the Hôtel de** in a state of semi-siege at the hands of the in- **Ville.** surgents.

Some of the soldiers threw away their cartridges and hob-nobbed with the demonstrators.

Towards evening, Ferry sent a letter to Thiers, which he entrusted to one of the municipal guard. Hardly had the latter shown his face in front of the Hôtel de Ville than he was shot down. A second messenger suffered a similar fate.

A council was hastily held. Ferry was in favour of sticking to his post and allowing himself to be assassinated in his " curule chair." His companions persuaded him of the futility of such a sacrifice, and he and his friends escaped secretly that night by way of the quays and sought refuge in the *mairie* of the first *arrondissement*, in the Place Saint-Germain l'Auxerrois. In the presence of the mayor they reviewed the situation. They still had a battalion of *gardes mobiles*, who, at the time of the disturbances of the 31st of October, had retaken the Hôtel de Ville from the insurgents under Flourens. The two Cambons questioned each of the officers in turn to find out whether they would consent to march out again. They refused, because, as they explained, they were not sure of their men.

Meanwhile, one of the mayor's assistants had revealed the presence of Ferry to the insurgents, who came in a mass and besieged the *mairie*. Men with lanterns subjected all who left it to a minute examination. Ferry and his brother, as also the Cambons, made their escape through a small court adjacent to the church of Saint-Germain l'Auxerrois, the door of which they prevailed upon the sacristan to open. Just as they were leaving, the church clock rang the tocsin. " Monsieur le Préfet," said the priest, " this is the bell that rang on the Night of Saint

Bartholomew. God grant that the coming night will not witness similar tragedies."

. . . .

Thiers' decision has often been criticised. He has been accused by some of having abandoned Paris to the rioters, and of having thus rendered possible all the outrages and horrors of civil war. Others, going even further, maintain that he desired such a war because he wanted bloodshed.

As a matter of fact Thiers, to anyone who understood his spirit and temperament, could not have acted differently. If a fulcrum is necessary to raise the world, for fighting an army is required. Now, had he remained in Paris, he would at any time have run the risk of being without an army.

Thus the removal of the Government to Versailles left the insurgents masters of the capital.

General Lecomte and another general, Clément Thomas, were recognised by the mob and shot the same day at Montmartre without trial. The assassination of these two men, for this is what it amounted to, gave the struggle from the very beginning that stamp of pitiless ferocity which it was destined to bear until the end.

As a contemporary writes : " Between Paris and Versailles there was a great gulf fixed." All attempts at reconciliation on the part of the mayors of Paris, the Freemasons and others failed, and were bound to fail, since the good-will of a few individuals had been broken by the fatal force of circumstances.

In Paris the Government of the Commune was more or less successfully established. The elections took place on the 26th **The Govern-** of March. The Paris deputies, the mayors and **ment of the** their assistants advised the electors to record **Commune.** their votes and thus sanction the authority of the future representatives. The central committee of the National Guard resigned its powers in favour of the new deputies.

On the 28th of March, in an atmosphere of feverish excitement, the results were proclaimed in the square before the Hôtel de Ville in the presence of a huge crowd. A red flag hid from view the equestrian statue of " the only King whose memory still lived in the hearts of the people." The members of the central committee, the abdicating power, some in black coats and white ties, others in the uniform of the National Guard, with a red sash round the waist, were on a platform. Military bands played the *Marseillaise* and the *Chant du Départ*. Everybody, civilians and military alike, congratulated each other. The latter were clad in the most varied uniforms— republican guards, estafettes, national guards, sharp-shooters, Garibaldians in red shirts with daggers in their belts and feathers in their hats, not to mention one or two *cantinières* in short skirts with a barrel slung over their shoulders.

In its external manifestations the Commune had a good deal of comic opera about it. But in Paris the theatre is nearly always to the fore.

The executive council consisted of 90 members, one for each quarter. The representatives of the revolutionary party **The Personnel** held a large majority. The moderates sent in **of the Com-** their resignation or failed to take their seats. **mune.** As is nearly always the case, the current which was to bear this assembly towards a policy of extremes and solutions of the utmost violence very quickly became apparent. The two men who headed the movement were Delescluze and Félix Pyat.

At the first elections, held on the 26th of March, 224,000 votes were registered, or over half the number of those entitled to the suffrage. This was a big proportion when it is remembered that large numbers had left the city.

At the final elections held on the 18th of April only 53,000 took part in the voting. Thus in less than three months the number of voters had decreased by four-fifths. There could not be a more conclusive proof that the majority in Paris felt they had been deceived.

An upright man, like Rogeard, the famous author of the *Propos de Labenius,* who was honesty personified, refused to accept this mockery of an election and sent in his resignation.

In the bosom of the executive committee a hot discussion on this subject took place between Delescluze, Pyat and Vermorel.

Nothing could have been more confused and nebulous and above all more fantastic than this programme. It contained a little of everything—the ideas of Rousseau, old revolutionary doctrines and socialistic theories. The *Declaration of the French People*, which was a sort of official manifesto, claimed " that the absolute autonomy of the Commune should be extended to all parts of France."

The Programme of the Commune.

It maintained that " the unity which up till that time had been imposed by the Empire, the Monarchy and by Parliamentary Government, was nothing less than a despotic, unenlightened and arbitrary or onerous centralisation.

" Political union such as Paris desired meant the voluntary association of all local bodies capable of taking the initiative, the spontaneous and free co-operation of all individual energies towards a common goal—the well-being, freedom and security of all."

These phrases have but little meaning, and the same can be said about all the documents of the Commune.

If there was a little of everything in the programme, there was also a mixture of everything in the officials, the ideas which animated it and the passions that directed it. It was at once a supporter of unity and of federation, of individualism and of socialism. Georges Duchesne, a contemporary journalist, gives us the following description of these conflicting tendencies :

" Hardly had Paris escaped from the talons of the lawyers than she fell into the hands of the idealists, as it were out of the frying-pan into the fire. The members of the Commune represented a number of sects with more or less barbaric names—Communism, Babouvisme, Collectivism, Individualism, Jacobinism, etc."

This so-called free Government quickly proceeded to destroy almost all freedom. The number of newspapers that were either suspended or seized grew day by day. Citizen Raoul Rigault, a ragamuffin who was pushed into the Prefecture of Police, heaped one arbitrary measure on another as fancy guided him.

The Acts of the Commune.

On the 21st of April, on the pretext of looking for hidden arms, the Gas Company's premises were searched. As the

36

search yielded no result, the till containing two hundred thousand francs was seized.

It is true this sum was returned on the following day. A number of priests and monks were arrested, certain of the churches were closed for worship, and religious establishments and convents were searched.

Meanwhile with great pomp and ceremony they set fire to the woodwork of the guillotine, oblivious of the fact that this was not the only instrument capable of speeding a man violently from life to death. A large gang of engineers, foremen and labourers took in hand the task of demolishing the Colonne Vendôme. This was the theatrical side of the Commune.

In all these acts there was a mixture of tragic gravity and childishness.

In all questions of money, the officials, it must be confessed, were on the whole extremely honest. Private property was almost always respected, and no attempt was made to touch the huge reserves of the Bank of France.

All efforts at conciliation having proved futile, a decision could only be reached by force, and a struggle was entered upon **Versailles ver-** which grew ever more terrible and atrocious the **sus Paris.** nearer it approached its end. Between Versailles and Paris it was war to the knife. But the result of the conflict was never in doubt. The Government of Versailles had the whole of France behind it. The isolated communistic outbreaks which took place in some of the large provincial towns, which followed the example set by the capital, were fairly quickly suppressed.

The Versailles Government possessed both organisation and discipline. The Paris Commune was incapable of securing either the one or the other.

Thiers, who had always felt a passionate interest in military matters, had undertaken the reconstruction of the army, which was destined to get the better of the Commune. The divisions withdrawn from Paris were re-equipped and imbued with a new spirit. The men were well fed and kept apart in comfortable quarters or barracks and provided with excellent cadres. The prisoners of war, both officers and soldiers, whom the signing of peace had set free, were arriving in large numbers.

Thiers appointed Marshal MacMahon Commander-in-Chief. Ladmirault, Cissey, Clinchant and Vinoy, with their respective corps, were sent round about Paris and proceeded to invest the city. Thus the second siege began.

The Paris army, a formidable body which grew larger every day, was an army only in name. And it was here that the innate incapacity of an insurrectionary Government to create a real military force for itself in a short space of time became glaringly apparent. If it does not find it ready made, the improvising of such a body is well-nigh impossible for it.

It was not in quantity that the Commune lacked soldiers, but in quality. At the beginning the number of its troops was considerably larger than those of Versailles. The National Guard, the organisation of which was undertaken by Cluseret, consisted of between 150,000 to 200,000 men, though this figure is purely theoretic. It was made up of mobile and garrison companies, the latter of which were preferred by the majority, whilst the former dwindled to an ever smaller minority. There was no cohesion, no discipline, and no confidence between the men and their leaders, or *vice versâ*.

The famous grand sortie of the 3rd of April was a failure. From Mont Valérien, which had remained in possession of the Versailles troops, a cannonade stopped short one of the columns commanded by Bergeret and Flourens. The latter, surrounded in a house in Rueil, was killed by an officer of the gendarmerie with his sword. The column operating to the south in the direction of Châtillon and Meudon was likewise repulsed after some initial success. Duval, who was in command of it, was made prisoner and shot.

Thus during the very first engagements the Communist army was deprived of its positions and some of its leaders. Moreover, it lost all hope of beating the Versailles army. In vain did the central committee from day to day change its generals, among whom they suffered terrific losses. Cluseret, a Frenchman who had become an American citizen after the War of Secession, Dombrowsky, a Pole who had served in the Russian army as a Staff officer, Rossel, a French officer who had escaped from the army in Metz, were each in turn given their chance; but in a moment they were worn out and discredited. In the end, despairing of their cause, the Commune gave the command to Delescluze, a civilian.

This holocaust of generals reminded the Parisians of the couplet of 1848 :

> " On sait d'une façon réelle
> Combien elle croque de gigots.
> Mais nul ne sait encore c' qu'elle
> Dévorera de généraux ! " [1]

After the abandonment of Fort Issy on the 9th of May, for which Rossel was accused of incompetence and even of treason, the fort of Vanves was occupied on the 14th of May by the Versailles forces.

In order to avoid the horrors of a bombardment and the shedding of blood, and above all the weariness of a regular siege, Thiers planned the seizure of one of the gates with the help of the not altogether disinterested complicity of one of the besieged. A certain man offered, in return for a fairly large sum, to deliver up one of the gates. Part of the Versailles army silently occupied the Bois de Boulogne during the night, in preparation for entering Paris as soon as the signal was given. Thiers was present in person by the side of General Douai. But the promised signal was not received, and at dawn the troops had to be withdrawn and the operation abandoned.

A week later, on the 21st of May, when it had been decided to make an assault two days later, Ducatel, an outrider in the service of the municipality, waved a white handkerchief from the ramparts near the Saint-Cloud gate. Some of the besiegers advanced and were informed by him that the gate was undefended. Troops accordingly entered without meeting with any resistance. Thiers, who was posted on the heights of Mont Valérien with Marshal MacMahon, noticed through his glasses an unusual movement of troops.

Entry of the Versailles Army.

A quarter of an hour later the good news was confirmed. A division of Douai's corps in two columns broke through the fortifications.

---

[1] "One knows pretty well the number of legs of mutton it consumes, but no one can yet say how many generals it will devour ! "

And thus the whole of the Versailles army entered Paris. Doubtless, if it had made a bold and rapid advance and taken the insurgents unawares, the capital would quickly have fallen into its hands, if not in a few hours, at least in a few days. But it advanced slowly and methodically with excessive caution, as the leaders were afraid that most of the quarters had been mined.

Thus the insurgents had time to prepare a war of barricades, to carry the most violent resolutions, and to put into execution the criminal designs of lunatics and madmen.

Their resistance was conducted without any attempt at co-ordination or method on the mere initiative of individuals.

Delescluze, the most violent of them all, endeavoured to rekindle enthusiasm and fight to the bitter end.

Thus when all seemed over a new siege began, more terrible and desperate than the first. Quarter by quarter had to be won and street warfare was opened.

The Commune in defeat was guilty of the worst excesses. Hostages, such as the Archbishop of Paris, President Bonjean **The Excesses** and the *curé* of the Madeleine, were massacred. **of the** Prisoners, Parisian guards, constables, monks **Communists.** and priests were seized by the federates and shot wholesale in an enclosure in the Rue Haxo.

While these crimes were being committed against innocent folk, others were perpetrated against the capital itself.

In order to hamper the advance of the Versailles army, but even more in order to satiate their own hatred, the federates set fire to public buildings one by one—the Tuileries, the Palais-Royal, the Hôtel de Ville, etc.

Owing to the shortage of coal there was abundance of oil, which had been distributed in large quantities.

Chance alone saved the Louvre, Notre-Dame, the Sainte-Chapelle and the Bibliothèque Nationale.

Barricades, shooting, burning, soldiers cautiously advancing, skirting the walls in fear of being shot from a window, hastily constructed defences taken by assault or strategy, searching of houses, anyone found in possession of arms or even suspected of having used them set up against a wall and shot on the spot, universal excitement and exasperation increasing as resistance was prolonged, prisoners herded together in thousands in every available space—such were the last convulsions of the Commune.

Delescluze, one of the leaders, met his death on the top of one of the barricades. Anybody who was arrested was immediately executed. Large numbers went into hiding and escaped.

It required a whole week, the bloody week, to win back Paris, from the eastern quarters to the Buttes Chaumont and the Père-Lachaise, where the last encounters took place.

On the 29th of May the fort of Vincennes surrendered, and the regular Government was master of the whole capital.

Consequences of the Commune

The Commune was on all sides guilty of terrible excesses. At no other period of French history, in which insurrections, revolutions and civil wars are not lacking, did Frenchmen fight and kill each other with such ferocity.

The Stubborn Nature of the Struggle.

The explanation of this fury is to be found in the circumstances out of which it grew. This civil war waged under the very eyes of an invading enemy had maddened one and all. The "Versaillais," and with them nine-tenths of France, were horror-struck at the idea that these convulsions and upheavals endangered the unity, nay, the very existence of the fatherland.

Anxious to reach a settlement as quickly as possible, they struck out with ever-increasing violence and lack of restraint.

The Commune, defeated sword in hand, and victory having been won without quarter or mercy, curious results followed for the peace and stability of the Government France had chosen.

The whole of the revolutionary party had been suppressed, some having been shot, and others sent in thousands to the prisons and gaols; all who could escape had crossed the frontier. Thus no fresh upheaval or revolt was possible against the Government, whatever it was like.

This, for nineteenth-century France, was quite a novel situation.

41

THE THIRD REPUBLIC

During this century the Napoleonic Governments alone, because they were Governments founded on force, and had no

The Suppression of the Commune secures Internal Peace. scruples about curtailing or abolishing the liberties of the people, and never hesitated on the smallest provocation to use shot and shell (Bonaparte had set the example from the very beginning)—the Napoleonic Governments alone had known the blessings of internal peace.

All the other Governments, on the contrary—the Restoration, Louis-Philippe and the Republic of 1848—constantly found themselves exposed to uprisings in the capital.

Louis XVIII and Charles X had no chance of thrusting firm roots into France. Between their rule, as it was conceived by the sovereign, surrounded as he was by the *émigrés* of the old regime with all their aspirations and habits, and the spirit created in France by the Revolution and the Empire, there was, from the political, religious, social and intellectual point of view, a great gulf fixed.

Owing its origin to a popular uprising in favour of the liberties that had been regained, the constitutional monarchy of Louis-Philippe might indeed have secured a compromise between monarchism and liberalism in France. But having sprung out of revolution, it was exposed to attack on the part of the disgruntled extremists, furious at seeing themselves thus deprived of the fruits of that revolution.

The King could only have held his own by means of a happy combination of conciliation and resistance, mildness and severity of demeanour.

But this happy mean, difficult enough to strike, was quite beyond the capacities of Louis-Philippe. Towards the end of his reign, more particularly, he was badly advised and persisted in an attitude of obstinate resistance, his refusal to allow the extension of universal suffrage demanded by an important section of the country being most foolish and inopportune. He ought, on the contrary, to have made the concession, since it would have provided the only possible safety-valve.

How much wiser the leaders of monarchist England had been eighteen years earlier ! In that country also the grave problem of the extension of the franchise had to be faced. The partisans

42

of the old state of affairs and the members of the privileged classes at first attempted to resist the innovation. But as soon as they felt that their assailants were too strong and that the revolutionary movement might get the better of them, they hastened to give way, and before it was too late gave their consent to the inevitable changes.

There are certain favoured beings who resemble travellers who regard with anything but pleasure the entry of fresh occupants into the compartment where they are so comfortably installed. If they can prevent them from getting in, so much the better. But if they cannot, wisdom bids them allow some to enter and share their privileges, and then the new arrivals can be used to defend them against a fresh invasion. And this the English thoroughly understood. But Louis-Philippe, unfortunately for himself, did not follow their example, for since his Government owed its existence to the barricades, he clearly had no right to be so unamenable.

Of the five forms of government to which France submitted in the nineteenth century (a large number indeed), those of the two Napoleons, Napoleon the Great and Napoleon the Little, fell owing to the faults, or one might almost say the follies, of their foreign policy. In both cases it was a foreign army that reached Paris and took upon itself the task of putting an end to the system. The three others, Absolute Monarchy, Constitutional Monarchy and the Republic of 1848, perished through the mistakes of their domestic policy.

The two kings, Charles X and Louis-Philippe, did not know how to be sufficiently liberal when the people were quiet, nor how to be energetic enough when they were restless. Rather than enter upon a struggle against a section of their subjects in revolt (their scruples do them honour, for a Napoleon would not have hesitated), they stoically went into exile, the road to which, as a matter of fact, they knew all too well.

The First Republic and the Republic of 1848 proved incapable of securing order, peace and discipline in the country, and this being the first duty of a Government of any kind, they thereby demonstrated their terrible inferiority.

But now by its pitiless repression of the Commune the new Government placed itself above all reproach or suspicion of weakness. Many who would have turned their backs on the Republic, because they felt it was founded on upheavals, insurrections and barricades, acquiesced in it when once they realised that these dangers were things of the past.

This meant so much ground lost for the advocates of a restoration of the monarchy.

But for the Commune, the new Government would have encountered the same dangers as the Government of 1848. At the first signs of disturbance the terrified country would inevitably have thrown itself into the arms of the monarchy. There is a well-known saying : " The Republic must either be conservative or cease to exist." And it was the Commune alone that gave the Republic the opportunity of being conservative. Otherwise it would have been impossible.

BIBLIOGRAPHY.—*Parliamentary Enquiry into the Insurrection of the 18th of March*, 1874 (3 vols.), published by the National Assembly. J. Claretie, *Histoire de la Révolution de 1870–71* (5 vols., 1875–6). Lissagaray, *Histoire de la Commune* (1876). L. Fiaux, *Histoire de la Guerre Civile de* 1871 (1879). G. Bourgin, *La Commune* (1907). M. Vuillaume, *Mes Cahiers Rouges au Temps de la Commune* (1910). General Vinoy, *L'Armistice et la Commune* (1872). D'Hérisson, *Nouveau Journal d'un Officier d'Ordonnance : La Commune* (1889). Général Appert, *Rapport d'Ensemble sur les Opérations de la Justice Militaire Relatives à l'Insurrection de* 1871 (1 vol.). A. Arnaud, *Histoire Populaire et Parlementaire de la Commune de Paris* (3 vols., Brussels, 1878). Cluseret, *Mémoires* (3 vols., 1887–8). Da Costa, *La Commune Vécue* (1903–5). F. Jourde, *Souvenirs d'un Membre de la Commune* (Brussels, 1877). Marshal MacMahon, *L'Armée de Versailles depuis sa Formation jusqu'à la Complète Pacification de Paris* (official report). Camille Pelletan, *La Semaine de Mai* (1880). V. Rossel, *Papiers Posthumes* (1 vol., 1871). L. Dubreuil, *La Commune*. H. Rochefort, *Les Aventures de Ma Vie* (1896). M. Du Camp, *Les Convulsions de Paris* (4 vols., 1878).

CHAPTER IV

THIERS' GOVERNMENT. FAILURE TO RESTORE THE MONARCHY

THIERS' GOVERNMENT

IMMEDIATELY after the civil war, which had followed directly upon the war with Germany, and had wrought untold moral and material havoc, France was like a man recovering from a dangerous illness, whose very existence has been in peril, but who returns to life again and recovers his strength very quickly.

Republic or Monarchy? Before proceeding to the work of reorganisation required in every department—financial, political, administrative and military—it was necessary to settle in whose name this task of reconstruction should take place, under what Government and what leader.

The question of the form of government had to be faced at once, and to judge from appearances the decision did not seem to be in doubt.

The National Assembly, representing the will of the people, was two-thirds composed of monarchists—the Legitimists and the Orleanists. As two out of three represents a clear majority, apparently nothing remained but to draw the conclusion from this state of affairs and restore the monarchy.

But what actually happened at this juncture was extraordinary. For this royalist majority, which held all the power and had the fate of the country in its hands, far from recalling the King, on the contrary, left France under the government of a *de facto* republic which inevitably tended gradually to grow into a republic *de jure*.

What is the explanation of this paradox? There is another problem equally difficult to solve. Far from proceeding without delay to upset the Government, which it had the means to do, it allowed Thiers, a temporary leader, to remain in power, although he was openly in favour of the Republic and on all occasions played the game of the Republicans if he did not actually support them.

To shed light on these two questions, which are inextricably involved, it is necessary to give a brief account of the years that followed the war.

The failure to restore the monarchy constituted a drama of which the cast was very small—the Comte de Chambord, the head

The Drama of Frohsdorf. of the senior branch, who embodied the principle of monarchy; the Orleanists, who, according to their own account, were ready for a coalition but incapable of ever realising it; and Thiers, who with the National Assembly represented the country. The Comte de Chambord played the principal part, as it was owing to his hesitation and scruples of conscience that the restoration eventually failed.

By nature upright and generous and endowed with a lofty nobility of sentiment, though but little inclined for action or for

The Psychology of an Exile. struggle, the Comte de Chambord was above all an exile, who having settled down in banishment and taken root, hesitated to leave it because in his heart of hearts he had no confidence in the throne upon which he was invited to take his seat. This explains his attitude throughout the course of the negotiations, his indecision and evasiveness.

The child of miracle was ten years old when his grandfather, Charles X, took him with him when he left France just after the July Revolution. In a chapter of his *Mémoires d'Outre-tombe*, Chateaubriand, who visited the royal family at Prague, has drawn a striking picture of the life led by the exiles.

" There is nothing sadder," he says, " than the life of fallen kings; their days are nothing but a tissue of reality and make-believe . . . they have the twofold inconveniences of Court life and private life—the flatterers, the favourites and the ambitions of the one; the affronts, the trouble and the gossip of the other. It is a continual masquerade of ministers and lacqueys changing clothes. These dethroned aliens are set under supervision in the middle of the world, spurned by princes as though they were plague-stricken with adversity, objects of suspicion to the people as being tainted with power. . . ."

Every line of this picture gives a vivid impression of sadness. And this sadness and discouragement weighed down the child from his earliest years, fashioned him and made him what he was. When he reached manhood he never succeeded in shaking himself free of it.

It was in the castle of Frohsdorf that the Comte de Chambord passed most of his life. On the invitation of Don Jaime de Bourbon, the Pretender to the Crown of Spain, and through his grandmother heir to the property, the author of the present work paid a fairly long visit to Frohsdorf.

Frohsdorf, *a Bourbon shrine*, and, as it were, the Mecca of the Legitimists, is situated about forty-five miles from Vienna, in a smiling and fertile valley. It is a large, square, two-storied building, with the arms of France on the façade, the three *fleurs de lis* surmounted by the royal crown. On the grand staircase are two portraits opposite one another—Louis XV and Louis XVI, full-length, a present from the two kings to M. de Calonne, and close by Charles X in his coronation robes. From the very entrance Bourbon souvenirs monopolise the attention of the visitor; they surround him, envelop him and refuse to leave him in peace; the walls are hung with portraits—the wonderful Louis XV as a child by Van Loo, Philip V, King of Spain, the Duke of Burgundy, the Duchess de Berry. A glass case holds the great silver watch which was in Louis XVI's coach on the day when he was arrested in Varenne, together with the prayer-book which he held in his hand on the way to the scaffold—there is a marker at the prayers for the dying. The library contains the register of Charles X's hunting parties, the minutes of the royal Council, etc.

Surrounded by all these souvenirs which served only to remind him of his exile and the misfortunes of his house, the Pretender, the last scion of the elder branch, passed his days. His state of mind when the grave question of his return to France was mooted, and the crisis of the white flag, can easily be understood by anyone who has spent only a few hours at Frohsdorf. The prince, hardened by exile and convinced that all that was best in him was summed up in a *principle*, an *idea*, found it impossible not to adopt an uncompromising attitude as soon as he realised that this principle, this idea, was at stake. The question should not have been put to him in the way it actually was put, unless he was to be driven to answer " No." The mistake made by those who wished for his return was to allow the discussion ever to take place on such a basis.

When a man has lived in exile from his earliest childhood he becomes adapted to his fate. The prince, who was a great huntsman, had made life tolerable for himself. The old burgh of Piten, a feudal castle perched on the top of a perpendicular rock, proudly dominating the valley below, afforded him a pleasant and picturesque hunting-box. A few miles away was the castle of Schwartzau, where, ever since he had lost his territories, his kinsman, the Duke of Parma, had lived surrounded by a large family. And thus two descendants of the Bourbons found themselves near neighbours, which, together with the close ties of friendship which bound them to each other, afforded consolation to them both.

For the restoration of the monarchy to have any chance of success it was in the first place necessary for the two Pretenders to come to some agreement, and for one or the other of them to give way to his rival. It was towards this end that the Royalists were working. As soon as the laws passed against the exiles had been repealed, the princes could return to France. In compliance with urgent solicitations, the Comte de Paris wrote to his cousin, the Comte de Chambord, that he was ready to present himself before the head of his House.

Unfortunately this reconciliation came from the lips rather than from the heart. The voices of the past were indeed too strong, and an ineradicable suspicion still persisted between them. The Comte de Chambord, in order to avoid misunder-

48

standing, insisted on making known his programme. He immediately raised the question of the flag in the manifesto of the 29th of January, 1872, which ended with the words: *Henry V cannot desert the flag of Henry IV.*

From that moment, no matter what efforts might be made, the die was cast. The prince, upon whom all kinds of pressure and persuasion were brought to bear, refused to depart from his idea : " But for my principle," he obstinately declared, " I am merely a fat limping man." This obstinacy and these scruples, which are nevertheless not devoid of beauty (a less noble and upright nature would have made all manner of promises with no intention of keeping them), were proofs of a will that nothing would move. The Pretender had a secret conviction—an intuition rather than an idea—that between himself and the France he would find there was a great gulf fixed. How could it be bridged ? The country would not move. So it would fall on him, the Pretender, to make all the concessions, and to what purpose ? With what result ? In order to be driven again in a few years or a few months' time like his grandfather along the road of exile ?

Such were the feelings and reflections that presented themselves more or less confusedly to his mind, and dictated his conduct. Every time that the question was opened afresh, his response and his attitude, in spite of appearances and misunderstandings, were always the same. Thiers' good sense and clear, unerring judgment guided him aright when he refused to embark upon the course of restoring a monarchy in which he did not believe and which was doomed in advance to failure. " The Republic," he declared, " is the Government which divides us least." And it was to the consolidation of this Government that all efforts should be directed, slowly and gradually and without giving offence. But how could this be accomplished with an Assembly in which the majority did not wish for a republic, although as a matter of fact it had but little idea as to how the system by which they proposed to replace it could be installed ?

As long as it was a matter of reorganising the country, the power and prestige of Thiers almost always won the day.

E

THE THIRD REPUBLIC

The most important task of all was to free the territory of the nation from the invader who was to occupy it until the whole of the indemnity had been paid. The raising of a loan of two milliards, which was subscribed in a single day, provided the necessary funds and secured the evacuation of the first slice long before the date fixed. The country was quickly restored to order. At a review in the Bois de Boulogne the army was greeted with acclamations, and its reorganisation was demanded on the principle of compulsory military service as in Prussia.

The Work of Reconstruction. Liberation of Territory.

In regard to the organisation of the municipal and cantonal assemblies, the reform of finance, the imposition of indirect taxation, and the raising of a second loan of three milliards, but for a few slight disagreements, Thiers and the Assembly were in complete accord. And from this collaboration the happiest results were obtained.

In September 1871, Thiers, who was only the head of the executive, was made President of the Republic. But this was only a provisional arrangement. The President was only the delegate of the Assembly, which kept its sovereign rights. Finally, Thiers was President of the Council as well as President of the Republic. The elections of the 2nd of July, 1871, signalised an undoubted victory for his policy and a defeat for the Royalists, at the same time proving that the verdict given under exceptional circumstances during the war did not represent the true opinion of the country.

From that moment the National Assembly could and ought to have been held in Paris, where order had long since been restored and where the Ministers had remained. But with a view to expressing its mistrust of the capital it deliberately chose to stay in Versailles.

Hence arose a strange situation. Paris always had been and still remained the *de facto* capital, and nothing in the world could deprive her of this position of superiority. But, as the result of an arbitrary decision, a real piece of make-believe, Versailles was promoted to the rank of *constitutional capital*.

Fortunately the two places were not far away from each other even at that time, for although there were no motors, a railway was already in existence. The incessant traffic between Paris and Versailles, the parliamentary trains, the arrivals and departures at the Gare Saint Lazare, the lunches at the Hôtel des Réservoirs, the anxious waiting for news, the days on which the grand sessions were held, were all characteristic of the political life of the period.

Nevertheless, disagreement between Thiers and the Assembly, who gave him but grudging support, was latent and inevitable. The success of the Republicans at the elections (the elections of the 9th of June, 1872, confirmed those of the previous July) was a blow to the Royalists, who felt that unless energetic and decisive measures were taken their cause would be irretrievably lost.

The struggle opened when the subject of finance came to be debated. Income tax, taxes on raw materials, the respective **First Incident.** merits of direct and indirect taxation—all these questions were raised in this debate, which in some ways was very similar to the discussions held on the same subject fifty years later. For when a State, like an individual, finds it necessary to put its finances in order, the alternatives offered and the remedies that can be applied are strictly limited in number.

Thiers was beaten when the question of raw materials was put to the vote. He sent in his resignation, but, at the pressing request of the majority of the deputies, he immediately withdrew it. The incident seemed closed, but it provided a warning of the approaching crisis, and proved that the Royalist and Conservative majority in the Assembly were resolved to separate as soon as possible from a chief with the essential item of whose programme they did not feel themselves to be in sympathy.

In short, the Assembly decided to submit to Thiers as long as it had a vague feeling that it could not do without his services. The first task, the liberation of the occupied territory, had not yet been accomplished. Large payments were still due to Germany, and the evacuation of several departments in the east, including Belfort, still remained to be carried out. This involved difficult negotiations. The Germans, and above all Bismarck, who was everywhere the leading spirit, were torn between two conflicting emotions—anxiety to receive their millions as quickly as possible, since what is good to receive is also good to keep, and the fear that France, whom they still thought was far more disorganised and revolutionary than she really was, might be shaken by a fresh convulsion which would inevitably postpone the payments.

Nevertheless, delighted as they were to pocket the money much sooner than they had expected, the fact that settlements were made before they were due and the facility with which they were carried out proved the astonishing vitality of their enemy and the miraculous rapidity of his recovery. And they consequently feared, or pretended to fear, that this all too speedy recovery would encourage their " hereditary foe " to seek revenge.

Hence the bad temper of Bismarck, upon whom the army tried to bring pressure to bear, his fits of rude and sometimes insulting behaviour when, as for instance on the subject of what he considered a scandalous acquittal (the murder of a German soldier by a Frenchman), he let himself go and published a note which was insolent if not a calculated outrage to the feelings of France.

Thiers was the only statesman capable of coping with all these difficulties and of securing by means of a judicious mixture of firmness and compliance the rapid evacuation of the occupied territory. The Assembly was not blind to this and accordingly left him in power.

The treaty of evacuation was at last signed on the 15th of March, 1873. Soon not a single German soldier would be left on **The Treaty of Evacuation.** French soil. The Assembly passed a resolution (it could hardly do otherwise) to the effect that Thiers *had deserved well of his country.* This was his Capitol. The Tarpeian Rock was close at hand.

Each victory won by the Republicans at the elections was a lash of the whip for the Royalist Assembly, rousing it to hasten events and secure the downfall of Thiers in order to put in his place a man in whom they had complete confidence for the execution of their plans.

The election in Paris of the Republican Barodet, which was due to the energetic intervention of Gambetta, was a set-back for Thiers, who had supported his friend Rémusat. This acted upon the Assembly like a red rag to a bull, and drove it to seek an immediate decision. This election pro-

The Barodet Election. vided the best possible proof of the extremely difficult situation in which Thiers was placed. The policy of the golden mean at which he aimed was opposed by the Republicans, who thought it too soft, and also by the Royalists, who considered it too favourable to their adversaries.

As the result of a certain incident in the Assembly, Grévy, the President of the Chamber, sent in his resignation and was succeeded by Buffet, who became a veritable **Buffet, President of the Tourney.** President of the Tourney. From this moment events moved rapidly. The members of the " right " united and organised a plot against Thiers. So sure were they of his defeat that they forthwith sought his successor. The Orleanists proposed the Duc d'Aumale, whom the Legitimists refused. A soldier who would inspire confidence in the army and if necessary be ready to carry out a *coup de force* seemed the obvious selection, and the conspirators agreed in the nomination of Marshal MacMahon.

Each side took up its position. Thiers, who knew all, awaited the conflict. It was opened by the Duc de Broglie, one of the **The Grand Session.** Orleanist leaders, in the course of a session which, on account of the beauty of the speeches and the dignity of the debates, was worthy of the greatest days of parliamentary history. Thiers, in spite of his age, was still too full of life and pugnacity not to hurl himself into the midst of the fray. The constitutional rules provisionally laid down gave him the right to do so, provided he sent a message demanding it. In a courageous and fundamentally able speech, he rent the veil, and, scorning all subterfuge, justified his policy. As he regarded the restoration of the monarchy as impossible, on account of the lack of unity among the Pretenders, he gave or rather confirmed his adherence to the Republic. If it went he too would go *to the left*—to use a latter-day expression. Finding himself in the minority he sent in his resignation on the 24th of May, 1873. The National Assembly, in keeping with the effect carefully prepared by the majority, appointed Marshal MacMahon in his place.

THE THIRD REPUBLIC

France at one of the darkest moments in her history had had the good fortune to find in Thiers a leader, and a great leader,

The Work of Thiers. who, but for a few mistakes which were difficult to avoid, took matters in hand, disentangled and conducted them with equal prudence and vigour.

For the continuation of war to the death and the conclusion of peace, possibly a more stubborn and militant policy, which would have aroused all the energies of the nation, might have secured somewhat better conditions for the country. But when once peace had been signed, Thiers' Government deserves nothing but praise. He held his own against the Commune and conquered it. With a rapidity which surprised everybody, and first and foremost the enemies of France, he raised and re-organised a country ruined by foreign and civil war. He restored order and confidence everywhere; the administration was reformed, the finances put on a sound basis. In a short time, at home as well as abroad, France returned to the position she had lost. Thiers (and this is perhaps his greatest claim to greatness), although in his heart of hearts possibly favouring government by a constitutional monarchy, a restoration of the July Monarchy, was quick to realise that the dissension among the Royalists on the one hand, and the marked development of the country on the other, *made any such restoration impossible.* And thus he made it his aim, in the interests of his country, to ignore this solution, which would only have served to provoke fresh revolutions and fresh upheavals. The safest plan was to wait and arrange for the question of what form of government should be adopted to be postponed as long as possible. The time thus gained was turned to account by the Republic in order to strengthen and consolidate its position. In applying and carrying out this wise and prudent policy this parliamentary Nestor displayed infinite care and skill. " Let us put our house in order as quickly as possible," seemed to be his message to all, " we shall have plenty of time afterwards to settle who is to be master of it." And thus, thanks to him, the upheavals and chaos which might have characterised the early days of the Republic, and which would gravely have compromised the recovery of the country, were avoided.

And now one of the two questions raised in the early days—

that of the conflict between the National Assembly and its chosen chief—was settled. The second still remained—that of the restoration of the monarchy. And to this **The Assembly and the King.** the Assembly at once turned its attention.

But in this case the difficulty, not to say impossibility, of finding a solution, was due not to the will of individuals but to the very nature of things.

MacMahon, the new President of the Republic, was above all a soldier with a very limited acquaintance with politics, of which he understood but little. His convictions inclined him towards a constitutional monarchy, but, loyal and conscientious as he was, he was of opinion that any such change should be brought about by *legal means* and not by a *coup de force.*

But the situation was so complicated, owing to the profound disagreement that existed between the two Pretenders, and by the obstinate refusal of one of them to bow before reality, that a legal and constitutional solution reached by means of an amicable agreement and the vote of the Assembly was practically impossible. Only a *coup de force,* which faced both parties with an accomplished fact, could have overcome this difficulty.

But would a solution reached by such means have proved enduring? This is another question. It most probably would not. Be that as it may, they persisted in trying to untie a knot which could only be cut.

The moment the Royalists in the Assembly had in the person of the President a man whom they believed to be on their side, they redoubled their efforts towards a restoration **The Comte de Paris at Frohsdorf.** of the monarchy. The first essential was to reconcile the two branches of the royal House.

Letters and messages having hitherto produced results that were far from satisfactory, the Orleanist princes, at the pressing instigation of certain of their supporters, decided to take a drastic measure and presented themselves before the Comte de Chambord at Frohsdorf, realising that by this visit they placed themselves under the orders of the head of their House (October 1873).

This was an event of the first importance. The son of Louis-Philippe, who to Legitimists faithful to their principles was only a usurper, rendered homage to the grandson of Charles X.

And thus the schism between the two families seemed at last to be ended.

But the reconciliation was more apparent than real. The Orleanist princes, and still more their supporters, were very far from regarding their adhesion to the Legitimist cause as absolute and unconditional. They were ready to follow the Comte de Chambord provided he could make up his mind to the necessary sacrifices and realise the changes that had taken place—if he were ready, in fact, to accept the throne of a constitutional monarch. As one of them remarked, they were not prepared to give the Pretender a *blank cheque.*

Now these conditions which they tried to impose, these limitations of his absolute power and his right divine, the Comte de Chambord had already on several occasions declared in the most formal manner his absolute refusal to accept. The attempt to hide this discrepancy beneath cleverly turned formulæ was vain, and the moment arrived when the veil of dissimulation was torn away and the discrepancy became apparent.

The question of the flag was merely a symbol. It stood for a fundamental principle, the principle of absolute monarchy, which, if it consented to certain limitations, insisted on deciding for itself what they should be instead of being guided by the will of the nation. Now after fifty years it was once again a matter of granting a charter.

The Symbol of the White Flag.

Imbued with such ideas and beliefs it was just as well that the Comte de Chambord, a Merovingian monarch, as his enemies called him, should not return. The fate of his ancestor, Charles X, would almost undoubtedly have been his.

It is questionable whether many of those who pretended to desire his return, the majority of the Orleanists, were really sincere in their protestations. There is room for every kind of doubt. Just about this time an article was published in the *Times* at the direct instigation, it was believed, of the head of the Government, the Duc de Broglie himself, which gave a clear summing up of the aims of the Orleanists. According to the article, the latter constituted a powerful party with whom the Pretender should make up his mind to reckon. They were ready to make concessions, but did not wish to be the only ones to do so. The Legitimist Pretender was urged not to sacrifice the *policy of Henry IV to the banner of Joan of Arc.*

Thus we see that the question always led to the same deadlock —the eternal problem of the flag which concealed and symbolised all the others. But on this subject any agreement was impossible.

Nothing affords a better illustration of the difficulties to be contended with and the contradictions to be met than the last

Last Attempt. The Chesnelong Mission. negotiations undertaken with the object of reaching an agreement notwithstanding, and endeavouring to reconcile irreconcilables.

The Orleanists, the most important party in the National Assembly, who had all the power in their hands and without whom, therefore, nothing could be done, rallied, at the invitation of their prince, round the Legitimist Pretender. But they refused to allow him to return *unconditionally.*

The Duc de Chambord was not disposed to accept any conditions. He had an innate mistrust, which amounted almost to horror, of the parliamentary world with its perpetual trafficking and intrigue. And so great was this mistrust that it extended even to the deputies of his own party. It was encouraged by those about him, it pervaded all his sentiments, inspired and explained all his actions.

This is the essential point to be constantly borne in mind, otherwise all that happened at this time becomes well-nigh incomprehensible. The constitutional guarantees that people demanded, or rather endeavoured to force upon him, he might at a pinch have accepted with his lips, although every time they were mentioned they would have put him into a state of lively irritation. But on the question of the flag, which outweighed all others, he showed himself absolutely immovable. All the attempts made to induce him to give way, however little, and accept a vague formula, a compromise, a make-believe, met with obstinate refusal on his part. In vain did they try to cover up the contradiction by vague nebulosities; they only made matters worse. At the critical moment, the prince, by some manifesto that echoed far and wide—a declaration or a letter—tore aside the veil, and the naked truth stood revealed.

A parliamentary commission consisting of nine members was

appointed to draw up the conditions to be accepted by the prince before the National Assembly would give its consent to the restoration of the monarchy. The most influential of the Legitimist leaders refused to support them, which was in itself very significant. Fully aware of the real attitude of their King, they were not inclined to come forward and undertake the responsibility of meeting with a rebuff which they foresaw and feared.

The guarantees demanded related to the constitutional laws—the executive power of the King, the legislative power of the two Chambers, ministerial responsibility and civil and religious liberty. At the express demand of MacMahon, a faithful interpreter of the wishes of the army, a last stipulation was added. It may be summed up in the following formula :— " The *tricolore* is to be retained, and can only be altered by consent of the King in conjunction with the representatives of the nation."

Without the *tricolore*, the President declared firmly, the army would not set one foot before the other. " The *chasse-pots*," he said, " would sally forth alone."

This last stipulation inevitably brought about the rejection of the rest.

When once the list of conditions had been settled, who would undertake the task of submitting it to the exiled prince and obtaining his consent to it? Knowing how thankless and how full of pitfalls such a task was, the most prominent personages and those best fitted for the charge among the Legitimists and the Orleanists prudently withdrew. One worthy man came forward whose only qualification was his worthiness, which in the circumstances was not enough, a man full of generous and upright intentions, but lacking experience—Chesnelong, a retired merchant who had recently rallied to the cause of monarchy. He did not know the prince and had never set eyes on him. He was an honest bagman; nothing more. Entrusted with this momentous message he asked for an audience, for which he was kept waiting. The prince received him at Salzbourg and listened to him for a long time, allowing him to speak much more than he spoke himself.

The question of the flag, which was the stumbling-block, was

58

at last raised. As the first interview had no result, it was raised again at a second audience after dinner, followed by a third and much shorter one at the moment of leave-taking. Chesnelong, anxious to reach a settlement at all costs, used every possible means at his command to find some loophole, some compromise. Since the problem as a whole seemed insoluble, he thought he would divide it up and cut it into three. The question of the flag need not be discussed. The prince could wait to settle it with the Assembly. At one moment Chesnelong hoped he had converted his interlocutor. Vain hope ! At the last minute the Comte de Chambord refused his consent to the essential clause dealing with his agreement with the Assembly on the subject of the flag. He insisted on settling the matter by himself in accordance with his own wishes, and refused to allow it to depend upon the will of Parliament.

A novice at negotiations of this kind, and taking the will for the deed, Chesnelong returned to Paris, honestly convinced that he had succeeded, whereas he had failed. A regular period of misunderstanding followed, which was prolonged into the following weeks and grew worse and worse. The Royalist deputies believed (some of the better informed only pretended to believe) that everything was settled, whereas nothing was settled, and that the prince had at last made up his mind to accept the *tricolore*, which was far from being the case. Thus they advanced on to the quicksands, which could only give way beneath their feet. Preparations were made almost openly for the speedy if not the immediate restoration of the monarchy. The stage was set for all the preliminaries and the parliamentary and military proceedings. The leaders of the Assembly drafted the law by which the descendant of a long line of French kings was to return to the throne. Gala coaches were ordered, and the Court tailor delivered a uniform decorated with the *fleur de lis*.

The Republicans, the Bonapartists, and all the adversaries of monarchy lived in constant expectation and dread.

Nevertheless, at the bottom of it all was a terrible, a tragic misunderstanding, which the moment an explanation was sought was inevitably doomed to vanish. And it was impossible for an explanation not to be demanded, since the interests of

The Misunderstanding.

59

too many people were involved. The Orleanists wanted the undertakings of the Pretender to be definitely stated. But at the first attempt to define them, and to put them, as the saying goes, into black and white, all was lost.

At Frohsdorf the prince, somewhat misled, was keeping an attentive eye on all these proceedings, which he found but little to his taste, and felt that an attempt was being made to involve him in a network of intrigue. His upright nature, incapable of duplicity, rose in revolt, and prompted by his feelings he wrote the famous letter of the 27th of October, which, at his formal request, was published in *l'Union*, the Legitimist organ, and gave the final blow to these attempts at a restoration of the monarchy. In it he once again declared his undying fidelity to the white flag.

The moment this message was made known, despondency and consternation filled the ranks of the Royalists, whilst the Republicans, on the other hand, were jubilant.

And thus, in spite of anything that men could do, all-powerful forces, over which no one had any control, inexorably produced the inevitable result. The deep and distant voices of the past dominated all the appeals of the present in the heart of the prince. His mind and character, shaped as they were by his ancestry, his education, his surroundings and a long exile, found it impossible to bow before the exigencies of the moment. The conditions offered for his acceptance were odious and intolerable. If he was required to return to the throne of his fathers he must be allowed to do so unconditionally. But in that case he would, according to all appearances, not have remained upon it for long.

At this juncture one of those curious episodes occurred which make history, and particularly the history of France, occasionally resemble a novelette. After the prince's message, **The Prince's Visit to Versailles.** it seemed as though all were over as far as he was concerned and that he had bidden his last farewell to a restoration. But this was far from being the case. Ten days had not passed when, acting on an impulse which was dramatic in its suddenness, he decided on the spur of the moment to set out in the utmost secrecy for Versailles in order to put himself into touch with MacMahon and to decide in a *tête-à-tête* with him all that the parliamentary intriguers and muddlers had only succeeded in confusing hopelessly. He took up his quarters *incognito* in the house of M. de Vanssay, one of his supporters, and demanded an interview with MacMahon. Caught point-blank with this unexpected request, the Marshal politely but firmly refused, saying that since he held all his powers from the sovereign Assembly he could not and would not do anything without its consent.

What mysterious and obscure motives can possibly explain this unexpected decision on the part of the Pretender? He was inspired by an idea which though right in theory was wrong in practice, that the restoration could only be brought about as the result of a swiftly accomplished deed, and that, far from facilitating it, the parleys and negotiations of the parliamentarians only served to delay it and make it impossible. It was for the King to show himself suddenly in the midst of his people, to return to his palace and take his seat on the throne of his fathers amid the acclamations of his subjects, filled with surprise and sudden delight by this bold step. What could be simpler? What could be more natural? What was the good of the haggling and bargaining of politicians who were jealous of one another and far more preoccupied with themselves than with the cause they pretended to defend?

The prince forgot but one thing, and that was the most essential—the accomplished fact, the *coup de force*, can only succeed at a moment of crisis or when it has behind it the power to support it. But any such power was totally lacking. At ordinary times, such as the one in question, all the power was in the hands of the parliamentarians whom he detested, and of the ministers and the President who were only their tools. Without their help, without their co-operation, nobody could do anything. Events soon convinced him of this.

The trial of Marshal Bazaine, which roused all the passions of the country, opened at Versailles on the 6th of October, 1873, in the salons of the Trianon.

The Trial of Bazaine. Under pressure of public opinion, Thiers, who at first was opposed to it, had allowed an inquiry to be held into the Marshal's case which inevitably led to this result. The famous words of Gambetta, " Bazaine has betrayed us," were on all men's lips and were fairly representative of the attitude of the country.

The Council of War, composed of generals who had held supreme command against the enemy and of divisional commanders, was presided over by the Duc d'Aumale. The charge brought against him was read by General Séré de Rivière, and on purely military grounds accused Bazaine of failing to do all in his power to prevent the necessity of capitulation before he delivered up to the enemy the fortress he was charged to defend together with his army.

The accused chose for his defence Lachaux, the celebrated assize lawyer, and defended his case with an apathetic dullness which was not altogether devoid of skill. His argument was that in the absence of a regular Government all his efforts had tended towards preserving intact for the country an army which, when peace negotiations were opened, would be able to play a decisive part.

The most stirring incident was provided by the reply of the Duc d'Aumale when Bazaine maintained since it was a revolutionary Government that was in power he was to a certain extent released from the duties expected of him under the military code. " Sir," exclaimed the Duke, " France was still in existence ! "

By a unanimous vote the Council condemned François Achille Bazaine, Marshal of France, to be degraded from his rank and put to death. The judges immediately sent a letter to the President, asking that the sentence should not be carried out, and MacMahon next day commuted the punishment to one of twenty years' detention in the island of Sainte-Marguerite opposite Cannes. The mildness of the climate, which was also accompanied by other advantages, made his captivity far from disagreeable. Urged on and helped by his wife, Bazaine arranged to shorten his sentence, and succeeded without much difficulty in making his escape, thus proving that he was not very strictly guarded. He sought refuge in Spain, where he died in obscurity and almost in want.

The inquiries that were demanded into the Bazaine case and the mystery with which people chose to surround it were due to the introduction of political considerations into a purely

THIERS' GOVERNMENT

military trial where they were quite out of place. If this aspect alone is considered the question admits of no doubt, and Bazaine's culpability stands clearly and indisputably proved.

This leader to whom Napoleon III so lightly entrusted the command of France's most powerful army had little or no knowledge of his profession. Marshal Foch in his brilliant studies on the war of 1870 has established this beyond doubt. Utterly incapable of commanding a battle he made no attempt to do so, and when it took place without him he did all in his power to end it. He showed an invincible tendency always to lead back his troops beneath the guns of the fortress, because this lazy solution required no effort and freed him from all responsibility.

As is often the case, mediocrity of character was combined with mediocrity of mind. Instead of using all his energies and resources for fighting and the attainment of victory, he allowed himself to be dragged into dubious political transactions in which he was the puppet of the Germans. The army which he ought to have used only to make war, and solely in the interests of the country, he tried to utilise on his own behalf, so that he might be in a position to play a part with the Emperor or the Empress if the Empire were restored, or else with the new Government. He failed to do his duty as a military leader, which consisted in fighting to the end and exhausting every effort in order to inflict as much damage as possible on the enemy.

Thus presented in its true light, the question is perfectly clear. The sentence passed against Bazaine was deserved a hundred times over. It was not a matter of deciding whether or not he was a traitor, which might indeed lead to controversy, but of finding out whether he had or had not done his duty as a military commander. The answer to this admits of no doubt. If Bazaine had done what he left undone, his duty, the issue of the war might have been different.

BIBLIOGRAPHY.—De Falloux, *Mémoires d'un Royaliste* (1888). De Meaux, *Souvenirs Politiques*, 1871-7 (1905). Ch. de Lacombe, *Journal Politique* (2 vols., 1907-8). J. Simon, *Le Gouvernement de M. Thiers* (1898). De Marcère, *L'Assemblée Nationale de 1871* (3 vols). H. Pessard, *Mes Petits Papiers*, 1871-3 (1888). E. Daudet, *Le Duc d'Aumale* (1898). E. Daudet, *Souvenirs de la Présidence du Maréchal MacMahon* (1880). De Dreux-Brézé, *Notes et Souvenirs* (1903). Chesnelong, *La Campagne Monarchique d'Octobre* 1873. Général du Barrail, *Mes Souvenirs*, 1894-6

THE THIRD REPUBLIC

(3 vols). Gambetta, *Discours et Plaidoyers Politiques*, II et III (1881). Loth, *L'échec des Restaurations Monarchiques* (1910). Du Bourg, *Les Entrevues des Princes à Frohsdorf* 1873 *et* 1883 (1910). *Souvenirs Inédits* of Comte de Vanssay, of which Gabriel Hanotaux gives numerous fragments in his *Histoire de la France Contemporaine*. P. F. Simon, *A. Thiers, Chef du Pouvoir Exécutif* (1911). *Procès du Maréchal Bazaine* (report of debates, 1874).

CHAPTER V

THE SEPTENNATE. THE CONSTITUTIONAL LAWS

The passing of the white flag. Consequences of this defeat. The temporal power of the Pope and *Kulturkampf*. The provisional Government made permanent. Struggle against the Republicans. Differences between the parties of the Right. Gambetta a parliamentary strategist. The constitutional laws. Fall of de Broglie's Ministry. The Cissey Ministry. Fall of the Cissey Ministry. Wallon's amendment. The powers of the President. The Senate. The Buffet Ministry. Character of the Constitution. A compromise. The President. The Senate.

THE mysterious visit of the Pretender, the Comte de Chambord, to Versailles, and the failure of this last attempt, which it is true was somewhat carelessly undertaken, sounded the death-knell of the Royalist hopes. From that moment any restoration of the monarchy seemed impossible; the candidature of the senior branch had just received its *coup de grâce*, whilst that of the junior branch would automatically have united against it the Legitimists, the Bonapartists, and the Republicans, whose power increased every day.

There is a tinge of tragedy in this " passing of the white flag." The prince was there, at Versailles, hidden in a small villa at the **The Passing of** bottom of a court. Not more than a dozen of his **the White** intimates knew of his presence in this hiding-place, **Flag.** where he was more or less in the position of a conspirator who had neither the power nor the wish to engage in a conspiracy.

He kept watch over events, and waited.

Waited for what? It would be difficult to say—for the head of the State, the President of the Republic, to come to him. Although MacMahon, in his heart of hearts, was inclined to favour a monarchical solution, he refused to go. An insurmountable obstacle seemed to stand in his path. The prince prolonged his stay, which ran the risk of being discovered at any

F

moment. Nothing happened. The National Assembly, which he mistrusted, went on with its work, passing laws for the establishment and consolidation of the existing system, and laying the foundations of the Republic. Doubtless he hoped—and this was certainly one of the motives of his journey—that the Assembly would prove impotent, and unable to secure a majority of any sort or come to any decision, and that this so-called *constituent* body would prove incapable of constituting anything at all. But this hope, like all the others, was doomed to disappointment.

After a fortnight spent in this way, a short stroll in Paris and a service at Notre Dame which he attended unnoticed among the crowd, he took his departure. Between him and the country there was a great gulf fixed which henceforward nothing could ever bridge.

The immediate result of this failure to restore the monarchy was to rally to the cause of the Republic a large number of members of the upper and middle classes who had **Consequences of this Defeat.** hitherto been hesitating and undecided. The two years that had just passed, the task of liberating the occupied territory and of reconstruction accomplished under the wise guidance of Thiers were proof that a Republic, which was conservative in the best sense of the word, wise and prudent and careful to avoid excess, was possible in France. Here indeed was something quite new and even astonishing, a kind of miracle. Since this miracle had been accomplished and had not passed away, since this republican system had proved itself capable of securing order, discipline and peace, why not abide by it? This from the beginning had been the opinion of Thiers, and it now became that of an ever-growing party among the bourgeoisie.

Strangely enough, and what a short time previously would have seemed paradoxical, the threat to peace came not from the Republicans but from their adversaries, and above all from the Legitimists. The reactionary mediæval ideas of their Pretender, the principle of monarchy by " divine right," seemed impossible in France and were alien and even odious to the majority of Frenchmen. Any effort to impose them on a people who did not want them could only lead to strife and revolt,

THE SEPTENNATE

probably to a fresh revolution. Such was the situation at home.

Abroad, the follies of the clerical party, representing the main body of the Legitimists, gave rise to still greater anxiety.

Temporal Power of the Pope and Kulturkampf. As soon as France, who was almost the only nation to uphold the temporal power of the Pope, had been beaten on the field of battle, an event took place which nothing in the world could any longer prevent—the King of Italy entered Rome, thus providing the last act in the drama of Italian unity. As there cannot be two sovereigns in the same capital, the Pope was henceforward a prisoner in the Vatican. One party among the French clergy, including certain bishops, refused to bow to the inevitable, and dreamed of revolt against the established state of affairs and of restoring the temporal power of the Pope by force. But this would mean war with Italy and probably also with Germany, who would support the latter. And it was not only against Italy that the clerical party adopted this rash attitude. Bismarck was engaged in a violent struggle, the *Kulturkampf*, against the German Catholics; and certain French bishops, not altogether oblivious of the possible result, unhesitatingly gave their open and official support to the persecuted Catholics against the Chancellor who was persecuting them, and joined in a quarrel which in no way concerned them. It may well be imagined that Bismarck, who was only too pleased to find an opportunity of showing his ill-feeling towards France, was not slow to lodge a sharp protest against the impropriety of the proceeding and to exaggerate the incident as much as possible, sending remonstrances mingled with threats to the French Government.

The large majority of Frenchmen were rightly indignant with this adventurous policy which risked embroiling France with her neighbours, and plunging the country into fresh disasters.

The excesses of the clerical party and the activities of the *Congrégation* had been largely responsible for the fall of the legitimate monarchy after 1815, and they now once again provided a reason for the country to turn its back on the Legitimists.

67

THE THIRD REPUBLIC

What course would the National Assembly, with its Royalist majority, adopt when it realised that the restoration of the monarchy was an impossibility? This was the question immediately raised by the head of the Government, the Duc de Broglie.

The Provisional Government made permanent.

The solution he adopted was to maintain the *status quo* as long as possible and to consolidate the provisional Government. He wanted to gain time. During the interval all sorts of things might happen—the Legitimate Pretender might die, for instance, and thus make possible a restoration which for the moment was out of the question.

Thus it was a matter of providing a solid and lasting basis to a *de facto* system and of prolonging the powers of the President of the Republic for a lengthy period of time. This solution, the acceptance of which the Duc de Broglie with considerable ability succeeded in securing, cut both ways; it possessed both advantages and disadvantages.

On the 19th of November, 1873, the National Assembly passed the Septennate law, prolonging the President's tenure of office for seven years. It was a constitutional law, one of the foundation stones of the present Republican Constitution. Thus one of the first stones was laid. Others followed. By this means the existing Government was in a sense consolidated; but this in itself meant the establishment of the Republic, for willy-nilly, this Government was in principle essentially republican. It was this that Thiers and Gambetta so clearly perceived. Everything that was afterwards done on constitutional lines could only serve the interests of the Republic which, being already in existence *de facto*, was to be consecrated by law.

Such were the disadvantages of this solution as far as the Royalists were concerned. The advantages, which for the time being were more apparent than real, were as follows—throughout this period the Govern-ment, being master of the situation, with the police, the army and the administration behind it, counted upon engaging in a struggle with the Republican party and on defeating its propaganda in every possible way. Thus it was really in a combative policy, although in the meantime all kinds of constitutional measures were being passed.

Struggle against the Republicans.

68

This struggle against the Republican idea, which could only increase in ferocity, and of which the logical conclusion was the crisis of the 16th of May, the religious crisis, which set up the power of the executive against the clearly expressed will of the nation, is characterised by a certain number of measures and incidents. The law relating to mayors (January the 20th, 1874) gave the Government the right of nominating the mayors in all the communes. Thus, as one of the Opposition deputies observed, they became so many electoral agents entirely in the hands of the prefects. This measure, together with certain others, those in particular which subjected newspapers to a strict system of supervision and restricted the freedom of the Press, proved in the end to be of doubtful value. This prospective dyke in no way prevented the water from following its course. The country was obviously in favour of the Republic, and in spite of all the pressure that was brought to bear, each new election (February–March 1874) was a triumph for the Republicans.

The Government found itself in a false position. The majority on which it relied was a solid body only in appearance, for the **Differences between the Parties of the Right.** embittered Legitimists, furious at seeing their hopes vanish into thin air, gave only half-hearted support to the work of consolidation, vaguely aware that the Republic was really the chief beneficiary. They were constantly deserting, opposing the Government schemes, and not hesitating to join the Bonapartists and the Republicans. The Duc de Broglie carried on as best he could in the midst of all these difficulties. He was obliged to tack and hedge. All his successors were handicapped in the same way.

This explains the bargaining and compromising nature of the constitutional laws that were eventually passed. They were not the result of a clear and definite policy, but half-measures between opposing ideals, the result of circumstances and sometimes of chance. The Commission entrusted with the task of putting the plans of the Government into practice worked in the utmost confusion. It consisted of a clear monarchist majority—twenty-five Royalists against five Republicans. All the measures drawn up by it and submitted to the Assembly should therefore, it would seem, have been definitely anti-republican. But they were nothing of the kind. The differences between the Royalists and the policy of despair instinctively if not consciously followed by a certain section of them, the Legitimists, were all in favour of the Republicans.

The latter possessed leaders round whom they rallied in an orderly way—Thiers, and above all Gambetta, who proved a **Gambetta a** wonderful parliamentary strategist. He was gifted **Parliamentary** in the highest degree with a sense of what was **Strategist.** possible, and kept a sharp watch in order to profit by every occasion and every opportunity. Political opportunism, which subsequently had such a deleterious influence, was at this time, when there was a Royalist majority in the Assembly, the only policy capable of producing satisfactory results for the Republicans. The latter would have risked losing everything if they had attempted to upset the Assembly or the head of the executive, who, with the army at his disposal, might have been tempted to make use of it. On the contrary, they had every inducement to hold themselves in reserve, to wait (for time was on their side) and to allow the disagreements between the two Royalist parties to increase and produce their inevitable result—the consolidation of the Republic.

The Legitimists had no leaders, and this explains most of the events that followed. Their true leader, the only one they had, was at Frohsdorf, in a state of disgruntled irritation. He took less and less interest in parliamentary affairs, and when he did intervene, as he did from time to time, it was by means of a letter or a high-handed angry message resembling an encyclical, and only serving to embroil matters still further.

Among the constitutional laws demanded by necessity, the question was, Which should be dealt with first—the prerogatives of the President, the power of the legislature, or **The Constitu-** the municipal bodies? The parliamentary com- **tional Laws.** mission appointed to undertake the work found itself faced with an impossible task. The one object it desired, the restoration of the monarchy, was beyond its powers. What it had the power to do it did not want to do, or rather it really did not know what it wanted.

THE SEPTENNATE

On a question of the order for the day, that of granting precedence to the municipal law, the de Broglie Ministry staked

Fall of the de Broglie Ministry. everything, and moved for a vote of confidence, without having first assured themselves that there was complete unanimity in the ranks of the Royalists. At the critical moment the Legitimists deserted and coolly joined the Bonapartists and Republicans. This alliance between the two extremes overthrew the Ministry. It was the first occasion on which the " light horse," as the supporters of the Comte de Chambord were nicknamed, openly went over to the enemy's camp. It was not the last.

In addition to success at the elections, the Republican party also won parliamentary victories in which they were largely helped by the paradoxical and unexpected support of the Legitimists, although the latter were really their most bitter opponents.

At this juncture, as had also been the case at the time of the Restoration, the most resolute partisans of monarchy by right divine showed themselves to be astonishingly devoid of political sense. This sense, however, was to be found among the leaders and rank and file of the Orleanists—de Broglie, Decazes, etc.; but, caught as they were and wedged in between the Republicans, the Bonapartists and the Legitimists, and reduced to their own forces alone, they were powerless.

On the fall of the de Broglie Ministry, MacMahon called upon General de Cissey to form a Cabinet, in which the Duc Decazes,

The Cissey Ministry. the extremely clever and able Minister for Foreign Affairs, and Fortou were the two most prominent members. They formed a fighting Government which engaged vigorously in a twofold struggle against the Republicans and the Bonapartists. The latter having just gained a success at the elections (Baron de Bourgoing, sometime equerry to Napoleon III, had won the election at Nièvre) had increased in confidence and were indulging in an extremely active propaganda in favour of the Prince Imperial.

As long as the object in view was a negative one—opposition to their adversaries—the Royalists acquiesced. But as soon as anything positive, such as passing constitutional measures, was mooted, differences at once appeared. A fresh manifesto from

71

the Comte de Chambord (2nd of July, 1874) came just in the nick of time to increase them. He protested against " the errors and falsehoods," expressed astonishment that " the proverbial intelligence of the French race " had not shown a better understanding of his last declaration, and denounced the " sterile struggles of Parliament."

The Government decided to suspend *l'Union* which had published this manifesto; hence the discontent of the Legiti-

Fall of the Cissey Ministry. mists. The Chamber adjourned until the autumn session. MacMahon, whose popularity his friends were anxious to increase, visited a certain number of the provinces. As soon as the Assembly met again, however, worse difficulties than ever arose. Once again, on a question of the order for the day, the Legitimists joined the Imperialists and the Republicans, and the Ministry, like its predecessor, was overthrown.

Thiers now had his revenge as he saw his prognostications fulfilled, and cast a disdainful eye on the increasing difficulties with which successive Governments and the Assembly had to struggle.

The impotence of the Royalist parties only served to favour the advance of the Republicans. For when leaders fail to agree and thus prove their impotence, how can disaffection in the rank and file cause surprise? And indeed disaffection among them increased day by day.

As de Broglie failed to form a Ministry, the Cabinet which had sent in its resignation continued in office. At last it was decided to attack the problem round which they had been hovering so long—the legal and constitutional establishment of the executive and the legislature, the rights of the President and those of the Assembly. And now the question which had been on the lips of all, and which every effort had been made to postpone, necessarily forced itself to the front—the question of the Republic.

There is a well-known English verse, though it is not precisely applicable at the present day :

> " I often think it's comical
>   How nature always does contrive
> That every boy and every gal
>   That's born into this world alive,
> Is either a little Liberal
>   Or else a little Conservative."

Similarly, a system must of necessity be either monarchical or republican. And this applied to the system by which France had been ruled ever since the war. In vain did the Orleanists and the Legitimists keep vigilant guard to prevent the word from being mentioned; the actuality was already established, which from their point of view was even worse, and by one channel or another the detested word had inevitably to be uttered. But how could this be done with such discretion and moderation as to prevent its enemies from immediately falling upon it and stifling it? This was the problem that the Republican leaders and the Assembly were now facing with all the skill and subtlety at their command.

A certain man named Ventavon, a Royalist and reporter to the Commission, suggested, as a way of avoiding the danger, to wait until the termination of the Septennate before definitely deciding on a Constitution. Meanwhile the President might be allowed to exercise almost unlimited power, with the right of nominating part of the Senate and of dissolving the Chambers. This system, derisively called the "Ventavonnate," was no solution. It was rejected. Was the word Republic to be mentioned in the text of the laws or not? This was indeed the main difficulty, and it was over this point that the struggle took place.

A certain Professor Wallon, a recent recruit to the Republican ranks, convinced, as was only reasonable, that no other form of Government was possible, proposed, with regard **The Wallon Amendment.** to the method of electing the President, his famous amendment, which was couched in the following terms—" The President of the Republic shall be elected by the Senate and by the Chamber."

This amendment, although it was rejected by the Commission, was passed by a majority of votes.

Obviously no republican system of Government ever had more modest or more humble beginnings, at all events from the legal point of view. A single majority vote was, it must be confessed, an extraordinarily fragile basis.

The most delicate part of any republican constitution is that connected with the executive, and particularly with the prerogatives of the head of the State. If the latter is made merely a nominee of the Assemblies who appoint him, he is necessarily their servant if not actually their slave. If, on the other hand, he is elected by the direct vote of the people, this very fact creates a separate power which may some day or other come into conflict with Parliament.

The Powers of the President.

A President elected by the people was an alternative of which no one either among the Royalists or the Republicans dreamt. The recollection of the 2nd of December was still too fresh. The Bonapartists alone, in keeping with their traditions, demanded that such an appeal to the nation should be made. And the very fact that they demanded it was a sufficient reason for nobody outside their ranks to desire it.

It was therefore decided that the President should be elected by the parliamentary Assemblies. What were to be his powers? The Royalists were instinctively inclined to make them as wide as possible, although on this point also they were far from being unanimous. The Legitimists shook their heads, fearing or pretending to fear that one of the Orleanist princes might one day become President of the Republic.

The Assembly refused to support the Commission, which wanted to give the President the right of dissolving the Chamber on his own authority alone. This right was accorded subject to the approval of the Senate. This measure, which deprived the President of an extremely important power, was only voted, and this is extremely significant, owing to the abstention of certain of the Legitimists. The right of revising the Constitution was vested in the two Assemblies.

The composition and method of election of the Senate remained to be settled. Since the President of the Republic could only dissolve the Chamber with the consent of the Senate, the latter, theoretically at all events, was endowed with considerable authority and importance. By whom and how was it to be elected? If it was to have the same, or almost the same, electoral basis as the Chamber, it would become a body more or less resembling the latter, which would diminish its power and authority. The Duc de Broglie, who knew his history, elaborated an extremely learned and remarkable scheme, which consisted in making of the Senate a Conservative organ in the full acceptation of the term, a body

The Senate.

74

representative of all that was best in the nation. The electoral body to which he proposed to entrust its election was to consist in each department of the following :

Deputies and former deputies ;
General Councillors and District Councillors ;
The representatives of the magistracy ;
The Archbishops, Bishops and *curés* ;
The Presidents of Protestant and Jewish consistories ;
The members of tribunals and of the Chambers of Commerce ;
Senior members and retired senior members of the order of advocates ;
The Presidents of the Chambers of notaries and attorneys ;
The Deans and Professors of Faculties ;
General officers and certain superior officers ;
Certain high officials who had retired ;
The Grand Crosses, Grand Officers, Commanders and Officers of the Legion of Honour ; and, finally, the largest taxpayers of each department.

In short, the picked members of every profession were to be called upon to elect a sort of grand national council which in some respects resembled a House of Peers.

This scheme, which deserved a better fate, was, curiously enough, received with indifference, almost with disdain. As was natural, the Republicans would have nothing to do with it, neither would the Legitimists, for the simple reason that the Duc de Broglie, who had drawn it up, allowed it to transpire that he hoped to offer the Presidency of this Upper Chamber to the Duc d'Aumale. This was all that was required to make the " light horse " turn away from it in horror. Broglie made a mistake in showing his cards too soon ; though he acted as he did partly in the hope of rallying around him the Orleanists, who had reproached him with putting Marshal MacMahon in the Élysée instead of one of their own princes. Thus we see that the position of the leaders was far from enviable. When they tried to please Tom and Dick they were almost sure to displease Harry.

Gambetta, who was more far-sighted, as soon as he heard of the scheme, exclaimed : " If the parties of the Right are only intelligent enough to accept it, the cause of democracy will be retarded by fifty years in France."

On the rejection of this scheme it was decided, as the result of a fresh compromise (22nd–24th of February, 1874), to have the Senate elected by a special college which should consist, in addition to the deputies and general councillors, of a delegate from each commune. This meant the certain predominance of the rural over the urban districts. And thus the Senate, to use Gambetta's expression, became the "Grand Council of the Communes." A quarter of its members, who numbered three hundred, were to be appointed for life by the Assembly.

As for the Chamber of Deputies, this was to be elected by the single vote system, which was contrary to the wishes of the Republicans, who, for theoretical rather than practical reasons since the system had fairly frequently worked to their disadvantage, demanded the multiple vote system.

As soon as the law organising the government bodies had been voted (24th–25th of February), the Buffet Ministry came into **The Buffet** office instead of the Cissey Ministry, which had **Ministry.** long since sent in its resignation.

With Buffet, who as President of the Chamber had proved his energy, the determined and combative nature of the Government and of the Ministry was accentuated. Unfortunately, however, the Cabinet was far from united, including as it did two representatives of the Right Centre —Dufaure and Léon Say, who got on very badly with their chief and on several occasions did not hesitate to express their disagreement.

It only remained for the Royalists, who had already made so many mistakes, to commit their last and perhaps most fatal error. A certain number of them, resigned and weary, and also perhaps moved by fear of Bonapartist intrigues and an Imperialist *coup d'état*, ended by supporting the Republicans and voting for the constitutional laws. But from the moment that the President of the Republic was obliged, in accordance with the Constitution, to depend on the Senate if he wished to oppose the Chamber of Deputies, and if necessary dissolve it, the parties of the Right should in duty bound have watched over the composition of the Senate with the greatest concern, and above all over the election of the seventy-five life members chosen by the Assembly.

Had they been united they could have introduced into the future Senate seventy-five of their own partisans, that is to say, a quarter of that body, and would thus have been in a position to decide its policy for a long time to come. But once again the Royalists failed to agree and only played into the hands of the Republicans.

There is no more curious and significant phenomenon than that presented by the intrigues to which the election of these seventy-five life members led. It immediately brought out into the limelight all the characteristics and defects of parliamentary assemblies. Private interests were mixed up with questions of principle and more often than not outweighed them. When once the representatives of the people were faced with the risk of not representing anything, they pushed their desire for re-election to fantastic limits. Whatever their origin or the party to which they belonged, they were ready to sacrifice everything, sometimes even their principles and their convictions, in order to secure their end. The microbe of re-election now began to work its ravages.

The Republicans soon got wind of the difficulties and disagreements connected with the drawing up of the Royalist list and sought to turn them to account. Under the guidance of experienced leaders, Gambetta and Jules Simon, they conducted their manœuvres with the greatest skill. They approached both the Bonapartists, who gave them their full support, and a party among the Legitimists, to whom, in return for their votes, they promised a certain number of seats in the Senate. A dozen of the " light horse " did not hesitate to accept this far from creditable bargain.

As one of them remarked to a colleague who had reproached him bitterly on the subject : " But I become a senator for life, whilst to-morrow you will be nothing at all." It would be impossible to go to further lengths of cynicism.

If the Legitimist party had been a real party, well disciplined and organised, and led by chiefs worthy of the name, they would

77

never have tolerated such proceedings, which had the immediate result of delivering up the keys of the citadel to their enemies.

But every party in France, whether Royalist or Republican, has the greatest difficulty in securing organisation and discipline. They in no way resemble the political parties in England and the United States, which are solidly constructed with a proper equipment of stringent regulations, cadres and leaders. Now the parliamentary system as it has been more or less faithfully copied by continental countries from England, "the mother of Parliaments," is based on the primary supposition that the parties are strongly organised. But the instinct of individualism, which is highly developed among the French, makes any such discipline and cohesion extremely irksome, and this tendency, which is an essential characteristic of the French Parliament, continued to develop.

At this time the Republican party presented a fairly united front, owing, in the first place, to the fact that in Gambetta it possessed a first-class leader, and also because the danger of a restoration of the monarchy or a *coup de force* on the part of the Bonapartists made such unanimity imperative. Nevertheless signs of cleavage began to appear. The extreme Left threatened to break away. In order to pass the Wallon amendment, for instance, which laid the foundations of the Republic, it was found necessary to beg and beseech Louis Blanc and his colleagues, and almost take them by force to the ballot-box.

But the moment that fear no longer held these elements together, when the Pretenders were dead or done for, and the Republic seemed to have no further cause for anxiety, these differences continued to become more and more pronounced.

The cartel, the paradoxical alliance between the Republicans, the Bonapartists and certain of the Legitimists, produced the following results in the election of the seventy-five life members (21st of December, 1875)—fifty-seven Republicans against ten Legitimists and seven Orleanists. Thus it was entirely in favour of the Republicans and against the Orleanists, whose chief leaders did not even secure a seat in the Senate.

Before rising the Assembly passed a law announcing the establishment of peace and raising the state of siege, except for the three great cities of Paris, Lyons and Marseilles.

THE SEPTENNATE

In order to judge the Republican Constitution which had just been established by a Royalist Assembly, the conditions and the time of its passing must be taken into consideration. In the first place, there was no such thing, as it is sometimes asserted, as a Constitution of 1875; there was only a collection of constitutional laws passed on various dates at more or less distant intervals.

Character of the Constitution.

The Constitution was above all a compromise between different and sometimes opposite parties and principles. This constituted its most prominent and characteristic feature. The Royalist parties were not in agreement; bitter quarrels of long standing, only half mended by superficial reconciliations, divided them. And their disagreements on more than one occasion afforded the Republicans the opportunity of realising their own views.

A Compromise.

The Republican Constitution, voted by a majority which was not Republican, was not the outcome, and for very good reason, of a uniform plan or of a general idea or principle. For the first time the Frenchman, who loves symmetrical constructions and logical developments, was perforce obliged to cast aside symmetry and logic. He carried on from day to day, obliged at every moment to tack and hedge and be guided by circumstances. He did not do what he would but what he could.

As France had lived since the war under a *de facto* Republic, a certain number of Royalist deputies, owing to force of circumstances, lassitude and the desire to end temporary measures, acquiesced in allowing this system to become a Republic *de jure*. They naturally made as few concessions as possible to Republican ideas and principles. Nevertheless on all essential points—universal suffrage, upon which the Chamber of Deputies, which in the last resort was the sovereign power, rested, the Senate, and the election of the President of the Republic—it was the democratic principle which in the end prevailed. It is therefore unfair to maintain, as is sometimes done, that the Constitution of 1875 was content to shelter Royalist wares beneath a Republican roof. And indeed events proved that this was not the case. When, after successive elections, the Republic grew ever more firmly established, it accommodated itself extremely well, except for a few slight changes, to the system originally drawn up. But if this had been Royalist in essence, force of circumstances would have obliged the Republicans to rid themselves of it.

As the principle of universal suffrage for the election of the Chamber of Deputies had been conceded without demur by all **The President.** parties, including even the Royalists, who had many a reason for regarding it with suspicion, the chief points in the Constitution were the method of electing the President of the Republic and the method of electing the Senate.

With recollections of the *coup d'état* still fresh in their minds, almost the whole of the Assembly was inspired with a feeling of hatred amounting almost to horror of the plebiscite. It was accordingly settled without further debate that the President should be elected by the united vote of the two Assemblies. Being a nominee of Parliament, what was to prevent him from becoming sooner or later entirely subjected to it? This question, which forms the stumbling-block of every republican constitution, was not only not settled, it was not even raised. Once again compromise and subterfuge intervened as well as differences between Orleanists and Legitimists, the latter not being over-anxious to increase the powers of the head of the State for fear lest an Orleanist prince might one day be elected President, and thus find the road to the throne ready prepared for him.

But when once the choice of the President had been vested in Parliament he never succeeded in securing any real power apart from the latter. All the prerogatives granted to him were more apparent than real. He might use them in a more or less prolonged endeavour to oppose the will of the Chamber and if necessary dissolve it. But in the last resort it was the will of the deputies directly elected by the people that won the day. The moment was sure to come when he was obliged to abandon the struggle and give way.

What happened in the case of MacMahon only a short time afterwards furnishes a striking proof of this. " Give way or give up," Gambetta's famous phrase, exactly expresses the truth. The example afforded by MacMahon, although he was at the time supported by the majority of the Senate, was not calculated to encourage his successors to stand up against the Chamber, no matter what the occasion might be. Dissolution, a measure to which he once had recourse, was never again resorted to by any of them. *It was inevitable that this should be so.* Similarly, none of them used or could use the more theoretical than practical powers conferred upon them by the Constitution —the right of sending a message, the power to postpone the promulgation of a law by demanding a second vote in Parliament, etc., etc.

The defeat inflicted on MacMahon in his struggle with the Chamber inevitably condemned his successors never to engage in any such conflict again. And thus the President of the Republic was destined to be deprived of all real power. Even at moments of ministerial crisis, the influence he exercised was extremely circumscribed. He was, it is true, able to choose the future head of the Government, but only on the lines laid down for him by the Chamber, which considerably restricted his choice.

The contention that the President of the French Republic has as much if not more power than a constitutional sovereign, and that all he lacks is the desire to make use of it, is a little bit wide of the mark. The spirit if not the letter of the Constitution forbids him to exercise this power, and if he allows it to lapse it is because, when all is said and done, he cannot do otherwise.

Next to the President comes the Senate. Is it possible for the latter to constitute a separate and effective power on its own **The Senate.** account? In order to answer this question it will be necessary to consider the difficulties attending the establishment of the Constitution.

In 1873 Thiers proposed that the Senate should be elected like the Chamber, by universal suffrage, with the proviso that the candidates should be chosen from certain definite categories, from a list containing the picked members of most of the professions.

The Duc de Broglie's scheme aimed at a Grand Council, which should only to a limited extent be dependent upon the elective system and would have as much in common with a House of Peers as with an elected Assembly.

Neither of these schemes was realised. The desire for safety and compromise again led to the establishment of a Senate two-thirds of which was elected, albeit by an extremely limited electorate.

G

Indeed so limited was it, that the Republicans, as soon as they were masters, felt the need of extending it, and straightway did so.

In spite of its origin, the Senate did not differ very greatly in fundamentals from the Chamber. The predominance of rural electors in the senatorial colleges certainly inclined the members to the exercise of a certain moderation. The upper Chamber acted as a brake on the lower Chamber, but it had no more power than the President to engage in any struggle with the latter, and it might almost be said that it never attempted to do so. The same influences and committees on which the election of the deputies depended also came into play in the case of the senatorial elections, and by the logic of things the Senate came to consist more and more of men who had once been deputies. The road to the Luxembourg lies through the Palais Bourbon, and thus the Senate became a haven of rest for the deputies, a port of calm and untroubled waters, a sort of place of retreat.

And thus in the last resort it was in the Chamber that all the power was concentrated, and became even more so as time advanced. It is here that the essential character-
The Chamber. istic of French parliamentary life, which we have already mentioned—the division and lack of cohesion of the parties and groups—is most forcibly felt. Instead of having two great parties as in England and America, both elector and elected have an invincible tendency to split up, a tendency which characterised the National Assembly from the very beginning, and which continued to grow. With such a multiplicity of groups, how can a Government possibly rely upon a solid and lasting majority? And as soon as a majority is lacking a ministerial crisis at once supervenes and a new combination is formed. But as similar causes produce exactly similar results the new combination has no greater consistency or length of duration than its predecessor. Thus a period of continual ministerial changes was inaugurated extremely detrimental to the efficient administration of public affairs.

It is impossible for the head of a Government, or a Minister who cannot count on the morrow and has no guarantee for the future, to tackle his task with the resolution demanding unceasing effort. Most of his time is wasted in defending himself against the plots and intrigues of those who will eventually take his place.

In England the parliamentary system is entirely based upon the existence of two great parties provided with strong cadres, well organised and strictly disciplined. If the alternation of the two were destroyed, everything would fall to pieces. Each party is led by a Committee, a veritable oligarchy which has all the funds and all the power in its hands, and appoints the candidates. And when these candidates are elected it keeps them in strict subjection. The Party Whip plays the part of sheep-dog to the members of Parliament, forcing them to be present at debates and exercising absolute power over their votes; he even goes so far as to prevent them from speaking.

Ministerial crises are negligible, as Cabinets, once formed, usually last as long as the elected body. Shortly before the latter reaches its term of existence, Parliament is dissolved and the decision rests with the electors. Such in bold outline is the English parliamentary system.

The rise of a third party, the Socialists, in addition to the Liberals and Conservatives, threatened to cause considerable confusion in this organisation. But the system continued to work notwithstanding, in the first place because the new party was organised on the same lines as its two predecessors, with similar cadres, trappings and discipline, and secondly because its strength and numerical importance had the effect of weakening the Liberal party whose place it gradually usurped.

In America also the existence and alternation of two great parties is an essential characteristic of political life.

In copying more or less faithfully the English system, the majority of European nations borrowed the externals, the façade, but omitted the most important feature—the internal structure. Without these parties, extremely limited in number and well disciplined, which secure the stability and continuity of the Government, any parliamentary system, no matter where it is established, is nothing but a caricature of the British system. But when Ministers are all powerful, and their authority is limited only by a vote in the Chamber, is it to be wondered at, especially in a country as centralised as France, where everything is done and settled in Paris and bureaucracy and officialdom are very strongly developed, that the possession of a ministerial portfolio should arouse the bitterest jealousy on the part of parliamentary candidates? The frequency of ministerial crises only serves to accentuate this jealousy. Every deputy is at liberty to ask : " After all, why should it not be I ? "

This curtailment of the life and weakening of the power of the executive can, at a pinch, be tolerated at ordinary times and periods of prosperity, when a well-to-do country and easily balanced budgets can stand a certain waste of strength and even extravagance. But at times of crisis, in the middle of a war, for instance, or when economic and financial difficulties have to be faced, the defects of the system stand out in sharp relief. How can a strong and lasting Government be formed, capable of indulging in the long-sighted plans and persistent efforts which can alone produce results? If the country is invaded or threatened, the Government in power, handing over the command of the armies to a generalissimo, is more or less obliged, as long as the peril continues, to ignore Parliament and become a regular dictatorship.

BIBLIOGRAPHY.—De Freycinet, *Souvenirs* (1878–93) (2 vols., 1913). J. Simon, *Le Soir de ma Journée* (1901). E. de Marcère, *Histoire de la République de 1876 à 1879* (2 vols., 1908). Ranc, *Souvenirs* (1913). Debidour, *L'Eglise Catholique et L'Etat* (2 vols.). Lecanuet, *L'Eglise de France sous la Troisième République* (2 vols., 1910). Léon Say, *Les Finances de la France sous la Troisième République* (4 vols., 1898–1901). M. Bodet, *Les Finances Françaises de 1870 à 1878* (2 vols., 1882). A. Esmein, *Eléments de Droit Constitutionnel* (1899). Faustin Hélie, *La Constitution de la France* (1880). E. Pierre, *Les Lois Constitutionnelles de la République Française* (1889). L. Duguit, *Traité de Droit Constitutionnel* (1909). *La Transformation du Droit Publique* (1915). Louis Passy, *Le Marquis de Blosseville* (Evreux, 1898). D'Eichtal, *Alexis de Tocqueville et la Démocratie Libérale* (1897). L. Jacques, *Les Partis Politiques sous la Troisième République* (1913). Gambetta, *Lettres* (Rev. de Paris, December 1906). Cheusi, *Gambetta, Lettres Intimes et Souvenirs de Famille* (1905). J. Lafitte, *Gambetta Intime* (1879). F. Laur, *Le Cœur de Gambetta*. A. Barboux, *Gambetta* (1879). Joseph Reinach, *Léon Gambetta* (1887). Bertol-Gravil et Plantié, *Gambetta : Souvenirs* (1883). Desmarest, *Gambetta* (1882). Depasse, *Gambetta* (1883). Sirven, *Gambetta et Chambord* (1883). Henri Thurat, *Gambetta* (1883). *Discours et Plaidoyers Politiques*, published by Joseph Reinach (2 vols. 8vo, 1881–6). Grenville-Murray, *Les Hommes de la Troisième République*. *Les Hommes du Septennat* (Paris, Sandoz, 3 vols.). *Les Portraits de Kel-Kun*. *Nouveaux Portraits de Kel-Kun* (Edmond Texier) (1876). Ignotus (Félix Platel) *Les Hommes de Mon Temps* (1878). Tchernoff, *Les Partis Républicain sous le Second Empire* (1906). G. Doré, *Album de Types de l'Assemblée Nationale*.

CHAPTER VI

THE SIXTEENTH OF MAY. CONSOLIDATION OF THE REPUBLIC

The parliamentary game. The 16th of May. Nature of the Conflict. MacMahon. The Dufaure Ministry. Resignation of MacMahon. Make way for the Greybeards! Jules Grévy, the Whiskered President. Death of the Prince Imperial.

WITH the disappearance of the National Assembly it was for the country to have its say. In whose favour would it decide?

If the elections which took place after the war afforded any criterion, the result was a foregone conclusion. And indeed it was the Republicans who won the majority of votes.

The senatorial elections took place on the 30th of January, 1876. The Republicans won ninety-two seats; the Right, the Conservatives, and the extreme Right, the Imperialists, one hundred and nineteen. There were in addition seventeen Constitutionalists. If these figures are added to those of the life members, we get a total of one hundred and forty-nine Republicans against one hundred and fifty-one Conservatives. Thus the Senate was divided into two almost equal halves. It was only through their clever strategy in the election of the life members that the Republicans succeeded in securing a Senate in which the parties of the Right did not have a very large majority.

The election of deputies (20th of February—5th of March) constituted a crushing defeat for the Right—three hundred and forty Republicans against one hundred and fifty-three Conservatives. Buffet, and this is a characteristic episode, after he had failed to be elected senator, was beaten in all the four constituencies which he contested. Immediately afterwards, on the 23rd of February, he resigned his Ministry.

85

Gambetta was successful in four constituencies—Paris, Marseilles, Lille and Bordeaux. A few fresh men also won seats in the Chamber.

Between a Conservative President of the Republic, a Senate **The Parliamentary Game.** divided into two almost equal parties, but inclining slightly to the Right, and a Chamber frankly Republican, how would the parliamentary game develop?

Though MacMahon was a Royalist he was too upright a man to attempt any *coup de force* against the majority in the Assembly. Any suggestion of the kind that was made to him he refused to listen to, just as a little while previously he had refused to lend an ear to the appeals from the Duc de Chambord. He found himself in a peculiar position, being called upon to collaborate in the consolidation of a system which did not inspire him with the smallest confidence. It required all the persistence of his Ministers to wrench from him his signature to the decrees dismissing officials who had been too badly compromised. His personal ties, his entourage, his general secretary d'Abzac, and his private secretary, the Vicomte d'Harcourt, were all influences driving him to the Conservative side. He ignored and wished to ignore the Republican world.

After the result of the elections, which filled the Conservatives with consternation, what course could the latter adopt? Use the weapons that still remained to them and engage in a struggle? Some of them contemplated doing so. The Vicomte de Meaux, in his interesting Memoirs, gives a description of a visit he paid to the Élysée for the purpose of advising the President to offer immediate and energetic resistance. The latter, however, immediately sided with the Duc de Broglie, who advised him to wait and see.

The conflict with the Chambers was none the less inevitable. It was not avoided, but only postponed.

The temporising policy recommended to the President by de **The sixteenth of May.** Broglie led to his endeavouring to govern, as far as possible, through the majority in the Chamber. He began by choosing an extremely moderate member of this majority—Dufaure.

Dufaure was a typical Conservative Republican. Is it

possible to reconcile these two terms, or was a " Conservative Republic," as J. J. Weiss maintained, " an absurdity "? As a matter of fact the Republic remained Conservative as long as it feared being strangled by its enemies. It was owing to this moderation at the beginning that it secured the support of a certain number of men whose feelings and tastes were inclined towards monarchy, but who turned away from it because it lacked one indispensable element—the monarch. But the moment the fear of a restoration or of a *coup d'état* had vanished, the Republic ceased to be Conservative and grew ever more and more democratic. Nothing could be more natural or inevitable than this development.

The same process took place in the union of Republican members. A man like Gambetta, a radical like Clemenceau, or a representative of the extreme Left like Louis Blanc, had very little in common with a moderate of the type of Dufaure. But the realisation of the danger which threatened the Republic in the throes of the crisis of the 16th of May, for instance, bound them closely together, though only for a while. When once the danger was past the differences between them reappeared.

The Dufaure Ministry was fairly representative of the opinions of the Chamber, although in a somewhat lower key. The question was, did Dufaure intend to follow a resolutely Republican policy? The Government declarations of the 14th of March seemed to indicate that he did. The word " Republican," however, was far from meaning the same thing to the various parties of the Left. Dufaure was in favour of a " pacificatory " policy, whilst Gambetta's main object was to bring about a coalition of the parties of the Left in both Assemblies, and form a single party of which his oratorical powers and prestige would make him the certain leader. He made the suggestion at a meeting of the parties of the Left before the convening of the Chamber. When the Ministry was formed, he conjured the Republicans to support his idea. But neither Jules Ferry nor Grévy, for personal reasons much more than as a matter of principle, responded. Thus the Left remained divided. This lack of unanimity was natural and inevitable. It was only the fear of immediate danger that was capable of uniting all the Republicans.

The Ministry confined itself to dismissing or changing a certain number of Prefects who had made themselves particularly conspicuous by their attitude during the course of the electoral campaign.

The conflict between the two Chambers began with the municipal law which proposed that the mayors should be elected in all the communes, except Paris, instead of allowing them to be appointed by the Government. Jules Ferry and the Ministry wanted the principle of election to be applied only to the rural communes, and for the arrangements already in force under the existing law to be continued in the case of the capitals of the cantons, the *arrondissements*, and the departments. The Commssion, for its part, was in entire agreement with Gambetta. But the President of the Republic lodged an energetic protest, and, according to the report published by the Paris correspondent of *The Times*, even threatened the Ministers with a dissolution if the Government measure were not passed without amendment. In the end the Commission supported the scheme, which was adopted by the two Chambers.

As President the Commission elected Gambetta, who in the exercise of the office brought his talent and activity to bear in full measure, constantly taking part in the debates, delivering wonderful speeches, and taking a particular interest in the War Budget. The Budget presented by the Ministry in April 1875 was frankly Conservative in spirit. Gambetta proposed an income tax, an old proposal made by the Republicans of 1848. Neither the Commission nor the Chamber would agree to it. Two simultaneous votes brought about the downfall of the Dufaure Ministry. On the 23rd of November, the escort of honour sent to attend the funeral of the musician Félicien David, who had died at Lyons, marched away because the ceremony was a civil one. On the 2nd of December, in an order of the day, the Chamber demanded from the Government recognition of the two great Republican principles—freedom of conscience and freedom of worship. On the same day Dufaure was defeated in the Senate on the Amnesty Bill, and finding himself in the minority he sent in his resignation (2nd of December, 1876).

The retiring Ministry had never been in more than superficial and apparent agreement with the majority returned by the last elections. Dufaure, though a sincere Republican, was at heart frankly Conservative. MacMahon, after holding a consultation with the Duc de Broglie, summoned the Presidents of the Chamber and the Senate, setting a precedent which his successors never failed to follow whenever there was a ministerial crisis. And these were to occur often enough in all conscience ! Neither Grévy nor d'Audiffret would undertake to form a Cabinet.

MacMahon, after vainly endeavouring to patch up the Dufaure Ministry, resigned himself to placing the Government in the hands of Jules Simon, who became Minister of the Interior, but was obliged to keep the same chiefs in the War Office and the Foreign Office. This was the first occasion on which the head of the Government was a member of one of the parties of the Left (12th of December, 1876).

The new Ministry soon found itself involved in the same difficulties as its predecessor. If it followed a frankly Republican policy, which would have secured the support of Gambetta and his followers, it would have alienated the Senate, and above all the President, who, although he had himself appointed Jules Simon, considered he had the right to exercise an active control over all his actions, and if necessary to oppose them on occasion. In fact he was determined to fight the tendencies of the majority in the Chamber.

From this moment conflict between the President and the Republican party, which was the indisputable master of one of **The Conflict.** the two Assemblies, was inevitable. It broke out in connection with the religious question. A law having been passed in Italy against the activities of the clergy, the Pope on the 12th of March invited the Bishops to bring pressure to bear with their respective Governments " for the purpose of removing all obstacles to the true and complete independence of the Head of the Catholic Church." This gave the signal in France for a campaign of charges and petitions, demanding intervention in favour of the sovereignty of the Pope. The official organ of Monseigneur Dupanloup, Bishop of Orleans, was conspicuous for its violence, and launched a regular ultimatum against the Government (2nd of May). Two days later, the Chamber, by a majority of 304 to 113, asked the Government to use all the legal means at its disposal to restrain the clerical agitation.

Thereupon MacMahon made up his mind to dismiss the Ministry. It was only a matter of finding a pretext. On the 15th of May the Chamber, without meeting with any opposition from Jules Simon, voted the partial abrogation of the law of the 19th of September, 1875, dealing with the Press; henceforward offences against foreign sovereigns and other delinquences were to be referred, not as hitherto to the police court, but to the Court of Assize.

MacMahon, dissatisfied with the attitude adopted by Jules Simon, held a consultation that night with his chief adviser, the Duc de Broglie, and on the following morning, the 16th of May, sent a letter to the head of the Government. In it he expressed his astonishment at the lethargy shown by the President of the Council and the Keeper of the Seals in the matter, and ended with the following words : " Some explanation is imperative; for although I am not responsible, as you are, to Parliament, I am nevertheless responsible to France, whom I am to-day more than ever called upon to consider."

Jules Simon presented himself before the Marshal and sent in his resignation, which was accepted. The Ministry, although it had not been put in a minority in the two Chambers, was dismissed by the head of the State, who appealed to a higher authority—his responsibility to the country—which was no part of the written Constitution.

On the evening of the 17th the new Ministry was formed and was composed entirely of partisans of the Right. Its choice of the Duc de Broglie as its chief, and of his colleagues,

A Fighting Ministry. clearly revealed its tendencies. It was entirely comprised of Legitimists, Orleanists and Imperialists. It presented itself on the following day before the Chambers, bearing as a sort of declaration a manifesto from the Marshal justifying his policy, in which he said that the two previous Ministries had been unable to secure a solid majority in favour of their ideas. Consequently it was impossible to form a Ministry without appealing to another faction of the Republican group (a union between Republicans and Radicals). The President declared that both his conscience and his patriotism

90

made him opposed to any such attempt, which would be disastrous for the country, and it was this reason that had guided him in his choice of the new Ministry.

In short, MacMahon insisted on choosing a Cabinet from the political groups he himself favoured and foreshadowed the dissolution which everyone was expecting.

In connection with this crisis, it has been maintained that there was opposition between the personal power of the President and the rights of the Constitution. This is a somewhat misleading way of presenting the facts. This opposition had no definite existence in reality. Matters were far more complicated.

Nature of the Conflict.

As there was no King, the National Assembly had elected for seven years a President invested with very considerable powers. A Republican Constitution had since been established in extremely confused and complicated circumstances by an exceedingly small majority. The President was honestly and sincerely convinced that the Constitution had not done away with his rights, and when the majority in the Chamber embarked upon a policy which he considered dangerous, he fought it with the weapons with which the Constitution itself had supplied him. In accord with the Senate, he appealed to the country, and in so doing maintained that he was strictly within his legal rights. He would only have infringed them if, when the country pronounced its verdict, it had returned the old Republican majority, even if it were slightly diminished, and he had then had recourse to a *coup de force*. At one time he had thought of this, but had quickly relinquished the idea.

The parties of the Left, feeling that the conflict was at hand, set to work to secure union among themselves. In the Senate, they expressed their conviction that the Upper House would never support any attempt made against Republican institutions. In the Chamber, 345 deputies, after a speech by Gambetta, passed a vote of censure, and by tacit consent Gambetta was made leader of the party.

When once it became a matter of an electoral struggle, no choice could have been better. On the 20th of May, 363 deputies addressed to the electors an appeal drawn up by Spuller, an intimate friend of Gambetta, in which they were invited to choose between a policy of reaction and a wise, peaceful and progressive policy, which had the sanction of previous elections.

Appeal of the 363. Gambetta assembled the directors of all the leading Republican journals in Paris, and in conjunction with them formed an opposition Committee. Young lawyers and officials who had been dismissed formed a second Committee charged with the work of propaganda, the distribution of leaflets and circulars, etc. The 363 signatories of the manifesto were invited to form working Committees in the capital of every canton.

The Government prepared for the struggle by making a complete change in the holders of the Prefectorial office. Between the 20th and the 29th of May, 207 Prefects and sub-Prefects were dismissed or changed. When the Chambers met on the 16th of June, each side took up its position. The Chamber in an order of the day passed a vote of lack of confidence in the Government. In the Senate, the Duc de Broglie brought forward a motion for dissolution, which was passed on the 20th of June by the Commission (by a majority of six out of nine), being opposed by Jules Simon and Béranger. The writ was issued on the 25th. According to the Constitution, the elections should take place within three months, that is to say, at latest on the 25th of September. A literal, though exceedingly dubious, interpretation gave the Government the right of convening the electorate for the 14th of October by a writ issued on September the 22nd. This meant an additional delay of a few weeks, which the Marshal's Government were anxious to secure in order to have a better chance of making preparations and cooking the elections.

An extremely violent campaign was immediately inaugurated in which the Government had recourse to all the devices employed under the Empire—the recommendation **The Electoral Campaign.** of official candidates by means of white placards, pressure brought to bear on all officials without exception, even those whose posts kept them furthest removed from political struggles, the suppression of street newsvendors in order to prevent the circulation of Republican papers, the closing of taverns and drinking booths, lawsuits against the Press, the dissolution of municipal councils, the dismissal of mayors and officials. As we see, nothing was neglected. The

Prefects were given instructions to make official circuits in their departments. The Marshal himself set the example, paying visits to the West, the Centre and the South-West, in order to influence public opinion. The tactics of the Government became clear with the publication of two manifestos (19th of September and 13th of October). The French people were invited to choose between the party of order and that of disorder, between the principle of authority and demagogy. Imbued with a sense of duty, which constituted a superior manifestation of the will of the people, the Marshal proclaimed that even if the elections turned in favour of " Radicalism " he would not be induced to abandon his post. He hoped that the word *Radicalism* would act as a scarecrow upon the electors. An incident which struck the keynote of the struggle was afforded on the 5th of July by Cuneo d'Ornano, a candidate of the Right, who wrote in the *Suffrage Universel des Charentes :* " We will make of the Republicans a mess of which even the dogs will refuse to eat."

As a counterblow to these tactics on the part of the Marshal and the Government, the Republicans presented Thiers to the electors as the candidate they had chosen to succeed the Marshal in case of the latter's defeat. The death on the 3rd of September of Thiers, the man who at the memorable session of the 16th of June had been greeted with the title of " liberator of the occupied territory," was a heavy blow for the parties of the Left. Jules Grévy was their candidate for Paris, and it was thereby hoped to show the moderates that Gambetta was not the successor chosen.

As a matter of fact it was Gambetta who was the soul of the movement. On the dissolution of the Chamber a Committee formed of representatives of the three Republican groups in the .Senate guided the electoral campaign. In conjunction with it another judicial Committee published pamphlets on the Government's abuses of power. The 363 outgoing members all presented themselves for re-election with the same programme; every Conservative candidate was opposed by a Republican. The Conservatives had only been able to supply 490 candidates for the 531 divisions (not counting the colonies). The Bonapartists terrified their Legitimist and Orleanist allies by the exaggerated language of their papers, so much so indeed that the Marshal was obliged to publish notes calculated to reassure the moderates.

Gambetta had prophesied that the 363 would return 400 strong. Although this prediction was not altogether realised, the elections were an undeniable victory for the Republicans. They won an aggregate of 327 seats as against 208 secured by the Conservatives, which constituted a strong majority.

On the 4th of November the choice of half the departmental councils confirmed this victory for the Left. In 45 departments the majority supported the Republicans, 41 remaining in the hands of the Conservatives.

And thus, in spite of the strongest official pressure that could be brought to bear, the elections signalised the defeat of the Marshal and his Government and assured the triumph of the Republicans. What was the reason of this? It was chicfly that the latter gave proof of political sense and adroitness, and submitted to an exceedingly strict discipline. The more violent and advanced among them, on the other hand, had the wisdom to give way to the moderates, who had every qualification for reassuring the country. Since Thiers died before the struggle began, it was Jules Ferry who took his place, whilst Gambetta, although he would have laid aside all violence and excess, and was a man capable of governing, had the wisdom to see that his name and programme might frighten a certain number of electors whose support was indispensable to him. Thus he intelligently gave way to an older and less advanced man than himself.

The Republican party had excellent leaders, a programme and a doctrine. It knew where it was going and what it wanted.

The case of its adversaries was very different, and this provides the main reason for their defeat. If they were victorious in the elections, what would they do? What were their designs and plans? If the Duc de Broglie, the most intelligent of them, had been asked this question, he would have been at a loss to reply. As a matter of fact this campaign on the part of the Right had not and could not have any far-sighted object in view. It merely aimed at consolidating provisional institutions, which was not a programme capable of winning the heart of a country. The restoration of the monarchy was not to be dreamt of. The same causes as had stood in the way of such a restoration three years previously would have prevented it again; indeed they would have been stronger than ever, since the majority in the Chamber was now Republican.

Moreover, to keep perpetually in power a President of the Republic who was reaching the end of his life and would soon be eighty was not a policy which offered much stability. Thus those who engaged in the struggle could see no solution, and it is not to be wondered at that, in the circumstances, they entered upon it somewhat half-heartedly.

To all this must be added the differences between the three factions—the Legitimists, the Orleanists and the Bonapartists, each of whom, as members of an alliance which was more apparent than real, preserved their own ideas and tastes.

Always in favour of a *coup de force* and of a policy of violence, the Bonapartists, by the exaggeration of their language and the violence of their campaign, naturally frightened many of those who had only too vivid a recollection of the misfortunes suffered under the Empire to have any wish to see it revived.

The excesses of the Legitimists, at whose doors the responsibility for the clerical agitation and the campaign in favour of the temporal power of the Papacy must be placed, were just as great. This campaign was a direct menace to peace. It caused profound irritation in Italy and literally pushed her into the arms of Germany. For Bismarck, feeling Russia escaping ever further from his grasp, especially since the outbreak of the Russo-Turkish war in the East, and anxious to replace her by Italy in the Triple Alliance, which was the object of his dreams, made excellent use of the weapon thus placed in his hands.

Moderation, wisdom, and peace at home and abroad were in the eyes of many people to be found not in a Government of the Right, but on the side of the Republicans.

What course would MacMahon adopt after the elections? Would he bow to the will of the country or would he continue the struggle? The dilemma enunciated by Gambetta, that he must either give way or give up, although fundamentally true, was not immediately realised. The Marshal, whilst refusing to abandon his post, at first thought of resisting. In this he was encouraged by one

MacMahon's Vacillations.

section of his followers, though once again his advisers were not in agreement. And it is this lack of agreement which explains the indecision and hesitation displayed in his attitude. A certain number of Orleanists, and first and foremost the Pretender himself, the Comte de Paris, had watched the struggle undertaken against the Chambers with complete lack of enthusiasm. They expected no good from it. When events proved them to be right they were all the less anxious to see it prolonged.

If the battle was to be fought, on what ground was it to be undertaken? In the political and parliamentary sphere it had already been lost; the solid block of Republicans in the Chamber who held the majority was bound, whatever happened, to impose its authority in the end. There remained the *coup de force*. The Bonapartists and certain of the Legitimists never ceased to clamour for this. But MacMahon, in his heart of hearts, felt that he had neither the desire nor the courage to undertake it.

For want of a better alternative he decided in favour of half-measures and a policy of semi-resistance which could not last very long.

The de Broglie Cabinet remained in office as though nothing had happened, but finding himself in disagreement with the Orleanist group in the Senate, de Broglie, who had been hard hit in the elections, sent in his resignation.

Who was to take his place? Would the Marshal choose a Minister from the ranks of the Republican majority in the Chamber? If he did, it meant nothing more or less than giving way, as Gambetta had predicted. Anxious to gain time, he had recourse to an extra-parliamentary Ministry, at the head of which he placed one of his old comrades, General de Rochebouët, who was in command of the army corps at Bordeaux.

Not unreasonably regarding this Ministry as an act of defiance, the Chamber refused to have anything to do with it. The Budget was held up and the parliamentary machine came to a standstill.

What was the way out of this deadlock? The Marshal had no alternative but to accept a Republican Ministry or else to have recourse to the bayonet and dismiss Parliament. A *coup d'état?* With what? Against what? In favour of whom?

To the last question above all it was impossible to find an answer, and it was this impossibility which provided the main reason for abandoning the scheme. MacMahon, urged on by certain of his advisers, contemplated calling out the army. General Rochebouët had already received orders to this effect. But would the whole army loyally obey? On this point opinion was divided. The situation was summed up by one of the generals present at the secret council : " Supposing the operation succeeds, what then ? "

A *coup de force* being regarded as out of the question, it only remained to give way. And this MacMahon decided to do. He sent for Dufaure, an old friend, one of those " useful men " who, under a parliamentary system, in which crises are of frequent occurrence, return periodically to the stage, like the supers in a play, and entrusted to him the task of forming a Republican Ministry.

This Ministry consisted chiefly of new men, including Bardoux and Freycinet, and marked the definite defeat of the President. The parliamentary system had got the better of personal power.

That evening at the Élysée MacMahon, on being presented with the edict nominating the new Ministers, had a moment of hesitation, but he quickly seized the pen and exclaimed : " Well, since I am forced to do so, I will sign." Then rising from his chair he fled rather than went out of the room.

From that moment he could only look on as a powerless and disarmed spectator at the measures passed by the new Government. When he disapproved of them, as he did in the majority of cases, he might postpone them for a while; but in the end he was obliged to resign himself to them.

The defeat of the Marshal meant the triumph of the parliamentary system, involving a weakening of the power of the executive, which in future could be and frequently **The Dufaure Ministry.** was changed by Parliament. It also represented the victory of the Republicans, which was marked, as was only natural, by a certain number of reprisals against the vanquished—many officials being dismissed and the law against the Press modified. The by-elections, owing to the momentum gained, did not fail to increase the Republican majority still further.

H

Freycinet, who had been a close colleague of Gambetta in the Government of National Defence, was one of the most prominent men in the new Ministry. It would be impossible to imagine anyone more different in character and temperament from Gambetta. A short, thin man endowed with a somewhat cold and forbidding elegance, clear and lucid even in conversation, his long life (for delicate-looking men who live as it were wrapped up in themselves give death but little hold over them) allowed him to span the interval of half a century between the last two wars.

The Public Works Department was entrusted to his care, and he managed it extremely well, drawing up and carrying out a colossal plan in connection with the railways and the canals and ports.

In May 1878 a Universal Exhibition was held in Paris, which attracted numbers of visitors from the country and abroad to the capital. It was one of those huge Fairs which were afterwards held every ten years or so.

They helped to a great extent in making Paris a sort of international city towards which the representatives of every race and every people, both in the Old World and the New, were drawn in ever larger numbers.

After the Republican party had gained possession of the Chamber, the task of conquering the Senate still remained, the former victory inevitably demanding the latter. In the elections of the 5th of January, 1879, held to fill the places of the outgoing third of that body, sixty-six Republicans were elected and sixteen Conservatives. The Republicans now had a majority of about fifty, and the Upper Chamber was no longer of a very different political complexion from the lower. This meant that all reason for disagreement between the two Assemblies had been removed.

Another consequence of this victory was that the higher officials in the administration had to be changed, since they had been largely appointed by Conservative **Resignation of MacMahon.** and more or less Royalist Ministries, and had inevitably to retire in favour of Republicans. To these changes, this " process of purification " as it has sometimes been called, the Ministry now turned its attention. So long as they dealt only with civilians, MacMahon, although very much distressed at heart, allowed them to do as they pleased. But as soon as it became a matter of dealing with military appointments, he rebelled, for he still regarded himself as the supreme head of the Army, which he considered his sphere and his alone. The removal of a few generals who had, as a matter of fact, reached or even passed the age limit, at first made him hesitate and afterwards refuse his consent. But as he had really made up his mind to go, he now found the opportunity for which he was waiting.

On the 30th of January, 1879, he sent in his resignation to the Presidents of the Senate and the Chamber.

His departure marked the termination of the temporary system which had been in existence since the war. It was the last barrier, which as a matter of fact was more apparent than real, that the Republican system had to remove.

But who was to take the place of MacMahon? There was one man whose prestige and talent everybody was bound to acknowledge, and who, with the exception of Thiers, had done more than anyone to bring about the consolidation of the Republic—Gambetta. He would surely be chosen President! The logic of things demanded that he should be asked to fill the vacant post without further discussion.

But the logic of things is not and is very far from being the logic of men, and above all of politicians. In the first place **Make way for** Gambetta had one very strong argument against **the Grey-** him—he was too young. Make way for the **beards!** greybeards! This was the motto that was destined to become more and more the rule, whether it was a matter of directing public affairs or important private concerns. Gerontocracy was inaugurated in the new regime, and its power and strength continued to increase.

It has often been said that it is difficult to achieve success in Paris. But what is difficult is not to achieve success but to last out long enough. Anyone who lasts out long enough is almost sure to " succeed " into the bargain. The best places, the highest appointments belong almost by right, not to those who might occupy them with the greatest brilliance, but to those who have long and patiently desired them, who have moved towards them with slow, sure steps, letting no opportunity slip, submissively following in the queue, careful only to see that they do not lose their place or allow any intruders to elbow their way in front of them.

In addition to his youth, his conspicuous and outstanding personality, his talent and superiority stood as obstacles in Gambetta's path. The Republic likes neutral tints and less pronounced outlines in its President, and regards second-class personalities as after all preferable to those of first-class rank.

Jules Grévy was elected on the 30th of January. Born in 1807, he was seventy-two at the time, which for Presidents and **Jules Grévy,** Popes is an excellent age. A lawyer by pro- **the Whiskered** fession, he was in 1848 a member of the Constitu- **President.** ent Assembly, where, as a matter of fact, he proposed the suppression of the office of President of the Republic, which it would seem was hardly calculated to fit him to become President himself. A member of the Legislative Council, the *coup d'état* of the 2nd of December forced him to return to the Bar. In 1868 the electors of the Jura returned him to the legislative body. Extremely reserved, cold and distant, this Jura peasant kept aloof from the fray less from distaste than from selfish motives, taking good care to keep out of the struggle in which he would have run the risk of being battered about. Initiative and courageous and energetic action were quite out of his line. He played no part in the Government of National Defence, he abstained from voting on the constitutional laws, and effaced himself during the crisis of the 16th of May.

But he kept his place quietly in the queue, certain that his turn would come. A grey and impersonal, frock-coated and whiskered President was the ideal he was destined to introduce into the Élysée. Nothing could have been more different and opposed to each other than Gambetta and Jules Grévy. They had nothing whatever in common and there was everything to keep them apart. The elder hated the younger with all his heart, the latter, for his part, returned the compliment handsomely. Grévy detested the younger man's gay bohemian bearing, his eloquence and above all his popularity, and was

110

determined to do all in his power to keep him as long as possible out of office.

With a man like Gambetta as President, at a time when the office was new and still capable of being modified in outline, the Republic would have had a more active and brilliant leader, who would have made his power and authority felt. But with Jules Grévy, on the contrary, it moved towards the conception which was ultimately to prevail—that of a sort of President Log.

The Dufaure Ministry had been merely a transition Cabinet, whose work it was to prepare the way. It naturally gave place to a more frankly Republican Ministry, in which the other groups of the Left were represented.

If he was not to be President of the Republic, Gambetta's destined sphere was undoubtedly the Presidency of the Council. Jules Grévy, however, was anxious to keep him out of this, and shunted him into the Presidency of the Chamber. Waddington, a diplomatist who had represented France very worthily at the Congress of Berlin, was entrusted with the work of forming a Ministry in February 1879. He carried out the task of liquidation, after which he was superseded by a Freycinet Ministry, which was merely a piece of patchwork.

Two important events mark its brief duration—the transfer of the seat of government to Paris, on the 19th of June, and the death of the Prince Imperial, who was killed in an ambuscade during an expedition against the Zulus, in which he had asked to take part as a volunteer.

There is an element of tragedy in the death of these sons of the Cæsars. The first, the King of Rome, "l'Aiglon," **Death of the** ended his life in an exile more or less resembling **Prince** imprisonment. The second fell in obscurity in **Imperial.** the depths of Africa, killed by the assegais of a handful of savages.

Fortune continued to favour the Republic. The rival who was really most dangerous to it had ceased to exist. The two Royalist Pretenders did nothing but cut each other's throats. The Legitimist candidate, the Comte de Chambord, also died four years later in 1883, leaving no heir. The incident which occurred at his funeral, and which prevented the Comte de

THE THIRD REPUBLIC

Paris from being present at it (he went to Frohsdorf, but as the Comtesse de Chambord refused to allow him precedence, he was not present at the interment, which took place at Goritz), proved that the breach between the two branches had not been healed. Rather than join the Orleanists, the more enthusiastic of the Legitimists preferred to give their allegiance, which, however, was more theoretical than practical, to the Spanish branch of the Bourbons, represented by Don Carlos.

Bonapartism, with its popular and demagogic side, a bit of Epinal ware, had struck fairly deep roots into French soil. When a period of crisis and disorder supervened, the Bonapartist idea, which above all represented authority, quickly rallied around it a large number of supporters.

But now the death of the son of Napoleon III, and the differences which arose between his heirs, Prince Jerome and Prince Victor, meant an appreciable weakening of Bonapartism.

BIBLIOGRAPHY.—See the bibliography for the preceding chapter.

H. Gautier, *Pendant le Seize Mai* (1881). Comte d'Ideville, *Les Petits Cotés de l'Histoire* (1885). L. Favre, *Histoire Politique de l'Année 1877* (1878). L. Teste, *La Monarchie sous la Troisième République* (1891). Barboux, *Jules Grévy*. A. Chuquet, *Le Général Chanzy* (1883). *Journal des Goncourt*. A. Houssaye, *Confessions* (1885-9). V. Fidus, *Le Prince Impérial* (1890). P. Ribot, *Le Suffrage Universel* (1874). Camille Pelletan, *Le Théâtre de Versailles* (1875). A. Picard, *Les Chemins de Fer*.

CHAPTER VII

THE CRISES AND THE MEN CONNECTED WITH THEM

Frequency of ministerial crises. The work of education. Gambetta and the Grand Ministry.

FROM this time forward one Ministry succeeded another more or less frequently, at intervals sometimes of months and sometimes of weeks; when they lasted for longer than **Frequency of** a year they may be considered to have enjoyed **Ministerial** exceptional good fortune. They were always **Crises.** more or less skeleton Ministries.

Nothing would be more tiresome and, moreover, more useless than to enumerate these interminable lists and omit nothing. Most of the names upon them have no personality, no distinguishing feature.

The reason for these changes of Government was connected less with questions of ideas and doctrines than with parliamentary intrigues and personal jealousies. In the absence of superior men who, when they make their appearance, are, as a matter of fact, worn out as quickly, if not more quickly, than other people, persons of average, not to say mediocre, ability are during their tenure of power spied and preyed upon by those who are impatient to step into their shoes. They resemble an organism which, continually exposed to the ravages of destructive microbes, resists them for a greater or shorter length of time, but is in the end forced to succumb.

The division of Parliament into sections and sub-sections gave rise in certain cases—and this is another important factor—to the most unexpected and frequently paradoxical alliances which led to a sudden upsetting of the majority.

Innumerable examples might be given. The following is a very typical one :

Jules Ferry, one of the most remarkable statesmen of the

103

period, a leader and even a great leader, made his tenure of office conspicuous for two great undertakings—the reform of education and colonial expansion.

In the first instance he was opposed by the parties of the Right, the clerical party, who were imbued with a bitter hatred against him. When the second measure was under discussion this hatred was not extinguished, and clerics and Conservatives had no hesitation in joining Clemenceau, the Radicals and the extreme Left, in their endeavours to overthrow the man they detested.

An incident like this multiplied a hundredfold was one among many reasons for the instability of the Government.

Born at Saint-Dié, Jules Ferry, journalist, member of the legislative body in 1869, member of the Government of National **The Work of Education.** Defence, and Mayor of Paris during the siege, was a man of abundant energy and fighting spirit, of which he gave proof on the famous 31st of October, 1870, which was a sort of dress rehearsal of the Commune. When the latter came into being he was the last to take his departure.

Elementary, secondary and higher education, and the various enactments by which the scholastic system under the Republic was established, were largely due to his initiative.

Elementary education was the basis of the whole, and in order to establish it on a firm footing it was necessary to found schools and provide masters. This was the greatest innovation and called for the most strenuous efforts and sacrifices. Elementary education was still partially subjected to the influence of the clergy, and it was a question of suppressing this influence and replacing it by another.

The elementary school provides free compulsory education, and the foundation of training colleges in each department produced the necessary masters. The instruction given is entirely secular. Denominational teachers, teaching in the free schools, have to obtain the same certificates of proficiency as the lay teachers in the State schools. Establishments for the secondary education of girls were opened. In the sphere of higher education Jules Ferry proposed to take away from the independent faculties the power of granting degrees. One of

104

the articles of his scheme, the famous article 7, forbade the giving of instruction in any of the three grades by members of unauthorised religious bodies. This was aimed against the Jesuits, and was not the first occasion on which the State, whether under a Republic or a monarchy, had directed an attack against this body. In this respect Jules Ferry only carried on the policy of Charles X, who was nevertheless far from having been suspected of an anti-clerical bias. This article, which gave rise to violent discussion, after having been passed by the Chamber was thrown out by the Senate. Nevertheless the Ministry decreed the dissolution of the Order of the Jesuits and the closing of the establishments belonging to it.

This organisation of education was in conformity with democratic tendencies. It was doctrinal and logical. Its only defect was that it was perhaps too much so.

The keystone of the edifice is the elementary school which gives to millions of children a sound and solid education on the whole equal, if not superior, to that provided in any other country. Owing to the increase in scholarships, it might almost be said that no pupil in these schools, however poor, should experience much difficulty in passing on to the *lycées* and colleges, and later to the Universities.

The only criticism that might be brought against this system is that it is too abstract and general, and does not take individual differences and the peculiarities of the various provinces into account. It almost completely overlooks local and technical requirements, and this for the children of the masses, who are chiefly sons of peasants, is a great disadvantage. It gives them the same discipline and instruction as if they were all destined to become barristers, solicitors or professors. And this leads to a general levelling of mind and a centralisation which is already exaggerated, and succeeds in killing all that remains of individuality and local characteristics.

This criticism, it must be admitted, would have greatly astonished the originators of the system, who deliberately aimed at making it of universal application, which was entirely in keeping with their doctrines and philosophy and their idea of establishing a democratic Government and order of society.

When Jules Ferry was removed from office on account of his Tunisian policy, Gambetta's turn arrived. As he was the most conspicuous personality in the Republican party it was inevitable that the time should come for the reins of Government to be placed in his hands. In spite of the opposition and dislike of President Grévy this time at last arrived. But it was of brief duration.

Gambetta and the Grand Ministry.

On account of the multiplicity of groups, Gambetta could only secure a Ministry which rested on a solid parliamentary basis if he came to some preliminary understanding with their leaders. But this in itself meant restricting his field of action and his activities. The same difficulty has since presented itself again and again to his successors, and above all to the most remarkable and energetic among them. Clemenceau, who at this time was opposed to Gambetta, was to have a similar experience later on.

Gambetta thought fit to forge ahead and to construct his Ministry, not of men of first-class ability but of his own creatures, who would be entirely subject to him because they owed him everything.

This was what was derisively known as the *Grand Ministry* because it was entirely composed of nonentities. Its fate was soon sealed. It was part of Gambetta's policy to use every possible means, including the revision of the Constitution, to increase the power of the executive, which threatened to grow weaker every day. His fears in this connection were only too well founded.

He also aimed, by the formation of a sort of national union, at grouping around him all the forces of the country, and thus exalting and strengthening French influence abroad.

But the majority of parliamentarians, instinctively feeling themselves more or less menaced, quickly formed a league against him, with the result that in the twinkling of an eye his Ministry was overthrown.

The great leaders having been shelved, it became necessary to have recourse to understudies, and second-rate men took up the reins of power, which they held for varying periods. As no party had a majority, a policy of concentration became ever more and more indispensable, and was destined to be the rule

THE CRISES

'or some time to come. It was one of the essential character-
stics of French parliamentary life, inclining sometimes to the
Right, sometimes to the Left. It continued to favour the Right
ıntil almost the end of the century and placed moderate Govern-
nents in power. But after the Dreyfus case, and especially
ıfter the Waldeck-Rousseau Ministry, the advanced parties,
;he Radicals, seized the reins of Government, which they
:ontinued to hold almost uninterruptedly up to the present
noment.

BIBLIOGRAPHY.—Rambaud, *Jules Ferry* (1903). J. Reinach, *Le
Ministère Gambetta* (1884). Tournier, *Le Cardinal Lavigerie* (1913).
General Zurlinden, *Souvenirs*. J. Simon, *La Réforme de l'Enseignement
Secondaire* (1874). Th. Ferneuil, *La Réforme de l'Enseignement Public en
France* (1879). De Laprade, *Le Baccalauréat et les Etudes Classiques* (1879).
Paul Deshanel, *Gambetta*.

CHAPTER VIII

FRANCO-GERMAN RELATIONS. THE ALARM OF 187?

Psychology of Bismarck. First tentatives towards a *rapproche-*
ment with Austria. His policy towards France. Preventive
warfare. The first alarm.

DURING the years following the war there was one question
which dominated Franco-German relations, and that was
the execution of the Treaty of Frankfort.

Thanks to the wisdom of his method of government, Thiers
succeeded in founding and establishing what many people

Psychology of
Bismarck.

both in France and elsewhere regarded as an
impossibility—a Conservative Republic, inspiring
full confidence in the moneyed classes, with the
result that the various loans raised for the liberation of the
occupied territories were subscribed with the greatest facility.
Whilst they were only too delighted to pocket the money, there
was no one more astonished than the Germans by the rapidity
with which France recovered, and this very rapidity inspired
them with fears for the security of their victory. Bismarck
was in the position of a man who, having reaped unhoped for
rewards, lives in constant dread of their being one day snatched
away from him, and accordingly uses every precaution to secure
them from danger. And these precautions always seem insufficient. In his opinion, and he did not attempt to hide it, the
victory so easily won over France, while it was undoubtedly due
to the superiority of the German military and diplomatic
preparations, was also indebted to the quasi-miraculous help of a
number of exceptional circumstances, all of which had worked
in favour of his country. So firmly was he convinced of this
that it explains his whole subsequent attitude and policy.
He continually repeated it in his Memoirs and conversations
with his confidants. The Germans, he maintained, would be

108

ery much mistaken if they supposed that because they had
eaten France without difficulty they could rely on beating her
gain if they wished. On the contrary, nothing was less certain,
nd instead of confidently lulling themselves to sleep they must
easelessly endeavour by every means in their power to make it
oth materially and morally impossible for the " hereditary foe "
o renew the attack. It is imperative to realise this state of
nind, shared by many of his countrymen, in order to understand
is efforts and manœuvres to secure the isolation of France in
Europe and prevent her from gaining allies and support which,
dded to her own resources and the elasticity of her race, would
nable her to dream of a war of revenge.

This idea of isolation, which thirty years later was to prove
 bugbear to Germany and become one of the causes of the
great War, was what Bismarck at that time aimed at realising
gainst France, and he worked day and night at constructing a
ort of diplomatic barrier against her.

His first efforts were made in the direction of Austria. And
ere he reaped the fruits of his wisdom and foresight when,
First Tenta- immediately after Sadowa, he had succeeded, not
ives towards a without great difficulty, in moderating the demands
Rapprochement of the Army, who, thinking only of the present,
with Austria. had but one idea—to exploit their victory to the
full and crush Austria. But Bismarck, who was more long-
sighted and thought of the morrow, resolutely opposed this
rash policy. He took care not to irritate Austria hopelessly or
to make the breach irreparable; and he succeeded. Never on
any other occasion did he prove himself so great a statesman.
Why did he not display a similar moderation and foresight in
his attitude towards France after 1871? Had he done so, the
peace of Europe might have been secured for much longer. But
Bismarck, who, as his recent biographer, E. Ludwig, has so well
shown, was a very hot-tempered man who did not always
succeed in controlling himself. And when it was a question of
dealing with France, he gave way both to the Army and his own
temperament. Wisdom and moderation here were much more
difficult than in the case of Austria.

This treatment of Austria made the task of reconciliation
much easier, and the constantly growing influence of Hungary,

which Bismarck turned to marvellous account, also facilitate
the *rapprochement*. From that moment Hungary became th
recognised bond of union between Germany and Austria. Th
Magyars brought all possible pressure to bear on Vienna t
induce the Government to draw the bonds with Berlin eve
closer.

The two Emperors met at Ischl and Salzbourg. Bismarc
made use of every opportunity to push Austria ever furthe
and further towards the East, which he thought wa
the surest means of turning her attention from Germany
For similar reasons, and also in order to embroil her witl
Italy, he afterwards pushed France in the direction o
Tunis.

Austria's Oriental policy, however, had the inevitable resul
of bringing her into antagonism with Russia, and oppositio
between the two countries was unavoidable. The day was t
come when Germany would be forced to choose between th
two. Bismarck did all in his power to postpone the necessit
for this choice, which was extremely distasteful to him, anc
continued as long as possible to have stakes on both sides.
When at last the time came for a definite decision, reasons whicl
he regarded as weighty and incontrovertible, and which he ha
explained at great length in his Memoirs, led him to decide ir
favour of Austria.

For the time being Germany was on the best of terms witl
both Austria and Russia. In September 1872 the three
Emperors met in Berlin. This meeting, about which the
German Press, inspired by Bismarck, made a great to-do, was
for Germany a sort of moral guarantee of her victories. The
great days of the Holy Alliance seemed to have returned.

But after these sentimental effusions the cold breath of reality
was not long in making itself felt. Full of majesty and self-
importance, Gortchakof, the Russian Chancellor, was only too
ready to regard Bismarck as his pupil, a part which the latter
was not at all prepared to play. Jealousy began to spring up
between the two, the jealousy of two tenors, which reached its
culminating point at the time of the alarm of 1875 and during
the Congress of Berlin.

110

FRANCO-GERMAN RELATIONS

Bismarck's policy towards France was twofold. It involved, on the one hand, hard and incessant toil in the diplomatic sphere in order to prevent the "hereditary foe" from reopening the question of his defeat. Ever watchful of events in France, and particularly of the possibility of the restoration of the monarchy, Bismarck was above all desirous that no such restoration should take place. He openly reprimanded von Arnim, his Ambassador in Paris, an intriguing mischief-maker, who was showing sympathy with the Royalists. Bismarck was convinced that under a Republican system France would find it impossible to make any lasting alliances. But in this his vision was at fault. He would have been very much astonished, had he lived, to see France not only allied to Russia, but bound by the close ties of an *entente* with England.

Policy towards France.

This diplomatic work was accompanied by military efforts calculated to provide Germany in all circumstances with an army far superior to that of her enemy, a superiority which she insisted should be undisputed and beyond dispute.

She almost regarded as an offence any effort on the part of France to reduce the gap which, from the military point of view, separated her from her adversary, or to catch up the start the latter had made. Germany was convinced, or appeared to be convinced, that if she lost this start, war between the two countries would automatically result. She therefore had the right, and was almost in duty bound, not to await that moment, but resolutely to forestall events and play her card while she was certain of success.

The theory of *preventive warfare* had already made its appearance. Promulgated by the Chief of the Staff, it penetrated deeper and deeper into the minds of the German people, who are extremely susceptible and have an innate tendency to believe, as though they were dogmas, any ideas which their rulers din into their brains. At every fresh military measure taken by the French Government, the German Headquarters' Staff gave vent to loud protestations, and Bismarck made no effort to conceal his displeasure. He said or allowed it to be said : " France is openly preparing

Preventive Warfare.

111

to attack us; we should be mad to wait; we must fall upon her before she has had time to complete her preparations."

Forty years later, when France, faced by the intensive arming of Germany, found herself obliged to revive the system of three years' military service, precisely the same attitude of mind was displayed across the Rhine, and the same language was used.

Pressure brought to bear by the Army on political circles and on Bismarck, and the latter's fear of a restoration of the monarchy, which would increase the power and prestige of **The First Alarm.** France both at home and abroad, were responsible for the crisis of 1875, the first serious alarm which occurred between France and Germany after the war.

Although the details of this crisis are common property, certain essential points still remain somewhat obscure, and especially the following—Was Germany really decided to attack France, or did she only wish to intimidate her, to make her feel her subjection, her inferiority? Had the Army, in which the movement had its origin, succeeded in winning the Chancellor and the Emperor over to its views?

This has never definitely been settled, any more than it was in connection with the two other grave crises which supervened between France and Germany, the crisis of 1905 (when the Kaiser landed at Tangier) and the crisis of 1911 (Agadir). It will never be known for certain whether Germany would have turned threats into action if France had not given way.

When the National Assembly, on the 13th of March, 1875, passed a law altering the cadres and forming a fourth battalion in each regiment, two of the official German papers complained that France was preparing for war. Diplomatic indiscretions, that of Radowitz among others, sowed the seeds of alarm in the capitals of Europe. The French Ambassadors in Germany and Russia informed their Government of their fears. The Duc Decazes, who was Foreign Minister, either filled by real anxiety or eager to exploit the incident in order to create in England and in Russia a current of sympathy for France, inspired Blowitz, the Paris correspondent of *The Times*, to publish a sensational article, which was copied by a large number of papers and spread apprehension far and wide. The bellicose preparations of

Germany, whose aim was the swift annihilation of France, were set forth and denounced in this article.

This was the first occasion on which journalism successfully intervened in foreign politics, but its power and the part it plays have increased ever since.

Blowitz, the Paris correspondent of *The Times*, was a typical representative of the great journalist, who exercises considerable influence, who sees the heads of the State and of the Government, Ministers and Ambassadors every day, giving them as much and often more information than he receives in return, making them serve his purpose and occasionally serving theirs. A Bohemian Jew, who had settled down in Marseilles before the war, and had become a naturalised Frenchman, he was introduced to Thiers, who appreciated his quick intellect and thought of making him a consul. But journalism offered him a more brilliant career. As correspondent to *The Times*, his energy, his *flair* and his shrewdness soon won him a position of considerable power.

His Memoirs, which it is well to read with a pinch of salt for Blowitz was exceedingly vain), are full of curious information regarding this alarm of 1875 and the Congress of Berlin.

In England public opinion was roused, and representations, couched, however, in most courteous terms, were made to Berlin. But it was in Russia above all that this effort, which included a fair amount of propaganda, to use a word widely current later on, produced most excellent results. Gortchakof, filled with hatred and jealousy of Bismarck, was not at all sorry to give him a lesson and to play the part of Mentor to him. During the course of a visit paid by the Tsar Alexander to Berlin, he gave Bismarck a warning. The latter protested loudly, calling on the great gods to witness that these rumours of war were figments of the imagination spread by his enemies.

Bismarck never ceased to maintain that, in spite of the pressure brought to bear by the Army, peace was never for a moment seriously menaced, and that Decazes and Gortchakof, anxious to win a diplomatic victory at his expense, had engineered the whole business, and that the latter especially had, with a very small expenditure of pains, arrogated to himself the credit of having saved France, whom nobody was thinking of attacking. There is probably some truth in these allegations.

I

THE THIRD REPUBLIC

The crisis of 1875 created in Europe a state of mind which was to have important results later on. England and Russia began to see in her true light a victorious and Prussianised Germany, somewhat intoxicated by victory, and anxious, in order to keep her conquests, to make her hegemony felt by all

This desire for hegemony, which no pains were now taken to conceal, did not fail to give rise at first to suspicion and afterwards to anxiety. And thus on this occasion they came to the diplomatic assistance of France, whom five years previously they had light-heartedly allowed to be crushed.

The seeds of the Franco-Russian Alliance and of the subsequent *Entente Cordiale* were sown at the time of this crisis.

BIBLIOGRAPHY.—A. Sorel, *Histoire Diplomatique de la Guerre Franco Allemande* (2 vols., 1875). G. May, *Le Traité de Francfort* (1909). Debidour *Histoire Diplomatique de l'Europe jusqu'en 1878* (vol. II); *Histoire Diplomatique de l'Europe jusqu'à Nos Jours*, 1914 (Paris, 1919–20, 2 vols.) E. Bourgeois, *Manuel de Politique Etrangère* (vols. III and IV). Hanotaux *Histoire de la France Contemporaine* (4 vols., 1903–8). S. Denis, *Histoire Contemporaine* (4 vols., 1897–1903). Valfrey, *Histoire du Traité de Francfort et de la Libération du Territoire* (2 vols., 1874–5), (1906). Gontaut Biron, *Mon Ambassade en Allemagne* (1906). *Les Dernières Années de l'Ambassade de Gontaut-Biron en Allemagne*, published by Dreux. Bismarck, *Pensées et Souvenirs* (French translation, 3 vols., 1899). *Mémoires de Bismarck*, edited by Maurice Busch (2 vols., 1899). Prince von Hohenlohe, *Memoirs* (3 vols., 1909). Marquis de Gabriac, *Souvenirs Diplomatiques* (1896). De Broglie, *La Mission de Gontaut-Biron* (1896). A Laussedat, *Les Délimitations de la Frontière Franco-Allemande* (1901) Blowitz, *My Memoirs* (London, 1906).

CHAPTER IX

THE CONGRESS OF BERLIN. THE TRIPLE ALLIANCE. THE FRANCO-RUSSIAN ALLIANCE. THE QUESTION OF EGYPT

The Russo-Turkish War. The Treaty of San Stefano. The Congress of Berlin. The Triple Alliance. Nature of the Triple Alliance. The Franco-Russian Alliance. Nature of this Alliance.

BISMARCK, who was furious with Gortchakof and the Russians, after the crisis of 1875, was not slow to take his revenge.

The Christians in the East, since certain among them had succeeded in freeing themselves from the Ottoman yoke, now expected but one conclusion to their agitations— complete and not merely partial liberation. When once this movement for independence had been set on foot, nothing in the world could stop it; it was bound to overcome every obstacle and reach its ultimate goal.

The Russo-Turkish War.

Whenever the Christian communities, tired of being trampled underfoot, lodge protestations or rise in rebellion, the Turks from time to time indulge in a massacre in order to keep their hand in. And this is what occurred in Bulgaria, where the Bachi-Bouzouks, let loose upon the country by the Sultan, vied with each other in acts of murder, incendiarism and violence. These " Bulgarian atrocities," together with the defeat of the Montenegrins and the Serbians, who had taken up arms, exasperated Russia, who, faithful to her ancestral dreams, asked for nothing better than to march out against the Turk.

The Russian Government, urged on by public opinion, which was whole-heartedly in favour of the Bulgarians, once again declared war against Turkey. The difficulties and reverses with which they met at first obliged them to seek support from Roumania, who, as it turned out, received but scant reward

115

for her pains. In the end their armies swept aside all obstacles, and, advancing to the gates of Constantinople, forced the Sultan by the Treaty of San Stefano, to consent to the practical dismemberment of Turkey in Europe.

The Eastern Question was now reopened. The great Powers considered that they should have a word to say **The Treaty of San Stefano.** in the matter and could not allow Russia a free hand.

Jealous and terrified by the latter's success, and of the moral and material advantages she was expecting to derive from it, two of them—Austria and England—quickly reached an agreement to circumscribe the results of the victory as far as possible.

As for Bismarck, whilst he was of opinion that the Eastern Question " was not worth the bones of a single Pomeranian grenadier," he was not sorry to play the part of go-between and reap the advantages of the position—making the Russians feel his dissatisfaction and obliging them to reconsider their treaty under his ægis, helping Austria to realise some of her ambitions and thereby winning her over to his side with a view to the alliance he already had in mind, and acting as intermediary between England and Russia, thus playing the part of peacemaker and all-powerful arbitrator in European politics.

The Congress of Berlin (June–July 1878) secured him the realisation of some of his plans. Russia, champing the bit, was obliged to give way. Austria and England, **The Congress of Berlin.** the not altogether disinterested champions of Turkey, each presented their bill and pocketed the proceeds—the reward in the former case being Bosnia and Herzegovina, and in the latter the island of Cyprus.

France, who received an official invitation to the Congress, could not refuse to take part in it. She played a deliberately retiring though honourable part, and derived a few advantages for her *protégés*, the Greeks and the Christians in the East, and for herself. Anxious to divert attention from her occupation of Cyprus, England pushed France towards intervention in Tunis, to which Bismarck, true to his policy of the balance of power, hastened to give his support.

Thus everybody had occasion to feel content, with the excep-

116

tion of Russia, who was the great loser in the matter, and it was inevitable that her discontent and irritation should weigh heavily in her future relations with Germany, pushing Bismarck all the more to a *rapprochement* with Austria and the realisation of the alliance which he had long been contemplating and preparing at his leisure. In order to bring it about he made use of his Hungarian friends, whose influence in Vienna was growing ever stronger. And it was a Hungarian, Andrassy, who on the 24th of September, 1879, signed the secret convention between the two sister Empires. This was the foundation stone of the Triple Alliance.

In persuading Austria to form a close alliance with Prussianised Germany, when only a few years previously Prussia had defeated her, and such an alliance inevitably meant that she was more or less held in tutelage, Bismarck overcame an obstacle which many would have regarded as insurmountable. But this initial success was not enough. He was literally thirsting for alliances, convinced that he would never have sufficient help and support from abroad to secure his victory, although it already had the protection of a formidable army. This was the dominant note, the *leitmotiv*, so to speak, of his diplomacy.

The Triple Alliance.

But where were these other allies to be found? Russia? Bismarck would indeed have asked for nothing better. But to hope for a union with Russia when he already had an alliance with Austria was like trying to square the circle or shooting the moon. It was no longer possible to harness Russia and Austria to the same chariot. Their aspirations were becoming ever more and more conflicting.

England, wrapped up in her policy of splendid isolation, had an instinctive horror for any continental alliance, and only made up her mind to forming one at the eleventh hour, when she was driven by imperative necessity and it was no longer possible for her to do otherwise.

Italy remained. But Bismarck showed a certain contempt in his attitude towards her, a contempt which was shared by his successors, including William II himself. Nevertheless, he argued that, taking everything into consideration, Italy was better than nothing at all. Moreover, he was by no means displeased at being able to give proof of his moral and material power by realising the apparently unrealisable, and in uniting and maintaining under his ægis those who but yesterday had been foes and adversaries. For after all nothing could better demonstrate Germany's magnetism and influence.

For various different reasons Italy responded to his advances. She allowed herself to be persuaded, but not enslaved. She was annoyed with France on account of the Tunisian expedition (1881), and also King Humbert, the successor of Victor Emmanuel, felt the necessity of consolidating his throne, which was threatened by both the Clerical and the Republican parties. The latter reason turned the scale. By associating herself, albeit somewhat unwillingly, with Austria under the hegemony of Germany, Italy secured a sort of insurance against every possible danger whether at home or abroad.

Nature of the Triple Alliance. The Triple Alliance was signed on the 20th of May, 1882, and thereafter was regularly renewed until the war.

What precisely was the significance of this treaty, the conditions of which were kept strictly secret and which had a greater influence than any other on the diplomatic evolution of contemporary Europe?

Its essential characteristics were based upon the respective positions of the parties to it, which in the end meant their strength. By reason of their aspirations and interests, each of the allies introduced an entirely different spirit into the alliance.

Austria—and this is an important point—was very far from being on a level of equality with Germany. Outwardly and in appearance she may have been, but in reality certainly not. The old Emperor at the Hofburg, granting forgiveness for injuries received, and quickly reconciled with his conqueror, certainly regarded himself as the equal of the latter, who always appeared to him in the light of a parvenu. But the Germans, as a whole, grew more and more accustomed to treating the Austrians, whether in the political, the diplomatic or the financial sphere, as their inferiors. German influence made itself felt ever more strongly in Vienna and Budapest, and was conspicuous for the powerful hold it won in the domain of business, industry, banking, journalism and University life, etc., etc. As an instru-

118

ment of penetration it made use of the Jews, who throughout Central Europe instinctively work in favour of Teutonism and are exceedingly numerous and active in the two capitals of the Dual Monarchy. The heavy hand thus laid by Germany on Austria, merely on account of the power she had acquired, did not cease to make itself felt more and more.

Austria resigned herself to it, in the first instance because she had no alternative.

In a household where one of the partners is very much richer, more energetic and decided than the other, the latter must perforce bow to the will of the former. And this was the case with the Viennese Government.

But, on the other hand, Germany's increasing " *drang nach Osten* " brought her into ever greater conflict with Russia, and ran the risk of precipitating a catastrophe of which, if Austria had only had herself to rely upon, the result would have been a foregone conclusion. The Government in Vienna was fully aware of this. A powerful Germany served them as a shield of defence. A few crises occurred, such as that of 1908, at the time of the annexation of Bosnia and Herzegovina, when Austria brutally presented the Serbians and their patrons the Russians with the accomplished fact. It was the unhesitating support of Berlin that secured a solution most favourable to Vienna.

At the most acute moment of the crisis, Pourtalès, the German Ambassador at St. Petersburg, used almost threatening language against Russia, advising her in perfectly plain and unequivocal terms to resign herself to the inevitable. The Russians, very much weakened by the Manchurian war and the revolutionary movement resulting from it, were indeed obliged, however unwillingly, to give way.

Berlin, however, as may well be believed, did not afford this protection for nothing. Such generosity and disinterestedness would have been entirely contrary to its nature. It got into the habit of regarding Austria as a " second-class " Power and treating her as such. The enterprises of Vienna in the Balkans were only tolerated by Germany to the extent to which they fitted in with her own policy. If they did not do so, she had no hesitation in refusing her consent to them. It would be easy to multiply examples. As long as Germany remained peacefully inclined the Austrians were never able to unloose the dogs of war, although on several occasions they would have liked to do so. On the other hand, the moment that Germany, for her own good reasons, became converted to the necessity for war, it did not fail to break out at the first opportunity.

While Germany acted as a protection for Austria against Russia, she also to a certain extent guaranteed Italy against her Austrian ally. An Italian diplomatist once observed, " Our position is such that we are forced to be either the allies or the enemies of Austria."

There is a good deal of truth in this remark. It was, in fact, the power and prestige of Germany that secured harmony in this strange *ménage à trois* which the Triple Alliance became.

The temporary irritation of Italy against France, and the feeling, exaggerated though it was, of her own weakness, led her to join this combination. But as each of these reasons gradually lost its force, she experienced an ever-growing desire to escape, in spirit if not in letter. The Triple Alliance had become a sort of prison to her. She automatically renewed the pact from time to time, but rendered it lip service only, attaching no further importance to it, and arguing that after all diplomatic arrangements were only of extremely relative value.

On the occasion of one of these periodical renewals in the early years of this century, Visconti Venosta, an extremely intelligent Italian statesman, declared to Barrère, the French Ambassador, "What the devil are you worrying about? Haven't you noticed that the Holy Alliance has never been publicly repudiated? Nevertheless, it is dead, dead as a doornail. What makes you think that the Triple Alliance will not meet with a similar fate?"

The formation of the Triple Alliance inevitably led by the very force of circumstances to a *rapprochement* between the **The Franco-** two Great European Powers who had remained **Russian** outside it—Russia and France. Certain con-**Alliance.** siderations might and indeed actually did succeed in postponing it, but they could not prevent it.

The chief of these, and the one which, even after the alliance had been concluded, was to make the working of it difficult, consisted in the difference, it might almost be said the incompatibility, of the systems established in the two countries— Russia being an autocracy, France a democracy. It is true that in former days we find his Most Christian Majesty, Francis I, in open alliance with the Grand Turk. But it was religion alone that separated them, and this, in the world of politics, is never a very serious obstacle. But the sharp contrast between the French and Russian systems of Government created a gulf which it was more difficult to bridge; the Russian leaders being instinctively inclined to mistrust the leaders of the Republic and to fear their instability and indiscretion. It required time and much perseverance gradually to overcome these obstacles. In Russia, the assassination of Alexander II (1881) placed upon the throne Alexander III, who felt himself much freer and less committed towards Germany. In France, President Grévy, a narrow-minded peasant from the Jura, looked with anything but favour upon this Franco-Russian *rapprochement*, for which he saw no necessity and in the solidity of which he did not believe. But when he was succeeded by Carnot in 1887 the outlook changed, and on both sides feeling improved. The situation abroad, and above all the all-powerful position of Germany, whose hegemony became more and more firmly established every day, made each of the two countries realise the serious inconveniences of isolation.

Austria, becoming daily more aware of Germany's support, developed her power in the Balkans. She was mistress of the situation at Belgrade, where the Obrenovitch dynasty was entirely subject to her, as well as in Sofia, where Ferdinand of Saxe-Coburg, an Austrian, had in 1887 succeeded Battenberg, who in spite of everything was inclined to favour Russia. Even in Bucharest, King Carol, a Hohenzollern, disregarding the aspirations of his people, drew his kingdom into the orbit of the Central Powers. And thus Russia found herself exposed to ever greater opposition and hostility in the Balkans.

France for her part continued to be subjected from time to time to outbursts of temper on the part of Bismarck, who, whenever he wished to carry an Army Bill providing for an increase in the forces (and Heaven knows this happened often enough), never failed to plead the danger threatened by the French thirst for revenge in order to silence all opposition. He blew hot and cold by turns in connection with the relations between France and Germany. The alarm of 1875 was followed by the alarm of 1886 due to the Schnaebelé incident.

Thus on all sides the reasons for a *rapprochement* between France and Russia became ever more numerous and definite. Bismarck, who felt the approaching menace, did all in his power to prevent it, using both persuasion and threats, and appealing to dynastic influences, and the old and cordial relations which existed between the Courts of Berlin and St. Petersburg.

He succeeded for a time in postponing the inevitable event, and as long as he remained in power and his master, the old Emperor, was alive, the Tsar, in spite of the increasingly friendly relations between France and Russia, hesitated to cross the Rubicon.

It stands to his credit that he did eventually do so, since the leaders in Germany did all they could to make things difficult for him. When a huge financial operation was being arranged in Russia for the conversion of the national debt, Bismarck openly inspired a campaign which made the co-operation of German finance, upon which the whole scheme depended, out of the question.

As this help was not forthcoming from Germany, it was France who came to the rescue. Hoskier, a financier of Danish origin, established in Paris, arranged for the raising in France of a preliminary loan, destined for the conversion of the 5 per cent. Russian stock (November 1888). This was the first of a long, a very long series of operations. The large capital available in France hardly existed in Russia, and, on the principle of communicating cisterns, the overflow from one market was periodically diverted to the other, and whenever Russia wanted money to exploit the natural resources of the country, she got into the habit of turning to France.

It was this financial support which to a large extent favoured the conclusion of the alliance, and afterwards facilitated the working of it. It was like oil poured from time to time on to the wheels of a machine to prevent it from grating.

As France possessed an excess of floating capital it was, after all, natural that she should invest it in a country to which she was bound by political ties, especially as these loans were accompanied by certain political and commercial advantages—the construction of railways rendering the mobilisation of Russian troops easier and securing orders for French goods, etc.

It was only a question of keeping within bounds, and it would be difficult for an impartial observer to maintain that this was always done. The Republican Government, which had no comprehensive policy regarding the best possible uses to which the national savings could be put, and was, moreover, exceedingly weak and helpless against the great banks, allowed the regular drainage of capital to continue on too vast a scale. The banks, who earned large commissions in this way, were naturally encouraged to send money abroad rather than to keep it in the country, either in France herself or in her colonies, where it might have been more usefully employed in the interests of the French people.

Moreover, it would also have been wiser to divide it up in all directions, of course omitting those countries which might one day become hostile to France, so as to avoid putting all the eggs in one basket, as they say. When Russia, owing in the first place to the war, and secondly to Bolshevism, which was a result of the war, fell to pieces, the loss inflicted on all the holders of Russian securities was enormous, and proved one of the many reasons for the impoverishment of France.

The accession of the new Emperor of Germany, one of whose first acts was the dismissal of Bismarck, released the Tsar Alexander III, and negotiations between Paris and St. Petersburg became more definite. The renewal of the Triple Alliance and the dread of a *rapprochement* between England and Germany caused considerable uneasiness in Russian diplomatic circles. Nevertheless the Tsar still hesitated to bind himself by any formal agreement, the chief motive preventing him from doing so being his fear of having such an arrangement divulged. He had no confidence in the capacity of French statesmen to keep it secret, and he was particularly anxious that it should not be known.

Failing a plain straightforward treaty, efforts were made on all sides to come to some arrangement which should be completed by a military convention. The French fleet received an official invitation to visit Kronstadt, and the Tsar came on board the Admiral's ship (25th of July, 1891). The proposed plan drawn up by the French Government had for its object definitely " to unite the two Powers." Eventually the *entente* was established on the following terms, drawn up by France and accepted by Russia—" The two Governments shall act in concert on all questions of a nature likely to jeopardise the peace of the world. In the event of peace being seriously threatened, and more particularly should one of the two signatories be menaced with aggression, both parties agree to the immediate and simultaneous adoption of such measures as the realisation of such an eventuality may impose upon the Governments of both countries."

Such was the abominable style, which certainly had nothing whatever in common with that of Voltaire, in which the majority of treaties were henceforward to be drawn up.

Monsieur Ribot, the President of the Council, in a speech delivered at Bapaume, made a discreet and veiled though sufficiently obvious allusion to this event. " Should a fresh situation arise," he said, " we shall know how to keep calm and dignified."

A military convention, the indispensable complement of this agreement, was signed on the 18th of August, 1892, by the army leaders of the two countries in the name of their respective Governments. It was arranged that each of the two Powers should come to the support of the other if either of them were attacked by a member of the Triple Alliance. They were to mobilise immediately on receipt of information that the enemy was mobilising. The troops to be furnished by each party for use against Germany were specified—France was to provide 1,300,000 men and Russia between 700,000 and 800,000. Co-operation between the high commands was also arranged for, and neither Government was to make a separate peace.

Through some of its clauses this convention exceeded the limits of a purely military arrangement and assumed a political complexion. In conjunction with the agreement which had already been signed it formed a regular defensive alliance between France and Russia.

In the last clause it was stipulated that the agreement should be kept absolutely secret, a condition about which the Tsar and his advisers were most emphatic. Although it was one which it was difficult to secure from a democratic Government, responsible to Parliament, it was nevertheless accepted, as one of the imperative necessities before which democracy and parliamentary control are forced to give way.

When the Russian fleet visited Toulon it was received with demonstrations of enthusiasm. After having won the Chancelleries the new alliance gained the support of the people.

France, after twenty years of isolation, was naturally filled with the greatest joy when she realised that this period was at an end. She was conscious of resuming her place in the diplomacy of Europe.

In order to understand the nature and scope of this agreement, it is necessary, as in the case of the Triple Alliance, to remember the state of mind of each of the two signatories and the objects they had in view. The preoccupations of each were different as well as their interests. Russia's chief concern, outside the financial support of France, to which she had abundant recourse, was almost exclusively the East. The encroachments made by Austria with the support of Germany caused her as much anxiety as irritation. If this pressure increased she wanted to be in a position to oppose it, and in order to do so to rely upon France to hold Germany in check.

Nature of the Alliance.

On the French side, the danger and menaces from the direction of Germany were the primary consideration. The alarm of 1875, the Schnaebelé affair, of which we shall speak later, proved that Germany was still in a position at any moment to have recourse to her usual methods of intimidation. The alliance with Russia would furnish the means, at least so it was hoped, of resisting her.

An alliance of this kind, concluded not without considerable difficulty and reserve between two States whose political systems were entirely different if not actually conflicting, and whose diplomatic interests were widely divergent, was bound to be anything but easy in practice. Each of the two parties would naturally be inclined to hold back their allies and prevent them from becoming whole-heartedly involved in affairs which to them seemed of secondary importance, whilst their partner, on the other hand, regarded them as essential.

In spite of the alliance, Russia still maintained cordial relations with Germany. Dynastic ties, which had always been very strong between the Courts of the two countries, only served to emphasise the friendship, and their influence was very great. The Tsar and the Kaiser corresponded directly with each other, without the intervention of Ministers and Ambassadors, through the channel of private *aides-de-camp* accredited at each Court.

Diplomatic differences between France and Russia had their inevitable repercussion in the military domain. Whenever it was a question of arranging the co-operation between the General Staffs of the two countries, France experienced the greatest difficulty in preventing Russia from planning to concentrate the greater part of her forces against Austria and thereby weakening her resistance to Germany.

Much care and patience were required to smooth over the various causes of friction.

When the Third Republic was first established, French influence was paramount in Egypt, which from the moral point **The Egyptian Question.** of view was practically a colony of France, and the recent cutting of the Suez Canal largely increased her power.

In the exploitation of the resources of the country, and its military and administrative organisation, etc., France had played an extremely prominent part. She had supplied the majority of the instructors, thanks to whose efforts great progress had been made.

As soon as an energetic Government had introduced a little order into the country, its resources and vast wealth had made the fertile valley of the Nile a veritable geographical miracle, one of the most prosperous and flourishing countries in the world.

Ismail, the descendant of Mehemet Ali, abused this wealth. His extravagant expenditure and mad prodigality soon jeopardised the finances of the State. The raising of one loan after the other led him where all those, be they Governments or individuals, who have recourse to them too freely, inevitably find themselves landed—the Bankruptcy Court. His European creditors, and especially France and England, were obliged to intervene and put him under the surveillance of a judicial council.

Whenever financial supervision of this kind is exercised by strangers it soon provokes discontent and anger in the breasts of those subjected to it. Ismail, who was short of money and ready to turn anything to account, resolved to sell his large interest (176,000 shares) in the Suez Canal Company. He offered them in the first place to the French Government. Filled with parliamentary scruples and fearing the opposition of the Chamber and the criticism of the Press, and, moreover, consistently feeble and vacillating, the latter had not the courage to undertake the responsibility of such a purchase, although it was offered under the most advantageous terms, namely, at the extremely low price of 568 francs. They were worth considerably more at the time, and everything pointed to the fact that they would show a steady rise. To-day they are worth from about four to five thousand gold francs, that is to say, almost ten times as much.

If the heads of the Government were doubtful whether they should enter upon the undertaking themselves, they could, if they had brought a little pressure to bear, have effected it by means of private enterprise—through the banks. But weakness and pusillanimity won the day. The British Government, however, adopted a very different attitude. They had no hesitation in buying the shares, and thereby acquired considerable influence in the administration of the canal.

This Anglo-French financial control aroused opposition in Egyptian Nationalist circles. A certain agitator named Arabi, the type of man who makes his spontaneous appearance in the Mussulman world as soon as there is any trouble, placed himself at the head of a movement which quickly assumed an attitude of hostility towards all foreigners, and culminated in a massacre of Europeans in Alexandria on the 11th of June, 1882.

And thus France and England, the two Powers chiefly concerned, were obliged, in addition to the controllers, to send armed men and soldiers to Egypt for the protection of the former. At the psychological moment France refused to make this effort, of which, as a matter of fact, she largely exaggerated the difficulties, but allowed England to act single-handed, and single-handed also to reap the benefit of her action. This was a real fit of weakness on the part of France such as several times occurred in her history. Everybody, both subjects and rulers, Parliament and public opinion, must be held responsible for it. The Freycinet Ministry set an example of weakness when, directly after the massacre, the Admiral of the fleet which had collected before Alexandria, and had been obliged to open fire on the forts, received a telegram telling him not to take part in the bombardment.

This initial weakness determined all the rest. When a little while afterwards the Government asked the Chamber for credit in order to occupy the Suez Canal in conjunction with the English, it was beaten by a large majority and obliged to resign. Clemenceau, resolutely and violently opposed to anything in the nature of a colonial expedition, ended his speech with the following words : " Europe is full of soldiers, the whole world is waiting, all the Powers are reserving their liberty of action for the future; France's liberty of action must also be reserved."

The problem could not have been more badly stated. France, it is true, kept her liberty of action, but by the same stroke she lost Egypt, at least politically. England, with whom she had refused to collaborate, was henceforward to dominate the situation alone. Shortly afterwards a small English expeditionary force was landed which dispersed the Egyptian army, mistakenly expected to keep it at bay, almost without striking a blow, entered Cairo and pacified the country with the greatest possible ease. England has been in Egypt ever since; she has remained there and will continue to remain there.

When diplomatists and rulers have been guilty of weakness they sometimes endeavour to make up for it by devious ways later on. In nine cases out of ten such efforts are absolutely useless.

The political and military masters of Egypt, it was impossible for the English not to stretch out their hands towards what was only its continuation—the Egyptian Soudan. They were all the less able to resist the temptation because they were very soon inspired by the grandiose idea of cutting Africa in half from north to south, and forming an uninterrupted chain between all their possessions from the Cape to Alexandria. It was therefore clear that any attempt to use the Soudan as a means for reopening the Egyptian question, which, in view of the impotence of France in the first instance, could never again be discussed, would be met by a categorical refusal on the part of the English. Since England was here faced with a question of the utmost importance to her, it showed a great lack of understanding to imagine that she would not go to any lengths, including the threat of war, in order to abide by her decision.

When the French Government somewhat hazardously, and without counting the cost, sent Major Marchand through the African bush from the Atlantic coast and Gabon to the neighbourhood of the Upper Nile, it clumsily created an imbroglio which, if they were not determined to settle it if necessary by force of arms (as they certainly were not), could only end in a defeat for France. After miracles of endurance and courage, Marchand, with a handful of Europeans, succeeded in crossing the greater part of the continent of Africa, through impracticable and almost unknown territories, and reached Fashoda on the Upper Nile. He certainly deserved every credit for his enterprise, which is more than can be said for those who sent him out so light-heartedly.

As was only to be expected, the British Government adopted a most determined attitude, whilst the French, after a rapid survey of the diplomatic, military and above all the naval situation, wisely decided to give way, a decision in which they were amply justified, and Marchand was recalled from Fashoda.

.　　.　　.　　.　　.　　.　　.

It's an ill wind that blows nobody any good. The Anglo-French condominium, if it had been exercised over Egypt, might easily have turned out badly. In collaboration of this kind, if any incident arises, the stronger and more resolute of the two parties generally ousts the weaker and more diffident. The Austro-Prussian condominium in the Danish Duchies of Schleswig-Holstein ended in war.) And England, less fettered by her continental policy, was in a better position than France. She was far freer, and her Government, protected from par-

K   129

liamentary crises, enjoyed a continuity of plan and outlook which was entirely lacking in France.

France, whatever her resources, cannot disperse and scatter her forces to all points of the compass. Her Empire in North Africa, owing to its proximity to the mother country, was bound to engross all her attention. Never was her diplomacy better advised or more far-sighted than when, by the famous agreement of 1904, which was the foundation of the Entente Cordiale, it abrogated all the political and theoretic rights possessed by France in Egypt, in return for complete liberty of action in Morocco.

From the very beginning England undertook that the moral influence of France in Egypt should be scrupulously respected, and it is only fair to say that on the whole this promise has been kept. All those who, by frequent visits at various intervals are well acquainted with Egyptian affairs, have been able to see for themselves that French influence, far from having diminished since the beginning of the century, has, on the contrary, grown even stronger, and owing to the flourishing condition of the French schools, French is more widely spoken than it was twenty years ago. The Suez Canal, one of the best organised and most prosperous concerns in the world, in which French and English work together in perfect accord, has remained under French control.

BIBLIOGRAPHY.—See the bibliography of the previous chapters, and especially Bismarck's Memoirs, the Memoirs of Prince von Hohenlohe which contain some extremely curious " portraits " of the Congress of Berlin, and the Memoirs of the King of Roumania.

Vsevolod Garchine, *La Guerre* (preface by Guy de Maupassant), 1889 Unpublished documents quoted by Hanotaux in his History. *Souvenir Inédits du Comte Schouvaloff*. *Souvenirs Inédits de Caratheodory Pacha*.

E. Driault, *La Question d'Orient* (8vo. edition, 1921). R. Pinon *France et l'Allemagne 1873–1914* (1914). A. Tardieu, *La France et le Alliances* (1910). P. Albin, *La France et l'Allemagne en Europe* (1913) A. Mevil, *De la Paix de Francfort à la Conférence d'Algesiras* (1909) H. Friedjung, *Das Zeitalter des Imperialismus*, 1884–1914. Pribram, *Di Politischen Geheimverträge Österreich-Ungarn*, 1879–1914 (1920) (which for the first time gives the official text of the treaties of the Triple Alliance and of all its renewals). *Livre Jaune sur le Congrès de Berlin* (1878) D'Avril, *Négociations Relatives au Traité de Berlin* (1886). Choublier *La Question d'Orient depuis le Traité de Berlin* (1897). J. de Witte, *Quinze Ans d'Histoire*. Baron des Michels, *Souvenirs de Carrière*. Katzenhoffer *Sur l'Occupation de la Bosnie-Herzégovine*. Baron de Stieglitz, *L'Italie dans la Triple-Alliance*. Comte Joseph Grabinski, *Alexandre de Battenberg*,

130

Correspondant, 25th of December, 1893). Wertheimer, *Graf Julius Andrassy* (1910). *L'Alliance Franco-Russe (Livre Jaune)*. J. Hansen, *L'Alliance Franco-Russe*. E. Daudet, *Histoire Diplomatique de l'Alliance Franco-Russe*. E. de Cyon, *Histoire de l'Alliance Franco-Russe* (1895). E. Laloy, *La Diplomatie de Guillaume II* (1917). Sir Sidney Lee, *King Edward VII, a Biography* (1925). *Affaire d'Egypte* (1880–81–82) *(Livre Jaune)*. De Freycinet, *La Question d'Egypte* (1905). *Souvenirs* (1913). Brehier, *L'Egypte de 1798 à 1906* (1907).

CHAPTER X

COLONIAL EXPANSION

Algeria. The conquest of the Sahara. Occupation of Tunis.
The Soudan. French Equatorial Africa. Indo-China. Madagascar.

IN 1870 the colonial empire of France included Algeria, the
Antilles, Saint Pierre and Miquelon, Guiana, Reunion
Island, the settlements in India, Saint Louis in Senegal
General   and the Isle of Goree, a few places on the coast of
Characteristics Gabon, New Caledonia and some archipelagos
of this   in Oceania, Cochin-China, and the protectorate
Expansion.   of Cambodia, making a total of 701,250 square
miles, with a population of 5 millions.

Just after the Great War the French colonies consisted of a
territory of 6,400,625 square miles (including North Africa and
the 304,375 square miles of Togoland and the Cameroons, which
were mandatory territories) with a population of 52 millions.
This was an area about nineteen times as large as that of the
mother country with a population one-fifth as large again as
that of France. The French colonial empire comes next to that
of England (which is 8,437,500 square miles, with a population
of over 400 millions), and is larger than the Dutch Empire
(which is 250,000 square miles, with a population of 48
millions).

The French expansion has been remarkable, well-nigh
miraculous in its extent and rapidity. But for Morocco and
Central Africa it had reached its full limit in 1900. This it had
taken barely thirty years to found. Such a growth is unique
in the annals of contemporary Europe.

England, indeed, had laid the foundations of her Empire
towards the end of the eighteenth century and had carried on
its development all through the nineteenth. Pre-war Germany,

132

who was a late arrival in the colonial movement, had to be satisfied with the non-occupied remnants—*tarde venientibus ossa.*

It seemed as though France had tried during the last twenty-five years to remedy the mistakes of the previous century.

The progress of this colonial empire seems at first sight to have been the result of a deliberate policy—the conquest of Tunis on one side and of Morocco on the other supplied Algeria with her two natural bastions; the linking of Senegal with the Niger, of the Soudan to the coast of the Gulf of Guinea, and the Soudan to Lake Chad and the Congo, forming a huge African empire two-thirds the size of Europe, to which must be added the Indo-Chinese empire extending over an area larger than that of France. This growth certainly gives the impression of resulting from a conscious striving after a given object.

But this, according to some, is pure illusion. This unity of thought and design had absolutely no existence in fact. It was chance, and an accidental concatenation of circumstances, that was entirely responsible. France, it has been said, won her vast Empire *without doing it on purpose.*

But any careful observer of the facts could not for one moment ratify such a statement, any more than they could agree to the fatalistic Asiatic theory of Tolstoy, that victories are won without generals and colonial empires founded without leaders, either civil or military.

The truth is quite the contrary. This vast movement of expansion across the sea was first and foremost the work of a small group of men who inspired it. The mass

The Men who inspired it. of the public, nine-tenths of the French people, it might almost be said nine-tenths of Parliament, allowed themselves to be pushed on without exactly knowing where they were being taken. Indeed this applies to almost all the great and fruitful works accomplished by democracies. They are always found to have originated in the firm action of a small body of men, an oligarchy which carried all before it. The whole history of England bears witness to this fact.

The taste for distant ventures, hazardous campaigns and expeditions for purposes of exploration and conquest had long existed in France. During the seventeenth and eighteenth centuries it had a period of extraordinary efflorescence. But it very soon met with opposition and jealousy on the part of England, who, owing to her geographic and economic position, and because she is an island, is far better adapted than France to uphold the pioneers of colonial expansion with all the power at her command. In France the Governments of the *ancien régime*, fettered by the exigencies of their European policy, could not or would not reconcile this policy with the desire and the need for spreading across the seas. " The snowclad fields of Canada " and the French possessions in India were time and again inexorably sacrificed to the demands of continental politics.

The Government of the Third Republic proved wiser and more far-sighted. It succeeded in establishing a fair equilibrium between its activities in Europe and in the sphere of colonial expansion. The development of the latter did not prevent it from being extremely alert and vigilant when it came to dealing with the former. It followed, though not always without offering resistance, those who were pioneers and leaders in the work of colonial expansion, who took the initiative with the utmost courage and shouldered the heaviest responsibilities, among whom the foremost and the greatest was Jules Ferry. He was fortunate in finding first-class men to carry out his policy—such men as Gallieni, Lyautey and Jonnart, to mention only the chief among them.

A nucleus of convinced and enthusiastic men, who had complete confidence in each other, were the apostles of the idea. By every means in their power, by speeches and by writing, they tried to arouse the interest of their fellow-countrymen, and eventually succeeded in doing so. The national energies, which had been curbed since the defeat, found in these distant enterprises the outlet they required. In the Army more particularly, all those who were possessed of a love of adventure, and would have choked in the atmosphere of small garrison towns, asked for and obtained posts in the colonies. Some of the foremost leaders in the Great War—Joffre, Gallieni, Gouraud, Mangin, Humbert, etc.—were colonials.

As a result of this apostolic fervour, coming both from within and without, colonial propaganda continued to increase in power and won fresh recruits. To some it became a second religion and had regular missionaries, among others Paul Bourde, the colonial editor of the *Temps*, a " lay saint," as Pierre Mille very rightly called him, who, although unknown to the great mass of the public, played one of the most active parts in this propaganda.

Republican France naturally came into contact with her old rival, England, in this sphere. The Fashoda incident, which at one moment brought the two countries face to face, was within an ace of leading to war. In the end wisdom and policy won the day, French and English alike realising that after all the territories to be divided were extremely vast and the world large enough for both of them.

The other European nations who might have been competitors only woke up somewhat late in the day to the advantages and profit to be derived from colonisation.

Italy for a long time held it in disgust owing to her adventure in Abyssinia.

Russia had Asia to devour, which proved quite sufficient for her appetite.

Germany, faithful to the doctrines of Bismarck, whose horizon was pretty well bounded by the limits of old Europe, and who knew nothing about world problems, proving that his intelligence as a statesman had its limitations, only came very late into the competition.

Bismarck thought he was extremely clever at first in encouraging France in her colonial policy, convinced that this was the best means of employing her strength and energies and of embroiling her with England and Italy. But this Machiavellian hope was doomed to disappointment.

In 1870 France had already been forty years in Algeria. The conquest of the colony was practically complete. It had

Algeria. Colonisation after the Conquest. demanded a great deal of time, effort and sacrifice due, to a large extent, to the mistakes made in the political as well as in the military sphere. Much time, for instance, had been lost in trying to treat with Abd-el-Kader. In order to avoid a momentary effort far greater difficulties had to be faced during the following years. Colonial history is full of mistakes of this kind, which were constantly repeated.

The rising of Abd-el-Krim, in the Rif, is only a repetition of the same old story.

After the insurrection of Kabylie in the spring of 1871, which was severely repressed without much trouble, France, except for small skirmishes on the borders of Morocco and the Sahara, was not called upon to make any further serious military effort.

Colonisation had followed step by step in the tracks of conquest. Uncertain and hesitating at first, and meeting with but little encouragement from the authorities, it neverthe-less showed a continuous development which bore witness to the wealth of the territory, and the energy and endurance of those who, by means of painful effort and the refusal to be discouraged by defeat, endeavoured to exploit it. A great many of the old Algerian families are descended from these pioneers who installed themselves from the very beginning in the country. In spite of every difficulty and obstacle, the majority of those who had once settled down were determined not to leave, so strong an attraction did the country exercise over them.

There is no place in the world where the Frenchman, whatever may have been his birthplace, so quickly feels himself at home. The natives of Provence and Languedoc find on the sea-coast, together with a warmer climate and more luxuriant vegetation, the same landscape and manner of life as those they have left. The vine, to the culture of which they quickly devoted them-selves with the greatest success, soon became one of the sources of wealth in the colony. This " Algerian Riviera " is backed by a region of lofty plateaux suitable for the cultivation of cereals and for pasturage. This high land slopes down to the Sahara, the land of oases and nomads.

How was a country so diverse and varied, where the French element, however great its importance, was in **The Policy of " Union."** the minority, to be governed and administered? Was the seat of authority to be Paris or Algiers?

At first the former alternative was tried. This was the period called the period of *union*. After the departure of

Chanzy, the military governor was replaced by a civil governor, and the Algerian administration being amalgamated with similar administrations in France. Algerian affairs were dealt with by eight different Ministeries, which, as may well be imagined, did not make decisions either rapid or easy. An official report by Jules Ferry pointed out the inconveniences and absurdities of this state of affairs.

The union, officially condemned in 1895, was modified by a decree of the 10th of May, 1896, which greatly increased the powers of the Governor-General. The decree **The New Form.** of the 21st of August, 1898, and the law of the 19th of December, 1900, provided for a separate Budget and instituted the *Financial Delegations*, a regular local Parliament, composed of three categories of colonial delegates (colonials, non-colonial Frenchmen and natives), who met separately and voted on the Budget proposals drawn up by the administration, together with a superior council reorganised with a majority of elected members for the revision of measures but without any right of initiative. Taxes could only be levied by means of a finance Bill in the mother country, which thus kept the right of exercising control over any fresh expenditure which the Governor-General alone might authorise. Military expenses, as in the case of the other colonies, were also borne by the mother country, with a guarantee of support for the railways. Algeria, provided with a Civil Service, had the right to raise loans and to give concessions for railways. Henceforward Algeria consisted of something more than the territories of her three departments, which were administered, as in France, by Prefects—there was Algeria herself endowed with a personality of her own.

As long as it existed this form of administration seemed somewhat of a compromise. The Governor-General was the common delegate of the different Ministers. The Prefects of the three departments played the same part and were endowed with the same functions as the Prefects in France. By the law of the 24th of December, 1902, the southern territories were made into a separate group with its own Budget and administration. These territories, which, as a matter of fact, were continually decreased, played the part of frontier States.

137

In order to start the system which granted Algeria a large measure of autonomy, the Republic made choice of excellent administrators—Jules Cambon, who was at the beginning of a brilliant administrative and diplomatic career, Revoil and Jonnart.

Jonnart, who was sent to Algeria by the Waldeck–Rousseau Ministry at the beginning of the century, just after there had been trouble owing to the anti-Semitic campaign of a certain agitator named Max Regis, held the office for over ten years. At the end of the war he returned to Algeria. By means of a liberal and intelligent policy towards the natives, his influence in parliamentary circles and his administrative capacity, he gave a wonderful impetus to Algeria, which at the present moment is not so much a colony properly so called as a part of the mother country.

The Great War, with all the consequences it involved, put the solidity of French institutions to the test. Algeria, which had revolted in 1871, except for a few unimportant disturbances in Aurès in 1916, never raised a finger during the four years of hostilities.

All the provinces of France, but more especially the southern ones, were represented in Algeria. A large influx of Italians **The Province of Algeria.** into the province of Constantine, and of Spaniards into the province of Oran, in no way affected the essentially French character of the colony. The sons of emigrants from the Balearic Isles, Alicante or Murça, who became naturalised Frenchmen, did their term of military service in the Zouaves and fought during the war with as much courage as the descendants of pure French colonists.

Only a few days before the battle of the Marne, during the memorable retreat across the plain of Champagne, the author of the present work, who was an officer in the Morocco Division, met a regiment of Zouaves in which almost all the soldiers spoke only Spanish; this, however, did not prevent them from fighting a week later with the same heroism as the French.

The race thus formed from a mixture of different nationalities, the type so brilliantly portrayed by Louis Bertrand in some of his novels, possesses all the qualities of the French peasant, but has in addition a characteristic absent in the latter—the

138

taste for and love of adventure. Great enterprises do not inspire it with fear. The Algerian colonist rarely puts his savings in a bank or a worsted stocking. As soon as he has any money to spare, and sometimes even before, he risks it in some new undertaking. There is no country where speculation in land—a very healthy form of speculation be it said, since it is based upon hard work and energy—has developed on so large a scale. The great vineyards round about Oran, Bône and Algiers, from the point of view of perfection of equipment and the use of the most up-to-date machinery, have not their equal in France. Lately the Algerians have taken up the cultivation of cotton with the most encouraging results.

The lofty plateaux are immediately followed by the country of oases and desert regions, the one being the continuation of **The Conquest of the Sahara.** the other. In order to make the occupation of the former secure it was imperative to conquer and occupy the latter.

The bond of union between the agriculturists of the lofty plateaux and the Ksourians who inhabit the oases, and whose chief means of livelihood is to be found in the palm and the date, is formed by the nomadic pastoral tribes.

In the early days of spring and in the autumn, at various passes between these two regions, and especially at El Kantara **The Achaba.** near Biskra, an uninterrupted procession of nomad tribes files through, either going to or returning from the desert. In the glaring sunlight of the far south, amid clouds of golden dust, a whole people on the march, men and women, young and old, animals and human beings, follows the ancient road of the periodic migrations. Fromentin, in his famous book, has given a magnificent description of this procession in which the magic power of creating colour by means of words has never been surpassed. This migration of the tribes is called in Arabic the *achaba*, which means the *search for grass*. And it is indeed the need of pasturage for the feeding of their flocks and herds that determines and at the same time regulates the movements of these pastoral tribes. Some of them, the Larba, for instance, penetrate during the winter a long way south of Ghardaia, almost as far as Ouargla, and return during the summer to the region of Teniet-el-Had, a journey of

625 miles there and back. Year after year, and even century after century, this movement takes place with absolute regularity and certainty. Time has glided by without making any difference to the migrations of these pastoral peoples. They are the same now as they were when Virgil described them in the Third Book of the *Georgics*.

" For days and nights, during whole months, the flocks and herds seek pasturage in these great deserts, never once sheltering beneath a roof—so vast is their expanse ! "

The conquest of the Sahara was a necessity and was brought about as the result of a sort of instinct rather than by means of any reasoned or methodical plan. A treaty concluded in 1862 with the Touaregs had remained a dead letter. Ouargla was occupied in 1871, El-Golea in 1873. Colonel Flatters, who was a member of a commission sent to survey the country for the building of a railway through the Sahara, reached Lake Mingou in 1880. He left in December and was murdered by the Touaregs on the 6th of February, 1881.

To the south of Oran, the insurrection of the Ouled Sidi Cheik, who were established on the frontier and had been roused to fanaticism by the Marabout Bou-Hamama, provoked the intervention of France. The revolt was crushed and the agitator sought refuge in Morocco. An outpost was formed at El-Golea. By the Anglo-French Convention of the 5th of August, 1910, the whole of the Sahara became a French zone of influence. In 1898 the Foureau–Lamy mission left Biskra to meet two other missions sent the one from the Soudan and the other from Chari. They met between February and April 1900.

By a fresh convention England recognised the right of France to the whole of the Sahara between Algeria, Lake Chad and the Soudan. From that time the route through the Sahara was open from Algeria as far as Timbuktu and the Niger. Ouargla, Ain-Salah, Hoggar, the land of the Touaregs, Timbuktu the mysterious, and finally the banks of the Niger, the country of the negro, these were the landmarks across these waterless regions.

The conquest and organisation of the Sahara districts were carried out with the utmost ease owing to the formation of the

corps of Meharists. They were a body of men who had been
brigands, but were promoted to the dignity of gendarmes and
patrolled the desert, establishing adequate security.

On the side of Morocco the incursions of robber bands were
held in check by means of the fortified outposts which France
had established in the Touat region. In 1899 Ain-Salah was
occupied, and the occupation was extended to the districts of
Tidikeld and Tafilelt, whilst the railway gradually advanced as
far as Ain Sefra and then Beni Ounif, the marvellous gateway
of the Oasis of Figuig, one of the most curious and variegated
in Southern Algeria, and finally to Colomb-Bechar.

The following years were occupied by the conquest of the
Touat district.

In 1881 Tunisia came under French rule. In North Africa
the mountain ranges run from west to east, and it is in this

**Occupation
of Tunisia.**
direction that throughout the centuries the great
invasions took place, first the Roman and then
the Islamic conquests.

France, on the contrary, through a sort of political and geographical paradox, had occupied Algeria, starting from the north
and going south, from the coast to the high plateaux and then
to the desert. But the demands of nature forced her to return
to the historic routes and to extend laterally—westward to
Morocco and eastward to Tunis. It was impossible for her,
without endangering her position in Algeria, to allow a rival
Power to set bounds to her expansion by settling down in
either of these two countries.

The occupation of Tunisia was planned and executed, with
the most consummate ease be it said, by the great statesman
who was responsible for the earliest French colonial conquests—
Jules Ferry.

Tunisia was governed by Beys of Turkish nationality and
inhabited by an extremely pacific people who spoke Arabic.
The extravagant expenditure of the Beys had led in 1852 to
their raising loans in Europe at such a heavy rate of interest
that in 1869 an international commission agreed to reduce the
debt in return for being allowed to administer their finances.
This was a difficult task, as the members of the commission
were not in agreement with the Ministers of the Beys, and the

European consuls were constantly quarrelling with each other. England and Italy were naturally opposed to French influence, and Wood, the English consul, who had held his position for twenty-three years, frustrated all the efforts of the French consul, Roustan. In 1874 England obtained the concession for the line connecting the French railway system in Algeria with Tunisia. As for Italy, she enjoyed an advantageous position on account of her geographic proximity and the number of her nationals established in the regency. Various incidents emphasised the opposition, and France was forced to have recourse to arms in order to protect her position in Algeria. But she had first to secure the consent of England, if not of Italy, and also have the support of public opinion. The Congress of Berlin granted her the former, and the Ministry of Jules Ferry prepared the latter.

In 1878, in Berlin, Lord Beaconsfield and Lord Salisbury informed Waddington, the French plenipotentiary, in plain terms that Great Britain would offer no opposition to French action in Tunisia. This was to counterbalance the seizure of Cyprus by England. The consent of England thus gained, Italy was notified of the new situation. In France public opinion was unable to face the prospect of this colonial expedition so soon after the disasters of 1870 without some apprehension, but parliamentary circles allowed themselves to be persuaded by Gambetta, who had himself been converted by Baron de Courcel, the head of the political department of the Foreign Office. The disapproval of Italy only served to hasten the intervention of France. The Tunis–La Goulette line, conceded in 1871 to an English company and sold to the French company to whom the Bône–Guelma line belonged, had been bought back after the cancellation of the sale by an Italian company at a price almost double that of the previous sale. Another somewhat shady financial deal (the Enfida affair, March 1881) gave Italy the opportunity of increasing her anti-French propaganda. A frontier incident, the invasion of Algerian territory by a band of Khroumirs on the 31st of March, 1881, finally determined the action of France.

The Jules Ferry Ministry obtained the necessary vote of supplies from Parliament without much difficulty, although the sum granted was extremely small (five million gold francs). In the Chamber barely fifty deputies abstained from voting, even Clemenceau supporting the measure. As a matter of fact the suppression of the Khroumirs was the excuse for the expedition and not its object ; but the Government, who were aiming at something very different than mere police operations, did not dare to confess its intentions to Parliament.

The first campaign lasted barely three months; a corps of 31,000 men drawn from France or Algeria were concentrated in two columns, one of which on the coast subdued the territory of the Khroumirs without difficulty, and the other, after a few small engagements, reached Kef, which threw open its gates. The greatest surprise of all was the apparition of the French troops before Bizerte, whither the rebel tribes might have sought refuge, and its occupation without a blow being struck by 8,000 men under the command of General Bréart (1st of May, 1881). And thus it was possible to invest Tunis from both north and west at once.

No diplomatic rupture had occurred between France and the Government of the Bey. The latter had merely refused to help the French to restore order. Roustan, the French consul, discovered that a relative of the Bey would consent, if necessary, to ascend the throne. On the 12th of May, General Bréart entered Tunis with a simple escort and the Bey accepted the Treaty of Bardo, which made his country a French protectorate. The military occupation was to be extended to every point regarded as necessary, a French Resident was to be the sole intermediary between France and the officials of the regency, and no transactions with foreign countries were to be carried on by the Bey without the consent of France.

The expedition had been brought to a close without Tunis having even been occupied by French troops, and about half the expeditionary force immediately quitted the territory of the regency. As it was the eve of the general elections, the Government thought it wise to limit the cost of the expedition as much as possible.

The French troops had hardly turned their backs when an insurrection broke out in the south and Sfax, Gabès and Kairouan, the holy city, fell into the hands of the insurgents. A fresh effort was absolutely imperative. On the 16th of July, 1881, Sfax, bombarded by the French fleet, was captured by a body of troops that had been landed; Gabès was the next to fall, on the 26th of July; 30,000 men were sent into the regency, bringing the aggregate of French troops up to 50,000. The commander-in-chief, General Saussier, first occupied Tunis (October), after which he directed three columns against Kairouan, one from Tebessa, one from Tunis and one from Sousse. They met with hardly any resistance, and Kairouan opened its gates without striking a blow (October). A year later (October 1882), on the death of the Bey Saddok, his brother Ali, in accordance with the laws of his house, succeeded to the throne, and on the 8th of July, 1883, the Treaty of Marsa completed the Treaty of Bardo.

Financial stability was established in Tunis with great speed and no trouble merely by handing over the control to high French officials. The budgets always showed a surplus. The agricultural and mineral resources of the country were considerable —cereals, wine, olive oil, etc., etc.

The plantation of huge olive groves covering thousands of acres to the south of Sousse and Kairouan was due to the really miraculous wisdom of Paul Bourde, General Secretary to the Government. As le Verrier discovered a planet by means of mathematics, so Bourde, from a careful reading of Latin authors and from the ruins of presses, deduced the existence in Roman times of huge olive groves in regions which for two hundred years had been uncultivated desert land.

Cattle are abundant in the northern region, where there is more rain. The chief wealth consists of phosphates. These are scattered all along the Algerian frontier, and concessions were granted to several companies. In 1923 the yield from the beds was 2,250 tons, which made Tunisia the greatest phosphate-producing country in the world, and superior to Algeria and Morocco, whose competition is nevertheless serious. The iron ore (774 tons) is almost all exported to England. The export trade (103 millions in 1900, 322 millions in 1913) reached 1,371 millions (gold francs) in 1923. In 1913, 41 per cent. of these exports went to France.

In this territory of 78,125 square miles there are 2,100,000 nhabitants (census of 1922), Mussulmans and Jews forming a large majority (about 92 per cent.), whilst the Europeans number about 156,000. The Italians outnumber the French, though the latter possess most of the wealth.

The numerical superiority of the Italians is due to the proximity of the peninsula and the fecundity of the race. This gives rise to a certain anxiety, inasmuch as the Italians hold strongly together and enjoy numerous privileges, particularly in the domain of education, which their Government, far from being willing to waive, would like to extend even further. The small colony has not, like Algeria, attracted many French families, the largest concerns being the property of great French landowners who are not resident in the country.

In 1870 the Soudan was almost unknown territory to the Frenchman. The districts occupied by France consisted only **The Soudan.** of the mouth of the Senegal, some settlements along the river, a few ports on the Casamance, in Rio Nuñez, Grand Bassam and Assinie and the future Ivory Coast. Of these possessions, the latter date from the second quarter of the nineteenth century, and Senegal from the end of the sixteenth century. Those were days when in the whole vast expanse of Africa only the mouths of rivers and a few carefully chosen points along the coast were regarded as possible settlements.

But Faidherbe, Governor of Senegal from 1854 to 1861 and 1863 to 1865, was more far-sighted. In the first place he transformed the colony by pacifying it and extending his zone of influence to the upper river. The war of 1870 prevented the French from continuing his work and pushing on, as Faidherbe had wished, as far as the Niger. Except in Senegal, French territory was confined to the coast. Faidherbe's plans, however, were taken up again under Colonel Brière de l'Isle, who was Governor from 1876. An enterprise was set on foot to connect the Senegal with the Niger by means of a railway between the extreme points at which the two rivers were navigable, Kayes and Bamako. Between 1882 and 1885 the railway was opened between Saint Louis and Dakar. The first section of the new line, the construction of which was authorised by the law of the 26th of February, 1881, had with

L 145

great difficulty covered about a quarter of the total distance b
1888. This advance brought the French into conflict wit
two native conquerors—Ahmadou, son of El-Hadj Omar, th
Marabout whom Faidherbe had subjected, and Samory, bot
of whom, at the head of their Mussulman warriors, practise
brigandage on the black inhabitants on both banks of th
Niger.

Captain Gallieni, who was sent on a mission (30th of January
1880), was held captive for almost ten months by Ahmado
(1880–81). Colonel Borgnis-Desbordes in three successiv
campaigns (1881–3) founded settlements at Keta and Bamake
and although he was unable, owing to the weakness of h
forces, to inflict a total defeat on Samory, he at least succeede
in extending the French zone of pacification as far as the rive
In 1887 Samory officially renounced all claim to the left ban
of the Niger, and Ahmadou accepted the protection of France

By the end of 1888 French Soudan consisted of a little nucleu
of subject States and a group of territories theoretically more c
less under French protection. France, solidly established c
the Niger, began to overflow to the north and south of the rive
But here she came into contact with neighbours—the Englis
while along the coast the territories of English Gambia, Port
guese Guinea, Sierra Leone, the republic of Liberia and Germe
Togoland set bounds to French expansion.

Except for the settlements on the coast the country inlar
belonged to the first comer, and there was great temptation
send exploring expeditions into the equatorial forests and ann
the territory thus won to the French Empire. As a matter
fact the Conference of Berlin (November 1884 to February 188
had recognised the rights of France in the Upper Niger, b
had decreed that possession must be followed by *effective occup
tion* of the territory. Thus there was a regular race on the pa
of the Powers established on the coast which was likely to lee
to incidents and quarrels. But in the River Senegal and tl
Upper Niger, the curve of the huge arc formed by the two rive
France held the trump card over her rivals, as she was in
position to reach the interior from both north and sout
Successive treaties allotted the various spheres of influenc
The boundary convention with Germany (December 188

146

with Portugal (1886) and with England (1882 and 1889) created the French colony of Guinea, the capital of which was Konakry.

On the Ivory Coast France had held ever since 1870 merely the settlements of Grand Bassam and Assinie, which she regarded as being of such little worth that she placed her interests there in the hands of a mere merchant, and they only began to acquire some value in her eyes after exploring expeditions had proved the wealth of the interior. The colony was organised in 1889 after a settlement of the frontiers with England.

Lastly, Dahomey, which was at first called the settlement on the Bight of Benin, included the country round Porto-Novo, over which the French protectorate, which had been established since 1863, was made effective in 1885, and the ports of Cotonou and Ouidah (1864–76). Béhanzin, King of Dahomey, was hostile to French influence, and of all the native sovereigns with whom France came in contact, proved the most formidable. He had a devoted army and a bodyguard of female soldiers. An expedition had to be sent (February 1890), resulting in a compromise by which the French were given Cotonou in return for paying rent for it to the King. Conventions with Germany (1885) had already settled the frontiers of the new State.

Thus the settlements along the coast were allowed to spread into the interior, where the native chiefs had to be subdued and England forestalled in the race for the mouth of the Niger. The exploring expedition so admirably conducted by Binger, a lieutenant of marines, who set out by himself, the only European, with a handful of natives (September 1887), crossed the States belonging to Samory and reached Kong (20th of February, 1888), the Mossi district and Ouaghadougou, returning to Kong and finally to Grand Bassam (20th of March, 1889), had corrected many erroneous ideas concerning the geography of the country, exploded the legend of the " Kong mountains " and proved the wealth of these districts. By treaties made with the native chiefs, Binger had joined up the Soudan with the Ivory Coast.

It was now a question of deciding whether France, who was established on the Upper Niger, or England, who exercised sovereignty over the Lower Niger by means of a chartered company, should obtain possession of the rest of the river.

Military leaders organising and commanding expeditions, explorers opening the road for them (the two are often confounded), treaties settling the boundaries, and feverish activity on all sides—such were some of the elements in the rush of the great colonising countries for the conquest of darkest Africa.

The work of pacification took time. Archinard, the commanding officer in the Soudan, undertook to break the power of Ahmadou in three campaigns (1888–90). After Sigou, his capital, had been taken, the latter was obliged to take refuge in the desert. But he reorganised his forces and was only finally conquered by a fresh campaign in 1893. He went away and died among the Sokoto in 1898. They were hard fights in which the odds were ten to one with extremely scanty forces, four or five small pieces of artillery against courageous adversaries who, however, were armed only with flint guns. The expeditionary columns contained a bare nucleus of Europeans, the rest being made up of black troops who, provided they had a solid cadre, very quickly learnt to use fire-arms without flinching. The commissariat was reduced to a minimum and there were no cumbersome convoys to hamper the march of the columns.

Samory was a more dangerous adversary than Ahmadou. His soldiers, " sofas " as they were called, used magazine rifles, and he himself knew how to choose advantageous positions for fighting. His troops were all the more devoted to him because the common booty, the fruits of pillage, were equally divided between them all. The campaigns conducted by Colonel Archinard and Colonel Humber, and in 1892 by Colonel Combes, succeeded in driving the *Toucouleur* chieftain either northward or eastward, and towards the end of 1893 the French possessions extended without a break from the source of the Niger as far as Macina.

The time had come to push on further. On his own initiative, Lieutenant Boiteux, who was in command of the small Niger flotilla, advanced on Timbuktu. On the 12th of December, 1893 he reached the mysterious city which since the days of Mungo Park (1805) had been visited by no more than four European explorers.

Boiteux and the ten Europeans who had accompanied him soon found themselves in danger. His second in command was murdered, and Colonel Bonnier, who had succeeded Archinard, marched with two columns to his relief. Whilst he himself was descending the river, Major Joffre led the second column by land to the left bank of the Niger. But Bonnier together with all his men was murdered while bivouacking by the Touaregs. Joffre made himself master of the town (9th of February, 1894), opening up all the approaches to it.

Owing to its gradual extension, the aggregate of French possessions in the Soudan made it necessary to reorganise the administration. The boundaries of the colony of French Guinea were fixed by new Anglo-French conventions (1891 and 1895). The Ivory Coast, where, owing to the timidity of the Colonial Minister, Colonel Monteil was unable to get the better of Samory's bands, who had penetrated into the country, was organised as an independent colony by a decree of the 10th of March, 1893. Lastly, Dahomey, where a revolt on the part of King Béhanzin rendered a double expedition under Colonel Dodds necessary and resulted in the capture and deportation of the negro prince (1892–4), was raised to the rank of a special colony in 1894.

It was necessary to establish some common bond between these colonies, to which Senegal and the Soudan were added. The Decree of the 15th of June, 1895, established a general government for French West Africa, which did not include Dahomey, and preserved the separate administration of each of the other colonies, but made the Governor-General, who was the Governor of Senegal, the head of all military operations.

The Lower Niger escaped the clutches of France. Three English companies were already established there. In 1879 they amalgamated and swamped the factories belonging to two French companies, who were unable to compete with them (1885). The union of these territories, which was called Nigeria, secured the navigation of the river in practice to England, although theoretically, according to the Berlin decision (1885), it should have been free to all. By a Convention of the 5th of April, 1890, the boundaries of the respective zones of influence were fixed. The French territory extended to the line joining Say on the Niger to Barroua on Lake Chad. England kept for herself the districts that seemed the richest and most populous.

149

She consented to acknowledge the right of France to the desert of Sahara, where, as one of her statesmen remarked, "the Gallic cock could make good use of his spurs."

In order to reconnoitre the French sphere, Colonel Monteil followed the boundary and, crossing Sokoto and Bornu and the whole of the Sahara, reached Tripoli, after an exploring expedition which had lasted two years. Lieutenant Mizon, who in 1890 was charged with the exploration of the country to the south of Lake Chad and the Benue, met with hostility on the part of the English agents of the Nigeria Company.

As their passage was barred in the north, the French turned southward through Upper Dahomey, the real subjugation of which was begun in 1892 and finished in 1894. Without relaxing their efforts, various missions joined up Dahomey to the Niger, to the Soudan and the Ivory Coast, or else explored the navigability of the river (the Toutée expedition in 1895, Lieutenant Hourst in 1895 to 1896), racing the English on the Lower Niger and the Germans in Togoland. Germany recognised the French zone in July 1897.

England, after a period of somewhat severe diplomatic tension, signed a convention with France on the 14th of June, 1898, which put an end to the struggle for the Lower Niger. A year later she redeemed the charter of the Royal Nigeria Company and made Nigeria a colony (1899). The year 1898 thus marked the end of the rivalry between the European Powers. It also saw the conclusion of the struggle with Samory, who was obliged to retire to the Kong district (1895), which was intersected by the roads running from the east and the north. His only hope of escape from the columns sent in pursuit of him was to flee westward to the outskirts of the equatorial forest and the most southerly of the French posts in the Soudan. He had with him about ten thousand fighting men in addition to a horde of over twenty thousand subjects, captives, women and children, who laid bare everything on their way.

In a district which was too barren to provide it with food, this huge caravan showed the road it had taken by the dead bodies it left in its track. After repeated skirmishes, Captain Gouraud succeeded in surprising and capturing Samory in his camp, together with his three hundred wives and three hundred and twenty children, without firing a shot. The conquered chief was deported to the Congo (23rd of September, 1898).

Thus the last and most powerful of the enemies of France disappeared after sixteen years of resistance. Except for a few risings on the Ivory Coast, the only important military operations took place on the right bank of the Senegal in the region of Adrar. This territory, which had remained almost unexplored until 1900, had had its boundaries fixed by a Franco-Spanish Convention of the 27th of June, 1900. Now the bandits of Mauritania, who were guilty of the murder of a French official, had succeeded in escaping punishment in spite of several punitive expeditions. Moulay Idriss, a cousin of Abd-el-Azis, the chief of Morocco, stirred up his bands against France, and during the years 1907 and 1908 several of these bands, setting out from the Adrar district, swooped down on French territory and ravaged it. Colonel Gouraud, the Government Commissioner in Mauritania, fought them in the defiles of Choummat and Amahil (December 1908 and January 1909) and, occupying Axar, the capital of Adrar, pacified the rest of the district without difficulty.

The creation of a single Government for French West Africa in 1895 was dictated chiefly by military requirements. The number and names of the colonies forming it were changed in 1899 by the suppression of the Soudan, the various districts of which were divided between the coast colonies, and in 1904 by the creation of the colony of Upper Senegal and Niger and the Niger territories and Mauritania.

With its eight colonies, West Africa is the largest of all the French possessions (2,915,625 square miles). The population, however, is very sparse, three or four inhabitants to the square mile (eight or nine in Dahomey and Guinea). This is due to the low birth-rate and the high rate of infant mortality. As is the case in the Congo, there is an insufficient supply of European doctors, and the knowledge of medicine among the natives is still in its infancy. This widely scattered population is entirely agricultural; the ground-nut (*arachis*) is the great source of wealth in Senegal, and its cultivation extends to the Soudan and Guinea; rice, which is grown in Upper Guinea, is an article in which a fairly large trade is already carried on. Copra, maize and tapioca are still only used as articles of food locally, but the coffee and cocoa plantations extend as far as Dahomey and the Ivory Coast, and the climate is such that there is no reason why these products should not be cultivated just as well here as in the neighbouring English colony of the Gold Coast. The production of rubber is negligible, as the rubber-bearing trees and creepers have been destroyed. Much is expected from the new plantations, but it is an industry which takes a long time to develop. The middle reaches of the Niger would be excellent for cotton, and this matter seems at last to be getting beyond the realm of inquiry. In this as in other respects the Great War has opened men's eyes. The whole of the cotton manufactured in France comes from the United States, Egypt or India, which is a heavy burden on the French exchange and a menace to her industry. But it will be many years before any important part of the three hundred thousand tons required for the French market can be provided from her own colonies.

The trial plantations made in West Africa have yielded good results, but the quantity is infinitesimal (three thousand tons). The chief obstacle to the growth of this industry, which requires a great deal of labour, is the sparseness of the population.

The wealth of the forests in the colony on the Gulf of Guinea is enormous. Here again systematic exploitation has begun since the war, but it is hampered by the scarcity of means of communication; kola, kapok and gums supply the materials for an export trade which could easily be made ten times as great. Lastly, cattle breeding is a prosperous industry in the Soudan and Guinea.

The harbours have been organised, and Dakar will become an important port as soon as some energetic authority has undertaken the task of sanitation. The Dakar–Saint Louis and the Kayes–Niger railways have long since been completed, and the line between Thies and Kayes was opened in 1924. Railways go inland from the coast, and, covering almost 1,875 miles, have shown unexpectedly large profits, the traffic in passengers and goods being far greater than was anticipated.

COLONIAL EXPANSION

In West Africa France had fairly formidable adversaries to contend with—Samory, who kept her on the *qui vive* for a long **French** time, and Béhanzin, who was quickly beaten. The **Equatorial** conquest of the territory of Gabon and of the **Africa.** Congo was accomplished without fighting the natives properly so called. It was only on the outskirts of the colony that a certain Mussulman Sultan, named Rabah, tried to bar the French advance. The conquest was a diplomatic rather than a military one, as these territories were regarded as No Man's Land—*res nullius*.

Before being occupied or even explored, the boundaries of these regions were settled by an international convention, the great colonising Powers staking out in advance the utmost limits of the territory they proposed to claim.

This colony, as was the case with its neighbour, had the most modest beginnings.

In 1841, in order to provide shelter for French vessels superintending the slave trade, France occupied the estuary of the Gabon. In 1848 Libreville was founded and enfranchised negroes settled there. The exploration of the country inland was only begun in 1856, and the voyages of discovery were made only up the rivers along which the villages were built. Between 1856 and 1872, du Chaillu, the naval lieutenants Braouzec and Genoyer, Aymes, Marche and the Marquis de Compiègne were the pioneers in the work of extending the French colony in the Gabon district.

But Savorgnan de Brazza was the real founder of the French Congo. An Italian by birth and admitted as a foreigner into the French Naval School, he became a naturalised Frenchman and joined the Navy with the rank of ensign. On his first exploring expedition, de Brazza surveyed the basins of the Ogowé and the Alima without, however, discovering that it was a tributary of the Congo. Sending back his escort he pushed further north by himself, and then resumed his homeward road. This journey, which was undertaken on an extremely small subsidy, Brazza supplementing his resources at his own expense, was conducted with the utmost regard for humanity— slavery was abolished in the Ogowé district, and the native chieftains won by presents and not by force. But at about

153

the same time Stanley, an Englishman who had become a naturalised American, had just descended the whole length of the Congo (1874–7), and on the day on which Stanley published the account of his expedition, Central Africa revealed part of her mystery to the world.

In 1876, Leopold II, King of the Belgians, collected a body of explorers and philanthropists together in Brussels and founded the International African Society, whose aim, a purely humanitarian one, was to be the abolition of slavery. Stanley's discoveries inspired Leopold with the idea of taking possession of the basin of the Congo in the name of the International Society, and with this object in view Stanley was despatched to Africa (1879).

If, therefore, Brazza wanted to secure part of this basin for France, he would have to be quick. Backed by a Committee of Inquiry and the Government, he returned to Gabon in December 1879. Once more ascending the Ogowé, in the upper basin of which Franceville is built, he reached the Congo in the region of the States of King Makoko, who accepted the protectorate of France (1880). Returning down the river, he founded Brazzaville and made his way back to Gabon. On the way he had met Stanley. The American explorer, in the description he subsequently gave of this strange encounter, depicted Brazza, the victorious apostle, with his dilapidated equipage, looking like a tramp with his uniform in rags and his hat battered in.

On his return to Paris he was given an enthusiastic reception, made a naval lieutenant and appointed Commissioner to the Government of West Africa. A third journey was undertaken, and Brazza, at the head of a mission consisting of soldiers, sailors and civil and native officials (soldiers or porters), was entrusted with the task of organising the huge new territory that had been acquired. One or two settlements were started and the mapping of the country completed. But Brazza did not succeed in fixing the boundaries of the French territories contiguous to the districts belonging to the International Association of the Congo, which afterwards became the Congo Free State, recognised by the Treaty of Berlin (1885). Conventions with Germany, who was established in the Cameroons

154

(December 1885), with Spain in Rio Muni, and Portugal, who was wedged in at Cabinda (May 1886), settled the frontiers of the new State, which in 1888 became the colony of Congo-Gabon. At one moment war almost broke out with the Congo Free State. The river Ubanghi formed the common frontier; troops from the Free State crossed it with the object of spreading northward. In order to put a stop to this attempt, which would have threatened the communications between her new possessions and West Africa, France sent Colonel Monteil to the district with a battalion of sharp-shooters. Negotiations conducted at Brussels closed the incident, and Colonel Monteil was then sent to the Ivory Coast, where he came up against Samory's bands.

Wedged in between the Free State and the Cameroons, the new colony could only extend in a northerly direction towards Lake Chad. But a plan was beginning to be outlined. The huge continent of Africa is divided on either side of the equator into symmetrical zones, the climate of which is the same. As France was extending her sway towards the bend of the Niger and the coast of the Gulf of Guinea, and by means of her explorers was insinuating herself inland as far as the tropical zone, Lake Chad suggested itself as the obvious centre of this empire. Similarly, since the basin of the Congo was already occupied, would it not be possible in Central Africa to join Gabon to the French settlements on the Red Sea by reaching the Upper Nile? Of these two projects, one was realised. The other almost led to the gravest complications with England.

From 1890 onwards the country between the Niger and Lake Chad was reconnoitred by a series of exploring expeditions. Colonel Monteil, after traversing the bend of the Niger, crossed the river at Say and advanced as far as Bornu. Cholet and Fourneau explored the course of the Sangha, Crampel set out from the Ubanghi district, and Mizon went up the Benue. Crampel was murdered in April 1891, and Dybowski, sent to find the remnants of his mission, was able to avenge his death. Mizon, after two journeys in 1892 and 1893, carried the French flag into the Adamowa district on the confines of the German Cameroons. But England and Germany, by the treaty of 1893, kept these territories, and France was deprived of them;

Baghirmi alone was recognised as a French possession, allowing free access to Lake Chad.

The country in this direction, however, was in the power of Rabah, a Mussulman at one time governor in the Egyptian service, who with a well-disciplined army derived his wealth from traffic in slaves. As soon as access to Lake Chad had been secured (the Clozel and Gentil mission, 1894–7), Rabah was attacked by three columns—the Foureau–Lamy mission, which crossed the Sahara, the Voulet–Chanoine mission, which became the Joalland–Meynier mission, and came from the Soudan, and the Gentil mission, which started from the Congo. The three columns met, and in the battle that was fought, Rabah was killed (April 1901). His domain became the military territory of Lake Chad. All that remained to complete the pacification of the country was to exterminate the slave-hunters who still remained there.

The whole zone north of the Congo bordering on the Cameroons was explored or had its boundaries fixed by Loeffler, Moll, Lancrenon and Lenfant, the last-mentioned of whom found in the east the sources of the Sangha and the tributaries of the Ubanghi. To the east of Lake Chad the Sultan of the Wadai district, a trader in slaves, was conquered and deposed, whilst the Sultan of Massalit massacred one of the French columns on the 4th of January, 1910. The general uprising that followed was repressed by Colonel Moll, who met his death at the moment of victory (1911). In 1912 the work of pacification was accomplished; the conquest of Borku and Tibesti in 1913, where the Senoussists with the help of the Turks had offered an energetic resistance to Colonel Largeau, was the end of the vast enterprise undertaken by France from the coast of the Mediterranean, across the Sahara to the edge of the Gulf of Guinea.

The Nile route was closed to her. In September 1882 the withdrawal of France had left England in sole possession of Egypt and put an end to the Anglo-French condominium. The French rights were still theoretically in existence, and the Government made a formal declaration to this effect in 1892, but did nothing to support its claims. Great Britain diplomatically prepared the way towards access to the basin of the Upper Nile. The idea of a trans-African Railway from the

COLONIAL EXPANSION

Cape to Cairo was launched, and on the 12th of May, 1894, a convention with the Congo Free State granted the latter a lease of the province of Bahr-el-Ghazal in return for allowing England a zone of 30 kilometres on the eastern frontier of the Free State which gave her an unbroken road to her possessions in East Africa. France protested. On the 28th of March, 1895, the British Foreign Minister declared in the House of Commons that a French expedition from West Africa towards the Nile would be regarded as an *act of hostility*. Nevertheless, so long as France sent out no expedition, England let her pretensions rest. But in 1896 the defeat of the Italians by Menelik warned Great Britain of the possible extension of the Abyssinians into the valley of the Nile. In order to explain the disaster of Adoa, the Italians had already maintained that French officers had trained the armies of the Negus. Thus there was the possibility of a union being formed between the French from Central Africa and the Free State in the lofty plateaux of Æthiopia, who by their joint effort might get the better of the Dervishes. The British Government at first decided to rid themselves of the latter by sending out Anglo-Egyptian troops against them. But France, exercising her just rights, forbade the Government of the Khedive to supply the funds required for the expedition out of the reserves of the Egyptian debt. Whereupon England advanced the money herself (February 1897). The expedition was methodically carried out by Kitchener, and at the same time a railway was constructed all along the Nile. The English advance, begun in March 1886, was never arrested, and on the 2nd of September, 1896, the Mahdi was conquered and Omdurman, his capital, was captured. But, ever since the 10th of July, the French mission under Captain Marchand had been at Fashoda on the Nile. In the race for the Upper Nile the French flag was easily first.

The decision to send out the Marchand mission had been made by the Bourgeois Ministry in March 1896. Officially it was to be merely an exploring party, but its real aim was to join hands with the Abyssinians, and in concert with them to forestall the English advance on the Upper Nile. It consisted of 150 Senegalese sharp-shooters secretly trained by Captain Mangin between May 1896 and January 1897. In July 1897

157

this strange Odyssey began. Setting out from Brazzaville, it went up the Ubanghi and down the Soué, a tributary of the Bahr-el-Ghazal. Marchand and Mangin were accompanied by Baratier, Largeau and Germain, who performed the miracle of cutting a boat fifty feet long into bits and carrying the pieces through 160 kilometres of bush and putting it together again.

The mission aimed at reaching the Nile with all their forces, and rather than cross the steppes they decided to get to the other side of the Bahr-el-Ghazal. The stock they carried was sufficient for them to be able to barter their goods in exchange for food, and on the 10th of July the column occupied the little ruined fort of Fashoda without having fired a shot. On the 25th of April two steamers full of Dervishes appeared before the walls. A few shots soon got the better of them, and Marchand signed a treaty with the native chief of the country, putting his territory under French protection.

On the 26th of September Kitchener reached Fashoda with six gunboats, and on instructions from his Government wanted to occupy it. Marchand informed him that he was holding it in the name of France. This time French and English pretensions clashed. But the British Government did not hesitate and showed that it was ready to go to war.

The French Government, thinking that the game was not worth the candle, gave way. By the Convention of London, signed on the 21st of March, 1899, the right of England to the whole basin of the Bahr-el-Ghazal, and the districts of Dar-Fur and Kordofan, and of France to Baghirmi, Wadai and Kanem, that is to say, the territory to the east and north of Lake Chad, were recognised.

And thus the aggregate of colonies was formed which a decree of 1908 united under the name of French Equatorial Africa. It was divided into sections for administrative purposes (Gabon, the Middle Congo, Ubanghi, Shari and Chad), each one of which was financially independent, under the supreme authority of the Governor-General residing at Brazzaville. In 1916 Chad was made a self-governing colony. Equatorial Africa was further extended in 1911 by the pacification of the Wadai district, whose Sultan was subjected after the capture of Abecher, his capital, and by the occupation of the districts of Borku and Tibesti. This huge territory of 1,375,000 square miles had in 1911 a population calculated at about four and a half million inhabitants. If statistics can be relied upon, this population was reduced in 1921 to 1,577,000 inhabitants, so that the loss due to epidemics was about 63 per cent. Even allowing for mistakes, the average density of population cannot be more than four inhabitants to the square mile.

The natives are the most backward of all the negro races. The poorness of the human material, the climate, which is unhealthy for the European, and the grave diseases, such as sleepy sickness, which attack him as well as the native, explain why Equatorial Africa is in practice the most neglected of the French colonies. The slowness of its development is due to the methods of colonisation at first employed; in imitation of the Congo Free State, the Government instituted the system of companies to whom concessions of large tracts of territory were made (there were forty of them), with the right of keeping the produce on a royalty basis. As ivory and rubber were about the only products, the system resulted in the forced labour of the natives. So great were the abuses that this system was abolished in 1907 and free trade was once more allowed. But the condition of the natives was still miserable. They have no regular food supply, they are lost in the bush; frequently at variance with each other, their families are broken up and their villages deserted. It is possible to wander about for days without meeting a human being. There are no roads except in Ubanghi; everywhere else there are only tracks and footpaths.

The wealth of the country has been but little exploited. The equatorial forests yield all kinds of essences. But it is only since the last war that exploitation has begun. Rubber, palm oil, ivory, coffee and cocoa are being exported in ever larger quantities; between 1908 and 1913 the trade was doubled, rising from 26 to 57 milliards. But the economic situation will only improve when adequate equipment is created or developed. Equatorial Africa is the only one of all the French colonies in which a railway has not been completed. In 1908 France consented to a loan of £840,000 to make a survey for a railway. The Congo and its tributaries afford good waterways, but the

Congo ceases to be navigable at 250 miles from the coast. Exports from the Middle Congo and Ubanghi have to be conveyed by the Belgian railway from Kinchassa to Matadi, on which the traffic is limited. In 1914 a loan of £684,000 was raised, and the laying of the line from Brazzaville to Pointe Noire, begun in 1922, has now covered a third of the distance. It is only when the railway is complete that colonisation will be possible, and wood, raffia, kapok, copal gum, and copper ore from Minduli will form important items for export. The economic prosperity of the Belgian Congo, the ethnographic and climatic conditions of which are very similar, gives ground for every hope.

As was the case in Africa, French expansion in Indo-China began before 1870.

France conquered Cochin-China in two stages (1861–7). The conquest was begun on his own initiative by a certain admiral, **Indo-China.** who, after an unfortunate landing at Bouram in order to avenge the massacre of some missionaries, took advantage of favourable tides in order to divert the forces at his disposal to the delta of the Mekong (1859). The country belonged to Tu-Duc, King of Annam, who was nominally a vassal of China. In 1863 France acquired the protectorate of Cambodia. Very little was known of the geography of the country, but discoveries in this sphere were made through the explorations of two naval officers, one of whom was Francis Garnier, who, after the campaign in China, went up the Mekong. Garnier discovered the Red River and came back down the Yang-tse-Kiang (1866–8). France was but little interested in this new world of which so little was known. A few merchants, whose attention had been directed to China, thought that Tonkin, the basin of the Red River, opened up the road to Southern China.

It was at this time that bands, called the Pirates of the Black Flag, were infesting the provinces of Southern China. Dupuis, a French merchant, was charged by the Chinese Government with the task of re-equipping the army which was acting against them in the province of Yün-nan. The Red River seemed to provide the most direct route. Dupuis went to Paris to ask the support of Thiers' Government for this

commercial expedition which might develop into a military
one. But he was disappointed. Leaving Haifung in November
1872, he carried out his mission and returned to Hanoi in
April 1873. As he had incurred losses at the hands of the
mandarins of Annam he claimed damages. The Governor of
Cochin-China sent Francis Garnier with 175 sailors, entrusting
him with the task of settling the dispute and concluding a
commercial treaty with Annam. As negotiations proved of no
avail, Francis Garnier, on his own initiative, had recourse to
force. He captured the citadel of Hanoi and in six weeks the
little forts on the delta. Negotiations were then resumed. The
Pirates of the Black Flag, who were now employed by the
Government of Annam, attacked the citadel of Hanoi. Garnier
repulsed them but was killed in a sortie. The territory he had
conquered was abandoned by the Government of MacMahon.
Private animosity also arose to complicate the situation. Dupuis
did not succeed in having his claims settled, and Garnier's
widow failed to receive her pension. The Treaty of Saïgon
(1874) recognised the sovereignty of the Emperor of Annam,
who was to have the support of France for the maintenance of
order and the control of foreign policy. The navigation of the
Red River was free, and all the ports open to commerce with
Europe. It was a *de facto* if not a *de jure* Protectorate.

The Emperor of Annam, in order to put a check on French
influence, chose to remember that he was a vassal of China.
In 1880 the Chinese Ambassador in Paris lodged a protest
against the treaty. The Pirates of the Black Flag attacked
the French posts. In order to settle these difficulties, the
Governor of Cochin-China sent Captain Rivière, a naval officer,
to Tonkin (1882), with orders to demand the strict execution
of the treaty. This meant a repetition of Francis Garnier's
exploits, which began and ended in the same way. Rivière, at
the head of 600 men, anxious not to waste time in endless
negotiations, demanded the surrender of the citadel of Hanoi
and took it by assault in April 1883. The Chinese Ambassador
in Paris immediately lodged a protest, but his claims were disregarded, France maintaining that the quarrel concerned herself
and Annam alone. Rivière seized the other forts on the delta
and, like Garnier, he was besieged in Hanoi, where he was

M

killed in a sortie by the Pirates of the Black Flag in May 1883.

Jules Ferry had been President of the Council since the 21st of February, and had already conducted the operations in Tunisia with the greatest skill. Public opinion was now beginning to take a greater interest in colonial expeditions, and he decided to deal drastically with the situation. Admiral Courbet with a naval division was sent to the delta and the forts were bombarded. As King Tu-Duc was dead, the Ministers who were carrying on the Government in his name sued for peace, which was signed at Hué on the 25th of August, 1883. It was called the Treaty of Harmand, after the man who drew it up. And thus Annam became a French Protectorate.

China now openly showed her hostility. As suzerain of Annam, she maintained that the quarrel concerned part of her territory, and first sent some regular troops to support the Pirates of the Black Flag in Tonkin, and afterwards declared war (October 1883). Thus a small colonial expedition developed into war against the Chinese Empire. The expeditionary force, raised to 9,000 men, took Sontay, and, with further reinforcements of 15,000 men, Bac-Ninh, Hung-Hoa and Tuyen-Kwang (May to June 1884). The whole of Tonkin was in the hands of the French. On the 11th of May, Li-Hung-Tchang, Viceroy of Pechihli, signed the first Treaty of Tientsin with Frigate-Commander Fournier, by which China undertook to recall her troops from Tonkin and recognised the treaties made between France and Annam.

Just as the matter seemed settled the duplicity of the Chinese Government reopened the whole question. The treaty had appointed the dates on which the Chinese troops were to evacuate certain places in Upper Tonkin. A French column on its way to take possession of Bac Lé ran into a detachment of Chinese regulars and was forced to beat a retreat. But Jules Ferry was not taken by surprise. On the 6th of June, 1884, the French Ambassador, who was on his way to Peking, had stopped at Hué and concluded a new treaty by which a French Resident was placed in Annam to deal with foreign policy, Tonkin was still to be autonomous as far as local administration was concerned, a head Resident was placed in Hanoi and local Residents

162

to superintend the Annamite officials, with the right of dismissing them. The war with China was carried on without a formal declaration having been made, which would have meant a debate in the Chambers. There was the bombardment of Kelung in the island of Formosa and the blockade of Formosa, the bombardment of Fou-Tcheou (August 1884) and the blockade of the Gulf of Pechihli, through which the rice for Peking had to go. China sent troops to Tonkin, and 15,000 men blockaded the little garrison of Tuyen-Kwang, where Sergeant Bobillot distinguished himself. General de Négrier with 7,000 men relieved it and drove back the Chinese regulars as far as the frontier (March the 2nd, 1885). But receiving reinforcements, the Chinese returned, and Négrier beat a retreat to the north of Langson and shut himself up there. He was wounded and handed over the command to a lieutenant-colonel who in a panic, although the place was in a position to stand a siege, evacuated it without striking a blow on the 28th of March.

This event led to the fall of the Ferry Ministry on the 30th of March. By that time the peace with China was ready to be signed. The negotiations for it had been in progress ever since January 1885, though there had been no lull in the military operations. The preliminaries were signed the day after the fall of Jules Ferry, on the 4th of April, and the treaty was confirmed on the 9th of June at Tientsin. China definitely renounced her suzerainty over Annam, and henceforward the matter was settled and the great work of conquest achieved.

Territorial expansion followed. In Annam, where General de Courcy, the Commander-in-Chief, had proposed the suppression of the dynasty and the annexation of the country, incidents arose which led to the deposition of the King and the appointment of a new sovereign (August–September 1885). As a result there was a rebellion, which, however, was suppressed without difficulty. Tonkin continued to be infested by the Pirates of the Black Flag until 1897, but these were the only disorders with which the French troops had to deal. Without meeting with any serious opposition France extended her sway in the basin of the Upper Mekong. Laos was a sparsely populated mountainous region whose princes, vassals of the King of Annam, were claimed as his subjects by the King of Siam.

But England, who since 1886 had been mistress of Burmah, was a neighbour of Siam, and along the Mekong a neutral zone of States belonging to Laos should have separated Siam from the French possessions. The French, however, occupied Laos. But Siam refused to recognise her capture and attacked the Annamite sharpshooters in the French service. Whereupon two French boats went down the Me-Nam to Bangkok, and the King of Siam gave way (October 1893). Laos with the Mekong as boundary was recognised as forming part of Annam and the port of Chantabun was handed over as a guarantee. England recognised the territorial clauses of the treaty. In 1904 the Anglo-French *entente cordiale* smoothed away the last difficulties with Siam; Chantabun was evacuated and Siam restored to Cambodia three provinces in the north-west which were inhabited by Cambodians.

Some mistakes, which were no doubt inevitable, were at first made in the organisation of the Indo-Chinese possessions. At the time of the conquest of Cochin-China, France had had no experience of colonisation. Napoleon III hesitated as to whether he should keep this territory and would have preferred to hand it back to the Government of Annam in return for a war indemnity. Moreover, the yellow world was entirely unknown to France. The military regime of the early days was altered by a decree of the 13th of May, 1879, and the colony was provided with a Governor and a Civil Service, a colonial Council and tribunals formed on the model of those existing in the mother country. In 1881 the colonists here were represented, like those in the older colonies, in the two Chambers. All the other States of Indo-China were included in the Protectorate, but Cambodia had her status changed after the new treaty of 1884. Annam was administered under a system similar to that in force in Tunisia. Tonkin, where there was no native dynasty, was governed by a Resident-in-Chief in Hanoi, and local Residents who supervised the native administrators. Laos kept her princes and chieftains, who were supervised by a Resident-in-Chief at Luang Prabang and his superintendents.

All these territories have ever since 1897 been under the general government of French Indo-China, to which the territory

164

of Kwangchow-wan, ceded by China, was added in 1898. The 450,000 square miles composing it contain about 21 million inhabitants. The most densely populated part is Tonkin (9 millions). Next comes Cochin-China with about 4 millions, while Cambodia has 1,200,000 inhabitants, and Laos, in 143,750 square miles, 700,000 inhabitants.

Indo-China is first and foremost an agricultural country. Rice is the principal crop to be cultivated and the chief article of export, and is responsible for most of the traffic in the port of Saïgon, making Indo-China, except for the British possession of Burmah, the largest rice-exporting country in the world. The quantity exported varies according to the year from one million to 1,800,000 tons. The other crops are of less importance for the export trade, but their yield, which could be largely increased, might make the French colony an important market. The cotton crop already reaches 9,000 tons, which, provided progress is regular and methodical on the "red earth" of Cambodia, might soon be sufficient for the needs of the country and later on possibly help to supply the French market. Jute, mulberries and cocoa are also being cultivated; the heveëne plantations made before the war in eastern Cochin-China and the south of Annam are beginning to yield very favourable results, whilst the mineral wealth is considerable, Tonkin providing 30,000 tons of zinc for export, while the export of coal reaches about a million tons.

Since the time of Monsieur Paul Doumer 1,250 kilometres of railway have been built, but the coast line which will run from Cochin-China to Tonkin is not yet finished. The waterways, which are abundant in these tropical regions, are obstructed by rapids and deposits of silt, and the management of the canals in Cochin-China constitutes an important part of the work of colonisation accomplished by France. Thanks to these works the production of rice has increased (the exports from Saïgon have trebled in twenty years), and the works already in existence have put an extra area of over 500,000 acres under cultivation.

Trade is constantly increasing. In 1913 it was about 650 millions, in 1924 it was almost 2 milliards. Rice represents 70 per cent. of the whole export trade. Cotton materials form the chief article of import. France is responsible for at least 50 per cent. of the imports, but only 25 per cent. of the exports go to her, a relatively small amount which, however, may become larger when more articles required by the mother country are produced.

The French rights in Madagascar are of very long standing. In 1626 Richelieu ceded this great island to a company which,
Madagascar. after founding some settlements on the coast, failed to carry on. The same fate overtook the East India Company formed by Colbert. In the eighteenth century Count Bengowski, a Hungarian magnate, charged by Louis XV with the task of colonising the island, proclaimed himself the independent king of Madagascar, and was killed by a French expeditionary force in 1786.

At the beginning of the Revolution no lasting establishment had been founded in this distant territory. General Decaen, Captain-General of the French settlements in the Indian Ocean, succeeded under the Consulate in occupying Tamatave. But in 1811 the English seized it. The treaties of 1814 and 1815 left Madagascar in the hands of France, in spite of the fact that England at one time maintained that as a mere dependency of the island of Mauritius it ought to have the same political fate.

The west is inhabited by an almost black race, the Sakalava. The central plateau is occupied by the Hova, a Malay people, who are more energetic and tried to subject all the various tribes to their rule. They succeeded and founded their capital at Antananarivo. Although it was still theoretically French territory, the island seemed much more like a British possession. The English sent missionaries there, who converted the Hova magnates and even their Queen, and acted as agents to spread British influence. Queen Ranavalo even went so far as to proscribe all the French (1861). A struggle ensued between the English and French missionaries, and treaties were concluded which were alternately favourable to France and England (1865 and 1868). In 1878 the Hova Government refused the right of holding property in the island to all foreigners, and on his death confiscated the estates of Jean Laborde, a Frenchman and a brigadier in the gendarmerie who had been cast ashore

166

in a storm in 1831, and by his activity and initiative and his friendly relations with the natives had succeeded in founding some flourishing settlements. In 1882 the Hova flag was planted on some territory on the west coast facing the island of Nossi Bé, which was officially under French protection. These two acts led to the intervention of France (1883).

The military and naval operations, which were carried out with insufficient forces, were hampered by diplomatic incidents with England and the changing of the high command three times. In May 1883 Admiral Pierre occupied Majunga and bombarded Tamatave. The Chambers, by voting a total credit of £680,000, had expressed a clear wish to uphold French rights, though the expenditure was to be limited. The negotiations conducted by Admiral Minot and the Consul-General Patrimonio, who had been summoned from Beirut, resulted in the treaty of 1885. The sovereignty of the whole island, and not only of the Hova, was given to the Queen, but she was forced to accept a French Resident-General at Antananarivo who was to deal with foreign affairs. France was given possession of the Bay of Diego Suarez together with an indemnity of £400,000. The aim of the negotiators was for the treaty to lead to a sort of protectorate, although the word was never mentioned.

Le Myre de Villers, the new Resident-General, and sometime Governor of Cochin-China, and his successors met with bad faith on the part of the Hova Government, and especially at the hands of the Prime Minister, who was the husband of the Queen. The latter wanted to treat with foreign Powers without the intervention of France, and the settlement of the indemnity due to the latter, owing to the raising of a loan on terms some of which were draconian, seemed as though it might lead to England seizing hold of the finances of the country. The Sakalava tribes, who were under French protection, were molested, and French colonists murdered. In 1894, Le Myre de Villers returned to Antananarivo bearing an ultimatum, which was rejected. This meant a rupture. In December Parliament voted a credit of £2,600,000, and on the 12th of December, 1894, Tamatave and on the 15th of January, 1895, Majunga were occupied without a blow.

The expedition lasted seven months, from the 1st of March to the 30th of September, 1895. It consisted of trifling encounters, and the manner in which it was conducted gave rise to severe criticism. The necessity for it having been long foreseen, and it had been made the object of studies and plans carried out concurrently by the War Office and the Admiralty. The latter had chosen the Tamatave–Antananarivo route, which was relatively short, but presented many obstacles—forests and pestilential districts to be crossed. The expeditionary force, it is true, was to consist chiefly of black troops, with a small reserve of marines, and revictualled by means of pack animals. The War Office preferred the route Majunga–Antananarivo, which, although longer, was easier at all events in appearance. On the pretext that the French troops were to defend the flag at all points where French interests were involved, General Mercier, the Minister for War, arranged that the expeditionary force should consist largely of detachments drawn from French regiments. But, as was to be expected in the case of young soldiers in no way acclimatised to tropical heat, the mortality was exceedingly high. At the instigation of the President of the Republic the conduct of the expedition was entrusted to the War Office, and the commander chosen was General Duchesne, who had distinguished himself in Formosa in 1885.

From the very beginning various incidents occurred to prevent the departure of the expedition; the supplies placed on the beach were partly washed away by the tide. Whilst the advance guard landed on the 1st of March, the main body did not arrive until April and May, and they had to make haste in order to profit by the dry season (May to September). They did not meet with much resistance on the way to Suberbieville, from which place the land transports were to start on the 9th or 10th of May. The making of the road, which was very difficult in the hilly country, was only accomplished at the rate of a little under two miles a day, and by the middle of July only 156 miles had been laid. Another 156 remained before Antananarivo could be reached. The battalions were decimated by sickness, and it was out of the question to imagine that the expedition could be accomplished before the rainy season. General Duchesne took the only decision possible—to form a

flying column of four thousand men who were not sick, with supplies carried on pack mules, who would advance at the rate of nine miles a day.

Setting out on the 14th of September, and victorious in fights on the 15th, 19th and 25th of September, this column skirted Antananarivo in order to make the assault from the east and the north-east. As soon as the first line of the heights was taken the firing of a few shells was enough to bring about the capitulation of the town. Out of a total of 18,000 men, the official figures for the losses were 6,000 dead from sickness, of whom 4,189 were Europeans, and 14 killed in battle. The losses of the light column on seventeen days of march were very low (22 dead and 52 wounded).

On the 1st of October, 1895, the French protectorate over the island was established by treaty. The Queen kept her Government, but a French Resident-General was to control the foreign policy and the administration. France was to provide the necessary military forces. The Protectorate, as it was defined by the treaty, did not last long. The French Government, mistrusting the native leaders, came to the conclusion that the annexation of the island by France was unavoidable. Queen Ranavalo accepted the change, and the annexation, duly notified to all the foreign Powers, transformed the island into a colony by the edict of the 8th of August, 1896. The civilian Resident was recalled and Colonel Gallieni, who was made a General, was sent to the island as Resident and Commander-in-Chief.

He remained in Madagascar from 1896 to 1905. Gallieni was the typical great colonial soldier. After having proved his capacity in the Soudan and in Tonkin, he reached Madagascar in the middle of a rebellion incited by the Hova Ministers who had been ousted from power. Two Hova Ministers were tried and put to death, and the Queen was deported to Algeria (1897). Gallieni, seconded by his chief of Staff, Colonel Lyautey, applied the system which was to be the basis of French action in Morocco. French troops were in effective possession of only an extremely limited zone, and the conquest of the whole island was imperative. In order to protect parts that had already been subjected it was necessary to occupy the others, if they were

not to become a refuge for rebels. This gradual extension had to be accomplished by a judicious mixture of policy and force. There were no isolated columns, but solid outposts composed of loyal natives with French cadres. As the work of pacification progressed the military organisation was replaced by a civil organisation. Unity of command was the pivot of the work, willingness and intelligence in every rank of the hierarchy the means for carrying it out. Gallieni's nine years' work could be measured by results. The whole country was at peace; the European staff, which was quite small, consisted of 310 officials as against 1,259 native clerks. In 1908 the island was placed under the authority of a civilian Governor-General.

The enduring results of this method of colonisation were the principles it laid down and the disciples it inspired, of whom the most remarkable was Lyautey.

Madagascar, together with its dependencies, supports a population of 3,382,000 inhabitants. The Hova element, which is more assimilable, accounts for less than a third of this number (about 950,000). The richest regions are situated on the east coast, which is the most unhealthy, or on the interior plateau. The construction of the railway from Antananarivo to the coast has led to the development of the rice industry, and 48,000 tons of rice were exported in 1923. Maize, sweet potatoes, and beans form the staple articles of diet for the native. A rich agricultural industry has been developed in the east, where vanilla, of which Madagascar is the greatest producer in the world, sugar-cane, coffee, cocoa and plants for the extraction of perfume are grown. There are large herds of cows and pigs which provide material for a tinned and frozen meat industry, the produce of which is sent to English South Africa, and for a large export trade in raw hides. The mineral wealth is very large, one article alone, graphite, in which Madagascar competes with Ceylon, being an important article of commerce. The island's wealth in precious stones is only just beginning to be methodically exploited. Recent surveys have revealed the presence of deposits of iron, coal, tin and copper. The trade figures reach 400 millions, of which France's share is in the proportion of about 50 per cent.

COLONIAL EXPANSION

Conclusion. A certain geographer has humorously remarked that France conquered a huge colonial empire " without doing it on purpose."

This assertion, as can be proved by a mere statement of the facts, is more humorous than true.

If we follow the progress of the French conquests in detail, whether in Africa or Asia, we find, as we remarked at the beginning of the chapter, that it owed its origin to two factors.

In the first place, there was in France a small body of men filled with faith in the colonising mission of their country, the members of which were closely united and who brought all their influence to bear on the Government to make the necessary decisions at the opportune moment. Chance ordained that from the beginning the reins of power should be in the hands of a man like Jules Ferry, who was a convinced believer in colonial expansion and determined to sacrifice everything, even his own political career, to what he regarded as a prime necessity. If Thiers was the liberator of French territory, Jules Ferry was the founder of the French Empire, two of the brightest jewels of which, Tunisia and Indo-China, she owes entirely to him. He opened up a path that others were to follow, and left colleagues and disciples behind him. The first successes which he gained in the face of every possible obstacle made similar successes in the future possible and in fact relatively easy. From that time forward every opportunity that presented itself for adding to the French possessions, and every time it was necessary to come to a virile decision, the same men, the same guardians of the sacred fire, were behind the Government forcing it to move. Very often, much oftener than is supposed, the Government resisted, on the plea that Parliament and the country were against further expansion. Between 1907 and 1909, just when France was on the point of being definitely engaged in Morocco, a certain Foreign Minister often used to say angrily to the writer of the present lines : " The ' colonials ' are doing all they can to hurl us into the Moroccan business. But I shall not give way. I shall get up on to the platform and denounce their machinations ! " Nevertheless this did not prevent Oujda and Casablanca from being occupied shortly afterwards by France.

171

This activity on the part of a small body of men at home ha
its counterpart in the colonies in the energy and audacity a
well as the intelligence and resource of the men who carrie
out the policy.

These were the two forces to which the French Empire owe
its existence. One would have been of no avail without th
other. With but rare exceptions, whenever it was necessar
to take the initiative on the spot, it was done and well done
Very often the Government found itself faced with an accom
plished fact, and as it seemed likely to lead only to happ
results, it ended by giving its consent.

Moreover, these practical pioneers, and this is an important
point, generally accomplished their task with the minimum o
means, without putting the country to heavy expenses o
demanding sacrifices against which it would have kicked. From
the very beginning the Army men showed a wonderful capacity
for recruiting, training and making use of native troops. And
this was the secret of their success. Nine times out of ten
except for the French cadres, who it is true never shrank from
sacrificing themselves if necessary, the losses were almost always
among the coloured troops. If it had been necessary to have
recourse very often to French soldiers, Parliament, we may be
certain, would very soon have imposed its veto. But the way
in which France succeeded in organising the raising of native
recruits without the use of force, and the art with which she
made use of them, is one of the things of which Frenchmen
have most right to be proud.

In this way a great empire was won *at very small cost*. That
was why the country allowed it to be done. Little by little,
as success became assured, and the value of the new acquisitions
became more apparent, the colonies, which were at first unpopular rather than the reverse, grew in favour.

There followed the war, which served to prove even to the
most sceptical the immense services which the empire was
capable of rendering to France. Owing to the scant interest
which France had shown in her colonies their economic equipment was as a rule most rudimentary. It would certainly have
been wiser to devote to them a few of the many millions that

172

he had invested with such a lavish hand in foreign countries—
Russia, Turkey, etc.

Nevertheless, in spite of their defective equipment in this
respect, the contributions made by the colonies were consider-
ble. In addition to 800,000 combatants, and 220,000 workmen, they supplied all kinds of produce that France would
otherwise have been obliged to buy from abroad. Since the
war the utmost effort has been been made to increase their
economic development. As three-quarters of the work of
restoring the devastated regions has now been accomplished, it
s in the direction of the colonies that French activity, enterprise
and capital should be turned.

BIBLIOGRAPHY.—Dubois and Terrier, *Un Siècle d'Expansion Coloniale*
(1902). M. Petit, *Les Colonies Françaises* (1902). *Bulletin du Comité de
l'Afrique Française depuis* 1893; *Bulletin du Comité de l'Asie Française
depuis* 1901. H. Lorin, *La France, Puissance Coloniale* (1900). P. Distère,
Traité de Législation Coloniale (4 vols., 1886–8). A. Rambaud, *Jules
Ferry* (1903). P. Gaffarel, *Les Colonies Françaises* (6th ed., 1899). De
Lanessan, *L'Expansion Coloniale de la France.* H. Vast, *La Plus Grande
France* (1909). Froelicher, *Trois Colonisateurs* (Bugeaud, Faidherbe,
Gallieni). General Mangin, *Regards sur la France d'Afrique* (1924).

ON ALGERIA.—Wahl, *L'Algérie* (4th ed., 1906). De Peyerimhoff, *La
Colonisation Officielle en Algérie* (2 vols., 1906). R. Aynard, *L'Œuvre
Française en Algérie* (1912). J. Cambon, *Le Gouvernement Général de
l'Algérie* (1918). A. Bernard and N. Lacroix, *La Pénétration Saharéenne*
(1906). Piquet, *La Colonisation Française et l'Afrique du Nord.* E.
Gauthier, *La Conquête du Sahara* (1910). A. Bernard, *Les Confins Algéro-
Marocains.* R. Recouly, *Itinéraires Algériens* (1922). E. Cat, *Histoire
de l'Algérie.* C. Rousset, *La Conquête de l'Algérie* (5 vols.). General
Daumas, *Mœurs et Coutumes de l'Algérie; le Grand Désert.* General du
Barail, *Mémoires.* Louis Bertrand, *Le Sang des Races. La Cina. Pépète
le Bien-Aimé.* Isabelle Eberhardt, *Dans l'Ombre Chaude de l'Islam.
Feuilles de Route.*

ON TUNISIA.—*L'Affaire de Tunisie,* 1870–81 (*Livre Jaune,* 1881). G.
Loth, *Le Peuplement Italien en Algérie et en Tunisie* (1905). Rafaelle
Capelli, *La Politica Externa del Conte di Robilan* (1897). M. Faucon, *La
Tunisie avant et pendant la Colonisation Française.* P. H. V. (d'Estournelles
de Constant), *La Politique Française en Tunisie* (1891). De Lanessan,
La Tunisie (2nd ed., 1917).

ON DARK AFRICA.—Terrier and Mourey, *L'Œuvre de la Troisième
République en Afrique Occidentale* (1910). Darcy, *Cent Ans de Rivalité
Coloniale. L'Afrique* (1904). S. de Brazza, *Conférences et Lettres* (1887).
E. Gentil, *La Chute de l'Empire de Rabah.* A. Lebon, "La Mission
Marchand" (*Rev. Des Deux Mondes,* March 1900). R. de Caix, *Fachoda*
(1899). G. Hanotaux, *Le Partage de l'Afrique. Fachoda.* Bruel, *L'Afrique
Equatoriale Française* (1918).

THE THIRD REPUBLIC

ON MADAGASCAR.—Gallieni, *Madagascar de 1896 à 1905* (2 vols., 1905). Lyautey, *Dans le Sud de Madagascar* (1903). *Lettres du Tonkin et de Madagascar,* 1894–8 (1920). L. Brunet, *La France à Madagascar ; Gallieni* (1903). Hellot, *La Pacification de Madagascar* (1901). *Guide de l'Immigrant à Madagascar* (3 vols., Vol. I., 1899).

ON THE FAR EAST.—Bouinais and Paulus, *L'Indochine Française* (2 vols., 1885). Cultru, *Histoire de la Cochinchine Française* (1910). Lyautey, *Lettres du Tonkin et de Madagascar,* 1894–8 (1920). L. Aymonier, *Le Cambodge* (3 vols., 1900–1904). De Lanessan, *La Colonisation Française en Indochine* (1895). Seauve, *Les Relations de la France avec le Siam,* 1880–1901 (1906). P. Doumer, *Situation de l'Indochine,* 1897–1901 (1902).

CHAPTER XI

BOULANGISM

The Schnaebelé incident. The wave of Boulangism. The night
of the election. The Exhibition of 1889. The elections of 1889.

THE elections of 1885 were conducted by means of the
multiple-vote system, and as the Republican party was
divided whilst their adversaries presented a united
front, they resulted, especially in the first poll, in victory for
the latter. But it was a barren victory, since the second round
to a large extent deprived them of the fruits of the first. For
when once the Republicans had restored discipline and unity
among themselves they had no difficulty in getting the better
of the Right.

And thus, fifteen years after its proclamation, the Republic
seemed to be solidly established and in a position to resist all
attack. Nevertheless the strength of this position was relative
rather than absolute, and due to the weakness of those who
had made their attacks with so little determination. Among
the pretenders to the throne, the Comte de Chambord, who
stood the best chance of ascending it, had not known how to
profit by his opportunity ten years previously, or else had
had no desire to do so.

The opportunity then lost never recurred. The Comte de
Chambord died without issue at Frohsdorf, and his death
sounded the knell to all monarchist hopes.

As the Prince Imperial, the Bonapartist Pretender, had also
vanished, it might have been supposed that the Republic really
had nothing more to fear from any quarter. And it was from
this, rather than from itself, that it derived its strength. The
Boulanger affair furnished sufficient proof of this, and laid bare
the weak spots in the system. It only required a little more
determination, energy and courage, on the part of those who

175

attacked it, to overthrow it. But on this occasion also the Republic had the good fortune to be faced by an adversary who was not very formidable.

Like Gambetta, Jules Ferry was also in his turn ousted from power on account of his colonial policy, though it had won a large empire and brought fresh wealth and strength to the country. The parliamentary system as it was established in France seemed, on account of the splitting up of parties, the lack of discipline in all of them and the eager competition for the possession of portfolios, to be becoming ever more and more a terrible destroyer of statesmen. It used them up with terrific speed. In the twinkling of an eye it led them from the Capitol to the Tarpeian rock, although it is true that those who were apparently most worn out succeeded after a while in regaining a place in front of the footlights without too much trouble. As Adrian Hébrard, who in his day was Rivarol and Chamfort rolled into one, remarked : " It is not the Seine that flows through Paris but the stream of Lethe."

When Ferry had been set aside, no leader worthy of the name was to be found. And a parliamentary majority was also as non-existent as a leader.

As Grévy had been re-elected President of the Republic, Freycinet, who, on the 7th of January, 1886, was called upon to form a Cabinet, gave the War Office portfolio to General Boulanger, at that time at the head of the infantry, who had been recommended to him by Clemenceau and almost forced upon him. Still young (he was only forty-nine), he had a fairly brilliant military career behind him—a campaign in Cochin-China, another in Kabylie, and the command of the army of occupation in Tunisia. As soon as he took up office his first concern seemed to be to give satisfaction to his Radical patrons. He sent away from the neighbourhood of Paris those cavalry regiments whose officers had given expression to Clerical and Royalist opinions. A circular, addressed to corps commanders, enjoined them to exercise strict neutrality, and to impose it on those who were attacking the Republic as well as on those who were defending it, the former, he declared, having hitherto been the only ones to enjoy every kind of latitude.

Meanwhile the General lost no opportunity of making himself
nown to the public. His handsome and commanding presence,
is pointed beard and his black horse, won for him the favour of
he Parisian people, always ready to make a popular idol of
ny military man who takes the trouble openly to woo them.
Vith this object in view he turned every opportunity to account,
nd if it did not come of its own accord, he had a marvellous
ift for creating it. He seemed to take a greater interest than
ny of his predecessors in the well-being and hygiene of his
roops, allowing the soldiers to wear beards, tasting their food,
tc. All these activities, which were carried on in full view of
verybody, were not long in producing their results.

At the review of the 14th of July, in the Bois de Boulogne,
Boulanger was acclaimed by the mob. As usual, the *café
oncert* played its part, and a well-known song sung by Paulus,
vhich in a few weeks, or rather in a few days, had spread all
ver France, consecrated the event :

> " Je suis le chef d'une nombreuse famille,[1]
> Depuis longtemps j'avais fait l'projet
> D'emm'ner ma femme, ma sœur, ma fille,
> A la r'vue du 14 juillet."

And the public in chorus shouted, " Hurrah for the
`eneral ! "

The Comte de Paris, who, on the death of the Comte de
`hambord, became head of the French Royal House, gave, on
he occasion of the marriage of his daughter with the Crown
`rince of Portugal, a brilliant reception in his own mansion, and
hose who organised it, as well as those who were present,
nanaged to turn the affair into a great Royalist demonstration.
`he Republicans saw in this an act of provocation, and retaliated
y a law forbidding the presence in the territory of the Republic
f the heads of any family that had once reigned in France.
nxious to outdo them, Boulanger not only struck out of the
rmy list the princes who figured in it, and first and foremost
mong them the Duc d'Aumale, but wanted to deprive them of
heir military rank, although this legally belonged to anybody

---

[1] I am the head of a large family, and long ago made up my mind to
ake my wife, my sister and my daughter to the review on the 14th of July.

who had won it. The Duc d'Aumale at once lodged a protest
against this decree, which he declared was arbitrary, and, in
order to wreak his revenge, allowed his friends to have published
a letter which he had received some years previously from
Boulanger, in which the latter expressed his devotion and
gratitude in terms that were little short of effusive : " It is you
who proposed that I should be made a General," he wrote
" it is to you I owe my appointment. . . . Blessed be the day
that will place me once more under your command."

Boulanger denied the authenticity of the letter; but as a
facsimile was immediately published, he was obliged to acknow
ledge it. This episode placed his treacherous nature in a very
unfavourable light, and made him appear as a man who was
anxious to push himself forward by any and every means
ready, as they say, to run with the hare and hunt with the
hounds, eager for notoriety, and impatient at all costs to play
a part.

Nevertheless, his popularity continued to grow. The
Nationalists came over to him, and Déroulède presented to him
the League of Patriots, of whom he was the President. The
most zealous of his adherents always called him " The General
for our revenge."

As usual, the German Government did not fail to make this
agitation the pretext for obtaining from the Reichstag a fresh
vote of credit for the army. This disclosed the possibility of
war and caused somewhat of a panic on the Paris Stock
Exchange.

Just at the psychological moment, as always happened when
the relations between France and Germany were strained, an
The Schnaebelé Incident. incident occurred. Schnaebelé, who held a special
appointment at Pagny-sur-Moselle, was enticed
by his German colleague to cross the frontier, on
the plea of having a conversation. He was arrested and taken
to Metz. It was a regular trap, the consequences of which
might have been exceedingly serious. Fortunately President
Grévy and Flourens, the Foreign Minister, kept calm, and
immediately displayed great clarity in pointing out the weak
point in the German argument—the legal aspect of the case

BOULANGISM

Whatever grievances the Germans may have had against Schnaebelé, the very fact that he had been invited to cross the frontier by his colleague made him actually immune. He at once became an envoy whose person was sacrosanct. This was the theory that Grévy at once advanced in Berlin, and it appealed to the old Emperor, who, whatever his faults, was by nature upright and honest. He commanded Bismarck to have Schnaebelé released.

The incident was closed, but the traces of it lingered for a long time, as was the case with everything that threatened to bring the two great countries into conflict. Following upon the scare of 1875, the Schnaebelé incident was the second serious alarm suffered by France. The landing of the Kaiser at Tangier in 1905 was the third, and the fourth was the despatch of a gunboat to Agadir. Each of these incidents proved to France how fragile and precarious was the state of peace that existed in the presence of a neighbour so formidably armed, who was aiming at the hegemony of Europe and certain, nay, more than certain of possessing a crushing military superiority.

By making the public excited and nervous and provoking its fears, the Schnaebelé incident necessarily provided much grist for the Boulangist mill. The General, adored by the mob, appeared in the eyes of many as the leader who would be capable at no very distant date of making headway against the provocations and bluster of Germany.

As the Ministry had fallen, the Republicans in the Senate who were older and wiser began to see clearly through the game, and declared that they would oppose any Cabinet of which Boulanger was a member. In order to remove him from Paris, where his popularity was becoming disquieting, the Government gave him command of the army corps in Clermont-Ferrand. His partisans immediately protested against this appointment, which they said amounted to exile, and accused the Government of trying to get rid of a man of whom they were afraid. On the evening of his departure a demonstration, which had long been arranged, was made on his behalf, and a large crowd besieged the Gare de Lyon. Boulanger had great difficulty in escaping from the hands of the thousands who were trying to hold him back, and in order to slip away from their enthusiastic attentions was obliged to get on to the engine of the train.

The Wave of Boulangism. The wave of Boulangism thus swelled visibly churning up clean and dirty water pell-mell in its swirl.

Many of the Boulangists were inspired by a patriotic sentiment which was all to their credit, and which was increased by the discontent, and in some cases the disgust, caused by the parliamentary system. Since the Republic had had nothing further to fear from the Royalist Pretenders, it was inclined to show too much of its worst side, and to appear in its most unkempt aspect, in shirt-sleeves and slippers, so to speak, which was not always an inspiring spectacle. In the midst of this relaxation and abandonment, Boulanger made his appearance as a man capable of restoring discipline, order and correct bearing where they were most wanting. The perennial desire for a strong Government, which exists in the heart of every Frenchman, once more made itself felt.

These reasons, however, do not explain everything. Other and very powerful if not decisive reasons were soon added. All the enemies of the Republic—Bonapartists, Royalists, and advocates of the Referendum—hastened to join the movement, which they regarded as the surest means of undermining the system and bringing about its downfall. They brought him adherents, votes, and, last but not least, money, a great deal of money. A committee was formed with the object of exploiting the enthusiasm in favour of the General by means of the most perfect and up-to-date methods of publicity—showers of placards, posters, chromos, circulars, etc. This was perhaps the first time that this method of commercial publicity, which is extensively used in the United States, and plays an important part in politics, was employed in France on so large a scale. But propaganda of this kind presupposes the existence of well-stored coffers. Revelations, which were made a few years later proved that it was chiefly the Royalists, and above all the Duchesse d'Uzès, who took upon themselves to supply the funds.

A crisis connected with the President, and which arose from a misuse of influence, occurred about this time. Wilson, the son-

BOULANGISM

n-law of Grévy, who was a deputy, was mixed up in several scandals—the sale of honours, in which two generals were compromised, correspondence sent under the President's stamp to avoid payment of postage, etc., etc. These scandals, which were published in the papers, could not be hushed up, and the Chamber ordered an inquiry to be held. The President was necessarily compromised by the misdemeanours of his son-in-law, who lived under his roof in the Élysée. He was urged to send in his resignation, but refused. The majority in Parliament, however, when they are really determined upon it, have the power to force a President to resign his position. All that is required is to make the formation of a Cabinet absolutely impossible. Faced by this, which puts a stop to the working of the whole parliamentary machine, the President has no alternative but to go. And this Grévy in the end decided to do.

As Ferry was still extremely unpopular, especially in Paris, as is often the case in Presidential elections, a nondescript man, somewhat obscure and retiring, Sadi Carnot, was elected by the Congress. An engineer, and deputy for the Côte-d'Or, he had been Minister of Finance and Public Works. A worthy man, conscientious, plodding and rather shy, he filled with zeal but utter lack of brilliance the high office to which he found himself suddenly raised.

This Presidential crisis and the scandals from which it arose proved a further source of advantage to Boulanger, and inspired his partisans with the idea of putting him forward as a candidate in the departments where there were vacant seats, although as an officer on the active list he was not eligible to stand. The Government became alarmed. They kept a strict watch on the General and found that he had several times left his post without permission and come in disguise to Paris. Thus the plot against the Republic became more clearly defined and the Government decided to take action. It deprived Boulanger of his post and brought him before a committee of inquiry, who put him on half-pay on account of serious misdemeanours in the service.

Boulanger, who was thus suddenly given freedom of action, was in a position to organise the agitation as he pleased. This was his opportunity for proving his talents as an organiser, his

181

political shrewdness and cleverness, as well as his determination and audacity.

The material means to do so were certainly not lacking. Chance circumstances rather than his own merits had placed him at the head of a large though somewhat miscellaneous party, consisting of the most diverse elements, but which nevertheless possessed a certain unity so long as it was merely a question of overthrowing the parliamentary system. When once this system was destroyed, however, and another had to be substituted for it, the temporary followers of the General would very soon have come to loggerheads. He had at his disposal the newspapers, all the money he required, and the support of the capital, which when the time came would have facilitated a *coup de force*. The Committee which was behind him and on which Rochefort, who was always out to destroy and was in everlasting conflict with somebody or something, rubbed shoulders with Déroulède, Senator Naquet and the deputies of the extreme Left, decided to present him as a candidate for all the vacant seats. This would amount to a sort of plebiscite.

Boulanger was elected time after time by huge majorities, first in Dordogne and afterwards in the North. In these two departments, however, be it noted, the Conservatives had been in the majority since the last elections. This proved that but for the heavy premium placed upon him by the Conservative and Royalist vote, Boulanger, from the electoral point of view, at all events, would not be a serious menace to the Republic. Among the Conservatives, it is true, the majority and all the younger members were now on his side. Only a few old parliamentarians, with whom principles, morality, and also a feeling for politics outweighed all other considerations, refused to cast themselves into this adventure, which under the guidance of a man of whom nothing was known might lead the country Heaven alone knew where.

As soon as Boulanger took his seat in the Chamber he introduced a scheme for suppressing the Senate, and indeed the whole of Parliament, and for abolishing ministerial responsibility and substituting the plebiscite in its place. This gave rise to an altercation between him and Floquet, which was followed by a duel in which the General was wounded.

Whereupon his propaganda became more active than ever. He was elected in three departments (19th of August)—the Nord, the Somme and the Charente-Inférieure. But these were all districts in which the Conservative party was very powerful, and where it only required the addition of a few votes from the Left, and from anybody who was dissatisfied with the existing system, to secure him the majority.

Now, to crown all, a vacancy occurred in Paris, and Boulanger's old patron Clemenceau, who had become his worst enemy, challenged him to face the verdict of the capital. It was an imprudent challenge, when it is remembered how captious the Parisian public is naturally inclined to be, ever ready to enthuse over a new-comer, and also that it had good reason not to regard the parliamentary system as it was carried on under its eyes as a thing of perfection.

In the electoral campaign that now took place all the Boulangist forces did their utmost, with the whole gamut of posters, songs, public meetings, circulars, etc. To oppose the General, who was a dangerous adversary if ever there was one, the Republicans could only produce a very dull candidate, a Radical called Jacques, whose very name was enough to make him ridiculous.

Boulanger was elected by 244,000 votes to 162,000. His success aroused the most violent enthusiasm among his followers, and nothing could better serve to show what this sudden rage for Boulanger was really worth. For it was a regular paroxysm. The women, whose opinion always counts for a great deal, were nearly all mad about the General. The Duchesse d'Uzès and Louise Michel, the one a very great lady and the other a revolutionary, who happened to meet at the bedside of a sick man during a consultation, became reconciled in their praise of him. It was certainly the only subject on which they could possibly agree. " We are communicants," remarked one of them, " in the body of Boulanger."

On the night of the election the General, together with his political staff, Rochefort, Thiébaud, Dillon and **The Night of** Naquet, were waiting in the saloon of the **the Election.** Restaurant Durand, in the Place de la Madeleine, the General in evening dress, with two large pearls in his shirt and

183

a red carnation, his favourite flower, in his buttonhole. As the results were being announced his followers invaded the restaurant, and arrangements had to be made to keep order to prevent the idol from being crushed to death. Improvised aides-de-camp had great difficulty in keeping the crowd in check, and only those who knew Boulanger personally were allowed to go upstairs and shake him by the hand.

The boulevards were black with people. Under the windows of the Boulangist paper *La Presse*, which was announcing the results, the crowd, which grew larger every minute, gave vent to shouts of jubilation. The police and municipal guards only kept it half-heartedly on the move; it was clear that their sympathies were with the demonstrators. And when a brass band struck up *En revenant de la Revue*, everybody, men and women alike, took up the refrain in chorus.

Some of his friends strongly urged the General to put himself resolutely at the head of the demonstrators. The League of Patriots, and the Boulangist associations, whose members were all in the streets that evening, asked for nothing better than to follow him, to march on the Élysée, which was but scantily guarded, and to turn out the President and seize the reins of power. The distance from the Madeleine to the Faubourg Saint-Honoré is not very great, and it seems clear that Boulanger, had he dared to take the step, could easily have traversed it. There is everything to show that a *coup de force* would have been successful. The police and the troops, even had they wished to do so, which is very far from being certain, were not in a position to offer him any resistance.

The revolution of 1830, as well as that of 1848, was carried out under far less favourable auspices. But what would have happened immediately after so easy a victory? How would the incongruous and in some respects opposing elements on whom Boulanger was temporarily relying have behaved? That is quite another matter. But if those who make revolutions were to ask themselves such a question we may be certain that they would never carry them out. On the night of the 27th of January Boulanger was the undisputed master of Paris.

BOULANGISM

Fortunately for the established system (and this was another stroke of luck among many others), Boulanger was quite devoid of determination, character and temperament. He gently but firmly declined to listen to all these suggestions. " I am certain," he said, " that I shall win the victory by parliamentary methods."

In this he proved how terribly short-sighted he was. Never for a moment did it occur to him that the opportunity offered him that day was unique. He had had the good fortune to take his enemies unawares, and to have behind him the whole of the capital, whose decisions, for better for worse, the provinces nine times out of ten endorsed.

In face of the danger threatening them, the Republicans were obliged to pull themselves together, to silence their differences, and to have recourse to the most energetic measures of defence. If Boulanger was master of the streets, they, for their part, were masters of Parliament.

In deciding to give battle on strictly parliamentary lines, Boulanger found himself engaged on unfamiliar and unfavourable ground, full of traps and ambuscades in the midst of which he was fairly certain to come to grief.

The Republicans, who were frightened, began by abolishing the secret ballot which they maintained, although it had been advocated by a large number of their own body, worked in favour of their enemies. They re-established the divisional ballot, which made any change of public opinion on a large scale practically impossible. They also threw out a reform Bill presented by Floquet. As this Bill was the first article on the Boulangist programme, it was playing the enemy's game to appear to support it.

The Ministry was formed, and consisted of men of energy, of whom Constans, who filled the most important post, the Ministry of the Interior, was the chief. He enjoyed the reputation of being a man of power who had largely contributed to the Republican success of 1881. He had more than one trick in his bag, as he was not slow to prove.

The vigorous attitude of the Government now became clear. The League of Patriots was dissolved and the Senate was constituted a High Court. Constans knew the weakness of his opponent and acted accordingly. The General's mistress was a certain Madame de Bonnemain, a divorced woman to whom he was passionately devoted. The police proceeded to frighten her, leading her to think that she was going to be arrested, and thus making her decide to go to Brussels. Boulanger, upset by her departure, and fearing that he too would be arrested, was not long in joining her. Love played a greater part in his breast than politics. As one of his followers contemptuously but justly remarked, " Cæsar was only a garrison Romeo ! "

As soon as he deserted the party in this way, it was lost to him. Never was wreckage so complete or collapse so sudden. Only the day before Boulanger had seemed a formidable adversary; twenty-four hours later, when he took to flight, he was nothing. He was merely a corpse; *jam fœtet*. Arthur Meyer, who was very acute, pronounced the famous words, " Good evening, gentlemen ! " by way of farewell to his old comrades in arms.

Boulangism let fly a few more sparks, like a piece of fireworks that is not quite extinguished; but he was done for. In the absence of the leader, the centrifugal forces made themselves felt and the whole of the strange, paradoxical coalition fell to pieces in the twinkling of an eye. The chief actors in it were tried by the High Court—Boulanger, Rochefort and Dillon— and condemned to deportation for life. Two years later, the General, half ruined, committed suicide in a Brussels cemetery over the grave of the woman he loved.

Nevertheless the Boulanger episode revealed the Achilles heel of the system, which in spite of its apparent solidity was extremely vulnerable. It was capable of being overthrown by a sudden attack, provided it was quickly and unhesitatingly carried out. But if the Republicans were given time to pull themselves together, and to organise a defence, they did so.

The notorious failure of this attempt was not calculated to encourage further efforts at a *coup d'état* for many a long day. The episode was hardly closed before many of those who had thrown themselves so light-heartedly into it, without examining either its aims or its methods, found themselves involved in considerable confusion.

BOULANGISM

The International Exhibition of 1889, which was held in celebration of the centenary of the French Revolution, drowned the last echoes of the Boulanger uproar in its triumphant success. Crowds from the provinces and from abroad thronged to it. The Eiffel Tower, the machinery section, the Palace of the Colonies and the Palace of Foreign Nations were the chief attractions offered by this international fair.

The Exhibition of 1889.

For the first time electricity, the magic new light, with its thousand and one jets of flame, was used for illumination on a large scale. Its advent and widespread use were destined to make a considerable difference in the life of mankind.

The elections of 1889, for which the multiple-vote system was used, constituted a victory for the Republicans, who captured 366 seats in the Chamber, whilst the Conservatives won 172 and the advocates of reform 38.

The Elections.

As soon as the system was thus consolidated, fresh adherents, as is always the case, did not fail to make their appearance. A certain number of Catholics were only too anxious to support it, and were encouraged to do so by the highest authority, that of Pope Leo XIII. Endowed with an exceedingly keen political sense, and realising that the Republican system, owing to the obvious impotence of all its rivals, was the only one capable of securing peace and order in France, he issued an encyclical in which he declared : " When a new Government is established, it is the duty of all to accept it."

A certain section of French Catholics accepted it in fact if not in theory. The extremists and irreconcilables, however, refused to bow their heads before the Freemason Republic, which had been guilty of passing the iniquitous secularisation laws.

BIBLIOGRAPHY.—Mermeix, *Les Coulisses du Boulangisme* (1890). J. Reinach, *La Politique Opportuniste* (1890). *Le Cheval Noir* (1890). Arthur Meyer, *Ce que mes Yeux ont vu* (1911). *Ce que je peux dire* (1912). Henri Rochefort, *Les Aventures de ma Vie* (5 vols., 1896). Maurice Barrès, *Scènes et Doctrines du Nationalisme*. Léon Marot, *Le Parti de la Guerre et la Ligue des Patriotes* (1887).

CHAPTER XII

THE PANAMA SCANDAL

IN every age finance and politics have gone hand in hand. The connection between them, call it collusion if you will, is not a recent phenomenon. Very far from it. And the nature of the established system makes no difference to the fact.

Under the monarchy the tax-farmers, to give but one example, obtained their concessions through the not altogether disinterested support of the great landlords, and the **Politics and Finance.** courtiers surrounding the King and his Ministers. When Louis XIV, on the advice of Colbert, instituted a *chambre ardente* to force the tax-farmers to disgorge, the shrewdest among them were careful to secure the help of all powerful personages in return for ready money. Thus they managed to escape prosecution at the cost of paying a heavy ransom to their rescuers.

In a Republic the King and his courtiers are replaced by Ministers and Members of Parliament. Between the latter and the financiers there are many points of contact, which increase with the growth of financial interests and when business affairs assume unexpected proportions. Many of the latter are closely connected with politics, since the authority of the State has to be exercised in one way or another, either at their inception or at some stage in their development. And if members of Parliament, who are masters for a day, and the holders of an altogether ephemeral power, are to be above temptation, they would have to be elected from the ranks of the saints. It must also be remembered that under the *ancien régime,* and even as late as 1870, the men who exercised power, or were in the immediate neighbourhood of those who did, were all more or less rich. If they were not rich before, they became so as soon as they took up their posts, which nearly always brought them substantial material benefits.

188

THE PANAMA SCANDAL

Under the Republic things were very different. Men from the middle classes, frequently of slender means, members of the liberal professions, small shopkeepers, and small landowners, came more and more to form the material from which Parliament was recruited. A candidate is elected. He comes to Paris, where his salary only enables him to live on a very modest scale. He becomes a Minister for a period which he knows is bound to be fairly short. His salary is raised, but his expenses are increased in proportion. He has his carriage or his car. Then comes a ministerial crisis (there are plenty of them in all conscience !), and lo and behold, he is on foot again.

But as an influential deputy, a member of important commissions, a possible or an actual Minister, he has to deal with matters which run into considerable sums, millions, sometimes hundreds of millions. And if he is the least bit weak or inclined to yield to temptation, it must be admitted that the inducements held out to him are frequently overpowering.

The Panama scandal affords a typical example of collusion of this kind between politics and finance. It owed its notoriety to the personality of some of those who were connected with it, to the sums involved, which were huge for that period, to the large number of persons convicted or suspected, and to the rivalry of the parties who used it in order to bring discredit or ruin upon their adversaries.

Ferdinand de Lesseps, the genius who had been responsible for the construction of the Suez Canal, had undertaken the opening of the Isthmus of Panama. The preliminary survey had been made as early as 1876. When the work of exploration had been completed it was decided to take a line running from Limon Bay on the Atlantic to the roadstead of Panama. The canal was to be seventy-four kilometres in length, without any tunnels or locks. A scheme of this sort presented the greatest difficulties. In a deadly climate, where those engaged in the work, and especially the Europeans, died like flies, the cost of clearing the ground alone reached a colossal figure. In order to avoid tunnels and locks it was necessary, in a country where earthquakes are frequent, to make a cutting 270 feet deep.

Nevertheless the name and reputation of Lesseps attracted subscribers and a Company was formed. The scheme was put into execution, and led from beginning to end to a gigantic " leakage " of capital between Paris and Panama, and to swindling on a colossal scale.

" Business means other people's money." Never was the truth of this adage proved on a vaster scale. The financial requirements of the Company, the capital to be raised, the cost of publicity, and the execution of the work ran into millions.

In this way resources were quickly exhausted, and the Company, in low water, was obliged to have recourse to a fresh loan. It decided to issue preference shares, for which the permission of the Chamber was necessary. It is here that politics intervened, and that Members of Parliament and the Directors of the Company came into contact. The fresh capital thus raised only served to fill a few gaps, the financial position of the Company went from bad to worse, and it was soon unable to face its obligations. Legal liquidators were appointed. In vain did Lesseps endeavour to form a new Company. All his efforts failed. Some of the shareholders and bondholders, suspecting, not without reason, that their money had been squandered, demanded that action should be taken against the Directors. A judicial inquiry was opened in June 1891.

The Government now found itself in a very awkward position. Could they allow Ferdinand de Lesseps, an old man covered with glory, Member of l'Académie Française, and Grand Cross of the Legion of Honour, to be dragged before the tribunal?

The information at their disposal proved that when the Company was formed and the Bill passed authorising the issue of preference shares, large sums of money had been distributed in the parliamentary world. Were they to open up all these sores and reveal the scandal to the eyes of France and the whole world?

The first effort on the part of the Government was to hush up the scandal, or at all events limit its scope. But the political world and political parties had already got wind of it, and names had begun to be whispered here and there. In 1892, in an order for the day, the Chamber called upon the Government to take energetic and prompt action.

THE PANAMA SCANDAL

The Attorney-General, Quesnay de Beaurepaire, having received all the papers, spent the summer of 1892 in studying them. He decided that proceedings would have to be taken against Ferdinand and Charles de Lesseps, Cotu and Marius Fontane, the Directors of the Panama Company. The *Libre Parole*, an anti-Semitic paper published by Drumont, did its best to turn the Panama scandal, which was a legal affair, into a matter of politics. It accused certain senators and deputies of having sold their votes when the Bill authorising the issue of preference shares had been passed.

Two events now took place, two incidents of the greatest moment, resembling the action in a sensational serial, on which the whole affair turned.

One of the financiers who was suspected of having acted as intermediary between the Panama Directors, who were forced to distribute the money subscribed by the shareholders, and the parliamentarians, Ministers, deputies and influential journalists, who sold their influence for ready money, was the Baron de Reinach. His father, a man of German extraction, had been ennobled by Victor Emmanuel in 1866. He himself, who had become a naturalised Frenchman, was the uncle and father-in-law of Joseph Reinach, a deputy and a Director of the *République Française*. The enemies of the latter, the Boulangist faction, whom he had violently attacked, did not hesitate to return blow for blow in their endeavour to reach the nephew through the uncle.

Suddenly the Baron, after having been cross-examined several times by the prosecuting counsel, died suddenly in such mysterious circumstances that everybody said he had poisoned himself.

Another financier, Cornelius Hertz, also of German extraction, but an American citizen and a Doctor of Medicine of the University of Chicago, who by the exercise of some mysterious influence had been made an officer of the Legion of Honour, and who it was said would have levied blackmail on the Baron de Reinach himself, hastened, as soon as the first rumours were afloat, to place the frontier between himself and his accusers. He sought refuge in England, where, by means of clever tactics, sometimes defending himself and sometimes attacking his enemies, he

191

from time to time carefully and systematically circulated confidential information.

From that moment the Panama case developed along two lines—the judicial and the political, events in the one sphere necessarily having their repercussion in the other, all manner of open or underhand connections being established between the two. The incriminated Directors were ready to plead in defence of their action that if they had rained part of the millions entrusted to them as it were like manna upon the political and journalistic world, they had not done so with irresponsible light-heartedness, but had been constrained by force of circumstances. In order to obtain from the parliamentary commission and then from the Chamber the vote supplying them with the requisite funds, they were obliged to pay the price. They merely paid a sort of toll, such as caravans in Arabia and in the Sahara allow the Touaregs and Bedouins to extort from them. In any case, which was the more guilty party, the one who bought or the one who allowed himself to be bought?

This little problem of legal casuistry was never, for very good reasons, completely solved.

A young deputy, Delahaye, took the matter before the tribunal of Parliament the day after Baron de Reinach's death, and charged over a hundred deputies of having taken bribes from Reinach and Cornelius Hertz to vote for the measure. A certain ex-Minister, he maintained, had alone received £16,000, which at that time was a large sum of money even for a Minister. One member of the Commission appointed to examine the scheme had had £8,000 assigned to him. Everybody agreed that this was too much for a mere deputy. It is true that chance, the fact that the Commission was divided into two equal parties of five for and five against, put the casting vote in his hands. Now a man in this position can always sell himself dearly. He was Monsieur Sans-Leroy, sometime deputy for Ariège.

These accusations raised a terrible tumult in the Chamber. Challenged to produce the names, the accuser refused, contenting himself with indicating his colleagues in a manner sufficiently clear for nobody to be in any doubt as to who they were. A

192

Commission of Inquiry was appointed. But the Government refused to grant it judicial powers, which reduced it to complete impotence.

The Directors allowed a number of semi-confidential rumours to be circulated, just enough to defend themselves and yet not too many, for fear of compromising too many people and increasing the scandal in which they found themselves involved. Public curiosity was stimulated to the utmost. The names of the " cheque-takers " as they were called were freely bandied about. In addition to these, it was said, there were others, many others. But how were they to be discovered?

Those who were exploiting the affair for political ends, the enemies of the Republic, Boulangists, Reformers and Royalists, would like to have secured complete lists. But where were they to be found? What proofs had they of their allegations? Without proofs their accusations rested on thin air. The Banque Thierée, in which Baron de Reinach had some funds, admitted that it had in its possession cheques received by a certain number of parliamentarians. It handed them over to the judicial authorities. Among others they bore the names of Albert Grévy, Léon Renaud, certain senators, etc., etc.

Faced with these revelations, which became ever more definite, the Chamber, on the demand of the Government, authorised proceedings to be taken against certain of its members—Emmanuel Arène, Jules Roche and Rouvier.

The Senate gave its permission for similar proceedings to be taken against Albert Grévy and Léon Renaud.

On the 10th of January the action brought against the Directors of the Company was taken to the Court of Appeal in Paris. The Solicitor-General in his speech for the prosecution accused the Directors of having " squandered " £56,000,000 of the public savings on an enterprise designated as " the most colossal swindle in the world." The five defendants received a fairly light sentence, a term of imprisonment and the payment of a fine.

As for the parliamentarians, some of them, such as Jules Roche, Thévenet and Emmanuel Arène, had been acquitted by the investigating judge (*juge d'instruction*). The others were summoned before the assize court, pell-mell, bribers and receivers

o

of bribes all mixed up together. Charles de Lesseps pleaded in his defence that the money he had distributed had literally been extorted from him by threats or, to put it more crudely, by blackmail.

All the parliamentarians were acquitted except one, Baïhaut, who had been a Minister at the time when the measure had been passed, and who was guilty among other things of not having been sufficiently careful to remember the famous dictum, *Never admit anything*.

A little while afterwards the Court of Appeal reversed the verdict and declared that all the defendants without exception were covered by the statute of limitations.

Thus ended the judicial side of the case. Its political con-sequences, and its effect upon the public, have been summed up in a book which, prejudiced though it is, since it is first and foremost a pamphlet against the parliamentary system, is a work of genius, *Leurs Figures*, by Maurice Barrès.

The author, who was elected at the early age of twenty-seven as Boulangist deputy for Nancy, was a new-comer in the parliamentary world, and he gives a striking picture of what took place as the scandal was gradually unfolded, the horror of those " cheque-takers " whose names were known, the breathless anxiety and fear of those who had not yet been denounced but were living in constant fear of exposure, the ruin and despair of some, the resistance of others, each acting in accordance with his temperament. The great session when Delahaye launched his accusation, when Déroulède crossed swords with Clemenceau, and Rouvier, suspected and well-nigh convicted, with his huge frame, his broad shoulders and his mighty fists, fought tooth and nail and held his own against the pack of his accusers, all this world of large and small fry is depicted with unforgettable touches reminiscent of the most vivid pages of Saint Simon. Barrès shows us Ribot, at that time President of the Council, carrying " his handsome pianist's head " high in the air; the cold and distant Waldeck-Rousseau, counsel for Ferdinand de Lesseps, " hard set in silence like a pike in aspic."

When the excitement created by the scandal was at its height, one of the deputies exclaimed, " What a pity that Boulanger was so foolish as to commit suicide in his Brussels cemetery ! "

And indeed Boulangism would have derived enormous benefit from the moral attacks that Parliament had just been forced to undergo. The mud slung at some of its members naturally splashed all the others as well. The whole system was discredited.

But this discredit, the moral consequences of which were destined to last, did not and could not have any very great practical repercussion. For want of something better to put in its place, the country was obliged to keep the established system, and to keep it functioning as it was, with all its habits, its parliamentary customs, the splitting up and rivalry of parties, which do not allow it to function in any other way.

The opportunists seemed to be the hardest hit. But the most energetic and vigorous of the Radicals, Clemenceau, was also involved, and for many years was destined to be exiled from the political world.

Some of the most prominent leaders being removed in this way, new men took their places, and Parliament was given a different set of leaders.

BIBLIOGRAPHY.—Quesnay de Beaurepaire, *Le Panama et la République* (1899). E. Bontoux, *L'Union Générale* (1888). Michel Chevalier, *L'Isthme de Panama* (1844). F. N. Mellet, *Etudes sur les Isthmes de Suez et de Panama* (1859). H. Dionne, *Le Percement de l'Isthme de Panama* (1875). A. Reclus, *Le Canal Inter-Océanique et les Explorations de l'Isthme Américain* (1879). L. Paton, *Le Canal de Panama et les Capitaux Français* (1886). G. de Belot, *La Vérité sur le Panama* (1889). Ponsolle, *Le Tombeau des Milliards Panama* (1890). F. Drumont, *La Dernière Bataille* (1890). *Statue de Neige et Visages de Bronze*. *La France Juive* (2 vols.). Armand Rousseau, *Rapport Presenté au Ministre des Travaux Publics sur sa Mission au Panama* (1893). P. Bressolles, *Liquidation de la Compagnie de Panama* (1894). Maurice Barrès, *Leurs Figures*. *L'Appel au Soldat*.

CHAPTER XIII

THE DREYFUS CASE

Its general outlines. The *bordereau* attributed to Dreyfus. The opinion of the experts and the arrest. The " secret *dossier* " and his condemnation. The traitor Henri. The trial at Rennes.

HOW was it that a mere judicial matter succeeded in absorbing, dividing and upsetting a whole country, and exciting, even beyond its frontiers, an extraordinary outburst of interest ? Such were the passions let loose that even to-day, when over a quarter of a century has elapsed, anybody who has made a careful study of the facts is apt, **Its General** if he is anxious, as he undoubtedly should be, to **Outlines.** reveal what he regards as the truth, to shock perfectly sincere beliefs and to hurt extremely worthy susceptibilities.

The reasons for this fact, which at first sight seems inexplicable, are numerous and varied. The whole matter is exceedingly obscure, combining as it does the dramatic and the pathetic, a thousand and one turns of fortune and theatrical effects. It also had its philosophic side, involving a conflict of doctrines and ideas, class prejudice and a curious element of patriotism which seemed opposed to the cause of justice and to the untrammelled pursuit of truth.

From the judicial it soon passed on to the political plane, and served as a platform and battle-ground for the various parties. All classes of society were, one after the other, caught up in this gigantic wheel—the Army, the industrial classes, and politicians alike. Even the mass of the public did not escape. Although it found it very difficult to understand and follow all the developments of this extremely involved story, it necessarily felt the repercussions of the conflict.

196

THE DREYFUS CASE

The essential facts are simple enough, but all kinds of accessory factors soon added complications.

By one of the most usual methods, by so-called " ordinary means," the Army Secret Service had obtained possession of **The Bordereau** letters and notes that the German military attaché **attributed to** had imprudently thrown into his waste-paper **Dreyfus.** basket. Among these documents there was a letter of advice accompanied by various pieces of information concerning the military organisation of France. This was the famous *bordereau*.

Who was it from ? Who was the traitor ? Inquiries were set on foot. The contents of the *bordereau* pointed to the author being an artillery officer attached to the staff of the Army. A search was made, but at first nothing was found, when suddenly, on a comparison of the writing of various persons being made, as soon as that of Captain Alfred Dreyfus came to be examined, the resemblance was found to be astonishing. So close was it, that when Dreyfus was first shown the *bordereau* he exclaimed : " Somebody has stolen my writing ! "

Dreyfus was a Jew, and at this juncture, and in such surroundings, the very fact that he was a Jew made matters worse for him.

Bertillon, one of the two experts consulted, who knew more about anthropometry than graphology, confirmed the allegation **The Opinion** in his report, with the qualifying clause that an **of the Experts** extremely clever forger might have copied the **and the Arrest.** handwriting of Dreyfus. It was decided to arrest the suspect. On the morning of the 15th of October, Dreyfus was summoned to Colonel Picquart's office and then taken to General de Boisdeffre. A note in which reference was made to the *bordereau* was dictated to him. Boisdeffre thought Dreyfus seemed agitated, and on this slender evidence he was charged and shut up in the prison of Cherche-Midi.

The charge made against him was exceedingly grave : the striking similarity of the writing, and the confirmatory evidence with certain reservations of an expert who might, however, be mistaken. On the other hand, all the moral presumptions were in his favour. He was rich both on his own account and by marriage. He was a member of an Alsatian family who were excellent French patriots; he led the most regular life, and, so far as it was possible to tell, was in need of nothing. Why, in these circumstances, should he have committed this terrible crime? He emphatically protested that he was innocent and continued throughout to do so.

Of all the members of the Government, Monsieur Hanotaux, the Minister for Foreign Affairs, fearing above all some diplomatic incident, was the only one who showed great foresight and good sense in opposing not only the trial of an officer on such slender evidence, but even the inquiry that would result from it. General Mercier, the Minister for War, rode rough-shod over his opposition.

The arrest of Dreyfus was kept secret. But is it possible to keep anything secret in Paris? On the 28th of October the news was published in the *Libre Parole*, Drumont's anti-Semite paper.

On the 9th of December Dreyfus was brought before the War Council. On the refusal of Waldeck-Rousseau, Maître Demange undertook his defence.

The "Secret Dossier" and the Condemnation. In order to amplify the charge, of which indeed the experts' report constituted the only piece of evidence, General Mercier, unknown to the defence, sent the judges certain documents which had only a superficial and apparent bearing on the case. This was the famous "secret *dossier*." The Minister afterwards explained that he had acted in this way because the trial in camera did not seem to him a sufficient guarantee of secrecy and that any indiscretion might give rise to grave diplomatic complications.

The defendant was unanimously condemned to deportation for life and detention in a fortress, and to be degraded from his military rank. On the 5th of January, in the court of the *École Militaire*, the sentence of degradation was carried out. As he was marched in front of the troops, Dreyfus exclaimed, "I am innocent." One of the few spectators, Pierre Giffard, the journalist, often described to us afterwards how deeply he had been moved by these protestations and cries.

The prisoner was sent to the Devil's Island, and obscurity and silence seemed irrevocably to have encompassed him.

. . . .

THE DREYFUS CASE

Stendhal, in his book on Love, mentions the phenomenon of *crystallisation* which takes place in the lover with regard to everything connected with the loved one. A thousand and one accessory feelings are, by the force of attraction, added to the chief emotion and impart to it a far greater force and richness.

Among those who judged and condemned Dreyfus, and who believed in his guilt, a similar phenomenon occurred. A number of extraneous elements became attached to the main proof. And thus the catalogue of charges brought against him seemed to grow. But it was in appearance only, for it would not have stood a moment's careful examination. In this mass of alleged charges (intercepted telegrams and so-called confessions of the prisoner when he was degraded from his rank, etc.) none could have borne minute scrutiny, none amounted to irrefutable proof.

This was one of the essential characteristics of the case, and the following is another equally important. The very fact that the judges on the War Council were given a *dossier* of which the prisoner and his counsel knew nothing, and which they could not discuss, constituted a flagrant breach of law which of itself was sufficient to vitiate and quash the prosecution. This point admits of no discussion. Those who decided to send the *dossier* may perhaps not have realised that they were thereby violating one of the fundamental rules of law and justice, *but the violation nevertheless existed.*

Dreyfus was in prison. His parents and family were still convinced of his innocence, which was only as it should be and redounds to their credit. They decided to leave no stone unturned and to spend all they possessed in proving it. They sought everywhere for evidence and proof; but where were they to be found? Everything was clouded in obscurity, and all they could do was to grope their way in the dark.

But it chanced that Colonel Picquart, the prisoner's commanding officer, who was an Alsatian, became in the course of a brilliant career the head of the Army Intelligence Department, and it was to him that the contents of the waste-paper basket from the German Embassy were handed over. A letter (the little blue letter) addressed to Esterhazy, and many other indications, formally convinced him that the author of the *bordereau* was Esterhazy and not Dreyfus, who was innocent.

Just as all the moral presumptions were on the side of the latter, who was a rich man well established in life, they were all against Esterhazy, the penniless younger son of a large Hungarian family, who was a needy adventurer, riddled with debt, hounded down by his creditors and leading an irregular, not to say dissolute, life. Picquart communicated his suspicions and misgivings to his chiefs. The latter were above all anxious not to allow this aggravating question to be opened up again on any pretext whatsoever, as it would be sure to create a newspaper war and give rise to the most virulent controversy. They told Picquart to hold his tongue, and in order to make sure of his silence sent him to the remotest regions of Tunisia. But before taking his departure Picquart confided his secret to his intimate friend, the lawyer Leblois, who passed it on to Senator Scheurer-Kestner, a politician who was resolved not to keep the matter to himself.

And thus the two threads, which had been separated until that moment, were in process of becoming joined. Picquart's discovery and the confidential information he had given lent to the investigations of the Dreyfus family, which hitherto had proved vain, the precision and strength which they lacked.

From that moment the case began to cause commotion among a small circle of well-informed people.

The first who with all the passion and ardour of youth betrayed their interest in it were the students of the Latin Quarter. The present writer has an extraordinarily vivid recollection of how, just at this time, one of his companions at the École Normale spent hours in expounding the chain of evidence which in his opinion established the innocence of Dreyfus. Although his arguments did not convince us they contained certain very disquieting points. Scheurer-Kestner called upon the Senate to insist upon the necessity of reopening the case, and the brother of the condemned man denounced Esterhazy as the author of the *bordereau*. From that moment all the machinery for resuscitating the whole inquiry was set in motion and nothing could stop it.

Event followed event in an automatic chain of cause and effect—the trial of Esterhazy, who was acquitted by the Council of War, Zola's letter " *J'Accuse* " in *l'Aurore*, and his famous trial before the Assize Court, ending in his being sentenced to a year's imprisonment.

From the circle of the initiated the matter had passed into the hands of the public at large, and the excitement aroused grew more and more violent every day. The reverberations grew ever louder and were necessarily re-echoed before the tribunal of Parliament. In vain did Ministers and leaders, fearing to face the responsibility, try to silence them. The more they did so the louder they grew. It would have been quite enough for one of these leaders to shut himself up for a few mornings in his study and have all the items in the *dossier* without exception laid before him to become convinced of the necessity for reopening the case.

It must be admitted in their defence that as the case developed it became more and more involved, complicated as it was by political squabbles and party passion. Both sides used it to attack and malign their adversaries. The Conservatives and the Nationalists, for whom respect for the Army and its leaders was a dogma, were firmly convinced that nobody connected with them could possibly have made such a blunder, and they denounced the activities of the " Jewish syndicate." They accused it of supporting the agitation to the tune of millions, and of sapping the basic institutions of the country by this means. Intellectuals, scientists and professors, who had hitherto lived amid the austere silence of their researches and studies, came down from their ivory tower and joined vigorously in the fray. This was one of the most curious and distinctive features of the affair. But for the Dreyfus case, certain well-known French politicians (Monsieur Painlevé, for instance, to give but one example) would never have thought of entering the sphere of politics.

The battle was now in full swing. Most of those engaged in it were animated by equal good faith and sincerity. The " revisionists," ardently convinced of the innocence of Dreyfus, demanded that the Court of Appeal should take the " fresh facts " into consideration and proceed to an immediate re-opening of the case. They expressed their indignation at the thought that there should be any excuse for keeping a condemned man in prison when he was innocent. Justice, the foundation stone of every nation, demanded that the case should be reopened. Every other consideration, however weighty, reasons of State, respect for the Army, etc., were insignificant in comparison. Although their ranks were continually swelled, they were as yet only an extremely small minority. The vast majority of the country, almost the whole of the political and military world, maintained, on the contrary, that judgment once given should be respected.

After a Council of War, duly appointed, after all the great military leaders without exception had declared that Dreyfus was guilty, how could anyone dare to cast doubt on their verdict? Even if one or two irregularities, which after all were insignificant, had been committed, it was the spirit of patriotism that had dictated them, with the object, in a matter of extreme delicacy, of avoiding incidents and complications of which it was impossible to foretell the gravity.

On the one side the demand for justice outweighed all else; on the other, reasons of State, love of the Army and patriotic considerations. Both sides were animated by convictions equally ardent and admirable. It would be necessary to go a long way back in French history to find an example of a similar conflict or so great a cleavage. The great trials of the eighteenth century, the trial of Calas, for instance, over which Voltaire waxed so eloquent, were insignificant by comparison.

In vain were passions let loose; it was impossible for the partisans of Dreyfus, in the course of their investigations, not to reveal the slender nature of the charges made against him. Suddenly a dramatic incident provided them with the proof for which they were seeking, the "fresh fact" upon which they could base their demand for a fresh trial.

Cavaignac, the Minister of War, when questioned about the case, maintained that he could prove the guilt of the accused **The Traitor Henri.** by producing a note from a foreign military attaché which would definitely establish his dealings with Dreyfus. A little while afterwards, his colleagues, after a careful examination of the note, had no difficulty in proving that the whole thing had been forged by

202

Colonel Henri. The latter confessed his guilt, and when he was shut up in the Mont Valérien prison he cut his throat with a razor.

This dramatic act of violence set the whole country agog. For many it was like a streak of lightning which suddenly lit up the darkness. When once it had been established that an officer of the Army had felt it incumbent upon him to forge an entire document against Dreyfus, it made the other documents cited against him appear exceedingly flimsy if not entirely fictitious. Prudence, reason and common-sense all pointed in this direction. Colonel Henri's confession provided the fresh fact which made the reopening of the case imperative. The Criminal Chamber of the Court of Appeal declared that the demand for a fresh hearing was in order. The Government, whom the Dreyfus case was, so to speak, slowly poisoning, anxious to manœuvre between the two parties, decided, in order to give satisfaction to both sides, that the verdict in the fresh trial should be pronounced not by the Criminal Chamber alone, as had always been the case hitherto, but by all the Chambers of the Appeal Court together. This measure, abrogating the rights of the Criminal Chamber, which was nothing if not opportunist, was passed. And Dreyfusards and anti-Dreyfusards fought over it as they had fought over everything else.

The Court sent up the accused to be tried again before a fresh Council of War. Brought back from the Devil's Island on the 3rd of June, 1899, Dreyfus appeared before his peers at Rennes. The battle now reached its height. An attempt was made upon the life of Labori, the counsel for the defence. Partisans and adversaries of Dreyfus quarrelled and exchanged insults and blows at the very doors of the Court. A verdict of guilty was again returned by a majority of five to two, but this time with attenuating circumstances, and the defendant was condemned to ten years' detention.

The Rennes Trial.

It was not a verdict, it was merely a compromise, explained by the circumstances and the time when it was given. For either Dreyfus was guilty of having written the *bordereau* and of having divulged the military secrets of his country to a foreign Power, or he was not. If he was guilty, no attenuating circumstance could possibly be advanced in his favour.

The Government of Waldeck-Rousseau decided, with very good reason, to have done with this agitation, and to pardon the condemned man. A few years later the Court of Appeal, by the joint action of all its Chambers, after a further examination of the whole case, rescinded the verdict of Rennes and once and for all reversed the judgment. And thus the case was legally ended.

But its consequences were destined to be profound and far-reaching. From the day on which it entered into the domain of politics until its termination and long afterwards, it may be said to have dominated the home politics of the country. It had brought about the resignation, one after another, of several Ministers of War; it had broken up more than one Cabinet.

After the sudden death of Félix Faure, who was found dead in his office on the 16th of February, 1899, Loubet was elected, owing to the support of the Left, instead of Méline, who was the Moderate candidate. The Nationalists, furious at this election, inaugurated a vigorous campaign. At the funeral of Félix Faure, Déroulède and some of his friends tried to win over General Roger's brigade. This badly organised *coup de force* failed, and Déroulède, who demanded to be brought before the High Court, was sent back to the Assize Court on a charge of having incited the troops to disobedience. He was acquitted.

Whilst Nationalists and Royalists tried to turn the case to account in order to overthrow the parliamentary Republic, the Socialists on their side were quick to use it as an excuse for entering upon an anti-militarist campaign. Both sides were equally guilty of excess, and the violence of their disputes was in danger of extending to the streets.

Fortunately a level-headed man came into power at this juncture—Waldeck-Rousseau, an old colleague of Gambetta and of Jules Ferry. He had all the qualities necessary for a Government leader—a feeling for law and order and for discipline. For the first time he gave a post in the Ministry to a Socialist, Millerand, and thus satisfied the advanced parties. But at the same time he also took on deck General Gallifet, who had the reputation of being a strong man, hated by the revolutionaries and Socialists for the part he had played during the Commune. Gallifet undertook and succeeded in the task of restoring peace and order in the Army.

The Waldeck-Rousseau Ministry, rallying in this way the parties of the Left which the agitations of the Nationalists had upset, opened the way for the Combes Ministry which was to succeed him, and French politics turned ever more and more in the direction of advanced ideas and parties.

This was another direct result of the Dreyfus case.

A further result was that Clemenceau, who had played no part in public life since the Panama scandal, and who had supported the cause of Dreyfus in his paper with all his polemical ability and ardour of temperament, found in it an excellent jumping-off board for his return to political life. A few years later he became President of the Council, and during the last part of the Great War he was one of the saviours of the country.

BIBLIOGRAPHY.—H. Dutrait-Crozon, *Précis de l'Affaire Dreyfus* (1909). J. Reinach, *Histoire de l'Affaire Dreyfus* (4 vols., 1901). Th. Reinach, *Précis de l'Affaire Dreyfus* (1924). Jean Jaurès, *Les Preuves, Affaire Dreyfus.* Alfred Dreyfus, *Cinq Années de ma Vie,* 1894–9 (1901). Maurice Barrès, *Ce que j'ai vu à Rennes* (1904). Esterhazy, *Les Dessous de l'Affaire Dreyfus* (1898). Bernard Lazare, *Une Erreur Judiciaire : la Vérité sur l'Affaire Dreyfus* (1896). *L'Affaire Dreyfus (Deuxième Mémoire)* (1897). Édouard Drumont, *La France Juive devant l'Opinion* (1886). Urbain Gohier, *Histoire d'une Trahison* (1905); *Leur République* (1906); *Le Procès Dreyfus devant le Conseil de Guerre de Rennes* (1899); *La Revision du Procès de Rennes : Débats de la cour de Cassation : Chambres Réunies* (2 vols., 1906); *La Revision du Procès de Rennes. Enquête de la Chambre Criminelle* (3 vols., 1908). F. de Pressensé, *Un Héros : le Colonel Picquart* (1897).

CHAPTER XIV

RELIGIOUS POLICY

The law regarding religious bodies. The elections of 1902.
Combes. The religious struggle. Conflict with the Holy See.
Consequences of the rupture. Home policy. The separation of
Church and State.

IN the Republican party, and especially among the Radicals,
who formed its most important section, there was an
anti-clerical strain that was only waiting to be aroused.
Many of Gambetta's successors, especially after a crisis
The Law   like that caused by the Dreyfus case, and even
regarding   more after the elections when they complained
Religious   of having been violently opposed by the clergy,
Bodies.   were ready to take up his famous battle-cry :
" Clericalism, that is the enemy ! "

Waldeck-Rousseau had a feeling that during the last period of
the Dreyfus case certain rich and powerful religious bodies,
Assumptionists and Jesuits, were behind the Nationalist
agitation, and by way of retaliation he wanted to strike a blow
at them and, as the saying is, have a hit at intriguing and
meddlesome, monks. First and foremost a jurist, it was his aim
by means of a general law against religious bodies to settle
their status definitely once and for all.

Nothing is more difficult than to handle such an undertaking
successfully, without allowing one's hand to be forced by
exaggerated party demands. It was a question of finding a just
and equitable balance between the powers of the State, the
rights of the religious bodies and those of the Vatican, which
would necessarily feel they were attacked by any measure
passed against them. When once the measure had been drafted,
Waldeck-Rousseau, had he been the sole master with power to
have it passed as it stood by Parliament and immediately put
206

into action, might perhaps have been able to arrive at a compromise which would not have upset either of the parties too much. But he was obliged to reckon with Parliament, who introduced important modifications into some of his provisions, and emphasised their aggressive attitude towards the religious bodies, thus provoking a crisis which shortly afterwards led to a conflict and breach with the Vatican.

During the debate on the Bill, Waldeck-Rousseau, who was a convinced believer in the Concordat, that is to say, the agreement made with the Pope, found himself continually overruled, first by the Commission appointed to examine the measure, and afterwards by the Chamber.

According to the Bill, the religious bodies could in future only be licensed by Act of Parliament, and not as hitherto by a mere Ministerial decree. All those that had not already been licensed were to apply for a permit within three months, in default of which they would be regarded as illicit. An article added by the Commission forbade any member of an unlicensed religious body to engage in the profession of teaching.

The Pope had already protested first at an interview and afterwards in a speech delivered to the Cardinals.

Eventually the law was passed on the 1st of July, 1901. Everything now depended on the way in which it was administered.

Meanwhile the general elections of 1902 had been held, when the clergy again took an active share in the struggle. The parties of the Left won about forty new seats, **The Elections of 1902.** although, if the actual number of voters is taken into account, the margin of difference between the votes cast for either side was extremely narrow.

This was not the first time that a minute difference in the number of votes led to a marked alteration in the number of deputies, which occasionally brought about a change in the existing majority in Parliament.

Elated by their victory, the one aim of the anti-clericals in the Chamber was to level a blow at their adversaries. And now, to cap all, chance provided them with a leader who was even more ardent than his followers. Immediately after the elections, Waldeck-Rousseau, who was tired out, sent in his resignation, and advised the President of the Republic to summon Combes to take his place.

Combes, a little old man of seventy, pugnacious and devilishly vindictive, was animated by a violent and ferocious hatred for **Combes.** the Catholic party, and this feeling dominated and stifled all others in his breast. His was the passion of the renegade. Once a seminary priest and actually a teacher in his institution, as well as the author of a thesis on St. Thomas Aquinas, Combes had sucked the milk of the nurse into whose breast he now set his teeth. Was it not Barbey d'Aurevilly who said that only he who had once been a priest could truly hate the religion he had left?

For Combes the hour had come. Among the advanced parties there were many who, as the saying goes, asked for nothing better than to dine off the parson. And Combes was the man to give them such a plateful that they would all have indigestion. Administered by him, the law, certain clauses of which, contrary to the desire of the man who had drawn it up, were already too severe, could not fail to become even more stringent. Combes made a beginning by closing the schools and institutions of non-licensed religious bodies. These measures gave rise to trouble in Brittany. The Nuncio and then the Vatican protested.

When it came to legislating on the applications for licences made by a large number of religious bodies, he decided, contrary to Waldeck-Rousseau's idea, to examine *en bloc* the applications he expected to refuse. Instead of giving careful consideration to each case, they were condemned wholesale, like cartloads of prisoners sent to the guillotine.

But this was very far from being the golden mean, the equitable balance that Waldeck-Rousseau had hoped to establish. But in opening the controversy and starting the hare which was bound to escape him, Waldeck-Rousseau had failed to show any greater political discernment than he had displayed when he had suggested Combes as his successor.

The battle was now raging, and passions waxed strong. In vain did Waldeck-Rousseau, in a speech delivered at Tréguier at the unveiling of a monument to Renan on the 13th September, 1902, and afterwards when he took part in a debate in the Senate, try to put a stop to this brutal and clumsy policy of which he realised all the drawbacks. The engine had been set in motion and nothing could stop it. Not only were all the religious institutions both for men and women dissolved, but the members of them were forbidden to teach for three years either in their own or neighbouring communes.

The Religious Battle. Conflict with the Holy See.

A conflict with the Holy See was thenceforward inevitable. Perhaps if Leo XIII had been alive he might have succeeded in avoiding it. But on his death at the end of July 1903, his successor, Pius X, immediately adopted a more uncompromising attitude. He sent a diplomatic protest against the visit of President Loubet to Rome, the first occasion on which the head of a great Catholic country had visited the capital of the Popes. Jaurès' paper, *L'Humanité*, through an indiscretion had succeeded in getting hold of the Pope's telegram, and this gave rise to serious consequences. The French Government recalled its Ambassador from the Vatican, leaving only a *chargé d'affaires* in his place. Whereupon fresh trouble arose in connection with two French bishops who had been summoned before the Papal Court. This time Combes broke off diplomatic relations and dismissed the Nuncio from Paris.

Such was the result of the anti-clerical campaign so lightly and imprudently undertaken. The engine, slipping away from the hands that had set it in motion, rushed down the slope with ever-increasing velocity. Owing to the conditions under which it occurred, and the animosity and irritation which it left in its train, the rupture between the French State and the Vatican gave rise to serious complications for France. It caused profound divisions in a country already sufficiently divided against itself, being at once devoutly Catholic and also anti-clerical, opposed, it is true, to the interference of the clergy in politics, but remaining nevertheless profoundly religious.

The Concordat had in its day been a model of wisdom, reason and political insight. Certain points in it might undoubtedly have been modified by consent of both the contracting parties. But to suppress it altogether was no solution.

Consequences of the Rupture.

It is only politicians with a parochial outlook who refuse to recognise the moral and material power of the Pope in the world. Two great Powers like France and the Vatican, instead of ignoring each other, have an obvious interest to serve in regulating their attitude to each other by common consent. As long as the Concordat was in force the French Government, which had a voice in the appointment of bishops, was able by this means to exercise a certain amount of influence over the clergy as a whole. But when the agreement was annulled the Pope became sole master. Gallicanism, which had already been undermined, disappeared altogether.

Abroad the results were even more disastrous. Catholics all over the world quickly turned against France, and when the war broke out the consequences of their violent hostility to her made themselves felt.

For centuries France had exercised in the Near and Far East a religious protectorate which served to maintain her power and supported her moral and material interests. But how could this be maintained after her rupture with the Vatican? The difficulty was practically insurmountable.

So great were the inconveniences, that almost immediately on the outbreak of war it became necessary, at first discreetly and then openly, to renew the bonds that should never have been broken. As soon as the war was over it was very wisely decided to make this *de facto* state of affairs one that was established *de jure,* and an Ambassador was once more sent to the Vatican.

A similar spirit of narrowness and intolerance characterised the home policy of the Combes Ministry. Immediately after **Home Policy.** its formation a circular, which became famous, was sent to the Prefects, and inasmuch as it seemed definitely to recognise and establish the rights of the Republicans, that is to say, the partisans of the Government, to posts in the administration, it inaugurated a new departure in public life.

The machinations of the " delegates " chosen by the Prefects in the reactionary communes embittered local disputes and exasperated the rural districts.

The enemies of the Cabinet continued to hurl ever more violent attacks against Camille Pelletan, the Naval Minister, whom they accused of introducing licence and disorder into his department.

210

RELIGIOUS POLICY

The attacks on General André, Minister for War, were even more violent. Pushing the principles of sectarianism to extremes, he had, on the pretext of exercising control over the political opinions of the officers, instituted a vast system of supervision which soon amounted to espionage over the Army, and which was carried on largely by the help of the Masonic Lodges. An employé of the Grand Orient Lodge having sold for ready money this unsavoury catalogue compiled from the " memoranda," the Opposition newspapers began to publish them. Whereupon General André was obliged to send in his resignation, and Combes, who became involved in the scandal, managed to keep his position a little while longer and then disappeared.

Some time before his retirement he had drawn up a plan of legislation on the separation between Church and State.

As relations with the Vatican had been broken off, the annulment of the Concordat made any discussion of the scheme, **The Separation** or a settlement of what the status of the Church **between** was to be, impossible. Complete separation, **Church** which was one of the planks in the Radical **and State.** programme, was therefore broached.

The parliamentary Commission entrusted with the task of examining the scheme chose as its mouthpiece a Socialist, who was a new-comer in the Chamber—Aristide Briand. Such was the memorable beginning of the public life of a man who, during the twenty years that followed, was destined to play a leading part in French politics.

Born at Nantes in 1862, Briand was at this time forty-three years of age. His rare oratorical gifts, his adroit and arresting eloquence, enhanced by a marvellous voice, won **Aristide** him a great reputation in Socialist circles very early **Briand.** in life. He became one of the leading spirits at " meetings " and on propaganda tours.

Ambitious, as he had every right to be, he was determined to leave at the first opportunity these surroundings in which his versatile spirit and his sharp though comprehensive intellect felt it was stifled.

The Separation Law came up for discussion at an opportune moment for him and gave him his chance. In defending the plan of the Commission he displayed, during the course of a long and heated debate full of snares and pitfalls, extraordinary resource and consummate ability. As frequently happens when it is a matter of reaching a compromise between two violently opposed policies, those whom he had to fight were not his political enemies but his own friends and supporters. In order to convince them and to reduce them to silence he turned all his gifts of persuasion to full account, and also made a display of liberalism which was entirely in keeping with his attitude. He was the great victor in the debate. Henceforward his reputation was made. Soon afterwards he became a member of Clemenceau's Ministry, and from that time forward, except for a few periods of varying length, he was a member, either as Minister or as President, of nearly all the Government combinations. His intellect is very far from being scholarly or concerned with abstract ideas. It would be useless to expect him to shut himself up with voluminous documents and to examine and annotate them as Poincaré and Millerand have done. His documents are human beings, the living, moving and talking world. It is in this alone that he is interested. He has no liking for frontal attacks on his enemy or for going bald-headed at an obstacle as Clemenceau does. Rather than engage in a struggle his temperament prompts him to try to make it unnecessary. He is a past master in the art of settlement and compromise, urged thereto by a certain nonchalance and desire to exert himself as little as possible. The war and its extraordinary prolongation, which he thought was useless and absurd, revealed the limits of a nature that was otherwise very attractive. About the autumn of 1917 he was convinced, as he has frequently assured the writer of the present work, that a little ingenuity in negotiation would and should put an end to hostilities, and that Germany, feeling that victory was impossible, would resign herself to a compromise acceptable to France, and would even go so far as to return Alsace-Lorraine. This showed that he instinctively believed that quarrels between nations could be settled in the same way and by the same methods as differences between individuals.

.   .   .   .

The Chamber unhesitatingly sanctioned the principle of

separation, guaranteeing freedom of worship, and declaring that the Republic did not recognise, pay or subsidise any religious body.

The main difficulty was to apportion the property of the religious bodies, and especially to establish a practical and convenient system which would allow freedom of worship. How was it possible to reconcile the neutrality of the State with the severe and rigid discipline of Catholicism, which subjects the clergy and their flocks to the supreme sovereignty of the Pope?

In order to reach a satisfactory settlement it would have been necessary to come to an understanding with the Pope and the bishops, a course which was contrary to the principle of separation.

In these circumstances any acceptable solution would have been more or less the squaring of the circle. Is it to be wondered at that such a solution has never been found?

BIBLIOGRAPHY.—A. Debidour, *L'Eglise Catholique et l'Etat* (2 vols.). See *Collection des Etudes (Revue de la Compagnie de Jésus)*. General André, *Cinq Ans de Ministère* (1907). P. Fesch, *Les Dossiers Maçoniques* (1905). Anonymous, *Les Fiches de Monsignor Montagbini* (1908). Captain Mollin, *La Vérité sur l'Affaire des Fiches* (1905).

CHAPTER XV

THE RADICAL GOVERNMENT AND THE GROWTH OF SOCIALISM

The Radical Government. Socialism. The Millerand case. Jaurès. The growth of Socialism.

ON the 17th of January, 1906, Fallières, President of the Senate, was elected President of the Republic in succession to Loubet, whose term of office had come to an end. He beat Doumer, on whom the Right and all the opponents of the " block " had relied, by 449 votes to 371.

The elections which were held a few months later (the 6th to the 20th of May) signalised a further success for the " block," who won about sixty seats from the Conservatives, the Nationalists and the Liberals. The Radico-Socialists, as also the united Socialists, won a considerable number of seats. From this moment the groups of the Left held the majority in the Chamber. This meant the triumph of Radicalism, which now assumed the reins of power and kept them until the War.

The Radical Government.

Clemenceau, the destroyer of Cabinets, who had always been in opposition hitherto, was summoned in the evening of his life (which was fortunately to prove a long one) to form a Cabinet in his turn. He went over " to the other side of the barrier " with alacrity.

The movement towards the Left, which, except for rare intervals, had been going on ever since the foundation of the Third Republic, now became clear and pronounced. It was marked not only by the fact that the Radicals and Radico-Socialists had seized the reins of power, but by the increasing number of Socialists elected to the Chamber.

If the development of the Socialist party and its doctrines between 1870 and the war is examined, it will be found that one

214

great question constantly dominated the debates and the Congresses—that of the relation between the Socialists and the parties in power.

Socialism. Two tendencies were constantly coming into conflict and continued to do so, without the ingenuity of those who sought a compromise, great though it was, and the complications and intrigues to which these compromises gave rise, and the meticulous hair-splitting of terms, succeeding in satisfactorily disguising the profound disagreement between them for any length of time.

The orthodox, the " pure " Socialists, those in whose eyes principles were more important than facts, believed that Socialism had nothing to gain, but on the contrary, a great deal to lose from any alliance, however feeble, with the bourgeois parties. The advantages to be gained from it, they argued, were more apparent than real, and the strength of their propaganda, which acted like a magnet on the masses, would be diminished and undermined by any such compromise, or collusion, as they preferred to call it. Socialism would at once cease to be what it ought to remain if it was to triumph—a faith, a real religion.

To this their opponents replied that every religion, however great the conviction and ardour of its disciples might be, had been obliged to take into account the conditions under which it had come into being and to adapt itself to circumstances. It would be impossible for Socialism to avoid the necessity of acting likewise. If it wanted to modify existing society from top to bottom, the first prerequisite was not to live and develop outside it, but, on the contrary, to permeate it through and through and to make use of every weapon that was offered and of every opportunity that presented itself. The electoral campaigns and the securing of votes furnished these weapons and these opportunities, and it behoved the Socialists to learn how to conduct the struggle with an ever more consummate display of skill. What mattered was not the means but the end, and the leaders of the Party were in duty bound not to hesitate over the choice of means. If, in exchange for substantial advantages, it was necessary for them to enter into temporary alliances with the bourgeois parties, even if they had afterwards to be repudiated one by one, where, after all, would be the harm?

This was the perennial problem that was raised at every Congress. Failing to find a solution, efforts were made to cover it up by means of more or less skilful phrases. Those who were elected deputies, all who had won or retained seats—for the very reason that they had retained them—those who by frequenting the Palais-Bourbon had become conciliatory and accommodating, were as a rule partisans of the second solution. But the mass of the " militants," the bulk of the rank and file, thought differently, and they subjected the leaders to constant control and supervision. On the alert for the smallest sign of weakness, they claimed the right to direct their decisions.

So tyrannical did their control become that many of the Socialist representatives in Parliament, especially those who were endowed with a masterful disposition, and were gifted with power, originality and talent, instinctively aimed at ridding themselves of this tutelage, which they had come to regard as humiliating and intolerable. It seemed to them unjust and even invidious to feel within themselves the capacity for becoming parliamentary leaders, and possibly great parliamentary leaders, with opportunities for reaching the Ministry, or the Presidency of the Council, possibly even the Presidency of the Republic, without being allowed to turn them to account, merely because a Congress, or rather a Committee, in which the ignorant and the envious were in the majority, had decided it should be so.

Socialism, owing to its daily practice and constant exercise in holding debates and meetings, is an excellent nursery, not only for orators, but also, which is quite as important if not more so, for electioneering and parliamentary strategists. Can it be wondered at, therefore, that the best and most highly gifted among its adherents wanted to make the utmost use of the faculties and gifts they had developed?

Socialism was like a hen sitting on duck's eggs. Its history for the last thirty years is full of cases of " defection."

First and foremost among these was the case of Millerand, who, in 1900, accepted the post of Minister of Trade in the Waldeck-Rousseau Cabinet. The inclusion of a Socialist in a bourgeois

Ministry gave rise to a terrific tumult. It is necessary to have recourse to memory and to read the newspapers of the day to form an adequate idea of the agitation. Those who screamed the loudest were not, as might have been supposed, the Conservatives and the bourgeois, terrified by the apparition of the Collectivist bogey, creeping like a wolf into the fold. On the contrary, it was the fellow-believers of the new Minister who waxed indignant at what they regarded as an act of treachery. Guesdists, Blanquists and Allemanists all rose in revolt against a " so-called Socialist policy which was made up of compromise and defection." It was impossible, they said, for the Socialist party to become a Ministerial party without committing suicide.

The Millerand Case.

Millerand set an example soon followed by others. Six years later, in 1906, Briand, another member of the Socialist brotherhood, also accepted a portfolio; shortly afterwards came the turn of Viviani. During the war, Briand, who was then President of the Council, remarked in his grave voice, with the suspicion of a malicious smile, to Albert Thomas, who was a Socialist also on the point of crossing the Rubicon, and of accepting an appointment as Under-Secretary of State for Munitions : " Thomas, the hour has come for you to become a renegade ! "

Whilst Millerand, Briand and Viviani had thus deserted the seraglio, and were preparing to win the highest offices of State, Jaurès, the greatest and most powerful Socialist orator and demagogue after Gambetta in the Third Republic, remained true to the tenets and discipline of his party, endeavouring by his speeches in and out of Parliament, by his articles in *L'Humanité*, a paper which owed its inception mainly to him, and by his pamphlets and books, to give the widest possible circulation to Socialist ideas and doctrines.

Jaurès.

Born at Castres in 1859, the eloquence of Jaurès was characteristically southern. Turgidity and emphasis, the least desirable elements of rhetoric, played too great a part in it. Nevertheless, a copious and powerful flow of language and an uninterrupted stream of words and thoughts carried along his speeches like a river rushing headlong down its course. The sincerity and ardour of his convictions, his wide culture, and an intellect at once swift and sure which enabled him to understand and master the most diverse and complicated questions, together with a mental inquisitiveness ever on the *qui vive*, made Jaurès the prototype *par excellence* of a great Socialist leader, capable of exercising great influence both in and out of Parliament.

These qualities were marred by serious defects. The narrow and rigorous discipline of Socialistic formulæ, the party spirit with which he was in the highest degree imbued, were constantly perverting and distorting his view of men and events. In foreign policy especially they led him into ridiculous errors of judgment, which made him by a process of *parti pris* and professional bias in many cases automatically side against the interests of his country. In speaking of the Triple Alliance, for instance, he maintained that it was the necessary counterweight to the Franco-Russian Alliance, an assertion which was little short of mad. The exact contrary was the truth. In discussing the question vital to the whole of Europe, the question of Germany, he was convinced, quite erroneously, as events afterwards proved, that the democratic and Socialist parties across the Rhine constituted a powerful force with which the Kaiser, the Army and the Nationalists would one day have to deal. Now this force, owing to the docility and malleability of the German people, which is obvious to any observer with the slightest clarity of vision, is absolutely non-existent.

The uninterrupted growth of Socialism, shown by the increase in the number of votes gained and the members elected to the **The Growth of Socialism.** Chamber, the Senate and the cantonal and municipal assemblies, constitutes one of the most marked features in the political evolution of the Third Republic. Socialism owes its success to its excellent organisation, the activity of its committees and the discipline of its party. It also owes it even more to the weakness, which occasionally amounted to lethargy, of the bourgeois parties, who, far from uniting to bar its path, on the contrary frequently thought fit to enter into alliance with it. In the south especially such alliances, long before the formation of the Cartel, were already frequent. Many electors voted for the Socialists without in the least believing in Collectivist doctrines, merely because in their eyes Socialism represented the most advanced of the parties of the Left, *the reddest*. Occasionally Conserva-

218

tives and Clericals, simply with the object of playing a trick on the Radical Freemasons and " devourers of priests," joined the Socialists and thus secured their election.

Thus Socialism profited and continued to profit considerably by the dissensions between the bourgeois parties.

The large number of votes it receives is thus very far from representing real and sincere conversion to Collectivist ideas. Possibly the bourgeois parties, although certain of their members are incredibly lacking in political sense, will in time perceive this truth which has hitherto been hidden from them. For the differences between themselves, however great, are as nothing compared with the abyss that exists from the financial, economic and political point of view between the real doctrines of Socialism, that is to say, Collectivism, and those of the bourgeois parties, whether Radical or Moderate.

In every country, in England and in Germany, to specify only two, in which the Socialists have succeeded in securing or in sharing political power, their dominion has been short-lived, and could hardly have been otherwise.

In Germany the influence of the Socialists quickly jeopardised the finances of the country and the balancing of the budget. It was immediately accompanied by a prodigious increase in expenditure, and a multiplication of officials in the various departments of the administration, and on the railways, etc. And this is a result which Socialism, however well-intentioned and intelligent its leaders may be, can never escape. It automatically leads to State control and the development of monopolies which necessitate a considerable increase in the number of Government officials.

From the national point of view, moreover, Socialism, imperatively urged on by its fundamental doctrines, finds it impossible to safeguard the essential interests of the nation in all matters connected with the Army, the Navy, and above all the colonies. The dangers to which it leads in this respect are such that they soon provoke a violent reaction.

In vain do its leaders, conscious of these perils, try to escape from the consequences of their doctrines. When once they are in power, Government obligations and a feeling of responsibility would soon lead them to lay aside their principles. But the rank and file, continually kept up to concert pitch by new relays of agitators who have not the same reasons as the former to declare themselves satisfied, do not allow them to do so. As soon as Socialism becomes connected with the Government, and for that very reason is tainted with bourgeois doctrine, it is threatened with the loss of part of its forces, which automatically go over to the more advanced and violent parties, above all to the Communists. The existence and development of a Communist party acts as a spur upon Socialism, while it also constitutes a permanent danger. That is why, in spite of appearances, the Socialist leaders dare not and will never dare to offer open and energetic opposition to the Communists. They are condemned to tack and hedge and to reach some sort of understanding with them.

BIBLIOGRAPHY.—M. Leroy. *Les Droits des Fonctionnaires* (1906). M. Leroy, *Syndicats et Services Publiques* (1910). J. Weill, *Histoire du Mouvement Social* (1902). Léon Blum, *Les Congrès Ouvriers Socialistes* (1901). Pelloutier, *Histoire des Bourses du Travail* (1902). J. Bourdeau, *L'Evolution du Socialisme* (1901). Zevaes, *Le Socialisme en France* (1908). P. Challaye, *Syndicalisme Révolutionnaire et Syndicalisme Réformiste* (1909). J. Sorel, *Réflexions sur la Violence* (1906). Paul Louis, *Histoire du Mouvement Syndicaliste en France* (1911).

CHAPTER XVI

L'ENTENTE CORDIALE

Edward VII. Uncle and nephew. Monsieur Delcassé. The two
Cambons. Establishment of the *Entente Cordiale*.

THE more one studies history, whether past or present,
the more one becomes convinced that, whatever may
be said to the contrary, there is no such thing as a
predestined event.

Everything that happens, or has happened, might just as
well not have happened or have happened differently. As the
march of history advances it reaches as it were cross-roads,
bifurcations where several paths might equally well be chosen.
And it is at these points that human energy and will intervene
to impose a certain direction, and transform *possible* into *actual*
events.

After the Fashoda crisis, when, without knowing exactly why,
England and France almost came to blows, up to the last
moment when a sudden access of wisdom on the part of France
succeeded in preventing the catastrophe, reason, good sense
and an accurate insight into European politics were prompting
both nations to settle their differences. Even for those of their
citizens who suffered from exaggerated greed, the world was
after all sufficiently large, and in the two hemispheres there was
enough land for all to have a share.

As far as Europe itself was concerned, several considerations,
but above all the growing menace of a common foe—Germany—
were calculated to bring them together. And thus an agreement was possible and in the highest degree desirable. But for
both parties a favourable moment was required, the turn of the
helm that would send the ship in the right direction.

The time arrived when, on both sides of the Channel, the men
were to be found capable of doing this. In England there was

221

first and foremost King Edward VII, and in France, Monsieur Delcassé, assisted by an excellent trio of Ambassadors, the two Cambon brothers and Barrère.

It is sufficiently often asserted that the King of England has less power than the President of the French Republic, who, as **Edward VII.** is well known, has none at all, and that he has not the right of dissolving Parliament, which the French Constitution has conceded to the President, but which as a matter of fact is never exercised.

This may perhaps be true *in theory*. But it is false *in practice*, which is all that counts, especially in England, where what is written is of far less account than the unwritten law of custom and tradition.

The Englishman is a past master at making his Constitution as convenient as his home. Whether it is a matter of a country house or of a law, what he aims at is comfort rather than symmetry. He has accordingly arranged that a mediocre or bad sovereign (such as have existed in the past and will do so again) should find it impossible to do any harm. All initiative is denied him, and he is bound hand and foot.

But when a monarch is recognised to be good, and when he has proved his worth both at home and even more abroad, these bonds are by common consent unloosed. Everybody is then extremely pleased to see him play a part, especially in foreign affairs, provided his intervention is in the first place discreet and tactful, and secondly in conformity with the general aspirations of his country.

The beginning of the reign of Edward VII conclusively proves to what extent this influence can prove a determining factor.

As long as old Queen Victoria was alive, with her stern and narrow outlook, her lack of sympathy with France, whom she did not understand and had but little liking for, there was small chance of any improvement in Anglo-French relations.

In this respect her son afforded a striking contrast. He knew France through frequent visits, and loved Paris, where he felt at home. Whenever he stayed in the country he made a point of having French statesmen, writers and artists presented to him. Above all he met Gambetta, with whom he lunched in a private room at the Café Anglais. The jokes and anecdotes of

General Galiffet, one of his favourite guests, amused him. He went to the theatre, and enjoyed French plays and books.

A lover of life in all its aspects, and refusing none of the pleasures it provided, under a thoughtless and occasionally somewhat frivolous exterior Edward VII concealed solid qualities and considerable gifts of mind and character. He was first and foremost a *gentleman*. His simplicity and free and easy ways were combined with a very lively sense of his own dignity and rank.

Brought up extremely strictly and austerely by his mother, and above all by his father, ruled with the iron rod of German discipline and culture, his independent nature emancipated itself very early in life, and rejected all that was too narrow in the education he had received. He was endowed with sound, clear judgment, solid common-sense, and a profound knowledge of Europe acquired not out of books or by diplomatic channels but, what was infinitely more valuable, from personal experience and mixing with men.

He was one of the first to be aware of the German menace, long before his people and its leaders had even begun to open their eyes. But this is one of the characteristics of a real states-man, that he has a clear perception of what others can scarcely see at all.

His sympathy with France and Frenchmen was as great as his mistrust of Germany, and above all of its sovereign, his own nephew, the Kaiser. The antipathy between the two was of long standing. The memoirs of the period and Sir Sidney Lee's important biography of Edward VII give the history of its origin and development.

Uncle and Nephew.

While his grandfather the Emperor and his father the Crown Prince were still alive, the future Kaiser, a few days before the arrival in Berlin of his uncle, the Prince of Wales, on the 13th of March, 1885, wrote to his correspondent the Tsar Alexander III : " In a few days' time we shall have the Prince of Wales here. I am not at all enchanted by the thought of his unexpected visit, because (you must excuse me, as he is your brother-in-law) his false and intriguing nature will certainly lead him to attempt by one way or another to uphold Bulgarian interests against Russia. Allah send him to hell, as the Turks say, and let him be content with carrying on his intrigues behind the scenes, *tête-à-tête* with a few pretty women."

The Prince of Wales was far too sensitive not to know immediately what the feelings of his nephew towards him were, and one event after the other showed the latter up in his true colours with all his vanity and histrionic turn of mind. The Prince soon came to the same conclusion about him as another person who was in the best possible position to judge him, his own father Prince Frederick, who in a letter to Bismarck, in which he protested against the communication of diplomatic documents to his son, wrote word for word as follows : " His lack of experience and his vanity and presumption, together with the high opinion he has of himself, may make him a public danger in any responsible position he holds."

This remarkable prophecy, alas ! was only too tragically confirmed by events.

. . . .

From the very beginning of his reign Edward VII's main object was to improve the relations of his country with France Extremely sensitive and shrewd, and a born diplomatist, he was fully aware, especially with regard to his own people, who are very slow to move, that one of the conditions of success was to advance slowly, step by step. He was fortunate enough to have behind him a Conservative Ministry, with Lord Lansdowne at the Foreign Office.

Tradition, temperament and religious influences had turned the Protestants of all sects, the Nonconformists, who form the backbone of the Liberal Party, more in the direction of Protestant Prussia than Catholic France.

The religious factor plays a far more important part than is generally supposed in the home and foreign policy of England. The strong dislike of certain Englishmen, Lloyd George, for example, for Poland is due to this.

It chanced that during the opening years of the century England had at the helm statesmen and diplomatists who were endowed with sufficient political insight and authority to respond to the advances made by Edward VII, and to do all in their power to bring about a *rapprochement* between the two countries.

224

L'ENTENTE CORDIALE

Its ministerial instability has often been a source of reproach against the Third Republic. While the indictment is only too well founded, it did not apply for some considerable time to its higher diplomatic officials, who directed the foreign policy of the country over the heads of the ephemeral Ministries.

And even as far as the Ministers were concerned, one of them, and the most important, Delcassé, remained for seven years at the head of the Quai d'Orsay. Now seven years is a long time in a parliamentary system, and it is only just to give the Republic its due.

Once a journalist, who had entered Parliament fairly young, this dark, energetic and obstinate little native of Ariège possessed all the qualities and defects of his native mountains —tenacity, the will to carry out any plan he had conceived, cost what it might, ardent patriotism, instinctive mistrust of Germany, and the feeling that France, if she were not to lapse into a condition of semi-subjection to the Power at her gate, would one day or other be obliged to cope with it and measure herself against it. This conviction entirely obsessed him, and he was anxious, in the event of a probable if not immediate struggle, to draw the bonds of the French alliance with Russia as close as possible, and cement the friendship with England.

Monsieur Delcassé.

It was towards these ends that he devoted all his powers, and his efforts were seconded by three remarkable Ambassadors— the two Cambons and Barrère.

The Great Ambassadors.

Pupils of Thiers and Jules Ferry, under whose auspices they started their careers directly after the 4th of September, the Cambons had previously served for a short time in the administration, having, as quite young men, held important posts as Prefects of large districts, residents in Tunisia and members of the Algerian Government, after which they took up the career of diplomacy.

Paul, the elder of the two brothers, was sent from Constantinople to London in 1898 and remained there almost a quarter of a century.

Jules, the younger, after playing a distinguished part at Washington, on the conclusion of peace between Spain and

Q

America went on to Madrid. In 1907 he was sent to Berlin, where he remained until the war.

The elder was more reserved and distant, the younger more friendly and genial. Paul, with his refined face and regular features, his pointed beard and the aristocratic elegance of his manner and bearing, immediately made an impression of authority and power. The frail and delicate-looking little man radiated nervous energy, as it were a mysterious, all-powerful stream. Usually cold and concentrated on the matter in hand, he became heated and animated at critical moments when the interests of his country were at stake.

Jules, with his blinking eyes scintillating with life and shrewdness behind their glasses, was unequalled in his judgment of men. He could weigh up their assertions at their proper value, and knew exactly what they were thinking and what they wanted. Endowed, like his brother, with a good classical education, always very well informed and in touch with events which he knew at once how to interpret, remaining young to an advanced age, and astonishingly youthful and vivacious, he was one of those who foresaw the bellicose intentions of Germany with the greatest certainty.

Camille Barrère, after a brief period of journalism, when Gambetta at once picked him out, was pushed by the latter into a diplomatic career. After having been Minister in Stockholm and Egypt and Ambassador in Berne, he was sent in 1897 to Rome, where he remained without being moved for twenty-five years. To re-establish cordial relations between France and Italy and thus deprive the Triple Alliance of all significance, was the difficult and prolonged task to which he devoted himself, and which he succeeded in bringing to a satisfactory conclusion.

These three men formed, during the ten or fifteen years preceding the war, the diplomatic buttress of the Third Republic. When the crisis of 1914 occurred it proved sound and solid.

Prudent and circumspect, Paul Cambon, who knew the English very well, and quickly succeeded in gaining their *Establishment* confidence, was aware that in negotiating with *of the Entente* them one of the first rules is not to ask for more *Cordiale.* than they wish or are able to give.

In the multitude of questions outstanding between the

226

two countries, logic and common-sense alike proclaimed
that it was better to proceed from the simple to the
complex, from the easy to the difficult. A beginning was
therefore made in clearing the road of the undergrowth that
blocked it—difficulties connected with Newfoundland, Sene-
gambia, Siam, Madagascar, the New Hebrides, etc., etc., after
which the two great questions which were to serve as a means
of barter—the questions of Egypt and Morocco—were entered
upon.

The conduct of these negotiations between England and
France is a pattern of what diplomatic negotiations should be,
and ought always to be held up as a model.

For England, Egypt, especially on account of the Suez Canal,
one of the chief arteries of her Empire, is of capital importance.
France had allowed the English to establish themselves there
alone. There they were and there they intended to remain.
It would have been useless for France to attempt to go back
upon her abandonment of her claims.

England was anxious that France should also abandon all
political interests in Egypt, though, on the other hand, she was
ready to acknowledge the great moral interest the latter still
possessed in the country. In this connection she gave the most
precise undertakings, which, moreover, she has loyally observed.

In exchange for the liberty allowed her by France in Egypt,
she granted France a similar freedom of action in Morocco,
which was of great importance, as it represented the indispensable complement of the French Empire in North Africa.

Egypt and Morocco—these were the two factors in the
agreement.

Whilst the negotiations with England were being carried on,
France, at the desire of the latter, succeeded in coming to an
arrangement with Spain, who also, on account of her geographical situation and traditions, enjoyed a privileged position
in Morocco. The two countries signed an agreement by which
Morocco was divided into two zones—one consisting of the
northern portion of the country from the neighbourhood of
Larache as far as the frontiers of Algeria, which was to be
subjected to Spanish influence, and the rest to that of France.

On the 8th of April, 1904, the Anglo-French agreement was

signed. *It was strictly limited in scope*, and dealt only with two questions that did not concern Europe. But the very fact that it had been concluded, and the way in which it had been done, could not fail to have more far-reaching consequences. Nothing affords a better proof of this than the name by which it was designated from the beginning—the *Entente Cordiale*. And it did indeed introduce a fresh element into the relations between France and England which up to that moment had been lacking —precisely in cordiality.

The importance of this event was naturally very great, and could not fail to make itself felt not only in the colonies but also in Europe itself.

That this should give offence to German diplomacy, which had hitherto relied upon the differences between England and France, was inevitable. It was also inevitable that proof of this displeasure should be given at the first opportunity.

It was in connection with Morocco that this occurred.

BIBLIOGRAPHY.—E. Bourgeois, *Manuel Historique de Politique Etrangère* (Vol. IV) (1926). A. Debidour, *Histoire Diplomatique de l'Europe depuis le Congrès de Berlin* (2 vols., 1916). Seignobos, *Histoire Politique de l'Europe Contemporaine* (2 vols., 2nd ed., 1924). Lavisse and Rambaud, *Histoire Générale : Le Monde Contemporaine* 1870–1900. Ch. Scheffer, *D'Une Guerre à l'Autre : Essaie sur la Politique Extérieure de la Troisième République* (1920). Wilhelm II, *Memoirs* (1921). *Tableaux d'Histoire* (1923). Prince Clovis von Hohenlohe, *Memoirs* (3 vols., 1909). Baron Beyens, *L'Allemagne avant la Guerre* (Brussels, 1916). V. Berard, *L'Angleterre et l'Impérialisme* (1900). *La France et Guillaume II* (1907). J. Bardoux, *Victoria, Edouard et George V* (1911). Prince von Bülow, *La Politique Allemande* (1914). A. Filon, *L'Angleterre d'Edouard VII* (1911). J. de Lanessan, *Histoire de l'Entente Cordiale* (1906). P. Mantoux, *A travers l'Angleterre Contemporaine* (1909). Juliette Adam, *Guillaume II* (1890–99) (1917). Raymond Recouly, *En Angleterre* (1909). Moysset, *L'Esprit Public en Allemagne Vingt Ans après Bismarck* (1911). André Tardieu, *Questions Diplomatiques de l'Année* 1904. *Le Prince de Bülow* (1909). Hanotaux, *L'Entente Cordiale* (1912). Sir Sidney Lee, *King Edward VII* (London, 1925). A. Mevil, *De la Paix de Francfort à la Conférence d'Algésiras* (1909). E. Lemonon, *L'Europe et la Politique Britannique* 1885–1911 (1912). R. de Caix, *Fachoda* (1899).

CHAPTER XVII

MOROCCO AND EUROPEAN POLITICS

A mediæval country. The special rights of France. The German
mailed fist. Danger of war. The Russo-Japanese War. Progress of Russia in the Far East. The sudden attack by Japan.
The Algeciras Conference. French penetration in Morocco.
The incident of the German deserters. An Anglo-Russian
agreement. The abortive agreement of Björkö.

OWING to an extraordinary concatenation of circumstances, Morocco, although it is situated at the very
gates of Europe, remained until the first years of this
century as far removed from the civilisation of Europe as the
most distant countries of Africa and Asia.

In the spring of 1903, the author of the present work travelled
by caravan from Tangier to Fez, and took seven days to cover
the two hundred or so miles which can to-day be
accomplished in a few hours by motor. It was
a marvellous journey, all the same, across the
plains and plateaux of Morocco, which at that season of the year
are like a verdant flower-strewn carpet. At night the tent was
pitched near the douars, to the accompaniment of Biblical
scenes—the return of the flocks in the evening, with clouds of
golden dust about them and the barking of dogs; groups of
young women, like those described in the Bible, coming home
from the fountain, resting their heavy stone pitchers on their
hips or their shoulders.

And thus Fez was reached, a mediæval city, one of the most
picturesque and variegated in Islam, where five times a day the
rumble of prayer was mingled with the murmur of running
waters.

Towards the end of the nineteenth century, the Sultan,
Moulay Hassan, ruled, after the manner of the princes of the
past, over this country which had remained unchanged for
centuries. He waged war against the tribes that had not been

*A Mediæval
Country.*

229

subjugated, going from one of his capitals to the other, cutting off the heads of rebels, which the Jews, after having put them in brine, hung up on the ramparts. His son, Moulay Abd-el-Azis (1894), was very far from displaying similar energy, but spent most of his time in squandering the coffers full of gold that his Grand Vizier had left him. Swarms of merchants and entertainers swooped down on his capital, ready to sell the young ruler anything he wanted, from lions for a menagerie to photographic apparatus in gold.

As invariably happens in Morocco, as soon as the central power is weakened, a pretender, a " rogui," immediately arose. The one who appeared at this juncture was called Bou-Hamara (the man with the she-ass). He recruited his followers from the region of Taza, not far from the Rif and the Algerian frontier.

The neighbourhood of Algeria and the length of the frontier on this side gave France an interest and special rights in Morocco. **The Special Rights of France.** When, as frequently happens, there are disturbances in the country, they immediately make themselves felt in the territories subject to French rule.

At the dawn of the twentieth century the condition of Morocco presented a paradox, an anachronism, which could only be accounted for by the opposition between the Powers who possessed the greatest interest there—France, England and Spain. As soon as these Powers came to an agreement, the situation, as far as it was possible to tell, could not help being quickly changed.

A few months after the signature of the Anglo-French agreement, France sent Monsieur Saint-René Taillandier to Fez as Minister, entrusted with the task of obtaining the consent of the Sultan to certain reforms which were regarded as indispensable. It was at this moment that Germany intervened.

.   .   .   .

During the ten years preceding the Great War, Morocco served as a lever to Germany in her political relations with France. German interests in the country were, at all events at first, almost negligible. But the German Government was anxious to keep the matter open in order to make France feel her dependent position whenever it seemed desirable.

Morocco and the Foreign Legion might either of them have

provided the pretext for war between France and Germany.
But Germany chose a third, the Balkans, because in this sphere
alone was she absolutely certain of being followed to the bitter
end by her ally, Austria.

Secretly supported by Herr von Tattenbach, the German
representative, the Sultan of Morocco refused his consent to all
the demands made by France.

On the 31st of March, 1905, the Kaiser in person landed at
Tangier. " My visit," he said, " is to the Sultan of Morocco,
who is an *independent sovereign*."

The German Mailed Fist. And thus German diplomacy, true to the traditions of Bismarck, rapped its knuckles violently
on the table in order to remind France, in case she might be
tempted to forget it, that Germany was still in existence, and to
make her feel that it was useless for her to come to an understanding with England, since the support of the latter would be
of no service to her so long as Germany also had not given her
consent. It was not merely the question of Morocco, which was
of secondary if not third-rate importance, that was now raised,
but European policy as a whole. And this Germany made
quite clear. A Press campaign, which from the German newspapers spread to certain French journals, was immediately
inaugurated, revealing once more the strategy of Bismarck, now
carried on in the Wilhelmstrasse by Baron von Holstein, who
had been trained by the great Chancellor himself.

As in Bismarck's days, Germany tried to interfere in the
internal affairs of France, and had recourse to similar tactics
of intimidation and intrigue. Henckel von Donnersmark, a
personal friend of the Kaiser, who late in life had married Païva,
the notorious *demi-mondaine* of the Second Empire, was sent to
Paris. He interviewed the journalists and mixed in political
and financial circles. The cause of all the trouble, he hinted,
was Delcassé, a megalomaniac and a Teutophobe, who had tried
to isolate Germany. This was the beginning of the isolation
theory of which the German Government was to make so much
account later on. If Delcassé were sacrificed, and made a
scapegoat, the relations between France and Germany would
immediately improve.

Delcassé had enemies in Parliament and even in the Cabinet.

Of what politician, especially when he has been seven years in office, can this not be said? Rouvier, President of the Council, who was above all a financier, inclined to regard everything from the financial point of view, thought his policy dangerous. He was, moreover, not the only man to believe, on somewhat superficial evidence, that a close economic union between France and Germany was possible and desirable, and that if it were achieved all difficulties between the two countries would easily be settled. Such, six years later, at the time of the Agadir crisis, was the attitude of Caillaux.

The German Government demanded, or rather insisted, that the question of Morocco should be referred in its entirety to the **Danger of** signatory Powers of the Conference of Madrid. **War.** To refuse this demand, and to hold out, was possible; and Delcassé wished to do so. But this meant danger of war. Was France ready for war either from the military or the moral point of view?

Now whilst Delcassé had been pursuing his policy, which in principle was unassailable, military and naval preparations had been seriously neglected by his Radical colleagues in the Cabinet. The Army, under the Ministry of General André, who was much more of a politician than a soldier, had just passed through a grave crisis.

Lastly, and this was the determining factor, Russia, the ally of France, was at the moment engaged with Japan in the Far East (1904-5), and quite incapable of rendering her the smallest assistance.

These reasons, which, it must be admitted, were extremely weighty, secured the support of the Cabinet for Rouvier's policy, and on the 6th of June, 1905, Delcassé sent in his resignation. The German Government had gained its ends, and over the question of Morocco had won its first diplomatic victory.

The advance of Russia in the East had, during the nineteenth century, been an uninterrupted sequence of successes, won, **The Russo-** curiously enough, not by generals but by diploma-**Japanese War.** tists. The reason for this was that the Russian, **Advance of** who is semi-Asiatic, is unequalled in carrying on **Russia in the** negotiations with the Chinaman and exercising **Far East.** the art of persuasion upon him. An astute negotiator, he is a past master at temporising. Whilst China was an object of envy to other nations—England, Germany, France and Japan—the Russian intervened at the psychological moment and carried off his share without striking a blow.

Japan, who after her victorious war against China (1894-5) had been prevented by Russia from reaping the rewards of **The Sudden** success, was becoming more and more irritated by **Attack by** the latter's encroachments. Scarcely had diplo- **Japan.** matic relations been broken off (February 1904) than, without any declaration of war, some Japanese torpedo boats entered the roadstead of Port Arthur and torpedoed two of the finest ships belonging to the Russian fleet.

A long and terrible war followed, at which the writer of these lines was present as Russian correspondent of the *Temps*.

Materially, and even more so morally, the position of the two combatants was very different. Russia possessed only one line of railway by which supplies could reach her army at a distance of over six thousand miles from its base. The war for her was merely a colonial expedition, in which she had but little interest, whilst for Japan it was a national struggle into which she threw herself heart and soul.

And this explains the results. In spite of a vigorous resistance on the part of the Russians, Liao-Yang and Mukden constituted two victories for Japan.

It was a strange war which was fought in a strange country— a country of ancient cities with great lines of ramparts, huge gates with triple roofs, pagodas and temples, vast, fertile plains swarming with people who looked on amazed at the strange armies, both equally detested, who came and laid bare their lands.

The Japanese had won victories which had cost them very dear. Count Witte, a clever diplomatist, was able to turn their fatigue and also the moral support of the United States to account at Portsmouth in order to secure a peace which on the whole imposed very slight sacrifices on Russia (5th of September, 1905).

Much more serious for the latter as well as for France, her ally, was the internal upheaval which the defeats in Manchuria had caused throughout the country. It allowed, or at least it ought to have allowed, clear-sighted observers, who examined not only the outside but also the inside of the edifice, to gauge how unsafe the structure was. The whole Empire was convulsed by one violent disturbance after the other—demonstrations, strikes (some of which were revolutionary in character), riots and firing in the streets of St. Petersburg and Moscow, peasant risings in the Baltic Provinces, disorders in the Caucasus, etc. All this, combined with the active opposition of the intellectual classes, the *intelligenzia*, as they are called in Russia, who with might and main demanded a Constitution, forced the Tsar, on the vigorous representations of Count Witte, to sign the famous manifesto of the 20th of October, 1905, by which a timid attempt at constitutional and parliamentary Government and the first attack on the autocratic system were made. The Tsar had no sooner signed this manifesto, however, than he regretted it bitterly, and could not forgive Count Witte, who had fallen into disgrace, for having forced it upon him. He did all in his power to limit, if not to destroy, the concessions he had allowed himself to have dragged from him.

Whilst Russia was thus occupied in the Far East, Germany had her hands practically free to make an attempt at intimidat-
The Algeciras Conference. ing France and forcing her to submit to her demands regarding Morocco. After the resignation of Delcassé, the French Government had no alternative but to accept the proposal of a conference put forward by German diplomacy. On the 8th of July an exchange of letters between Monsieur Rouvier and Prince Radolin, the German Ambassador in Paris, recognised the principle and settled the programme of the conference.

The place chosen was Algeciras. Situated on the extreme edge of Europe, this little semi-African city, with its white-washed houses, its crooked streets, its gardens full of palms and orange trees, in the midst of which there is an excellent hotel, run on English lines, and frequented by winter visitors—the Maria Christina—faces the sunburnt rock of Gibraltar. It was here that the diplomatists met.

France, by dint of repetition, succeeded in having her claim to special rights in Morocco recognised. Germany, indeed, had no cause for congratulating herself on having raised the matter before a European assembly. If the fact of having forced

France to consent to a conference was a triumph for Germany, the conference itself was on the whole more of a triumph for France. In more than one instance, Italy, though an ally of Germany, did not hesitate to side with France.

It was here that the results of the excellent work carried on for many years in Rome by the French Ambassador, Camille Barrère, made themselves felt. An agreement made in the greatest secrecy with the Marquis Visconti Venosta, the Minister for Foreign Affairs, had resulted in the Convention of 1902, by which the two countries were allotted a sphere of influence in Morocco and Tripoli respectively. Signor Prinitti, who succeeded Visconti Venosta, after renewing the Triple Alliance, consented to sign a Convention with France by which Italy undertook to remain neutral in the event of France, owing to some act of provocation, or in order to defend her own interests, should be led to declare war on Germany. From that moment the Triple Alliance lost, as far as Italy was concerned, much of its menace to France.

France, having secured the major share in the policing of the ports and the management of the State Bank, and to a large
French Penetration in Morocco. extent free to do as she pleased, continued to prosecute her policy of penetration in Morocco. But as soon as she began to get a footing there, she was led by force of circumstances to settle down more and more. The " hold " on Morocco could not be secured by half-measures. All kinds of obstacles both at home and abroad were opposed to its development, but a sense of the great interests involved, the active influence of the same small group of energetic men who had succeeded in developing the French colonial empire, and rightly convinced that the acquisition of Morocco was indispensable for France, overcame them all.

In March 1907 the murder at Marrakesh of Dr. Mauchamp, a French subject, led the Government to decide upon occupying Oujda, not far from the Algerian frontier. On the 30th of July European workmen engaged on a task in the port of Casablanca were massacred by the inhabitants, and the French Consul was threatened. A body of troops was immediately set ashore to occupy and protect the town. This was the thin end of the wedge, and from that time forward operations were bound to increase. General d'Amade seized the Chaouia, the vast and fertile plain surrounding Casablanca. Oujda on the east and Casablanca on the west formed the two arms of the pincers which on the occupation of Fez were bound to close before long.

The incident of the German deserters from the Foreign Legion gave rise to fresh difficulties between Germany and France.

The Incident of the German Deserters. The German Government demanded apologies and the release of the deserters. The French Government retaliated by asking for the recall of the German Consul. In case of refusal, it suggested recourse to arbitration. Germany, after a fairly lively resistance, ended by consenting.

Monsieur Clemenceau, at that time President of the Council, seconded at the Foreign Office by Monsieur Pichon, his intimate friend and faithful lieutenant, upheld the rights of France with great energy.

After a fairly long disappearance from political life owing to the Panama scandal, the Dreyfus case had furnished him with the opportunity of making a conspicuous return. In 1905, during the crisis provoked by the landing of the Kaiser at Tangier, his articles sounded a vigorous call to his country to rouse its energies and offer determined resistance to German intimidation. " The yoke they offer us," he wrote, " does not fit our neck. Neck or yoke, one or the other of them must be broken ! " The phrase was characteristic of the whole man.

Events led to France extending her sphere of action and sending more and more soldiers to Morocco. The feeble Sultan, Abd-el-Azis, openly compromised in the eyes of his people by his dealings with strangers, was dethroned by his brother Moulay Hafid (1908), who was soon afterwards compromised in his turn. A revolt forced the French Government to occupy Fez (21st of March, 1911), and afterwards Meknes and Rabat.

Germany watched with jealous eyes this series of encroachments which was inevitably bound to lead to what she termed the " Tunisification " of Morocco. An attempt at economic and financial collaboration, made after the incident of the deserters from Casablanca, with the object of making a combined use of French and German capital in the colonies, resulted in nothing.

The French Government has been accused of being responsible

or this failure. It has been maintained that if Germany again struck her fist violently on the table in 1911, it was because the hopes she had based upon this economic agreement had been disappointed.

Such reproaches are without foundation. The collaboration was bound to fail for the simple reason that each of the two partners understood it in a different way—Germany expecting to play an important part, while France expected her to play an insignificant one.

Once again reasons based chiefly on the general political situation were to lead Germany to show her ill-temper against France. The *Entente Cordiale* had continued to grow stronger ever since its establishment. The rulers of the two countries and their leading statesmen had exchanged visits, and the death of Edward VII in 1909 had in no way affected their cordial relations. Neither did the ousting of the Conservatives by the Liberals make any difference. Sir Edward Grey, who succeeded Lord Lansdowne at the Foreign Office, carried on the policy of his predecessor. This reserved, cold and correct " gentleman," who showed himself as little as possible in public, hid beneath a frigid exterior an ardent attachment to the interests of his country and to peace, and he was of opinion that the maintenance of intimate relations with France constituted one of the guarantees of peace.

As the friendship between England and France became stronger it could not fail to react upon the relations between Russia and **The Anglo-** England. After the Russo-Japanese War the **Russian** British Government had not the same reasons as **Agreement.** before for fearing the undue aggrandisement of Russia in Asia, and the idea occurred to it of concluding with the latter Empire a similar colonial agreement as that which had succeeded so well with France. French diplomacy did all in its power to encourage England in this direction, and Monsieur Iswolsky, who had become Minister of Foreign Affairs in Russia, was an enthusiastic supporter of an *entente* with her. During his long tenure of office in Copenhagen he had learned to know and respect the English. Negotiations were opened. They resulted in an agreement which settled matters almost everywhere in Asia—Persia, Afghanistan, Tibet and the Persian Gulf,

—which presented outstanding difficulties between the two countries (1907).

Like the *Entente Cordiale*, the Anglo-Russian agreement was bound to pass from the colonial to the European sphere. To balance the Triple Alliance there had now come into being another group to which the name of the Triple Entente was given.

Germany and above all the Kaiser did not fail to show their displeasure. In vain did the latter bring his personal influence **The Abortive** to bear upon the Tsar in an attempt to turn **Agreement of** Russia away from England and bring her back into **Björkö.** the wake of Germany. In 1905, towards the close of the Russo-Japanese War, he had met Nicholas II at Björkö on one of the fjords of Finland. Profiting by the irritation of the Tsar at the attitude of England, who was openly supporting Japan, he made him sign a treaty of alliance against England in which France was to be forced to join. Feeble and irresolute, the latter allowed his signature to be cajoled out of him. Later on, when his Ministers, whom he had failed to inform in the first instance, learnt of the affair, they had no difficulty in pointing out to him the grave dangers of this secret treaty, and the opposition it would provoke on the part of France, who would have just cause for complaint at not having been consulted. The Tsar, giving way to these arguments, informed William II that since the treaty had not been ratified by his Ministers, it must be considered void. Thus the efforts and intrigues of Germany ended in smoke.

After 1870, Bismarck's one object had been to keep France isolated in Europe. For a long time he succeeded, but he could not do so for ever. It would have been unreasonable to expect it.

Imbued with the Bismarckian principle that France was to stand alone in Europe, the leaders of Germany had come to regard as an act of defiance, almost of provocation against their country, the fact that France was seeking and finding allies and friends. The Triple Entente, from the moment of its inception, and as it became more firmly established, irritated them more and more.

The fear of themselves being isolated haunted the minds of the Germans and became an *idée fixe*. It developed into one of the main causes of the war. Germany never ceased openly to complain that she was surrounded by enemies—England, Russia and France—and that this was driving her to make formidable and overwhelming military preparations.

Were these complaints sincere or feigned? It is difficult to be certain. Did the leaders of Germany use them as a pretext to justify their rush to arms? The docility and credulity of the German people, who are like wax to receive any impression, led to this fear of isolation becoming an obsession which spread more and more among the masses. Thus Germany reached the sincere conviction that she was living in a world of enemies who were only awaiting an opportunity to hurl themselves against her. It never entered her mind that she herself had created this hostility by the brutality of her policy.

BIBLIOGRAPHY.—Pierre Loti, *Au Maroc*. André Chevrillon, *Un Crépuscule d'Islam* (1906). De la Martinière, *Souvenirs sur le Maroc* (1919). H. Gaillard, *Une Ville d'Islam, Fès* (1905). Eugène Aubin, *Le Maroc d'Aujourd'hui* (1904). Roud el Qartas (*Le Jardin des Feuillets*) (translated by Beaumier). A. Bernard, *Le Maroc* (4th ed.) (1916). Rouard de Card, *Documents Diplomatiques pour servir à l'Histoire de la Question Marocaine* (1911). Léon l'Africain, *Descriptions de l'Afrique* (translated by Ch. Scheffer). A. Tardieu, *La Conférence d'Algésiras* (1907). De Torcy, *France et Espagne au Maroc* (1909). Raymond Recouly, *La Guerre en Manchourie* (1905). *Le Tsar et le Douma* (1906). *Correspondance de Guillaume II et de Nicolas II* (1914–18). M. Baring, *With the Russians in Manchuria* (1905). Sir Ian Hamilton, *A Staff Officer's Scrap-book during the Russo-Japanese War* (London, 1905). Iswolsky, *Autour de l'Entrevue de Bjoerkoe*. A. Cheradame, *Le Monde et la Guerre Russo-Japonaise* (1906). V. Bérard, *La Révolte de l'Asie* (1905). A. Gérard, *Ma Mission en Chine et au Japon*. Comte Witte, *Mémoires*.

CHAPTER XVIII

THE STORM IN THE BALKANS

Austria a harlequin. Von Aerenthal puts fresh life into Austrian policy. The Young Turk *coup d'état*. Ferdinand of Bulgaria. The Austro-Bulgarian *coup*. *Quieta non movere*. Italy in Tripolitania. The Balkan agreements. On the verge of war.

A T the beginning of the twentieth century, Austria, in spite of an apparently constitutional and parliamentary system, was still governed as if she were under an absolute monarchy. There was a Parliament in Vienna and another in Budapest. But they were mills that generally had nothing to grind. The deputies, who were of different races and languages, debated and disputed and sometimes fought with each other without the Crown attaching much importance to their disagreements or their blows. The parliamentarians might do as they pleased, but the King-Emperor nearly always succeeded in governing without them.

Austria a Harlequin.

The Austrian Empire, which extended from Switzerland as far as the gates of the East, presented a strange and curious medley. There were the purely German provinces, the Tyrol, and Upper and Lower Austria; the territories in which the people and the language were Italian, the Trentino and the region of Trieste; the ancient Kingdom of Bohemia, which was almost entirely Slav; and next to the northern Slavs the southern Slavs of Dalmatia, and the province wrested from the Turks by the Congress of Berlin, Bosnia and Herzegovina, which was half Mussulman and half Slav.

In the Kingdom of Hungary the population was no less heterogeneous. In the centre, in the plains, and along the Danube and the Tisza, which is *par excellence* the river of Hun-

240

gary, there was a pure Magyar element. As the plain begins to rise in slight undulations on every side, north, south and east, different races make their appearance—Slovaks, Ruthenes, Roumanians in Transylvania, Serbs and Germans in the Banat, not to mention the Jews, who are more numerous here than anywhere else, flowing in an endless stream from the hills of Galicia to Budapest, "their capital," often called, not without reason, *Judapest*.

This multiplicity of races and diversity of peoples did not weaken the central power as much as might be supposed. There were powerful bonds uniting the vast assemblage, first and foremost among them the prestige and dignity of the Crown, which had remained as powerful as in the preceding century. Vienna and its magnificent palaces, the Hofburg, the old Emperor, who had occupied the throne for over fifty years, the etiquette and pomp of the Imperial Court, all acted as a magnet on these races and their leaders.

In addition to the Crown, the Army, organised on the German system, put all the recruits it raised as it were into the melting-pot, whilst the administration, which was excellent, with its solid cadres, and a whole host of traditions, also formed a powerful instrument of unification.

This empire in its entirety still held together fairly well, though only on condition that no external crisis, such as a war, supervened to shake it and put it out of balance. It was like the wall in the Archbishop's Palace described by Anatole France, which though tottering and on the point of collapsing, neverthe-less remained standing so long as no imprudent hand dared to touch it.

In 1906, in succession to Count Goluchowski, who was a great Polish nobleman, too indolent and careless to take any important initiative, which, for an Austrian diplomatist, was really the height of wisdom and sagacity, Baron von Aerenthal became Minister for Foreign Affairs. He had been Ambassador in St. Petersburg for a long time, both during and after the Russo-Japanese War. Well acquainted with Russia, he knew her weaknesses, and was aware that, hard hit as she was both at home and abroad, she

Von Aerenthal and Austrian Policy.

was not in a position to oppose an energetic policy on the part
of her rival Austria in the Balkans. The idea occurred to him
to profit by her embarrassment in order to increase the power
of Austria in such a way as to master the Serbs, who ever since
the bloody tragedy of Belgrade (1903) and their change of
dynasty had shown an ever-growing desire to escape from the
tutelage of Austria. The Revolution of the Young Turks came
in the nick of time, and provided him with the opportunity for
which he was waiting.

Turkey, even more than Austria, was an anachronism in
Europe at the beginning of the twentieth century. Her empire

The Young Turk Coup d'état. was still enormous, stretching from Macedonia to the Persian Gulf. The Sultan who ruled it exercised absolute and uncontrolled power. But her strength was more apparent than real, it was a survival from the past, a façade behind which there was very little.

Every Friday, Abdul Hamid went for the Selamlik to the
mosque near his palace, between a double row of Albanian
soldiers, who with their backs turned to him, raised loud cries
when the carriage of the Padishah and after it the whole host of
great dignitaries made their appearance. This typically Asiatic
spectacle might impress tourists and foreigners, but those who
lived in Constantinople and knew Turkey well were better aware
of her decrepitude. No one was more fully conscious of it than
the Sultan himself, the most interested party. He accordingly
took great care, in his wisdom and experience, to avoid any
crisis or war as long as he was master. He was fully aware
that a war, whatever its issue, could not but prove fatal to his
country.

Full of suspicion and mistrust, living in constant terror of
being the victim of the dagger, poison or some plot against his
life, he sent into exile in the depths of Macedonia any officers
whom he felt he could not trust. But it is sometimes extremely
imprudent to send suspicious characters too far away, as it is
impossible to exercise supervision over them. These officers
helped by a few officials belonging for the most part to old
Jewish families in Salonica who had turned Mussulman
organised, under cover of Freemasonry, a military plot which
was well laid and entirely successful.

242

THE STORM IN THE BALKANS

As soon as they felt they were masters of a part of the Army an ultimatum was sent to the Sultan demanding the immediate granting of a Constitution to his people. The Sultan, having no one to support him, was obliged to give way. The moment when the whole or a part of the Army rebels, nothing is easier to overthrow than an autocratic system. The Tsar of Russia was to have a similar experience during the war.

This *coup d'état* on the part of the Young Turks was at first greeted with enthusiasm by the Liberals of the West, both French and English, who little suspected that what is known as Liberalism is above all a question of latitude and longitude. They made the same mistake ten years later when Tsarism was overthrown. Certain Frenchmen thought it was a direct blow at German influence, which was all-powerful in the Turkey of Abdul Hamid. But they, too, soon sang a different tune.

The real aim of the Young Turk *coup d'état* was, as everybody soon realised, the victory of the Nationalist idea in Turkey.

Her immediate neighbours, the Balkan States, who all considered themselves as more or less her presumptive heirs, could not fail to be upset by this. But if the old man, who was sick unto death, suddenly changed his system of rule, their succession to the property would be retarded.

Hardly had they seized the reins of power than the Young Turks made a bad blunder which furnished certain of their neighbours with the pretext for which they were waiting.

They claimed, on extremely slender evidence, that they had the right of having deputies for the future National Assembly elected in countries over which, for some considerable period, Turkey had only exercised a nominal sovereignty—Bosnia and Herzegovina and Eastern Roumelia. It was hardly to be expected that the Austrians and Bulgarians would find this claim to their taste.

In Vienna, von Aerenthal thought the moment had come for putting fresh life into Austrian policy in the Balkans, which he considered had become somewhat slack, and came to an agreement with Sofia. He had no difficulty in converting Ferdinand, who had been champing his bit for a long time, chafing at the thought that he was only a Prince Regnant instead of a King like all the others.

THE THIRD REPUBLIC

Among the prominent figures of our day, Ferdinand of Bulgaria, on account of his curious personality, his scheming temperament and the crookedness of his character and policy, has won a place of his own.

Ferdinand of Bulgaria.

A descendant of the House of Coburg, which, during the course of the nineteenth century, supplied many reigning princes for various countries in Europe, Ferdinand, while still a young man, responded to the appeal of certain Bulgarian statesmen who, after the melodramatic deposition of Alexander of Battenberg, scoured the capitals of Europe, like Diogenes, in search of a man who would deign to rule over them. He left Vienna almost like a fugitive, with considerable difficulty eluding the Austrian police, who wanted to nip his adventure in the bud. But he was urged on by a strong ambition which constituted the dominant characteristic of his nature.

The Crown, or rather the semi-Crown he was offered, however, was not a particularly tempting bait. The fate of his predecessor should have inspired him with serious doubts. How would he get on among the rough, uncouth Danubian peasants, who loved conspiracy and had no hesitation in taking violent action? How was he to manœuvre his way between Austria, who would never cease to remind him of his origin, and Russia, who had been accustomed to regard Bulgaria, which was entirely her creation, as her vassal?

Like the bat in the fable, Ferdinand turned, as necessity required, first to the one and then to the other. He had no hesitation in knocking at the door of each, and sometimes at both at once, and having two strings to his bow. He went even further. A grandson of Louis-Philippe through his mother, the Princess Clementine, who, as long as she was alive, exercised an active influence in his favour, he never failed whenever he met Frenchmen to remind them that the blood of their kings flowed in his veins.

In order to curry favour with the Russians, he decided to make his eldest son a member of the Orthodox Church, in spite of the fact that he had entered into a solemn agreement with his first wife, a Princess of Parma, who was a devout Catholic, to have him baptised in the Church of Rome. But with him promises were like pie-crusts. His wife, when she learnt of his decision, directly after her confinement, was so furious that she threw a cup of boiling broth at her husband's head. The writer of these lines was told this story by a relative of the Princess herself.

Proud of his physical resemblance to Francis I, Ferdinand, who should have lived at the time of the Renaissance, had a pathological love of flowers and rare birds, as well as of precious stones, which he delighted to handle, and had them placed in a bowl always within reach. His complicated, tortuous nature was in many ways reminiscent of one of the characters in Huysmann's celebrated novel *A rebours*. There was one great desire that obsessed his mind—some day to make a solemn entry into Constantinople and to be crowned Emperor in the basilica of St. Sophia.

When Austria annexed Bosnia and Herzegovina, Ferdinand broke the last bonds that bound Bulgaria to Turkey and, pro-

The Austro-Bulgarian Coup. claiming his independence, arrogated to himself the title of Tsar.

These two events, which were of the greatest importance, since they changed the established state of affairs in the Balkans, the *powder-magazine of Europe*, were quite unexpected and took everybody by surprise.

The Serbs were the first who felt that they were menaced, and took no trouble to hide their discontent and fury. The two provinces that had become definitely joined to Austria were peopled chiefly by members of the Serbian race.

In Russia also the fire of resentment burned hot and fierce. Government circles and public opinion were on the side of Serbia. Had Monsieur Iswolsky, Minister for Foreign Affairs, during his interview with von Aerenthal been warned by the latter of the inevitability of this annexation? Had he allowed his consent to be more or less dragged from him? He ardently denied the suggestion later on. At all events the Russian Government quickly made it known that it did not regard the annexation of Bosnia as a *casus belli*. This would have meant throwing down her cards too soon. Whatever it might have said or done later on, Austria was well aware that she was running no risk. Von Aerenthal had been right. He found his enemy disarmed. He accordingly met the Russian proposal that an International Conference should be summoned to examine the whole Balkan question with a blank refusal. He would not hear of it at any price. In vain did Russia insist; her efforts were bound to result in a failure commensurate with the ardour of her desire to secure it.

As the Serbs, mistakenly thinking that they had the support of Russia, increased their agitations, Austria and Germany decided one fine day to have done with the matter. Pourtalès, the German Ambassador in St. Petersburg, adopted a determined, not to say threatening attitude towards Russia, informing her that if she did not definitely abandon the idea of a conference, Germany would leave Austria, who was only awaiting the signal, free to punish the Serbs. This step closed the incident. Much the same attitude was adopted six years later, in 1914, when Pourtalès again warned Russia, under threat of retaliation, not to interfere, but to allow Austria to settle her differences with Serbia single-handed.

This crisis bore within it—and it was this that endowed it with grave significance—the seeds of other far graver crises. The imprudent, not to say foolhardy, spirit of the Viennese leaders, who instinctively introduced questions of prestige into everything, was here made abundantly clear. Russia, disorganised by the Russo-Japanese War and threats of revolution at home, on this occasion bowed her head; but she would not always do so. And when the day came that she refused, the worst complications were to be feared.

Quieta non movere is a motto which applies most aptly to the Balkans. As soon as an attempt is made to change the existing

Quieta non movere. equilibrium, however unstable it may be, complications are sure to arise of which it is impossible to measure the extent. And this was true in the case of the steps taken by Austria and Bulgaria.

In foreseeing the consequences of his move, von Aerenthal had judged aright. Nevertheless, it is possible that he did not foresee quite all, for it was from this moment that the antagonism between Austria and Serbia in its most acute form was to grow more and more desperate as time went by, until it became one of the main causes of the war. Irritated by what they considered an act of provocation, a piece of impertinence, Austro-Hungarian military circles talked of mobilising a few army corps

246

in order to go and chastise Serbia, that nation of pork-butchers, as she was commonly termed in Vienna and Budapest.

From that time forward, whenever the situation became strained, or any incident occurred, the Austrian staff got into the habit of having recourse to military measures, and reinforcing the troops on the frontier. But all such measures cost dear, and the day arrived when they grew tired of continually threatening but never striking, and of brandishing the sword without using it. And on that day they proceeded to take active measures at the risk of provoking a catastrophe.

When France, after the Agadir incident in 1911, took steps to organise her protectorate over Morocco, the Italian Government, in order to maintain the balance of power in the Mediterranean, also made up its mind to claim possession of the rights in Tripolitania accorded to them by England and France.

Italy in Tripolitania.

Their allies, Germany and Austria, not only took no steps to dissuade them from the scheme, but even encouraged them, in the hope that Italy, who would thus be occupied for a long time by the African expedition, would have her attention diverted from Albania and the Balkans.

The Italian army occupied Tripoli and the coast fairly easily. But as soon as it became a matter of penetrating inland, obstacles of all kinds arose. Turkish officers arrived to organise the natives, who offered a most stubborn resistance to the advance of the Italians. The latter now found themselves obliged to make a far greater military effort than the Government in Rome had anticipated; hence their irritation and ill-humour. Many Italians suspected that the resistance offered by their adversaries was fostered by a contraband trade in arms, and help from Tunisia. Two French steamers, *Le Carthage* and *La Manouba*, were stopped by Italian torpedo boats and searched (January 1912). The incident aroused considerable excitement, which Monsieur Barrère, the French Ambassador in Rome, was fortunately able to calm, though it did not fail to leave its mark on the relations of the two countries.

Thus the Austro-Bulgarian proceedings of 1908, together with the Italian expedition of 1911-12, meant that within the space of a few years two blows had been struck at Turkey, the latter being much more serious than the former, since it deprived her of a fairly vast tract of land which she had long held in full sovereignty. But it was to have other important consequences. The Austrians and Bulgarians had taken the first bite in 1908. But what they took was after all only what they already in fact possessed. But three years later Italy cut off a slice of the cake, and encouraged by her example the young Balkan nations, Bulgaria, Serbia, Greece and Montenegro, showed their teeth and made ready to pounce upon the enemy.

Scarcely was Italy's declaration of war against Turkey made known than Monsieur Guéchoff, the Bulgarian Prime Minister, who happened to be at Vichy, cut short his cure, and took the train to Paris, where he stopped a few hours (the 4th of October, 1911). Here he had an interview with Monsieur de Selves, the Minister for Foreign Affairs. In Vienna he met two of his colleagues, and drew up a memorandum, sketching the outlines of an alliance with Serbia in view of the eventual partition of Macedonia, to which he obtained the sanction of King Ferdinand. When he arrived in Belgrade he held a consultation with Monsieur Milanovitch, the Minister for Foreign Affairs. In the course of a discussion lasting several hours, the two statesmen tried to reach an agreement.

The Balkan Agreements.

But this was no easy matter. It reminds one of Charles V's famous words : " My cousin Francis I and I are in agreement with regard to Milan. He wants to take it and so do I." It was an agreement of this nature that the Serbs and Bulgarians were endeavouring to reach. The negotiations were long and difficult, necessitating much discussion and bargaining, " bazarlik " as they say in the East. Macedonia was divided into several portions, and the territories in dispute were hotly contested. At last, on the 7th of March, 1912, a preliminary agreement was signed, and a week later the treaty was concluded at Sofia and supplemented by a military convention between the two Army staffs.

From the very beginning the Russian Government had been kept informed of these transactions. Its agents in the Balkans did everything in their power to smooth over differences and facilitate a solution. On the 1st of April, Monsieur Iswolsky, the Russian Ambassador in Paris, notified the French Government of the agreement, by which, he said, the *status quo* in the Balkans would be maintained, and the two signatories also promised to take no steps without the consent of Russia.

Thus it is impossible to maintain, as some have done, that Russian diplomacy entirely concealed this important event from its ally.

Nevertheless, Russia only revealed half the truth. The arrangement, as a matter of fact, had a very different object in view than the mere maintenance of the *status quo* and a promise of mutual assistance. It provided for the eventual partition of Macedonia, which was certainly a strange way of respecting the established order. Russia, it is true, was to be consulted by the sharers in the spoil, and was at liberty to impose her veto. But was this anything more than a flourish of words? Certain indiscretions let slip by a Russian diplomatist, the *chargé d'affaires* in Sofia, pointed to the fact that Russia might very well only be consulted after the step had been taken, and would merely be presented with the accomplished fact.

Whilst he was carrying on negotiations with Serbia, Monsieur Guéchoff, encouraged by his initial success, did not remain inactive with regard to the Greeks. On the 29th of May, 1912, he came to an arrangement with them, and in September a military convention was concluded. Montenegro remained. Here too diplomatic negotiations were energetically pursued. By a strange irony of fate, it was during the course of a visit paid by the King of Montenegro to the Emperor of Austria, under the very roof of the Hofburg, that the representatives of Bulgaria and Montenegro drafted the terms of their alliance, the consequences of which, as time was to prove, were to cause Austria so much annoyance.

Thus the close web of diplomatic agreements, of which the secret was extremely well kept, was completed. The young Balkan States, the heirs of Turkey, had arranged among themselves to enter upon their heritage as quickly as possible. If the " sick man," whose property they were waiting to share, made up his mind of his own accord to pass from life to death, well and good. But if life persisted, and he made his heirs wait too long, the latter, who were in a hurry, would not hesitate to hasten the end.

They had strength on their side, and were well aware of it. Since the military arrangements had been made in the nick of time to complete the diplomatic agreements, they felt certain of getting the better of Turkey. They also knew that the Great Powers, always slow to move and divided into two conflicting groups, would lose time in palavers and negotiations, and would not be in a position to intervene effectively in order to prevent war, when once it had been declared.

Russia, moved more by public opinion than by her Government, upheld the pretensions of the Balkan States, and was not sorry to have her revenge in this way on Austria for the affair of 1908, in which her rival had had the last word.

The events which took place in Turkey during the summer of 1912—the mutiny of the garrison in Adrianople and the rising **War in the** in Albania—furnished the necessary pretext, and **Balkans** demonstrations were held in Sofia, Athens and **Imminent.** Belgrade, more or less encouraged by the respective Governments. On the 14th of August, Count Berchtold proposed the decentralisation of the Turkish administration in Europe. On the 25th of August there was a meeting in Sofia of the charitable organisations of Macedonia and Adrianople. Just as Bulgaria, Serbia and Greece were preparing to act, an emissary from the King of Montenegro arrived in Sofia to arrange for concerted action. Feeling that he might have much to gain, the monarch of Tchernagore insisted upon taking part in it. He placed his conditions in the hands of his future allies to take or to leave, and they accepted them.

They were all agreed as to the necessity for immediate action, and the date for the attack was fixed. It was like the Great War, when the exact moment when the troops were to leave the trenches was arranged beforehand. But the Montenegrin Government was too impatient to wait. It anticipated the date and advanced single-handed, declaring war on Turkey on the 8th of October, a few days before the time decided upon for a joint declaration.

It has been maintained, not without good reason, that this

sudden blow, which by its very unexpectedness took public opinion in Europe by surprise, was used as a cloak for a Stock Exchange deal, the results of which were extremely profitable for the participants, and enabled them to pocket a few millions from the Paris and Vienna markets. The operation was carried out apparently through the agency of an Austrian financier living in Paris, a certain Rozenberg, whose name was connected two years later with the scandal of the Rochette case.

As always in human affairs, tragedy and comedy went hand in hand. The old Montenegrin patriarch, king of a country hardly larger than a county, and, moreover, poor and barren as the mountains of the moon, presented a curious spectacle. Father-in-law of the King of Italy, and of two Russian Grand Dukes, a gifted schemer who knew very well how to guide his bark between the jealousies of his powerful neighbours, with one hand he knocked at the door or rather on the coffers of Vienna, while the other was held wide open to St. Petersburg.

BIBLIOGRAPHY.—B. Auerbach, *Les Races et les Nationalités en Autriche-Hongrie*. H. Wickham Steed, *The Hapsburg Monarchy* (1913). Raymond Recouly, *Le Pays Magyar* (1903). René Henri, *Question d'Autriche et Question d'Orient, des Monts de Bohême au Golfe Persique* (1908). V. Bérard, *La Révolution Turque* (1909). G. Gaulis, *La Question d'Orient* (1903). Krusky, *L'Annexion de la Bosnie en 1908* (1912). A. Gauvain, *L'Europe au Jour le Jour* (6 vols.). R. Pinon, *L'Europe et la Jeune Turquie*. Magafir, *Notes sur la Jeune Turquie* (1911). Feld Marschal Conrad von Hoetzendorf, *Aus Meiner Dienstzeit* (4 vols., 1922–23). R. Poincaré, *Les Origines de la Guerre* (1921); *Au Service de la France* (3 vols., 1926). *The Black Book* (Russian document published by the Soviets), French translation (1921). Iswolsky, *Mémoires* (1920). *Livre Jaune* (*Les Affaires Balkaniques*). Guéchoff, *L'Alliance Balkanique* (1915). E. Laloy, *Documents Secrets du Ministère Russe* (1919). H. de Weindel, *François-Joseph Intime* (1905). Alexandre Hepp, *Ferdinand de Bulgarie Intime* (1910). Balkanicus, *La Bulgarie, ses Ambitions, sa Trahison* (1913). Bellessort, *La Roumanie Contemporaine* (1912). Boucabelle, *La Guerre Turco-Balkanique en 1912* (1913).

CHAPTER XIX

FRANCE, GERMANY AND THE BALKANS

The *Panther* at Agadir. France again gives way. Caillaux.
Difficulties of the negotiations. Mutual discontent. Germany's
armaments. The French reply. What the Kaiser confided to
the King of the Belgians. The Balkan Wars, the prelude to the
Great War.

THE AGADIR CRISIS

ON Saturday the 1st of July, 1911, the German Ambassador
in Paris visited the Quai d'Orsay in order to make an
exceedingly unexpected communication.

It is curious to note that it was preferably towards the end
of the week on a Friday or a Saturday, that Germany, or her
ally Austria, hurled their diplomatic bombshells.
For on Saturday morning, and sometimes sooner
in the summer, English statesmen leave their
offices for the sacred *week-end* holiday, which nothing in the
world, even the destruction of the universe (*si fractus illabatur
orbis*) would induce them to forgo. During the whole of this
interval diplomatic communication between England and
France is practically broken off.

The Ambassador announced that, owing to disturbances in
the south of Morocco, his Government found itself obliged to
send a gunboat with all speed to Agadir.

There was great excitement in the Chancelleries. The trouble
in Sous demanding the protection of German interests was
clearly only a pretext. And indeed nobody was deceived by it.
Germany in 1911 was repeating her action of 1905. The gunboat for Agadir was merely a repetition of the Kaiser's landing
at Tangier. It was as much general political considerations as
anything connected with Morocco, if not more so, that led

252

Germany to take this high-handed measure. Once again it was a question of making France feel her dependence, and proving to her that her *Entente* with England and Spain would be of no avail as long as she had not come to an understanding with Germany, and in order to obtain full liberty of action had paid her some sort of ransom.

The attitude of the German Press, and certain articles implying that the Wilhelmstrasse would demand compensation in the Congo in return for waiving all claims in Morocco, clearly indicated that it was towards some such negotiation or bargain that France was to be driven.

What was France to do? Resist and risk the danger of war, or give way?

France again gives Way. Once again France gave way. Instead of sending a gunboat to Agadir, as she might have done, to keep watch over the German ship, she resigned herself to negotiate, and paid the ransom.

On the German side the Agadir surprise was planned, prepared and carried out under the direction of Kiderlen-Waechter, who, two years previously, had succeeded von Schön at the Wilhelmstrasse.

This southern German, this bantering, sneering Swabian, had, at the beginning of his career, accompanied the Kaiser on his voyages and kept him amused by his jokes. His letters show how disrespectfully he spoke of the " old Queen " (Queen Victoria), of " fat Wales " (the Prince of Wales), and of the " oxen " (the English) during his stay for Regatta Week at Cowes.

Having fallen into disgrace on account of his private life—an old liaison which shocked the narrow-minded prudery of the Empress—he had been left, for a long time as Minister in Bucharest. His energy and intelligence, however, eventually succeeded in impressing his chiefs, the German diplomatic service being notoriously lacking in men of distinction.

Brought up on Bismarckian traditions and methods, a great worker, and a realist endowed with great vigour and clarity of mind, he thought that Germany ought to claim her place in the sun, assert her power and have her rights respected.

253

He argued that since England, in exchange for non-existent rights in Morocco—for after all she had no shadow of claim on that country—had claimed from France compensation in Egypt, why should not Germany, who was quite as powerful, also obtain satisfaction? Why should she not also have her reward?

Such was the attitude adopted by Kiderlen-Waechter out of which the Agadir incident arose. When once he had embarked upon the enterprise he insisted on its being energetically pursued to the end without allowing any qualm to stand in his path, and in his opinion the only way to force France to give way was to make her understand that she ran very grave risks in holding out.

But he was also anxious—and this is very important—that Germany should cease from pursuing a policy of provocation and pin-pricks against her neighbour. Whenever vital interests were not at stake she should, on the contrary, endeavour to live on the best of terms with France. Above all, care should be taken in connection with the Balkan problem not to allow Austria to dictate to the Triple Alliance. Nothing could be more dangerous than this, for Austria, as he maintained, and he was not far wrong, was led by incompetent chiefs.

If Kiderlen-Waechter, who, although he was still comparatively young, was laid low with apoplexy in the following year, had been in power in 1914, it is possible that events might have followed a different course.

In France, the President of the Council was Joseph Caillaux, and it was he who conducted the negotiations over the head of **Caillaux.** the Foreign Office. The son of a former Minister of the 16th of May, a member of a well-to-do bourgeois family, an Inspector of Finances, deputy for the Sarthe district, and Finance Minister in the Waldeck-Rousseau Ministry, Caillaux had moved very quickly to the Left and become one of the leaders of the Radical party. Endowed with quickness of intellect and extraordinary vivacity and mobility of mind, with a capacity for changing his direction at a moment's notice, impetuous and daring and a born fighter (as he proved in all the various parts he played), lacking in balance and equilibrium, with a lively taste for intrigue in every shape and form, and an absence of discernment regarding the men about him, Caillaux, in whom the financier outweighed the diplomat, considered that France could and ought to find the basis for a colonial and economic agreement with Germany, and that it was essential to her interests to do so. In his opinion the advantages to be gained by securing the consent of Germany to French policy in Morocco would provide ample compensation for the abandonment of a few stretches of land in the Congo.

There was much to be said for this idea. Indeed from the moment it was decided not to hold out against Germany, but to enter into negotiations, it was necessary to bring the discussion to a satisfactory conclusion under the best possible conditions.

The mistake that Caillaux made was to use devious and underhand ways and means, for which he always had a secret preference, and to employ more or less unqualified emissaries, often without the knowledge of the official agents of his country.

One day the author of the present work called upon him at the Ministry of the Interior, in the Place Beauveau, and was told : " If you want information, for heaven's sake don't go to the Quai d'Orsay, where they are a pack of mediocrities and snobs who will tell you nothing because they know nothing."

It was this spirit that led him to negotiate directly, without the knowledge of the Quai d'Orsay or of Monsieur Jules Cambon, the French Ambassador, with Baron Lancken, adviser to the German Embassy in Paris. But a telegram from Lancken, in which he gave details of his conversation with Caillaux and the promises made by the latter, was deciphered by the Foreign Minister, and provided proof of these transactions. This was the affair of the " *documents verts*." When an inquiry regarding this agreement was held by a senatorial Commission, Monsieur Caillaux nevertheless maintained, though nobody had asked him (he was involved up to the hilt), that he had never engaged in any secret negotiation. Whereupon Clemenceau, like the gifted fencer he was, immediately called upon Monsieur de Selves to confirm this declaration. On the latter refusing to do so, Caillaux, openly convicted of misstatement, sent in his resignation and thus brought about the fall of the whole Ministry.

As is always the case in any discussions with Germany, the negotiations were difficult and strained. They were prolonged **Difficulty of** for forty days in the middle of a stifling **the** summer, one of the hottest that Paris has ever **Negotiations.** known.

As soon as a decision seemed to have been reached, some fresh claim on the part of Germany put everything once more into the melting-pot, and in August and September there were a few critical days when war loomed on the horizon. According to information received after the event, the German leaders apparently seem to have contemplated this, and it was chiefly financial considerations, and the opinion in banking circles that the country was not prepared to bear the expense of recourse to arms, which decided them against it. England in the most uncompromising terms (speech of Lloyd George, at that time Chancellor of the Exchequer, in the Guildhall on the 21st of July, 1911) let it be known that she would support France.

After lengthy discussions an agreement was eventually reached, and Germany, in exchange for allowing France the protectorate of Morocco, obtained a territory of 171,875 square miles in the Congo. The French Parliament, without the smallest enthusiasm, ratified this arrangement, the deputies for the East abstaining from voting.

As is often the case with unwilling bargains, one side thought it had given too much, and the other that it had received too **Mutual** little, so that, far from being improved, the rela- **Discontent.** tions between the two countries only became more embittered. In France it now became obvious, even to the most confirmed pacifists, that Germany's attitude must inevitably sooner or later lead to war. Twice at least during the six years, from 1905 to 1911, Germany had sought a quarrel with France and forced her to give in. *But she could not continue to give in for ever.*

In Germany, moreover, the Agadir incident caused considerable excitement and exercised a disastrous influence, and in Nationalist circles no effort was made to hide their discontent and indignation. The Government was subjected to the severest criticism, and accused of having made a fool's bargain in handing over Morocco to France (as if Morocco belonged to

Germany) in exchange for what was dubbed a few stretches of marsh land in the Congo. France, it was maintained, derived all the moral and material advantages of the treaty, whilst the prestige of Germany had suffered a severe blow.

These grievances were aired at full length in the papers, and conveyed to the Reichstag when the treaty was discussed. In one of the galleries the Crown Prince in uniform and certain princes of the Imperial House might have been seen frantically applauding the orators who denounced the agreement. This state of mind spread from the ruling classes to the mass of the public, and its effects were soon seen. The fact that Germany had not received greater advantages was due, it was maintained, to the insufficiency of her forces. It was necessary for her to speak more loudly for her voice to be heard. Hence the necessity of increasing the army without delay.

As soon as this decision was taken, the Army, which was still all-powerful, the Government and Parliament hastened to secure the increase of the forces. *In less than three years* (end of 1911 to 1914) Germany did more for the aggrandisement of her military power than during *the whole of the preceding twenty*.

Germany's Armaments.

Here are a few details that cannot be disputed. In 1911 the Imperial Government had passed its quinquennial military estimate providing for a slight increase in the Army. Everybody thought it would be satisfied with that, as had been asserted when the Bill was passed by the Reichstag. But in March 1912 there was a fresh increase four times greater than that of the preceding year—namely, 37,000 combatants, being two supplementary army corps, one on the French, the other on the Russian frontier, with full complement of auxiliary services—Commissariat, Engineers, etc. Lastly, and this is of supreme importance, the increase, instead of being spread over a period of several years, as had always been the case previously, was to be carried out in a few months, before the 1st of October, 1912.

In order to explain the reasons for this increase and haste, General von Heeringen, the Minister of War, expressed himself before the tribunal of the Reichstag with characteristic military candour :

s

" The experience of last year (Agadir)," he said, " has proved to us that our army has not been sufficiently increased."

But was Germany going to be content now? Certainly not. Ten months later, in 1913, she proceeded to fresh and even more extraordinary armaments. After the increase of 40,000 men in 1912 she arranged for 1913 an increase of 80,000 men, together with another 80,000 for 1914, that is to say, 160,000 in all. At the end of 1913 Germany's active forces would consist of 800,000 to France's 500,000. In 1914 it would be, compared with the French army, in the proportion of 17 to 10, that is, almost two to one.

In order to raise the money required for this huge increase, a milliard marks (£50,000,000), the Government, on the initiative, it is asserted, of the Kaiser himself, decided to have recourse to exceptional taxation, *a regular war tax*, to be levied on all fortunes above twenty thousand marks (£1000).

In the face of measures such as these, which Germany had not adopted since 1870, France, in spite of the pacific tendencies of her leaders, was forced, unless she wished to sign her own death-warrant, to put herself in a state of defence. On the downfall of the Caillaux Ministry, Raymond Poincaré took up the reins of power, and from President of the Council and Foreign Minister he became, in February 1913, President of the Republic.

The French Reply.

A level-headed native of Lorraine, with a mind gifted for detail and precision, cousin of the famous mathematician Henri Poincaré, a great lawyer and a giant for work, he has no rival in the art of sifting and solving the most intricate problems. A lover of order and method, he prefers written notes to conversations, as they have the advantage of leaving nothing in obscurity, and of avoiding confusion and misunderstanding. The alertness and rapid working of his mind, which is always on the *qui vive*, and the absolute reliability of his memory are phenomenal.

The need for precision and clarity, a sense of equity, whether in dealing with home or foreign affairs, a passionate love for his country, to whom he has once and for all dedicated his activities, and his very existence, intellectual and moral uprightness,

258

absolute disinterestedness, regulating the material side of his life by means of a strict and meticulous discipline, and under an apparently cold and somewhat distant reserve hiding a deep fund of good-nature and fidelity to friends, and perhaps also a certain timidity—such are the dominant characteristics, the rare qualities of his nature.

It would have been impossible during the critical years before and during the war to have had at the head of the country a better balanced, sounder or more stable personality. Indeed to anyone who knows him or has had anything to do with him, nothing is more incomprehensible and absurd than the accusations that have sometimes been brought against him, the charge of " Poincaré the war-lord ! " If ever there was a man who by nature and temperament had a horror of war, it is certainly Poincaré !

France, on account of the sparseness of her population, not possessing, as Germany did, a superabundance of conscripts, had only one resource open to her if she wished quickly to catch up the advance her formidable neighbour was about to make—and that was to revive the system of three years' military service. Upheld and encouraged by the Government, public opinion turned towards this solution with ever-increasing insistence. Significant proofs of this were given in almost every direction both in Paris and in the provinces. The supreme War Council, when consulted on the subject, declared itself unanimously in favour of it. The Cabinet adopted it, and the Government, in spite of the opposition of the Socialists, had the measure passed in Parliament.

It was not, as may well be imagined, an easy matter to carry through. For a democratic and constitutionally governed country, in which parliamentarism was everything and opinions were very advanced, to abrogate a measure which was regarded as final, the law of two years' military service, and to increase this period of service by a whole year, must have seemed an almost impossible task. Nevertheless, the impossible was achieved. Fortunately at this juncture the country had as President of the Council Monsieur Louis Barthou, a vigorous and resolute native of Béarn, who spared himself no pains to

secure the passing of this salutary measure. He put his whole
energy and resource into the matter, and by sheer dint of determination and spirit, giving a vigorous hoist of the shoulder
every time the cart became stuck in the mud, at last succeeded
in having the measure passed.

Thus Barthou, who has sometimes been depicted by his
enemies as a calculating and extremely shrewd man, threw
himself eagerly and without hesitation into the thick of the fray,
and succeeded in accomplishing a regular *tour de force*, and
carrying through, after an interminable discussion, lasting three
months, in which he was opposed by some of the Radicals and
all the Socialists, an indispensable measure of reform without
which the war would probably have been lost.

The passing of the measure, as the newspapers of the day
bear witness, filled Germany with astonishment which soon
developed into fury. Many Germans refused to believe that
their rivals were capable of such a sacrifice. Thus the trouble
they had taken to outdistance them once and for all was pure
loss; the lead they hoped to have secured had been wiped out.
Hence arose a burning hatred of France which no effort was any
longer made to conceal, many Germans regarding the re-establishment of the system of three years' military service as little short
of an act of provocation on the part of France.

If the causes of the war are to be understood, it is essential
to bear in mind that the attitude of a large number of Germans
may be described as follows : Germany was to have the right to
take all the diplomatic and military measures which she regarded
as indispensable for her security, but when her adversaries
retaliated with similar measures, she might complain and
protest as if she were about to be attacked.

From this time forward signs of the coming storm, some of
them extremely grave, became ever more frequent. A certain
military order connected with immediate preparations, the
necessity for an offensive, and the advantages to be derived
from a victory regarded as certain fell into the hands of the
French War Office in March 1913.

But the following was an even more alarming incident. In
November of the same year, during an official visit of the King

of the Belgians to Berlin, William II, taking his guest aside, informed him that war was inevitable and close at hand. **What the** He declared that he was certain of victory on **Kaiser Confided** account of the superiority of his army. **to the King of** In order to give further weight to these state-**the Belgians.** ments they were repeated to the King of the Belgians by von Moltke, the head of the German Staff.

These confidences, which were immediately communicated by the Belgians to Jules Cambon, the French Ambassador in Berlin, had a twofold object—to sound the attitude of the Belgian leaders and find out how they reacted, and also to deprive them in advance of any desire to intervene in a struggle the issue of which could not be in doubt. It was after this conversation that Jules Cambon sent his famous telegram of the 22nd of November to Paris. We will quote it in full, for it will ever remain one of his titles to glory.

As years begin to weigh heavily on William II, family traditions, the reactionary feelings of the Court, and above all military influence gain ever greater ascendancy over him. Possibly he is moved by a certain jealousy of the popularity won by his son, who flatters the passions of the Pan-Germans and considers that the position of the German Empire in the world is not commensurate with her power. Possibly France's reply to the last increase in the German army, the object of which was to place the superiority of Germany above dispute, also has something to do with his bitterness, for, whatever may be said to the contrary, one feels that things cannot go on as they are much longer.

It was during 1913, after the moral victory of Agadir, when the Prussian Headquarters Staff was increasing armaments at all possible speed, that William II reached the turning-point and definitely decided in favour of war. Among the motives which determined him there were many, if one can judge him aright, which belong to the lowest category—theatricality and the tenor's jealousy of the Crown Prince, who, in Nationalist and Chauvinist circles, was beginning to rob him of his popularity.

His own father, who, for his part, was a gentleman, had summed him up only too well at a very early age when he passed the terrible verdict upon him which we have already quoted.

In 1905 and again in 1911, Germany had meditated war against France of which Morocco would have been the pretext. But on neither of these two occasions did she feel herself sufficiently prepared either morally or materially for the conflict. It was afterwards that she decided upon having recourse to arms. Wedged in between France and Russia, she was obliged to rely upon her ally, Austria-Hungary, and to bind her to her body and soul in the struggle. But Austria, however dependent she was on Berlin, would certainly never have supported her whole-heartedly over Morocco, in which she had not the slightest interest. It was therefore necessary to find some other pretext for war, some vital question, or one that was considered vital to Austria. And this was found in the Balkans.

. . . .

After the agreement of Agadir, France, who had now secured freedom of action in Morocco, established a protectorate which was officially recognised on the 30th of March, 1912, by the Sultan Moulay Hafid. It was largely modelled on the French system already established in Tunis. As in the case of the latter, a Resident-General represented the protecting Power at the Sultan's Court, and had the control of most of the services. This elastic system, which had stood the test of time, allowed the spiritual and moral power of the Sultan to remain untouched and interfered as little as possible with the structure of Mussulman society.

In April 1912 a general uprising of the Tobors, the native troops, took place in Fez, and a number of French instructors were murdered. An expedition was sent to relieve the capital of the Cherif, and Moulay Hafid abdicated in favour of Moulay Ioussef, with whom France has since had no difficulty.

The next task was to conquer and pacify the greater part of the country with the smallest possible number of troops, in order not to deplete the Army of the mother country more than was absolutely necessary—a difficult undertaking indeed. In order to bring it to a successful issue, France fortunately had to hand one of her best colonial servants, a man who combined the qualities of a great administrator with those of a great soldier—Lyautey.

Like Poincaré, Lyautey was a native of Lorraine, a member of a family of high officials and soldiers (his great-grandfather had been a general in one of Napoleon's armies). When he was a young captain, an article he wrote for the *Revue des Deux Mondes* on the moral obligations of an officer had already attracted attention. Long sojourns in the colonies—Indo-China and Madagascar—where he was a disciple of Gallieni, had accustomed him to dealing with colonial matters. When he was sent to Algeria, in command of the Oran division, it was towards the frontier of Morocco and Morocco itself that his attention and activities were turned.

By the time the Government appointed him Commander-in-Chief of the troops, Lyautey was in possession of a technique and a doctrine which he was destined to bring to perfection on the spot and to put into practice for many a long year. This doctrine, based on a deep understanding of the Mussulman soul and character, consisted in using force " in order to be able to do without it," and in filling the minds of the natives with a profound respect for the protecting Power, and whilst safeguarding their rights, their traditions, their beliefs and their social system, making them understand that life is better and more agreeable in a civilised and peaceful country, where every man is at liberty to enjoy what he has, than in a land given up to anarchy and plunder. The natives did not take long to realise these advantages.

As for Lyautey's military theories, which more than once brought him into conflict with the Headquarters Staff, who were instinctively inclined to centralise everything, they were founded on the belief that colonial operations, unlike wars in Europe, required different strategy and tactics and more supple units than the army in France. In addition to the commander of a column there was a political chief who knew the regions and the tribes among whom operations were taking place and was ever on the watch for an opportunity of supporting the military manœuvres by means of political action.

THE THIRD REPUBLIC

The application of these methods yielded excellent results. But Lyautey had hardly begun the work of pacification (Taza was only captured in 1914, thus definitely opening up communications between Algeria and Morocco) when the Great War broke out and put his whole system to the touchstone.

In spite of the instructions of the Government, who, in order to recall the greater part of his troops immediately to France, asked him to evacuate the interior of the country and to retreat with his columns to the coast, Lyautey, realising that such an evacuation would be a catastrophe giving rise to a general insurrection, and would hand over the country to fire and sword, undertook, even with an exceedingly small army of occupation, consisting chiefly of territorials who replaced the regular units, to maintain order throughout the country. He was better than his word, for, though the war was in full swing, he contrived to extend the zone of occupation very considerably.

At once an administrator and a soldier, carrying his activities into every branch of life, building railways, roads and ports, careful, for the first time in the annals of French colonial history, to preserve artistic treasures and safeguard the picturesqueness and local colour of the native cities (he forbade European houses to be built in the middle of the old towns), developing trade, industry and colonisation, and patronising a large number of French enterprises, Lyautey was in the strictest sense of the word an inspirer. He took short cuts, and accomplished in ten years what would otherwise have taken half a century to secure.

" Blithe and joyous "; these epithets might well have been applied to the Balkan Wars (October 1912). With concerted **The Balkan** action and irresistible impulse all the Balkan **Wars, the** Christians hurled themselves against the Turk, **Prelude to the** their hereditary enemy and oppressor, who stag- **Great War.** gered and soon fell beneath the onslaught.

Admirably organised and trained, the Bulgarian army accomplished marvels. Manœuvring in accordance with a well-conceived strategic plan, its divisions crossed the Balkan passes, and throwing the Ottoman Army into confusion, passed it, and having invested Adrianople advanced swiftly in the direction of Constantinople.

The success of the Serbs and the Greeks was quite as great.

FRANCE, GERMANY AND BALKANS

In the space of a few weeks what was known as Turkey in Europe had practically ceased to exist.

These dazzling victories and the sudden collapse of a great empire, which many still regarded as extremely powerful, created great surprise everywhere. Hailed in some countries with joy, in others they provoked displeasure and even anger. A moral and material success for the Russians, whose prestige in the Balkans was now vastly increased, they constituted on that account alone a defeat for Austria, who, possibly inadequately informed regarding the activities and plots of the Balkan States, and above all never believing that they could be successful against the Turks, had taken no precautions in advance. Germany, the powerful friend and protector of Turkey, whom she supplied abundantly with instructors and material for her army, was also hard hit by her defeat, or rather her collapse.

The Cabinet of Vienna made no effort to hide its displeasure. Having failed to intervene either before or during the proceedings, it tried its hardest to do so afterwards. A conference was held in London which was attended by the belligerents and the Great Powers. Austria, supported by Germany, emphatically demanded the withdrawal of the Serbian troops from the coast of the Adriatic, and the creation of an Albanian principality to which was to be added the town of Scutari, at that time being besieged by the Montenegrins. The latter soon afterwards captured it, and it was only with considerable difficulty that they were forced to give it up. Similar inflexibility and determination obliged the Serbs to retire from the coast of the Adriatic, where, not without some show of reason, they were demanding an outlet to the sea—Durazzo, which they had conquered. The Vienna Cabinet, supported by Rome, insisted in peremptory tones that they should not be allowed a foothold on the coast (March 1913).

The dismemberment of the Ottoman Empire had hardly taken place before bitter dissension arose between the sharers in the spoil. Convinced that they had done everything or almost everything in the war, the Bulgarians were animated by hatred and fury against the Serbs, whom they accused of laying hands on the greater part of Macedonia. Having quarrelled over the bear's skin while the bear was still alive, the two

265

hunters, as soon as he was killed, prepared to renew the struggle, armed to the teeth.

Austrian diplomacy, becoming more and more irritated with the Serbs, and seeing a growing menace in their aggrandisement, sought every possible means of obscuring the issue, and putting everything into the melting-pot once more. There can be no doubt that she encouraged the Bulgarians in the plot a certain section among them were hatching. When it is a matter of a surprise attack, no very great effort is required to make the Bulgarians move. They are a hot-headed people who easily lose control of themselves, together with all sense of responsibility and fear of consequences.

A crisis of this kind was convulsing the soul of Bulgaria. The militarists, furious with Serbia, whom they had grown to hate even more than the Turks, and secretly urged on by Austrian emissaries, decided to take action. General Savok, the mouthpiece of the Macedonian committees, who would willingly have sacrificed the whole world for the smallest grievance, wrung from Ferdinand his consent to a sudden treacherous attack on the Serbian army (June 1913).

Ferdinand was too clever not to realise all the drawbacks of this act of aggression, but Savok frightened him, as he did the politicians, and he gave way. The whole nation, wild and intoxicated by an unexpected series of victories, had completely lost all sense of reality, and was incapable of distinguishing the possible from the impossible.

As soon as it heard of this fratricidal struggle, the Russian Government sent furious telegrams to Sofia. M. Danef, at that time President of the Council, tried to stop the offensive, thus giving the Serbs and the Greeks time to recover and prepare to march forward, with the result that the Bulgarians in the end reaped no advantage from their act of treachery.

No sooner was the Bulgarian attack made known than Roumania also decided to intervene. On the first occasion she had remained a mere spectator, but she soon perceived that the victories of the Balkan States and their unforeseen aggrandisement were upsetting the balance of power in the Balkans. As soon as an unexpected opportunity presented itself she had no hesitation in turning it to account. As one of the leading

Roumanian statesmen remarked, " We have allowed the train to go once without getting in, but as soon as it stops again we have made up our minds not to be left on the platform ! "

Everybody, including, as was only natural, the Turks themselves, decided to take advantage of the opportunity offered. Enver Pasha, gathering together the remnants of his army, rushed in pursuit of the Bulgarians and succeeded in recapturing Adrianople. Bulgaria now found herself invaded from all sides at once; she was obliged to confess herself beaten, to lay down her arms and place herself at the mercy of the victors. The latter, at a meeting held in Bucharest, under the ægis of the Roumanian Government, who took the lead in the negotiations, imposed whatever terms they chose on Bulgaria, among others the handing over to Roumania of the town of Silistria and a strip of territory with a population of 400,000.

.   .   .   .

Austria as well as Turkey had been worsted in these Balkan wars. She had not known how to prevent them or to foresee the results in time.

The first mistake she made was in 1912, when she thought that the Turkish army, the strength of which she over-estimated, would easily account for its adversaries. But the second mistake she made, when she urged the Bulgarians to advance, little imagining that she was leading them to a catastrophe, was far more serious. The Army and the diplomatists shared the responsibility for this error, and the leading men in Vienna had really only themselves to blame. But they were embittered and disgruntled, furious at having allowed so many opportunities to slip, and seeking in every direction for the means of making good their mistake.

From that moment their one thought was of war against Serbia, convinced that this was the only remedy.

In the month of August 1913, anxious to take military measures against the Serbs, they laid their plans before their allies, Germany and Italy. The strange revelations made during the Great War by Signor Giolitti shed a bright light on these bellicose intentions on the part of Austria. On the 9th of August, 1913, the Marquis de San Guliano, the Foreign Minister, telegraphed to his chief, Signor Giolitti : " Austria-

Hungary has communicated to us, as also to Germany, her intention of taking action against Serbia. She describes her action as being one of self-defence, hoping to provide the Triple Alliance with the *casus fœderis*, which I do not think is valid. I am using every effort, together with Germany, to prevent this step being taken. But it may become necessary to state clearly that we do not regard such an action as defensive, and thus do not believe that the *casus fœderis* is established. Please telegraph to me in Rome if you approve of my procedure."

Signor Giolitti replied: "If Austria takes action against Serbia, it is clear that no *casus fœderis* is established. It will be action taken on her own account. There can be no question of defence in such case, since nobody is dreaming of attacking her. It is necessary to state this to Austria in the most formal terms. It is to be hoped that Germany will succeed in her efforts to persuade her ally not to embark on this perilous venture."

This exchange of telegrams was unequivocal. It made the attitude of the Viennese leaders as well as that of Italy perfectly clear. It was a rehearsal of what was to take place a year later. Italy informed Austria that she refused to have anything to do with any dangerous act or policy of aggression. Her position was absolutely sound and her arguments unassailable.

It is probable, and indeed certain, that if Italy alone had barred her path Austria would have brushed her aside. But on this occasion she was held back by Germany, anxious not to alienate Roumania, who was bound by a military convention to the Central Powers and governed by a Hohenzollern. For it was under the ægis of Roumania that the Peace of Bucharest had just been signed. Any attempt on the part of Austria, therefore, to destroy the treaty could not have been regarded with indifference by Roumania.

Thus the Austrian Government found itself obliged willy nilly to resheath the sword. But its one thought was to draw it again at the first opportunity, to abrogate the Treaty of Bucharest, to which it could not resign itself, and to take action against the Serbs, and if necessary against the Russians.

This bellicose spirit became more clearly defined during the winter and the spring of 1914.

Thus—and there are innumerable proofs of this—the Austrian

Government turned its face ever more and more resolutely in the direction of war.

But at this precise juncture a similar movement was also carrying away the German Government. As long as the Berlin Cabinet was acting as a brake upon Austria the danger was not very great, since Austria would not and could not act without her powerful ally. But on the day that Germany not only ceased to restrain Austria, but actually urged her on, the conflict was inevitable, and would break out at the first opportunity.

BIBLIOGRAPHY.—Nippold, *Le Chauvinisme Allemand* (French translation, 1917). *Yellow Book* (on the Agadir negotiations). L. Mauriac, *La Politique Marocaine de l'Allemagne* (1916). A. Tardieu, *Le Mystère d'Agadir* (1912). P. Albin, *Le Coup d'Agadir* (1912). *D'Agadir à Serajevo* (1915). Caillaux, *Agadir* (1919). R. Poincaré, *Au Service de la France* (*Le Lendemain d'Agadir*) (1926). Kiderlen-Waechter, *Mémoires* (1924). Sir Thomas Barclay, *Thirty Years : French Reminiscences* (1915). Baron Beyens, *L'Allemagne avant la Guerre*. Nekludoff, *Souvenirs Diplomatiques* (1920). Baron von Schoen, *Mémoires* (1922).

CHAPTER XX

THE CAUSES OF THE GREAT WAR

Uncle and nephew. The illness of Franz-Ferdinand. The
romance of the Archduke. The conversations of Konopicht.
The leaders of the monarchy. The crime of Serajevo. The
mystery of Serajevo. Its effect on Europe. Count Tisza.
The secret of the ultimatum. Presentation of the ultimatum.

DURING the spring of 1914 alarming rumours were
current regarding the health of Francis Joseph, the aged
Emperor of Austria. It was not the first time this had
occurred. For many years the editorial departments of all the
leading papers had had the obituary notice of the senior
sovereign of Europe ready for publication. On
this occasion, however, as the news seemed bad,
everybody turned their eyes to the heir to the
Crown, the Archduke Franz-Ferdinand.

Uncle and
Nephew.

At Court and in diplomatic, high official and army circles
Franz-Ferdinand had aroused violent dislike.

High-handed and brutal, ready to sacrifice everything to the
smallest whim, he so far abused his power on the rare occasions
that the old Emperor temporarily entrusted him with making
appointments in the army that he very soon had to be deprived
of his right " of signature." Francis Joseph had but little
affection for him, as is only to be expected and frequently
happens in the case of a sovereign with regard to his heir, and
never allowed an opportunity to pass for showing his dislike.
In order to emphasise it still further he overwhelmed with
solicitude the next in succession, the Archduke Charles, husband
of the Princess Zita, who theoretically should have mounted
the throne on the death of Franz-Ferdinand, as the latter's
children, owing to the morganatic marriage of their father,
were excluded from the succession.

As soon as Franz-Ferdinand, who hardly ever stayed in

270

Vienna, left home on one of his frequent visits to St. Moritz or Brioni, the Emperor used to make his grand-nephew Charles take his place at official ceremonies, a favour he but rarely granted to the former.

Strange stories about the heir to the throne had long been current in well-informed circles. It was said that in his youth **The Illness of** he had contracted a grave disease, and that from **Franz-** time to time violent crises occurred, during which **Ferdinand.** he became a prey to frenzy and broke everything he could lay his hands on. When the crisis was over he would fall into a state of prostration.

Moreover, he was hardly ever to be seen at Court, but lived by himself with his wife and children in his castle at Konopicht in Bohemia, at Miramar near Trieste, or in the little island of Brioni not far from Pola.

During a cruise in the Adriatic on a friend's yacht, the author of the present work stayed for a week in this delightful spot, which is a favourite resort of the best people in Austro-Hungarian society. A lively and energetic hotel-keeper, who was an excellent man of business, had succeeded in "making" Brioni in a very short space of time, and establishing it as a fashionable watering-place. Franz-Ferdinand spent nearly every winter there, living quite simply with his family and one or two aides-de-camp.

We were told that he used to be the victim of regular fits of madness. They were a common topic of conversation among people in the hotel and the servants.

In addition to this his wife gave cause for grave anxiety. She was an ambitious woman who apparently, when once her husband was on the throne, would not have resigned herself to the subordinate position allotted her by her morganatic marriage.

Romance or tragedy, fairly frequently both, had for long played havoc with the lives of members of the ill-omened House **The Romance** of Hapsburg. The marriage of the heir to the **of the** throne with a penniless Tchech countess was **Archduke.** indeed a romance. When he was on a visit to a certain Archduchess who wanted him to marry one of her daughters, Franz-Ferdinand suddenly fell in love with the

271

young Countess Chotek, who was only a lady-in-waiting, and in spite of universal opposition made up his mind to marry her

The Emperor, after violently opposing the marriage, eventually gave his consent. But Franz-Ferdinand had formally and for ever to renounce his children's right to succeed to the throne.

From this time forward his wife slowly and gradually climbed ever higher and higher, in spite of the obstacles and rules of etiquette that barred her path. She was made a princess and then Duchess of Hohenberg. Extremely clever, she turned the smallest opportunity to account in order to mount all the steps one by one. The Marquis de Reverseaux, who was for many years French Ambassador in Vienna, has described to us the discreet overtures to which he was subjected in order to induce him to give dinners in honour of the Duchess which would allow her to meet on the neutral ground of the Embassy personages whom she could otherwise never have known.

Among those who were anxious to court the Archduke there were many, as may well be supposed, who eagerly seized upon meetings of this kind, and William II was one of the first to use this method. He heaped honours and favours on the wife of Franz-Ferdinand, hoping thereby to bind her husband closely to him.

When once the latter was Emperor would not his wife use every effort to sit on the throne beside him? Endless complications and difficulties might be foreseen arising from such a contingency.

On the 12th of June, 1914, William II paid a visit to the Archduke at his castle of Konopicht. He was accompanied by **The Conversations of Konopicht.** Admiral von Tirpitz, his military adviser, who stood high in his favour, thus emphasising the political nature of the interview. Count Berchtold, the Viennese Foreign Minister, was also invited.

As soon as he returned to Vienna from Konopicht, Berchtold although laziness was his pet vice, set to work, and drew up a memorandum on the situation of Austria in the Balkans " This situation," he wrote, " is becoming intolerable. Russia is aiming at creating a Balkan Confederation in opposition to the ruling House of Hapsburg, and with this object in view is trying to win over Roumania, whose relations with Austria have become extremely strained."

The conclusion of his report was equivocal, not to say menacing, with regard to Russia.

The Leaders of the Monarchy. Tired and worn out, the aged Emperor had ceased to rule. He signed the papers presented to him, and that was all, and acted more or less as he was told to do.

The Foreign Minister was Count Berchtold, who had succeeded von Aerenthal. A member of the high nobility and extremely rich, running after pleasure and putting entertainment above everything else, he was reminiscent of some of the characters in the *Reigen*, Arthur Schnitzler's celebrated play, in which he gives an extremely amusing picture of certain Viennese types drawn from life.

Berchtold used to frequent the smaller theatres, make love to the actresses and amuse himself like a boisterous student. Frivolous, superficial and vain, devoid of any serious knowledge or culture, he unconsciously allowed himself to be drawn into the whirlpool.

The man who was the real leader at the *Ballplatz* was Count Forgash. It was he who in 1909 had been entirely responsible for the Agram trial, who invented a bogus conspiracy, made use of forged documents, and finally covered himself with ridicule as well as infamy. But this case, in which Austrian diplomacy had appeared in a very bad light, had in no way hindered his promotion.

As for the military leaders, the most influential was the future generalissimo, General von Hoetzendorff. In his souvenirs, which have been published, he admits with a certain candour, that the moment he was made chief of the Staff, a few years previously, he had advised the Emperor to make war on Italy. " As we shall have to fight her some day or other," he said, " the sooner the better ! "

At the beginning of June the newspapers announced that military manœuvres on a large scale were taking place in Bosnia **The Crime of Serajevo.** under the leadership of the heir to the throne, who, on Sunday the 28th of June, was to make his solemn entry into Serajevo, the capital. This was the anniversary of the famous battle of Kossovo, which is a

T

day of national mourning for all the Serbs, those of the kingdom of Serbia as well as of Bosnia.

The choice of this day was a very clear warning to the Serbs which it was impossible to misunderstand, and the official papers did not fail to emphasise it.

On the Sunday morning, about nine o'clock, the Archduke and his wife, the Duchess of Hohenberg, arrived by motor-car. As soon as the first houses were reached a bomb was thrown at them. The chauffeur accelerated his speed and it fell on the hood of the car, from which the Archduke with great presence of mind threw it out into the road. As soon as they arrested the perpetrator of the crime, Franz-Ferdinand exclaimed : " Make haste and hang him, otherwise Vienna will send him a decoration ! " On arriving at the Hôtel de Ville he hardly had the patience to listen to the lengthy harangue of the burgomaster, who, with a singular lack of appropriateness, vaunted the loyalty and fidelity of the inhabitants of Serajevo.

As he was about to return in the same car he tried to send his wife back to his hotel. But she obstinately refused. " No," she insisted, " it is precisely at a time of danger that you have most need of me." (*Nein, gerade in der Gefahr brauchst du mich !*)

After the first attempt on his life, the most elementary prudence should have dictated the adoption of the most careful precautionary measures. But none were taken. As Count Harrach, a member of the Archduke's suite, expressed his astonishment, General Potiorek, the military governor, took him sharply to task. " Do you imagine," he said, " that Serajevo is full of assassins ? And don't you know that there are never two attempts made on the same day ? " [1] Thus reassured the procession set off. In one of the extremely narrow streets, just as the car had to slow down in order to turn a corner at right angles, a youth standing on the pavement had only to stretch out his arm in order to discharge two shots from a large revolver at close range at the Archduke and his wife.

[1] All these details are taken from the account of an eye-witness, Monsieur René Gourdiat, who was in Serajevo at the time as correspondent to the *Matin*. His pamphlet, *Serajevo, 28 Juin, 1914*, is one of the most interesting and circumstantial documents published on the subject, though very little use has been made of it.

THE CAUSES OF THE GREAT WAR

When the car, accelerating its speed, reached the Governor's house, it was found that both the occupants were dead. Franz-Ferdinand and his wife had been killed on the spot.

A disquieting mystery hangs over this tragedy which brought about one of the most terrible wars that has ever devasted **The Mystery of Serajevo.** humanity. The murderer, who was arrested with very little difficulty, was a student named Gabrilo Prinzip, a Serbian by race, but born in Bosnia, and thus an Austro-Hungarian subject. How was it that he had been allowed to take up his position at this spot in order to commit the crime with the greatest possible ease? How was it that no control and supervision were exercised at a time when everything pointed to the necessity for the most stringent precautions?

It was not the first time that great personages had paid an official visit to the capital of Bosnia. In 1910 the Emperor Francis Joseph had been received there with great pomp and ceremony; and in 1914, only a short time before, another Archduke, Francis Salvator, had gone there on Corpus Christi Day. All the streets had been lined with soldiers and police, and for several days beforehand all travellers arriving at the station had been carefully scrutinised. During the procession the Archduke had marched surrounded by a strong cordon of Hungarian soldiers.

But on the present occasion none of these precautions were taken. There was no organisation for keeping order and no troops lined the streets.

Was this negligence accidental or deliberate? The question gives rise to manifold suspicions, including the darkest.

William II was at Kiel on his sailing yacht, going the round of the regattas. Busy and excited as he always was, and giving **The Effect on Europe.** his orders right and left, he suddenly saw a torpedo boat approaching his yacht and trying to come alongside. With a peremptory gesture he waved it away. But the boat continued to approach, and Admiral Müller, standing near the wheel, waved a paper he held in his hand. Then placing it in his cigarette-case he threw it cleverly on deck. On opening the case William found the telegram announcing the murder of the Archduke. He grew pale, and letting the telegram fall merely said : " *We must begin everything over again.*"

The murderers of the Archduke were two extremely young Bosnian students. The Viennese Cabinet immediately maintained that the crime was the outcome of a vast plot hatched in Belgrade, and from a mere assassination it suddenly developed into a political conspiracy aimed at a neighbouring State.

Intent upon exploiting to the utmost the unexpected opportunity thus offered, Viennese diplomacy immediately set to work. On the 4th of July Count Hoyos, the head of the Cabinet and Berchtold's right-hand man, took to Berlin an autograph letter from Francis Joseph in which it was definitely stated that a conspiracy had been hatched in Belgrade.

Szogyeni, the Austro-Hungarian Ambassador in Berlin, lunched with the Kaiser at Potsdam and handed him the missive from Francis Joseph. After lunch an extremely important meeting was held at which war against Serbia, and if necessary against Russia and France, was definitely settled.

The Austrian Ambassador, in reporting his interview with the Kaiser, wrote :

" William II is of opinion that we should not wait long before taking action against Serbia. The attitude of Russia will certainly be hostile, but if war breaks out between Austria-Hungary and Russia, Germany, with her usual loyalty to her allies, will side with us."

In his Memoirs Prince Lichnowsky declares : " I afterwards learnt that during the memorable discussion of the 5th of July at Potsdam the demands of Vienna received the unconditional consent of all the authorities with the further addition that there would be no harm if war with Russia were to result."

Preparation of the Ultimatum. As soon as Count Hoyos returned to Vienna, the Austro-Hungarian Government held an extremely important Cabinet meeting on the 7th of July.

The Austrian Red Book has published the account of it.

" The Serbs," said Berchtold, " must immediately be rendered impotent ; the German Government has promised its full support. If this results in war with Russia, it is better for it to come now than later on."

Count Tisza, President of the Council and Prime Minister of Hungary, expressed a different opinion. He refused his consent to a sudden attack on Serbia without any previous diplomatic action having been taken.

Tall of stature, dry and emaciated, with a badly trimmed beard and untidy appearance, brutal and deliberately cynical **Count** in conversation, Tisza conducted both his home **Tisza.** and foreign policy with violence and occasionally with bloodshed.

If on this occasion he intervened, albeit extremely cautiously, in favour of Serbia, it was certainly not because he was animated by any affection for that country. It was merely that he possessed a wider and more intelligent view of all the complications that might arise out of war with Serbia. His was a powerful and vigorous mind, very different from that of Berchtold.

Nevertheless it was not long before he too allowed himself to be converted to a bellicose policy, and he collaborated with Berchtold in drawing up the ultimatum. It was arranged that the terms should be such that it would be impossible for Serbia to accept.

It was essential that absolute secrecy should be preserved, and that nobody in the camp of the eventual adversaries, **The Secret** Russia, France and England, should suspect what **of the** was taking place. Like all wicked deeds, this one **Ultimatum.** was hatched in the dark. The results obtained in this respect were prodigious. The Note to Serbia, of which none of its members had received any intelligence, at all events none that was sufficiently reliable, took the Governments of the Triple Alliance completely by surprise.

Their Ambassadors were all away on holiday. Monsieur Poincaré, the President of the Republic, and Monsieur Viviani, President of the Council, were setting out on their official visit to St. Petersburg, after which they were to proceed to the Scandinavian capitals. The Viennese authorities, in concert with Berlin, postponed the presentation of the ultimatum for an hour, in order that the news might not be known in St. Petersburg before the departure of the French guests.

The financiers, as usual, were better informed than the diplomatists. Whilst the Chancelleries allowed themselves to be lulled into flaccid optimism, the Exchanges in Vienna, Budapest and Berlin became more and more depressed. There was a sudden slump in the markets, and everybody tried to sell out.

Had they been better informed, the Cabinets of Paris, London and St. Petersburg might have tried to intervene before the Note was despatched to Belgrade, and perhaps have made it less harsh. But knowing nothing, they could not and did not do anything.

On the 23rd of July, at six o'clock in the evening, the Austrian Minister to Serbia presented the ultimatum to the representative The Presenta- of Monsieur Patchich, who was away at the time. tion of the The Note enumerated all the grievances that Ultimatum. Austria-Hungary had against Serbia. It demanded a formal disavowal on the part of the Serbian Government of its propaganda in Austria-Hungary, the dissolution of the societies fomenting it, the dismissal of all the guilty officers and officials, a list of whom would be supplied by Austria, the opening of a judicial inquiry against the originators of the plot, in which the Austro-Hungarian authorities were to take part. Coming after all the rest, this last clause more particularly, which demanded the interference of foreign agents in a judicial action, could hardly be accepted by an independent State.

The time granted for a reply was extremely short—forty-eight hours.

BIBLIOGRAPHY.—The various Government books, Yellow (French), Blue (English), Orange (Russian), Green (Italian), Blue (Serbian), Grey (Belgian), White (German), Red (Austrian).

Karl Kautsky, German documents relating to the origin of the war. Complete collection of official documents (French translation, 4 vols., 1922) (of prime importance). J. Reinach, *Histoire de Douze Jours* (1914). J. W. Headlam, *The History of Twelve Days* (1915); *Correspondance de Guillaume II et Nicolas II* (1924). R. Poincaré, *Les Origines de la Guerre* (1921). James W. Gerard, *My Four Years in Germany* (1917). H. Morgenthau, *Vingt-six Mois en Turquie* (1919). A. Dumaine, *La Dernière Ambassade de France à Vienne* (1922). M. Paléologue, *La Russie des*
278

THE CAUSES OF THE GREAT WAR

Tsars pendant la Grande Guerre (1922). Conrad von Hoetzendorf, *Aus Meiner Dienstzeit* (4 vols., 1922). Giovanni Giolitti, *Mémoires de ma Vie.* E. Bourgeois and Pages, *Les Responsabilités de la Guerre* (1921). Renouvin, *Les Origines Immédiates de la Guerre* (1925). A. Gauvain, *L'Europe au Jour le Jour* (Vols. VI to XIII). V. Giraud, *Histoire de la Grande Guerre* (1918). *J'Accuse*, by a German (1917). *Le Crime* (3 vols.), by the same author. Lord Grey, *Twenty-Five Years*, 1892–1916 (1925). Wickham Steed, *Through Thirty Years*, 1892–1922 (2 vols., 1924).

279

CHAPTER XXI

THE TRAGIC TEN DAYS

Feeling in the capitals. Attitude of Germany. Serbia's reply.
German intervention. German mobilisation. The crux of the drama.
The declarations of war.

IN its exceptional and crushing severity and the brief interval allowed for reply, the Note assumed the character of a regular ultimatum. And it was regarded in this **Feeling in the Capitals.** light in all quarters. The impression it made gave rise to the utmost alarm.

A question was immediately raised which overshadowed all others—would Germany support Austria or not? If she did not, everything could easily be arranged. But if **Attitude of Germany.** she did, the menace to peace could not be greater. The reply to this question was given on the following day, when the public learnt, in spite of a certain reticence on the part of the Quai d'Orsay, of the grave message conveyed by Herr von Schoen, the German Ambassador in Paris, to Monsieur Bienvenu-Martin, who was temporarily acting as head of the French Government.

At the end of a long Note, of which he refused to submit a copy, but which he read over twice to the latter, the German Ambassador emphatically called the attention of Monsieur Bienvenu-Martin to the following sentence :

" The German Government considers that the question at issue is a matter concerning Austria-Hungary and Serbia alone, and that the Powers have the gravest reasons to restrict it to the two interested parties. It ardently hopes that the conflict will be localised, since any intervention on the part of another Power will, as the natural result of existing alliances, give rise to incalculable results."

On the morning of the 25th the author of the present work

280

had occasion to have a long interview with Herr von Schoen, the German Ambassador. He came away from the meeting with feelings of the deepest pessimism. On the main point at issue he found him absolutely immovable. " There is no alternative but to leave Austria and Serbia to arrange matters between them," he kept obstinately repeating. " The intervention of a third party would lead to the most terrible misfortunes."

Even more significant than these words, which kept recurring like a *leitmotiv*, was the aspect of the Embassy; on the stairs, and in the corridors and vestibules, the servants were doing up parcels and nailing down cases. The whole place seemed to be in process of packing up.

The argument of the German Government can be summed up as follows :

1. The German Government declared at every opportunity, by the mouth of all its representatives, that it did not know the text of the Austrian Note, and that Vienna did not take the trouble to consult it. This assertion may seem somewhat extraordinary when the docility, to say the least, of Austro-Hungarian diplomacy towards Berlin is borne in mind. But, as frequently happens in the case of liars, carelessness on their own part suddenly reveals the fact that they have lied. While the German diplomatists in Paris, London and St. Petersburg kept repeating this assertion, which nobody believed, the President of the Bavarian Council in Munich was caught out when he declared to Monsieur Alizé, the French Minister, who immediately reported it to Paris, that the contrary was true. ". . . The President of the Council told me to-day," wrote Monsieur Alizé, " that the Austrian Note, the contents of which he knew . . ."

This lie, which was the first of a long series, proved at one stroke both Germany's preconceived plan, as well as her bad faith. It vitiated in advance all the arguments that the Germans might afterwards bring forward in their effort to prove that they were not responsible for the war.

2. Having been ignorant, as they maintained, of the contents of the Austrian Note, which they nevertheless approved and supported with all their might, the Berlin Government proceeded

to inform everybody, including Russia, whose interests were more particularly involved, as well as France, that Austria should be left alone to deal with Serbia, that the matter she was about to settle in a high-handed way concerned her and *her alone*, and that any intervention on the part of Russia would automatically bring Germany into the game and thus set fire to Europe. This was what German diplomacy quite clearly meant when it spoke of " incalculable results."

Bolstered up with falsehood, this pretension on the part of Germany cannot be maintained either *de facto* or *de jure*.

The Austrian Note, which was delivered in Belgrade on Thursday the 23rd at six o'clock in the evening, only became known in the various capitals on the morning of

Reply of Serbia. Friday the 24th. The President of the French Republic and the head of the Government were at that moment far away in the Baltic, on the cruiser which was bringing them back to Denmark from Kronstadt, where they had taken leave of the Tsar. In England, Ministers, diplomats and Members of Parliament were all ready to go away for the sacred week-end rest. Most of the Ambassadors were on holiday, and the head of the Serbian General Staff was taking the cure at a German watering-place.

But the time allowed to Serbia for an answer was exceedingly short. The Governments involved hardly had time to consult together before it expired.

On the advice of France, England and Russia, the Serbian Government sent Austria a reply couched in the most conciliatory terms. It accepted all the Austro-Hungarian demands with but one exception—the participation of foreign agents in the judicial inquiry to be held on the conduct of those suspected of complicity in the Serajevo assassination. Making this one reservation his excuse, Giesl, the Austrian Minister, left Belgrade with all the staff of the legation. Thus diplomatic relations were broken off. Warlike demonstrations were held in Budapest and Vienna. On the following day Austria took drastic military measures—the mobilisation of a certain number of army corps, the suspension of constitutional liberties, the adjournment of Parliament, etc.

In Paris, as in St. Petersburg, there was a well-defined feeling that only the adoption of a determined attitude by England towards Germany would prevent the latter from moving and ward off the catastrophe. Unfortunately England at this juncture, in view of the attitude of her leaders and of the public, and fettered by tradition, habit and routine, was neither willing nor indeed in a position to take any such steps. And thus the situation now became tragic.

The key to the attitude of Great Britain is afforded by the English Ambassador in Berlin, who, when Jules Cambon observed that a few determined words from England might save the situation, replied: " I agree with you, but I am not authorised to pronounce them."

Sir Edward Grey, who for many years had directed the foreign policy of the Radical Government, was a philanthropist and a lover of peace, almost a pacifist. During that terrible week two men were fighting in his soul—the diplomatist, who, on information received from his agents, could not be ignorant of the fact that Europe was rushing headlong into war, and the idealist, who could not make up his mind to be responsible for any word or deed that might be interpreted as a threat and would in his opinion precipitate England into the war. For from the very beginning he was afraid, and this fear paralysed him, that if he made it quite clear that the British Government was determined to intervene, this fact alone would encourage France, and above all Russia, to adopt an attitude that was far from conciliating towards Germany and Austria.

The Simile of the Cave.
In one of his most famous similes Plato depicts prisoners shut up in a cave who mistake for the objects themselves what are really only their shadows cast on to the rock.

It is well to bear this comparison in mind if an understanding of the week preceding the war, which was so full of incident, is to be reached.

The semblance, the shadow of the substance cast on the wall of the cave, were the diplomatic facts. The military events alone, the almost universal setting in motion of the formidable organism known as mobilisation, constituted the reality. Whilst Ministers and Ambassadors were vainly agitating in the front of the stage, making endless overtures and communications,

283

and exchanging Notes which crossed and recrossed with every capital in Europe, from the very first days the Headquarter Staffs of the Powers which might be termed " aggressive," first Austria and soon afterwards Germany, set to work.

Whilst awaiting definite orders for mobilisation, all the steps were taken which constituted the necessary preparation for it, or rather which practically amounted to mobilisation itself. Russia, who was directly threatened, since she ran the risk of having to deal with two assailants, and very soon France also were bound, unless they wished to commit suicide, to retaliate without overmuch delay by taking similar measures. Thus in one country after the other the vast machine was put in motion. And the faster it moved the more difficult it became to stop it.

The mobilisation of Austria, the inauguration of military action against Serbia and the bombardment of Belgrade (29th of July), which aroused great excitement in St. Petersburg, constituted the first act. The reply of Russia, which was at first partial but soon became complete, constituted the second. The placing of Germany on a war footing, soon to be followed by an ultimatum to Russia, was the third.

It was not merely by words and diplomatic notes, which became more and more menacing, but by deeds that the bellicose intentions of Germany were made manifest. As **German Mobilisation and the French reply.** early as Saturday the 25th and Sunday the 26th the German regiments in Alsace were placed on a war footing. Officers on leave were recalled by telegram, which forced the French Minister for War to take similar action. On the following day, the 27th, Germany definitely continued the work of arming herself.

On the 28th the German reservists were called up to reinforce the frontier in Alsace, horses and vehicles were commandeered, the air-force was mobilised, and the families of officers stationed on the frontier were sent back, etc., etc. Then came even graver news. Monsieur Jules Cambon telegraphed that a preliminary notice of mobilisation had been given to the whole of Germany.

On the 29th of July Monsieur Poincaré and Monsieur Viviani arrived back from Russia. They reached Paris at the Gare St. Lazare, and all along the road to the Élysée the leaders of the country and of the Government were greeted with acclamations which were at once hearty and subdued. From that day the sacred unity of the nation was proclaimed in the most moving fashion.

Immediately on the return of the Presidents two Cabinet meetings were held. Between these two meetings the famous visit of Herr von Schoen to Monsieur Viviani took place. The German Ambassador, in tones that were almost menacing, commented on the military measures that the Government of the Republic was taking, adding that France was at liberty to act in this way, but since these preparations could not be kept secret from Germany, public opinion in France should not become alarmed if Germany retaliated.

Up to that moment the French Government had not called up a single reservist and no movement of troops to the frontier had occurred. General Joffre, who was head of the General Staff, was insistently demanding that protective troops should immediately be posted, as any delay might mean disastrous consequences. The Cabinet decided to wait a few days longer before coming to a decision.

On the 30th of July German troops took up their fighting positions on the frontier and constructed defensive works, and a concentration of troops was reported in the neighbourhood of Trèves. General Serré, the military attaché in Berlin (who was killed in Alsace), telegraphed that Germany, anxious to start proceedings with a lightning blow, was feverishly hastening on her preparations. At a Cabinet meeting, Monsieur Messimy, Minister for War, communicated General Joffre's demand for the immediate mobilisation of all the frontier regions and all the cavalry divisions.

The Government found itself in an exceedingly embarrassing position. For military reasons it was obviously necessary to accede to Joffre's request. But diplomatic reasons were equally imperative in their insistence on the need for the greatest prudence and circumspection. After lengthy deliberation the Cabinet decided to sanction the posting of protective troops, making, however, the following provisos—that only the units that could be moved by road were to take up their positions, that no reservists were to be called up yet, and lastly, that the protective troops were to be kept at a distance of *six miles from the frontier*, so that the German and French patrols might not come into contact.

This last stipulation laid the Government open to the severest criticism. From the military point of view it undoubtedly had some inconveniences, which, however, should not be exaggerated. But from the diplomatic standpoint it made an excellent impression everywhere, more especially in England, whom it was to the interest of France to treat with the utmost solicitude. It clearly and definitely defined the attitude of France, who only decided to go to war because she could not do otherwise.

We now come to that most critical day, Thursday the 30th. Early in the morning the French Government had been informed that German troops were barricading the roads across the frontier, and sending back pedestrians and horse-drawn vehicles to France, but keeping the motor-cars. At half-past twelve a special edition of the *Lokal Anzeiger*, a semi-official paper, published in Berlin the news that general mobilisation had been ordered. This edition was seized a few minutes later and Jagow, General Secretary for Foreign Affairs, telephoned to Jules Cambon that the news was false, and begged him to send " urgent " information to his Government to that effect.

Jules Cambon has himself told us more than once that he attached no credence to this denial. He was convinced that mobilisation had been decided upon on the previous day, but that owing to various reasons—an exchange of telegrams between the Kaiser and the Tsar, and above all England's declaration that she reserved to herself complete liberty of action—these grave measures were postponed.

But what was happening in Berlin? We now come to the crux of the drama. The Kaiser and the leaders of Germany

The Crux of the Drama.
had rushed into the affair convinced, in the first place that Russia, on account of the unpreparedness of her army, would give way, and secondly that England would keep out of the conflict.

But this conviction was to be proved doubly wrong. It was clear that Russia was decided to go on to the bitter end, whilst England declared that she could not stand aside. And indeed, on the 29th of July, the day before this declaration was made, the famous council of war had been held at Potsdam, under the

286

presidency of the Emperor, at which the Headquarters Staff had succeeded by dint of ever more emphatic insistence on brushing aside the last scruples of the civilians and securing that the order for mobilisation should be given on the following day. Hence the news published in the *Lokal Anzeiger*. That night, immediately after this meeting, Bethmann-Hollweg called upon the English Ambassador, and informed him in fairly plain terms of the impending catastrophe. " If England," he said, " will consent to stand aside, the Imperial Government is ready to give her every assurance that in case of victory it will seek no territorial aggrandisement at the expense of France in Europe. It refuses, however, to give a similar undertaking with regard to the French colonies. It says very little with regard to Belgium, as the operations which Germany may consider necessary in that quarter will depend upon the action taken by France."

This communication on the part of Germany, on the gravity of which there is no need to insist, made a very bad impression in London.

Sir Edward Grey had already informed Prince Lichnowsky, the German Ambassador, that Germany should not count upon " the neutrality of Great Britain under all the eventualities that might arise."

The extremely determined attitude of Russia as well as that of England provided sufficient food for reflection at the last moment for the civil leaders of Germany. Feeling the terrible weight of responsibility resting on their shoulders, they had at the eleventh hour a sudden access of hesitation, and were moved by one last scruple. They made an attempt to draw back and to stop the movement of the formidable machine which had begun to be set in motion. This explains the countermanding of the order for mobilisation and the denial of the news published in the *Lokal Anzeiger*. But the military party returned to the charge with greater determination than ever and quickly broke down the last efforts at resistance.

On the following day, the 31st of July, Jagow informed Cambon that in view of the mobilisation of the Russian army, Germany found herself obliged to take precautionary measures. Her Government had come to the conclusion that there was danger of war. Moreover, and this was quite as serious, if not more so, it was sending an ultimatum to St. Petersburg, calling upon Russia to cease all warlike preparations within twelve hours, in default of which Germany would give the order for general mobilisation.

It further demanded a declaration from the French Government within eighteen hours as to whether, in case of war between Germany and Russia, France would remain neutral.

The instructions which led to this action on the part of Herr von Schoen concluded with the following *secret clause :*

" If, as there is very little reason to expect, the French Government declares that it will remain neutral, I beg Your Excellency to inform them that, as a guarantee of neutrality, we must demand the surrender of the fortresses of Toul and Verdun, which we will occupy and return as soon as the war is over. The answer to this question must be made known here before four o'clock to-morrow afternoon."

The declaration by Germany that danger of war existed, which practically amounted to mobilisation, combined with the steps taken by her Ambassador in Paris, obliged the French Government to take the military measures which General Joffre was demanding with ever-increasing insistence.

On Saturday the 1st of August the latter sent a note to Monsieur Messimy couched in even more emphatic terms than his previous communications, protesting against any delay. He was given audience by the Cabinet.

As Germany, he argued, owing to the facilities afforded by her system of government, was able to gain a fairly considerable start of France, it was imperative to retaliate against all the measures that had been taken by a general mobilisation, failing which, Joffre declared, he would no longer be able to shoulder the crushing responsibility of his office.

The Cabinet decided to accede to this demand. Nevertheless, anxious to do all in its power up to the last moment to preserve peace, it allowed Monsieur Messimy to keep the order for mobilisation in his possession for a few hours longer.

At half-past three the second in command on the Headquarters Staff came to the Minister's office to fetch the document. At a quarter to four it was taken to the post office in the Rue

de Grenelle. It consisted only of two lines : " Mobilisation of
all land and sea forces. Sunday the 2nd of August will be the
first day of mobilisation." That was all. In two or three
hours the whole of France was to be set in motion as though an
electric button had been pressed. There was not a village or
hamlet tucked away in the depths of the country, whether in
Brittany or the Pyrenees, that did not receive the news. Where
there was no telegraphic communication the tocsin was sounded
instead.

France, morally quite prepared, immediately rose to arms.

In the midst of these tragic days there was great excitement
in the capital over a trial that had just been brought to a conclusion. Between the 20th and the 29th of July,
The Pulse of Paris. Madame Caillaux, who a few months previously
(16th of March) had assassinated Gaston Calmette,
one of the directors of the *Figaro*, in his office in the Rue
Drouot, had been appearing before the assize court over which
a magistrate, who was on the side of the defendant, had presided
with obvious partiality.

The trial, in which politicians and well-known writers were
called as witnesses, gave rise to great commotion. The incidents
which took place in the Palais, the way in which the case was
conducted, and the acquittal, which a great many people
regarded as scandalous, all combined to raise public excitement
to fever-heat. But the fever soon subsided beneath the grave
rumours of war which rose from every quarter of the
horizon.

The same thing happened when Jaurès was murdered, shot
by a revolver, on the 31st of July, in a restaurant near the
Bourse. Some were afraid that the act would provoke Socialist
demonstrations and lead to a disturbance of the atmosphere of
sacred unity. But nothing of the kind took place.

A procession made a timid attempt to overrun the boulevards from the heights of Montmartre. But the shouts of the
demonstrators were literally drowned in the wave of emotion
and grave enthusiasm which was making itself felt in Paris at
the moment.

About one o'clock in the morning, just as the cafés had closed
and the boulevards were still full of people, the resounding echo

U

of a troop of cavalry advancing was heard in the distance in the direction of the Porte St. Martin. The hoofs of the horses clattered on the roadway. A voice exclaimed, " The curassiers ! " and an electric shock passed through the crowd. Windows were thrown open on every floor. People climbed on to benches and got on to the tables in the cafés. Headed by a troop of children and young people, the horsemen advanced in war kit, their helmets covered, looming tall as giants in their ample cloaks. A great shout rose from the mouths of all : " *Vive la France ! Vive l'armée !* "

General mobilisation took place in Germany and in France almost simultaneously. That day, at one o'clock, the Chancellor sent to Pourtalès, the German Ambassador, the text of the declaration of war against Russia which, in the event of the latter refusing to accept the ultimatum addressed to her the previous day, he was to present to Sazonof at five o'clock that same afternoon. The declaration of war ended with the melodramatic words : " His Majesty the Emperor, my august sovereign, accepts the challenge in the name of the Empire, and regards himself as being in a state of war against Russia."

The Declarations of War.

It sounds remarkably like the tourney in *Lohengrin !*

Having declared war upon Russia, what action was Germany going to take against France? The question did not fail to cause her considerable embarrassment. The German Government were hoping that in view of the violations of the frontier committed by the German troops, the French Government would take the initiative in declaring war, which would have allowed Germany to throw the responsibility upon France. But the Cabinet in Paris took care not to fall into the trap. Even after the German Ambassador in Paris had asked for his papers, Jules Cambon telegraphed to his Government begging them not to instruct him to do likewise. " You must let me be turned out ! " he said.

At dawn on the 2nd of August the German troops invaded the Grand-Duchy of Luxemburg, and the French Minister only just had time to escape in his car. During the night of the 1st to the 2nd, violations of the frontier had occurred at various places, near Cirey, at Longwy, Boron, and Delle. A French

290

corporal, named Peugeot, was shot by a revolver on French soil by a lieutenant in command of a German patrol.

The French Government was content with lodging a diplomatic protest.

Realising that France, in spite of every provocation, would not take the initiative in declaring war, the German Government decided to take the step. But it was only on Monday the 31st that it telegraphed to von Schoen to present the declaration at six o'clock in the evening.

The German Government gave as its excuse for declaring the existence of a state of war, alleged violations of the neutrality of Belgium, over which French airmen were said to have flown, and bombs thrown by aviators on the Eifel district, at Carlsruhe and at Nuremberg.

Never had so many falsehoods been collected together in so few words. This declaration will remain famous in history under the heading *The Bombs of Nuremberg*. Nobody, not even the Germans themselves, could possibly believe such a tale. It had, moreover, been denied by the Prussian Minister in Bavaria himself. But of course it was necessary to find a pretext.

At the last moment, in the absence of any other, and as time was short, they had recourse to this one.

In the British Cabinet, from the very beginning of the crisis, opinion had been very much divided, but was on the whole against intervention. Only the Prime Minister, Mr. Asquith, Winston Churchill, and to a certain extent Sir Edward Grey, were inclined to be in favour of sending help to France. All the others were against intervention. Winston Churchill, who is endowed with great energy, took upon himself the responsibility of deciding to keep the fleet, which had just ended its grand manœuvres, ready mobilised. This was an exceedingly important decision. When England, somewhat late in the day, decided to take action, she had in the Navy an instrument that was ready to strike at once.

The Attitude of England.

Lloyd George, at that time Chancellor of the Exchequer, was one of those who hesitated most.

Naturally impressionable and volatile, and a ready prey to any influence brought to bear upon him, he received on the 30th of July an important deputation of big financiers, who

291

told him that England should not on any consideration take part in the war. Even if the conflict lasted only a short time, they declared, it would have the inevitable result of plunging the whole world into unprecedented financial chaos. (This prophecy was to a certain extent justified.) The only way to save mankind, therefore, was to keep England out of the dispute, so that she might remain the great market and economic arbiter of the world.

Deeply impressed by this argument, Lloyd George declared himself opposed to intervention, which only served to increase the indecision of the Cabinet. The Ministers met every day, sometimes twice a day, without being able to reach a settlement. On the day of the famous Council of Potsdam at which war was decided upon, and after Bethmann-Hollweg had offered the English Ambassador a shameful bargain if Great Britain consented to remain neutral, Paul Cambon called upon Sir Edward Grey, who addressed him substantially as follows : " The Imperial Government would be mistaken," he said, " in thinking that England would remain out of the conflict in the event of the failure of all the efforts made to preserve peace. But it is only fair to let you know," he added, " that, on the other hand, public opinion in this country does not regard the present crisis in the same light as the Moroccan crisis which occurred a few years ago. The question then at issue was one of prime importance to us and had been the subject of a special agreement between the two countries. But to-day we are faced by a struggle for supremacy in the Balkans between the Teutons and the Slavs with which we are in no way concerned."

" That is a very subtle distinction," replied Paul Cambon, who explained the situation of France, pointing out that neither materially nor morally was she in a position to promise Germany to maintain neutrality in the event of the latter attacking Russia. He returned to the subject again on the following days.

But Sir Edward Grey refused to make any promise, and took refuge behind the feeling in Parliament and in the country, which was not in favour of intervention.

On Saturday the 1st of August Paul Cambon again called upon Sir Edward Grey just as he was leaving the Cabinet.

The cause of intervention had made no progress. Sir Edward Grey told him to inform Paris that no decision had been reached.

" I refuse to send any such news," replied the Ambassador, and insisted, not without deep emotion, upon all the proofs afforded by France of her peaceful intentions—her resistance to the Headquarters Staff who were urging the Government to mobilise, and the withdrawal of the troops to a distance of six miles from the frontier. Finally, he drew attention to the following important point—the whole of the French coast in the north and west, the Pas-de-Calais, and the Channel and Atlantic coasts were entirely defenceless and could be attacked by German squadrons with impunity. And indeed, by the naval agreement between the two countries, France had undertaken to guard the Mediterranean, whilst England had made herself responsible for the North Sea. Was England going to fail in this undertaking? When the violation of Belgium was openly being arranged, was she going to allow the German ironclads a free hand to bombard Cherbourg and Brest? This last argument seemed to impress Sir Edward Grey.

" Those were the darkest hours of my whole life," Paul Cambon afterwards told us.

The President of the Republic had just written a moving letter to the King of England which a diplomatist from the Quai d'Orsay had brought in person to London. The King, although his personal feelings were very different, confined himself to replying by means of a missive couched in the vaguest of terms and dictated by his Cabinet, in which he declared that the British Government did not yet know what course it would adopt.

On Sunday the 2nd of August there was another Cabinet meeting. One of the greatest financial magnates in the city, Lord X., had been summoned to attend. Still no decision was reached.

It was only in the evening that Sir Edward Grey brought Paul Cambon the assurance for which he was waiting. He came and told him that the Government had resolved to give France the support of the British fleet. In the event of the German squadrons attempting to enter the Pas-de-Calais, the

British fleet would oppose them and England would consider herself as being in a state of war against Germany.

This was something; it was, in fact, a good deal. The leader of the Conservative party, after an important meeting at Lansdowne House, sent an official deputation to the Prime Minister to inform him that, in the event of the Government deciding to intervene on the side of France, it might rely upon the whole-hearted support of the Conservatives. This had a great influence in bringing the Cabinet to a decision.

Violation of Belgian Neutrality. The violation of Belgium happened just in time to remove England's last scruples and persuade her to intervene with full strength on the side of France.

On the 31st of July the French Government had informed Brussels of her intention to respect Belgian neutrality. On the 1st of August this promise was categorically renewed. But the German Government, on the contrary, was maintaining a silence which began to cause uneasiness in Belgium and also attracted the attention of England. On the 2nd of August the news of the violation of the Grand-Duchy of Luxemburg was made known in Brussels and in London.

At one o'clock on the same day the German Minister in Brussels went to the Ministry of Foreign Affairs and asked for facilities to be given for the transport of German reservists residing in Belgium (there were enough of them, in all conscience !) who were anxious to return to their own country with all possible speed.

This was the only communication he had to make. At three o'clock the Belgian vice-consul in Cologne informed his chiefs that troop trains were leaving the station every three or four minutes in the direction not of France, but of Aix-la-Chapelle, on the Belgian frontier. That same day the German Minister, in an interview published in *Le Soir*, gave his solemn assurance that his country was animated only by friendly intentions towards Belgium. " Your neighbour's roof may burn," he said, " but your house will be safe."

But at seven o'clock he asked for an immediate interview with Monsieur Davignon, the Minister for Foreign Affairs, and

294

presented him with an ultimatum demanding a free passage for the German armies through Belgium.

In the case of Belgium as in that of France, German diplomacy had not even taken the trouble to find a plausible pretext for its ultimatum.

The fact was that the German diplomatists were merely instruments in the hands of the Headquarters Staff, who, for their part, wasted no time in searching for good reasons. In this connection also Kautsky's valuable book throws the most vivid light on the subject.

The hour appointed for the reply from Belgium was fixed for the following day, Monday, at seven o'clock in the morning. A council was held during the night at the Palace under the presidency of the King. Neither the sovereign nor the statesmen had the slightest hesitation. They decided that their country would resist the German demands with all the power at its command. The council rose at about midnight. At seven o'clock in the morning, a few minutes before the limit of time appointed, the Baron de Gaiffier, General Secretary to the Ministry for Foreign Affairs, presented the reply at the German Legation.

Germany's ultimatum and the violation of Belgian neutrality produced great excitement in England. At one stroke all
England's Ultimatum. hesitation on the part of the Government and of public opinion was swept away. On the 4th of August Sir Edward Grey telegraphed to his Ambassador in Berlin to lodge an energetic protest against the violation of Belgian neutrality, and to demand before midnight on that date the assurance that the threat held out to Belgium would not be carried out, otherwise the Ambassador was to ask for the immediate return of his papers.

But Germany had now gone much too far to retreat. On the political leaders and the Kaiser the threatening attitude adopted by England at first produced a feeling of astonishment and afterwards of rage. Nothing sheds a greater light on the mentality of Germany than this astonishment and rage. When it is remembered that both Belgium and her neutrality were the direct creation of England, how was it possible to suppose that the latter would not bring armed intervention to bear in defence of her own work? Nevertheless the German statesmen were surprised, and their surprise was quite genuine, the reason being that they judged others by themselves. They could not understand that a Government should attach so much importance to its engagements and its signature. When he received the English Ambassador for the last time in Berlin, Bethmann-Hollweg declared that the steps taken by the British Government were "terrible in the extreme." For a mere word "neutrality," a mere "scrap of paper," Great Britain was about to make war on a country that was related to her and asked for nothing better than to remain her friend.

He repeated these words in the Reichstag and even enlarged upon them.

"We are forced," he candidly remarked, "to brush aside the justifiable protestations of the Governments of Luxemburg and Belgium. *The injustice*—I am speaking quite openly—*the injustice of which we thus become guilty*, we shall make good as soon as our military aim has been achieved. Anyone who is menaced as we are and is fighting for his very existence must think only of how he is to cut his way through."

This was the famous theory of the scrap of paper, and that "necessity is its own law."

Later on, German diplomacy and propaganda, realising the disastrous effect produced throughout the whole world by this confession, and these words of the Chancellor, which were at once cynical and imprudent, tried to explain them away. They brought forward as an excuse certain documents that were supposed to have been discovered in Brussels proving that the Belgian Government had already violated the neutrality of their country and had forfeited their liberty of action with regard to France and England.

For the time being, however, certain of victory, they gave no thought to such precautions.

Italy, who was bound by a formal treaty to Germany and Austria, cited a clause of that treaty, the famous Article 7, in order to maintain that since the action taken by Austria against Serbia was aggressive, the *casus fœderis* did not arise. She informed Berlin and Vienna of her decision, and in spite of all the arguments used by her allies, insisted on abiding by it. In vain did the German Government urge the Vienna Cabinet to make some concessions to Italy in order to induce her to throw in her lot with the Central Empires. Every effort was useless. On the 2nd of August the Cabinet officially decided that Italy would remain neutral. William II made one last effort. He sent one of his aides-de-camp in hot haste to Rome bearing an autograph letter to the King from the Kaiser. But even this had no effect.

Thus from the political and the diplomatic point of view the war opened somewhat badly for both Germany and for Austria, who had now become of minor importance. Owing to the violation of Belgian neutrality, England ranged herself from the very beginning on the side of France and Russia, and Italy proclaimed her neutrality.

But from the military point of view, which after all was the only one that mattered, the Germans had laid their plans so well, they had thought out every detail of their offensive and set their formidable machinery in motion with such meticulous care, that they felt certain of success—success, moreover, that would be complete and crushing. And this explains their conduct. Every other consideration gave way before it.

Their calculations in this respect, it must be admitted, were not built upon air; very far from it. The military organisation which for many years Germany had been perfecting was terribly powerful, and it came within an ace of sweeping away everything that stood in its path.

BIBLIOGRAPHY.—See the bibliography of the preceding chapter.

Raymond Recouly, *Les Heures Tragiques d'avant Guerre* (being accounts collected by the author from the chief actors in the drama—R. Poincaré, General Joffre, Viviani, Messimy, Paul and Jules Cambon, Camille Barrère, Baron de Gaiffier, Take Jonesco, etc.) (1922). Prince Lichnowski, *My Mission to London* (London, 1919). D. J. Hill, *Impressions of the Kaiser* (New York, 1918). Hillferich, *Die Vorgeschichte des Kriegs* (Berlin, 1920). Take Jonesco, *Les Responsabilités de la Guerre* (1921). Von Tirpitz, *Memoirs* (1923).

CHAPTER XXII

THE GREAT WAR

Germany against France. Stabilisation of the Fronts. Change in the High Command. Ludendorff's offensive. One-man command—Foch.

GERMANY and Austria, on the one side, presented a solid and compact block of about a hundred million inhabitants, and with France, Russia, England, Belgium and Serbia on the other this formidable conflict involved the greater part of Europe. Certain countries who at the beginning had stood aside were only awaiting an opportunity for hurling themselves into the fray—Turkey, Italy, Bulgaria and Roumania. From Europe it was destined to spread through the whole world. First Japan, and then China, Brazil and lastly America were to take part in it.

Owing to the number, the power and wealth of the countries engaged, this war far surpassed any that had been waged before and which were trifles by comparison.

Moreover, for the first time in history it was to be shown what a really national war meant in which not only a professional army, as had been more or less the case before, but a whole nation, both at the front and behind the lines, combatants and non-combatants, were alike swallowed up. All the material and moral resources of the country, all the reserves collected for centuries, were to be hurled into the fray and quickly consumed. For this reason the war demanded expenditure and even waste on a colossal scale, and a frenzied destruction such as had never before been witnessed.

If the population and wealth alone of the block of countries on the side of the Entente are taken into account it would appear to be much stronger than that formed by the Central Empires. Unfortunately, however, it was only apparently a block. Its geographical situation as well as its political condition condemned it to fight for a long time in scattered formation. Between Russia, on the one side, and England and France on the other, there were practically no easy means of communication after Turkey had entered the war. Thus the huge Russian Empire, which is more than half Asiatic and stood in great need of moral and material help from its western allies, being unfitted to carry on a war lasting any length of time, was condemned to isolation. And this was one, if not the chief, of the causes of its downfall.

The Central Empires, on the other hand, possessed what military men term the interior lines. Germany, by an easy turn of the wheel, could transport her forces from the Eastern to the Western Front and *vice versâ* in a few days. Moreover, from the very beginning she assumed diplomatic and above all military control of the coalition. She ruled it and was destined to do so ever more and more. Unity of leadership and command, which the Allies were to take so long to secure, and which, moreover, they only succeeded in establishing imperfectly, existed in the case of Germany from the very beginning.

And now once more the two great adversaries who had so often confronted each other on the field of battle were again

Germany against France.
face to face.

The military prowess of their soldiers and the warlike qualities of their race were about equal. Prussia, "the male organ of Germany," as it has aptly been termed, had Prussianised the whole empire, especially from the military point of view. The Bavarian, Hessian, Saxon and Wurtemburg troops were as good or almost as good as the Prussian.

Since the warlike qualities on both sides were pretty well equal, the deciding factor which would lead to a lack of balance, and to the victory of one side and the defeat of the other, consisted in the material equipment, the training and organisation of the army, and above all the merits of the Headquarters Staff and the High Command.

As regards equipment, Germany possessed a marked superiority over France. She had devoted more care and money to her army. In this respect her system of government had been of considerable service, the power of the Emperor, the supreme War

Lord, not being limited by the rights and opposition of Parliament. As regards material of war, the importance of which plays an ever greater part in modern warfare, superiority lay on the whole on the side of Germany. Her rifle was newer and better than that of the French. The French seventy-five was better than the German field gun, but Germany had a far larger supply of the latter than the French. But above all the Germans possessed formidable heavy artillery, consisting of the most recent and most perfect guns at a time when the French had very little with which to meet it. Owing to the civil leaders, who were only too ready to cut down the army estimates, and even more to the military authorities, who, believing in letting well alone, were convinced that the seventy-five, that Jack-of-all-trades, was sufficient for every need, the French army went into the field with practically no heavy artillery at all. And this put France in a position of inferiority which was to make itself acutely felt as soon as the struggle began.

In the French Army there was one seventy-five gun to every six hundred and seventy men, which is a far lower proportion than the four guns to every thousand men prescribed by Napoleon. The supply of machine guns was also quite as inadequate. Here again the Germans had learnt much more from the wars that had recently taken place, and above all from the Russo-Japanese War. They were also much better acquainted than the French with the use of wire entanglements, improvised entrenchments and field fortifications. All this side of military instruction had been culpably neglected in the French army.

There was a similar superiority on the side of Germany in regard to all accessory war material—the telephone, the telegraph, instruments of all kinds, explosives, trench mortars, etc., etc. The German uniform was more practical and less visible than the French, which, in spite of every effort and experience of all kinds, still insisted on keeping that anachronism —the red trousers. But the fact that the material side had suffered such neglect in the French Army was not entirely due to apathy and *laisser-aller*. The influence of ideas and novel theories on questions of tactics had to a large extent contributed to it. As a reaction against the extremely reasonable and wise method advocated by Bonnal and Foch, a young school, repre-

300

sented by Colonel de Grandmaison, had succeeded in spreading the notion that a determined offensive, and the engagement of all the forces from the very beginning along a wide front, was all-sufficient. There was no other method, they maintained, except immediate and wholesale attack.

These were elementary and extremely rash conceptions which owed much more to Souvarof than to Napoleon, and took no account of the terrible havoc wrought by quick-firing appliances of all kinds.

The proportion of reservists, who must of necessity be less well trained, was appreciably less in the German armies than in the French, forming, as they did, three-fifths in the French active units and two-fifths in the German.

This inferiority in various respects, as well as certain strategic mistakes made at the beginning, is sufficient to account for the unfortunate results of the first battles. Thanks to the elasticity of the French temperament and the innate capacity of the race for getting out of a scrape, they were speedily rectified as far as it was possible to do so. A few weeks in the field made the reserves, which were very inferior at first, equal or almost equal to the active army. Lastly, the High Command, after a few initial mistakes, was clearly superior on the French side.

The German Headquarters Staff had, ever since the conclusion of the agreement between France and Russia, faced the possibility of having to wage war on two fronts, and **The Plan of Campaign.** under the influence of von Schlieffen, their chief since 1891, conceived a gigantic plan of attack which consisted in crossing Belgium and thus turning the strong line of fortresses protecting the French frontier on the east; whilst a few German army corps, acting on the defensive, were to endeavour to the best of their ability to hold back the Russian offensive on the Eastern Front, the main body of the German armies was to turn the French defences, and attacking France at her most vulnerable point, where she was denuded of fortifications, reach the capital and bring her to her knees in a few weeks. Thus it was on the north across Belgium that the German Staff counted on making its main effort.

Its intentions were known. Certain obvious signs, the construction of stations and railway wharfs in the Eifel, gave the

301

French General Staff sufficient warning of the German plan of operation. The mistake made by the French was not with regard to the fact that Belgium would be crossed, but, and this is extremely important, the method of its accomplishment. The French Staff were convinced that Germany's enveloping movement would not reach further than the Meuse, and would not extend to the left bank of that river.

On what did this conviction rest? On a calculation estimating the number of divisions which the Germans would have at their disposal at the beginning. Given the stretch of territory to be covered from Alsace, they concluded that she would not have sufficient troops to extend the front to the left bank of the Meuse. This is typical of Staff reasoning which, starting from doubtful and frequently false premises, deduces with inflexible certainty and logic conclusions which are equally false. The French, both civilians and military men, and the latter even more than the former, who regard the world as being ruled by logic, are somewhat apt, both by temperament and nature, to be guilty of mistakes of this kind. As a matter of fact, Germany, owing to the superabundance of her forces and the high efficiency of her troops, was able from the very beginning to put more divisions into the field than her adversary knew she possessed.

To meet the German plan, the French plan of campaign, arranged in April 1913 by the Supreme War Council, consisted, as soon as the concentration of troops had been carried out, in attacking the German armies on both sides, on the east in Lorraine and on the west to the north of the line Verdun–Metz.

This plan of attack as well as the disposition of the forces had of necessity to be modified as the German offensive developed and became clear. After some hesitation and delay, the French Staff was obliged to give heed to facts and acknowledge that a very considerable proportion of the German forces were crossing Belgium and preparing to attack France on the north-east. Hence an important modification in the disposition of the French armies and the permission accorded to General Lanrezac, who was in command of the left wing, to move in a north-westerly direction.

But for this, the plan of the French General Staff was more or less carried out—the First and Second Armies attacking in Alsace and Lorraine, and the Fourth Army through Belgian Luxemburg.

All these offensives failed. The French army on the left wing, which had advanced as far as Belgium, lost the battle of **The Battle** Charleroi. It was obliged to beat a hasty retreat, **of the** together with the three divisions of the English **Frontiers.** Expeditionary Force which were operating in conjunction with it.

The battle, called the battle of the frontiers, was lost.

The reasons for this defeat are to a large extent similar to those given above—the superior equipment of the German Army, which had a far larger number of machine guns than the French, the heavy artillery, the bad choice of position for the French offensive, above all that conducted by the Fourth Army, numerous mistakes in tactics, troops hurled madly forward without sufficient preparation, absence of communication between the units, and the obvious incompetence of some of the generals.

The situation had become seriously compromised. But a leader, a very great leader, was found to save it.

Either by chance, or by the intervention of Providence, as has happened more than once at the most critical moments of **General** French history, the man on whom the fate of his **Joffre.** country depended at the time was endowed with the qualities, the temperament and the character to bear the crushing load without flinching.

An officer in the Engineers, after a brilliant career in the colonies, Joffre had reached the top of his profession and had been head of the General Staff for three years. A native of Rivesaltes in the Pyrenees, he was a cold southerner, with fair hair and blue eyes. Broad shouldered and heavily built, he conveyed above all an impression of robust energy and massive force.

Napoleon, who was not without experience in such matters, asked himself the following question in the solitude of St. Helena: " What are the qualities that make a great general? " It is very rare, he said, to find them all in the same man. The first essential is a balance between intellect and character. It is necessary, said Napoleon, for the gifts of mind and will to be harmoniously adjusted. A general who possesses more intellect than character is like a ship with too much sail and not enough body; the slightest gust of wind is enough to upset it. If, on the other hand, it has too much body and not enough sail the ship will not move.

Joffre was endowed with this harmonious equilibrium between the gifts of mind and of will. His optimism was unshakable, and was founded not on beatific confidence, but on the profound conviction implanted in his breast that a great country like France, provided she did not give way and stiffened herself to bear the full brunt of the trial, could not and should not be overwhelmed. Such was the faith that animated him and which he communicated to his colleagues, to all the generals and to the whole army. Had mistakes been made? Then they must be rectified. Had it been shown that the troops were inadequately trained and disciplined? This must be attended to without delay. Certain generals, many too many generals, had been found incompetent for their work; they must immediately be superseded. Joffre at once applied himself to this essential side of his task, and there was nothing that demanded more courage on his part. Many of the generals who were to be sacrificed, *stellenbosched* as the saying is, were his comrades and friends. Many had behind them the most powerful patrons who, after having secured their appointment, would not readily resign themselves to seeing them hit in this way. No matter! None of these considerations had the slightest weight. Joffre had but one object in view—the interests of his country and the necessity for choosing the most capable men to lead the troops to victory. And in this respect he gave proof of infallible judgment. All the leaders who were destined to gain distinction in the war were appointed by him during the first few days— Foch, Pétain, Franchet d'Esperey, Mangin, Humbert, Maud'huy, etc., etc. And thus dozens and dozens of generals were immediately deprived of their commands, and those who took their places proved excellent.

The Battle of the Marne was won above all because, unlike that which took place in 1870, when the French leaders only too often failed to support one another, there was now from one end to the other of that vast front the most perfect understanding and collaboration between all who participated in the action.

Faced by the defeats of the early days and the lightning advance of the enveloping wing of the German armies, a re-arrangement of the French forces became impera-tive. It was necessary to gain time and obtain a foothold.

The Retreat from the Marne.

Whilst his right wing, fastened on to Nancy and Verdun, held firm, Joffre ordered his left wing to fall back. This retreat gave him the opportunity of restoring order in the units and of taking the troops in hand and completing their training and equipment.

And now began that memorable retreat of a vast army, which every day ceded a fresh strip of territory but nevertheless kept its morale, its confidence and its will to victory intact. It retreated because the generalissimo had decided that it must retreat and not because the Germans seemed to have gained the victory. Whenever the order came to face the enemy, the retreating forces immediately turned round and held their own and very often beat the foe. This happened in the case of Lanrezac's army at Guise and the fine Moroccan division at La Fosse-à-l'Eau. Many other instances might be given.

This is a point which cannot be too often insisted upon, for otherwise the victory of the Marne appears almost in the light of a supernatural and inexplicable event.

In a general order of the 28th of August, Joffre gave instruc-tions for the formation within the fortified area of Paris of a strong army under the command of General Maunoury, together with the formation in the centre, between the Fourth and Fifth Armies, of another army to be commanded by Foch, who had been recalled in hot haste from Lorraine.

The formation of Maunoury's army on the extreme left and of Foch's army in the centre—these were the two measures which led to the victory of the Marne. They were the seeds that brought forth the fruit.

Whilst Joffre was indefatigably visiting the greater part of the front, calling upon the army commanders and keeping in close touch with each one of them, and changing two of them, Lanrezac and Ruffey, before the battle, Moltke, the German generalissimo, did not move from his General Headquarters in Luxemburg, several

The Battle of the Marne.

hundred miles from the front, but allowed the plan he had made to be carried out as it had been concerted and arranged beforehand, leaving the execution of it to his various lieutenants.

The German is naturally inclined to believe that a plan or an organisation is in itself a thing of value. No greater mistake could be made. Strategic plans owe much more to the manner in which they are carried out than to the way in which they are conceived. Napoleon, who was always on the spot, and directed everything in person, was so little a slave to his plan that sometimes, on the very eve of a great battle, he would change every detail of it. Jena is a case in point.

Even in 1870, Moltke gave up the idea of conducting operations himself and allowed each of his generals to manage as best he could alone. Foch, in his book *La Conduite de la Guerre*, has proved this up to the hilt, and given chapter and verse. The only reason why the Germans were victorious was because they were opposed by French generals, the majority of whom were incompetent. In 1914 similar mistakes were again made by the German High Command. But on this occasion they were more serious, as the front was far wider and the troops in action far more numerous. Moreover, the mediocre German Command had to deal with French leaders who knew their business. And this to a great extent explains the difference in the result.

Following his uncle's example, Moltke's nephew set the machine in motion once and for all. He thought it was enough to start it without worrying about the various obstacles and accidents that might arise.

The army commanders, who received extremely vague directions from their chief, did pretty well as they pleased with regard to his instructions. It is curious to note the attitude of Moltke whenever he was disobeyed. Instead of taking the delinquents severely to task he veiled their acts of disobedience in silence, persuaded that, as in 1870, success would crown his efforts in spite of all.

As a result of this silence, acts of disobedience increased, more especially in the case of von Kluck, who had been entrusted with the principal rôle, that of turning the enemy's flank.

Von Kluck was on the turning wing, which may literally be

said to have turned with devilish speed. If one follows his movements from day to day, across Belgium and the north of France, one is astounded and stupefied by their rapidity. His advance was a regular torrent far from easy either to keep back or to regulate. Orders from General Headquarters chased after him but could not catch him up. When eventually they reached him, the situation was frequently very different from what it had been at the time they had been drawn up.

On the 3rd of September three out of von Kluck's five army corps had already crossed the Marne. It was at this moment that he received the order to echelon his troops in depth behind the Second Army commanded by von Bülow. Such an order was a clear proof that General Headquarters had not the faintest notion of the exact position in which von Kluck's army corps were situated at the moment. It imagined they were not nearly so far south as they actually were. As in 1870, it was in a thick fog regarding the movements of its armies.

When Gallieni on the evening of the 3rd of September learnt of von Kluck's rapid advance to the south, he immediately communicated with Joffre and suggested a flank attack on the German army by Maunoury's army. Joffre decided to stop the retreat and launch an offensive all along the line, and on the 5th of September he circulated his famous order for the day, which contained the following words : " Any body of troops which finds itself unable to advance further must keep the ground it has won, cost what it may, and must be wiped out on the spot rather than give way."

Both morally and materially this sudden half-turn on the part of the French, this swift change from a retreat to an advance, created the greatest surprise among the German armies. Bad psychologists as the latter were, and instinctively inclined to under-estimate their enemy, whose temperament and qualities they could not understand, the Germans, intoxicated by a triumphal march lasting over a fortnight, imagined that their enemy was no longer able to turn round and face them.

Maunoury's offensive overtook von Kluck as inevitably as March overtakes Lent. Exposed to a simultaneous attack on his right and his centre, von Kluck was obliged to make his army corps beat a hasty retreat. Some of them rushed into the lines of communication of the neighbouring army, and the result was dire confusion. " Kluck's ninth corps," writes von Bülow, " was covering the right wing of the Second Army, so that one of our corps, the seventh, was completely paralysed on the 6th of September and could not move." The result was that the sudden retreat of von Kluck's army in a northerly direction created a huge gap between his own and the neighbouring army which, harassed by the English divisions and Franchet d'Esperey's army, found itself in a more and more critical position. In vain did von Kluck endeavour to turn Maunoury's army. In the centre von Bülow and von Hausen tried at all costs to break the lines of Foch's army in the Marais de Saint-Gond and at Fère-Champenoise. For the German High Command had changed its plan. Feeling that no decision could be reached on the right wing, owing to the stubborn resistance with which von Kluck's army had been met, they tried to obtain it in the centre by driving in the enemy's front on both sides of Fère-Champenoise, where Foch's army was placed. All their efforts were in vain. The French stood firm everywhere. The German attack in the centre had failed, and the situation on the right was becoming more and more critical, on account of the growing gap between the armies of von Kluck and von Bülow. Still the German generalissimo did not move from his head-quarters, far away though they were, and insisted on directing nothing in person, but allowing himself to be represented by a mere lieutenant-colonel—Hentsch. It was the latter who on his own responsibility gave the order for retreat along the greater part of the front.

This in rough outline is the explanation of the Battle of the Marne, which may be said to have been lost by the Germans even more than it was won by the French, a remark which as a matter of fact applies to almost all the battles. What was called a victory was nearly always won by scraps and remnants of the forces. For a long time both sides remained equally balanced, the slightest additional weight being sufficient to turn the scale one way or the other.

But this in no way detracts from the courage, the endurance and the heroism of the soldiers, and the merits of their leaders, and above all of Joffre—quite the contrary.

THE GREAT WAR

The mediocrity of the German High Command was proved in other ways besides the failure to direct operations. Some time before the Battle of the Marne it was guilty of a mistake of the utmost gravity, which also to a large extent contributed to its defeat.

The Russians had launched a vigorous offensive in East Prussia, and, driving back the German forces, which were inferior as regards numbers, had penetrated into the territory of the Empire. This success caused a panic in Berlin, which was all the greater because the family estates of most of the large landowners were situated in this province. The latter brought influence to bear in high circles, with the result that the Government decided, cost what it might, to put a stop to the Russian offensive. Two army corps were accordingly recalled from the Western Front and sent in hot haste to East Prussia. Hindenburg, recalled from retirement to active service again, seconded by Ludendorff, was given the command of these troops, which were reorganised and reinforced. On the 25th of August, 1914, he won over the Russians, who were caught in the middle of their offensive, and whose two armies, although they were operating on extremely difficult ground, had practically no communication with each other, the brilliant victory of Tannenberg.

East Prussia was saved; but Germany lost the Battle of the Marne and with it the whole war. The two army corps, which had been withdrawn precisely from the right wing, where the High Command had most need of them, were responsible for a serious deficiency in the battle. Had they been there the result might have been different.

In this instance political and sentimental reasons were allowed to outweigh purely military exigencies, which in any vigorously and intelligently conducted war ought always to take precedence.

Stabilisation of the Fronts. Trench Warfare. A few days after the Battle of the Marne, the front, which until then had been mobile, was stabilised. The German Army, which knew more than the French did about the judicious use of trenches and of wire entanglements, which a few well-placed machine guns could defend, broke up the ground and dug

themselves into strongholds which became more and more perfect every day, and which enabled them to arrest the advance of the pursuing armies. The fact that an uninterrupted line of hastily constructed fortifications, extending over hundreds of miles of country, and soon reaching to the North Sea, was able to resist all the attacks and hold back the onward rush of the enemy, was the greatest surprise and a veritable revelation to many.

One of the most energetic leaders of the French Army, with whom the writer of the present lines happened to be, had given the order on the 13th of September that his division was to push forward before nightfall to the other side of Rheims. About ten o'clock in the morning, as no further advance had been made for the last two hours, his aide-de-camp came to him and timidly suggested : " Shall I order lunch here, General ? " He was sharply snubbed. " Are you mad ? " the General replied. " We shall lunch at Fismes. Surely a little paltry barbed wire is not going to prevent us ? " However, to reach Fismes took more than four years.

A new form of warfare was now begun, trench warfare, which has frequently been contrasted with war of movement. But the distinction is only apparent and is due to a superficial view of things. As a matter of fact the stabilisation of the front and trench warfare were nothing but a confession of impotence on both sides.

The art of war consists above all in securing as perfect an equilibrium as possible between the three factors —war material, the morale and discipline of the troops, and the intelligence and courage of the military leaders. If any one of these factors is lacking or present in insufficient strength, the equilibrium is upset. It then becomes impossible to reach any decision.

Immediately after the Battle of the Marne, there was a grave shortage of war material. Both sides, but France far more than Germany, were faced with a terrible crisis connected with the supply of munitions.

Both the belligerents tried to fill the void, and a race began between them, in which each side brought all its resources and ingenuity to bear.

THE GREAT WAR

But it was not the supply of munitions alone that was lacking, but also the method of using them.

It was necessary to discover new strategic and tactical methods for this new form of warfare. The stabilisation of the fronts, and their great length, which gave no opportunity for enveloping manœuvres, set the High Command an exceedingly difficult problem.

The solution which at first presented itself to the mind, the famous "breaking of the line," which for a long time hypnotised both the French and the Germans, was a delusion, a will-o'-the-wisp. This breach could never be made so long as there were sufficient reserves in the rear to fill the gap. The outer crust might be broken, but it was closed again immediately. Every effort made in this direction was pure loss. This was true of the French offensive in Champagne in 1915, and of the German offensive at Verdun the following year. The German staff in this case introduced an element of *surprise*, of which it tried to make more and more use in its later offensives, and which it learnt to conduct with consummate mastery. But this factor was not enough to ensure success. The Verdun offensive took place along too short a length of the front. The Germans endeavoured during the course of the battle to extend it by continuing their efforts on the left bank of the Meuse.

But it was too late. The reserves of the French Army were too large for them not to be in a position to put in an appearance. All the divisions of the army, like the links of a chain, were hurled one after the other into the fray. They were left for a certain length of time in the fighting line until they had suffered a settled proportion of casualties and been subjected to a given amount of wear and tear, and were then withdrawn and replaced by fresh troops.

The problem to be solved, in short, but which it took both sides a long time to discover, was not how to break the front, but how to use up enough of the enemy's reserves for him to have no more left to put in the field.

The French offensive on the Somme, during the summer of 1916, showed a vast improvement in this respect. It was made on a far wider front and the forces engaged were very large. It

almost attained the desired end—the exhaustion of the enemy's reserves.

As a result of this battle Germany suffered from a shortage of men which was far graver than a shortage of munitions, because it was much more difficult to make good. If the French Staff had maintained its efforts, it might have been able at the end of that year or the beginning of the next to have reached a decision.

But for this it was necessary to follow the Somme offensive by another, carried out as quickly as possible, after the shortest interval, so as not to allow Germany the time to raise fresh reserves.

The German Staff, faced by a shortage of men, left no stone unturned. They enrolled all who could possibly be enrolled. And from that moment they turned their attention towards making their western front considerably shorter, so as to be able to hold it with fewer divisions.

This afforded the best proof that the last Anglo-French blow had gone home.

Unfortunately, political influences arose at this juncture to obstruct the military plans. They interfered with their execution and jeopardised their success.

During the first period of the war, Parliament had left the High Command fairly free. When the Germans were advancing on Paris, the Government and the Chambers had moved to Bordeaux. They remained there a fairly long time. Gradually they drifted back; but as the front became stabilised and the danger appeared to be less imminent, the interference of Parliament in the conduct of the war began to make itself felt more and more.

This interference had some happy results, connected, for instance, with the supply of munitions and war material.

But the longer the war dragged on, the more difficult did it become to maintain that sacred unity which had existed at the beginning. Ambition, parliamentary intrigue, and party jealousy inevitably came into play once more.

Joffre, the victor of the Marne, was subjected to ever greater criticism, and a campaign, starting in Parliament, was inaugur-

ated against him, with the result that towards the end of 1916 he was superseded.

Who was to take his place? If military reasons alone were to be considered, which are the only ones which should have any

Change of Generalissimo. weight when a war is being waged, all the evidence and the claims of justice were in favour of Foch.

He had been second-in-command to Joffre, an extremely brilliant second, when, immediately after the Battle of the Marne, it was necessary, in conjunction with the British Army, to stem the German advance in the north towards Calais.

He had been put to the test on the Somme, and he possessed the full confidence of the English, with whom he was in complete accord, an extremely important consideration.

But purely political reasons were responsible for his being passed over. He was considered as being too religious, too Catholic.

"He is a mystic," a certain President of the Council once remarked to the author of this work. For very good reasons, however, he did not take the trouble to explain wherein his mysticism lay.

If Foch was set aside, there remained Pétain, who had just conducted the Battle of Verdun with great brilliance. The politicians considered that he was not sufficiently amenable.

In the end Nivelle was chosen, who was an excellent army leader, but certainly did not possess, in the same degree as Foch and Pétain, the combination of those rare and lofty qualities which are indispensable in a generalissimo.

The appointment of a new generalissimo at this precise juncture had a disastrous effect on the progress of the war. "Better not swap horses in mid-stream" is an adage the truth of which was never more apparent.

Joffre, profiting from all that had been learnt on the Somme, had arranged for a far more important Franco-British offensive to be launched at the beginning of February 1917 on both sides of the extremely sharp salient formed by the German lines in the direction of Noyon. But it was precisely this salient that Ludendorff was preparing to evacuate, as it was so difficult to hold, and the date arranged for this great retreat was precisely during the first weeks of February. The Allies' offensive would, therefore, have taken place just as the Germans were evacuating or preparing to evacuate their position, which is an exceedingly delicate operation, more especially in trench warfare, which entails the use of vast quantities of war material extremely cumbersome to move.

Thus there was a combination of the most favourable conditions for this Allied offensive, undertaken on a wide front with a plentiful supply of men and munitions, which might have resulted in a signal success.

The change in the command had one immediate result which was in the last degree disastrous—it postponed the date of the offensive, thus giving the German Staff time to carry out the retreat perfectly quietly without being disturbed, and with no loss of either men or guns.

When this great retreat had been successfully carried out— a triumph for the Germans—the problem which now faced the French Command was very different and the accompanying conditions undoubtedly less favourable.

The plan of the offensive had to be changed, a necessity to which General Nivelle was not sufficiently alive. The modifications he introduced were far from adequate, and the scheme upon which he eventually decided was full of defects. It was too simple and elementary and insufficiently worked out both as a whole and in detail. It made the mistake of arranging the second act before the first, and of exploiting victory rather than actually winning it. He launched the attack against the strongest and most difficult of the German positions, taking, as the saying is, the bull by the horns, which is often a bad method of dealing with the beast. Lastly, he did not inspire confidence —and this is a most serious defect—in some of those entrusted with the task of carrying out the plan.

In spite of all, the offensive took place, although it had given rise to unfortunate disagreements between the Government and the High Command, and between the latter and the executive Staff, leading General Nivelle to send in his resignation, which, however, he withdrew.

THE GREAT WAR

This was certainly a bad beginning for an operation of such magnitude.

Its failure, which was obvious, led to a change of generalissimo, and the appointment of Pétain, and gave rise to serious loss of confidence in the army, which might have led to a catastrophe. Mutinies broke out among the troops, though they were fewer among the units in the fighting line than among certain regiments at rest, who were poisoned from the rear by the defeatist propaganda which had been inadequately suppressed by the police and the Ministry of the Interior, though it was the essential duty of the latter to see to such matters.

General Pétain had to take in hand and restore the morale of an army which had just suffered defeat and whose confidence had been undermined.

But now once again, as had been the case before the Battle of the Marne, France had the unexpected good fortune of finding a leader who possessed every qualification for the task.

Tall and of commanding presence, cold and somewhat distant in appearance, with polished manners, attentive, deliberate and sparing of words, Pétain, beneath a stony exterior and deliberately ironic expression, hid a nature in which the highest sensitiveness was perhaps mingled with a certain shyness.

Joffre and Foch, the two other great leaders in the war, were southerners. Pétain, on the other hand, came from the north, and bore a certain resemblance to Turenne.

In his case spontaneity and dash, and therefore recklessness even more so, were bridled, disciplined and even repelled. His was a comprehensive and methodical mind, endowed with an innate sense of order and a brain of exceptional clarity and lucidity, a head divided into watertight compartments in which everything had been marked and classified from the very beginning. He set to work from the first moment at the task of reorganising the army both materially and morally. He visited the front from end to end, inspected each division separately, regiment by regiment, interviewing the officers, talking to them, and explaining to them in plain and simple language the most important points in their duty, and solicitous for the well-being, comfort and health of the troops. In a few weeks the army had recovered, proving that nothing was fundamentally wrong with it.

Unfortunately there could no longer be any question for a long time to come of an offensive on a large scale, particularly as just at this moment an event occurred, the results of which were incalculable—the almost complete collapse of the Russian front owing to the revolution of 1917, the downfall of the Tsarist regime, the disbanding of the armies (July and August), followed by the Bolshevist *coup d'état*, placing Lenin and his followers in power. The latter were ready—and they took no trouble to hide the fact—to forsake their allies in the middle of the war and conclude a separate peace with Germany on any terms.

And thus Germany and Austria were suddenly freed from all further anxiety on the Eastern Front and able to concentrate all their efforts against their enemies in the west.

The first step they took was to strike a violent blow against Italy, which immediately had the most important results.

The German Headquarters Staff was now in a position to send a few divisions to this front, which, in conjunction with the Austrian forces, fell upon the Italian troops, who were badly led and also poisoned by defeatist propaganda. They inflicted a defeat upon the latter at Caporetto, one of the most important in the war. The whole Italian front was shaken, and it was necessary, in order to prevent it from collapsing also, for the French and English to rush with all speed to the rescue. French and British divisions were despatched in hot haste to Italy and succeeded in stemming the German advance.

The year 1917 ended badly for the Allies. It had brought them only disappointment instead of victory, which, but for the mistakes that had been made, might and should have been theirs. For victory—and it is impossible to emphasise this point too strongly—might have been won by them as early as 1917. But it was snatched from them owing to military mistakes originating in political mistakes, and above all in the change in the High Command.

If the war had been won in 1917, that is to say, a year earlier than it actually was, it would have meant for the Allies, and above all for France, an aggregate of material and moral advantages on the importance of which there is no need to insist.

As hostilities were prolonged, the expenditure of human life and money increased in geometrical progression, and bled France white, poor as she already was in man-power. It devastated French territory and disorganised the finances of the country for a very long time.

In this respect it may be said that the year 1918 alone was as ruinous as the three preceding years.

After the war had ended on the Eastern Front, the French and English had to expect the enemy, who was now free to transport the greater part of his forces to the Western Front, to redouble his efforts and try to make an end of the matter by a series of decisive attacks.

Ludendorff's Offensives.

There were all manner of reasons urging Germany also to end the war as quickly as possible—the economic situation, which grew every day more serious, the shortage of raw material, the material and moral misery of the people, the ever-present possibility of the defection of her ally, Austria, whom she was practically supporting.

Thus Germany, eager to reach a decision, was about to make supreme efforts; at sea, by submarine warfare to the death, she hoped to oblige England to capitulate in a few months, and on land by means of powerful offensives she counted on breaking the Franco-British front.

These offensives, one on the 21st of March, 1918, in the direction of Amiens, where the French and English forces joined; and others on the 9th of April in Flanders, on the 27th of May at the Chemin des Dames, and on the 15th of July in Champagne, were from the tactical point of view conducted with consummate superiority and skill.

The element of surprise played an important part, especially in the first three. Owing to miraculous precautions being taken, making the troops march by night and reducing the artillery preparations to a minimum, the German Staff succeeded in massing its troops for the attack which broke the enemy's line without his adversary getting wind of it. But here the truth of what we have already said was again proved—the breaking of a front leads to no final decision as long as there are sufficient reserves in the rear to fill the gap.

The first of these attacks cut to pieces, literally pulverised, a whole British army, and that at the most critical point, where the English and French fronts met.

And now events themselves, and the danger of a catastrophe, demanded more peremptorily than ever the settlement of the **The Single** problem which the French and the English had **Command :** to their cost postponed for so long—that of unity **Foch.** of command.

It was at last decided at the Conference of Doullens, in March 1918, that Foch should be entrusted by the Governments of both countries with the task of " co-ordinating " the military efforts of the French and the English. This was the first important step in the direction of establishing unity of command.

The scope of Foch's mission was necessarily defined and widened during the weeks that followed, and he became Commander-in-Chief of the Allied forces.

A native of the Pyrenees like Joffre, born at Tarbes, and also a cold southerner like the latter, Foch, while he was still a young man of the rank of lieutenant-colonel and colonel, had gained a reputation through the famous course of instruction he gave at the *École de Guerre*, the lessons of which he has published in his two books—*Les Principes de la Guerre* and *La Conduite de la Guerre*.

All his ideas and doctrines are to be found in these two works. After formulating and summing them up in the first book, Foch shows their practical application in the second, which is a profound and illuminating study of the war of 1870.

Neither tall nor short, fat nor thin, robust without being heavy, and at once vigorous and refined, his most striking features are his eyes, which are sometimes cloudy and deep, at other times extraordinarily vivacious, shooting out a keen and penetrating glance from beneath their somewhat heavy lids. His speech is jerky and a little abrupt, and his voice has an indefinable touch of surliness. The prevailing impression he gives is one of frankness, loyalty and clarity, and if a motto had to be chosen for the Marshal, the following would be most appropriate—*Voir clair*.

He is a man who looks facts fairly and squarely in the face, who can see them as a whole and in detail, and allows nothing to come between himself and reality. No preconceived notion distorts his vision or perverts his judgment. He weighs up his enemy's forces at their just worth and lays his plans accordingly. The extreme vividness of his impressions and his swift imagination, which he owes to his southern blood, is tempered and held in check by imperturbable good sense, and calm clear judgment which is accustomed to take good stock of things, to weigh all the advantages and disadvantages carefully, and only to decide on good evidence, but, when once a decision has been taken, to carry it out to the end with minute attention to every detail and never allowing any obstacle to stand in the way. These qualities may seem contradictory, and, as a matter of fact, in nine-tenths of mankind they exclude one another. But in Foch they exist side by side in harmonious agreement, and it is to this combination that what may be called his genius is to be ascribed.

" What is the question at issue? " is the formula he is most fond of using.

The problem with which he was faced from that moment consisted first and foremost in preventing at all costs the breach between the French and English fronts at which Ludendorff was aiming.

When, at a council of war, at a time when the situation was most critical, the English General, Wilson, asked him point-blank the following question, "If you were obliged to sacrifice Paris or the Channel ports, which would you choose? " Foch replied, without a moment's hesitation, " I should defend them both."

This reply is characteristic of the whole man. And he did indeed succeed in defending both by means of a prodigious feat of equilibrium and an unstinted expenditure of wit and energy. A judicious use of his reserves, and the growing confidence which the English, and soon afterwards the Americans, came to have in him, enabled him, come what might, always to find sufficient forces to stem the German advance.

319

Throughout the whole war the strategy of the Germans was far inferior to their tactics. The point for the first attack had been admirably chosen by Ludendorff. But the same could not be said of those that followed. Ludendorff was guilty of the grave mistake of continuing each of his offensives for too long, after the advantage to be gained by them obviously became less in proportion as the hollow made in the enemy's front became deeper.

The results of the first few days were excellent and the advance terrific. At the Chemin des Dames, for instance, some divisions advanced as much as thirty miles in four days, which practically amounted to a return to a war of movement. But little by little the advance fizzled out ; it gradually grew less, and generally came to a standstill on the tenth day.

A really clever generalissimo would have realised this, and, rather than persist in futile efforts and sacrifices, he would have turned his attention elsewhere, and launched a fresh offensive at some other point along the front.

This is what Foch actually did a few months later.

But Ludendorff was guilty of another mistake, which was quite as serious and, moreover, developed from the first one. As he spent all his forces in each of his attacks, he was obliged to prolong the intervals between them, in order to have time to reconstitute his storming divisions.

But these intervals gave the enemy an incalculable advantage, as they allowed him to recover and to prepare and increase his reserves.

Now, as at the beginning of the war, the Germans, in keeping with their nature and temperament, imagined that, when once a plan had been thought out in every detail, all that remained was to carry it out on every occasion in order to be certain of obtaining the same results each time. But the element of surprise, which had been one of the principal reasons of their success, was bound to become less and less as time advanced.

After the three first offensives the French and English saw clearly through the enemy's secret. They sought and found the means of meeting it, which consisted in vacating the first lines, so that the hammer-stroke fell as it were on the void, and conducting the main defence from the supporting positions.

320

This system, which they carried out in combination, worked wonderfully well, and on the 15th of July it stopped and paralysed the fourth German offensive, which was to be the last.

From that moment, Foch, who never allowed an opportunity to slip, took the initiative, which he never again abandoned.

Each of the deep or shallow pockets made in the French lines by Ludendorff's offensives was admirably adapted for the making of flank attacks. While he was still forced to act on the defensive, and even at the most critical moment, after the Chemin des Dames, Foch always had the possibility of an offensive in view. For it was not his nature to receive blows without returning them. The plan he had prepared with the greatest care and secrecy arranged for a vigorous attack by the two armies under Mangin and Desgouttes on the flank of the German armies to the east of Villers-Cotterets. This offensive was launched on the 18th of July, only three days after Ludendorff's last attack. It met with signal success. The advance made by the French troops was considerable and the number of prisoners taken very great.

Foch had tested the enemy, and from that moment he had an intuition, characteristic of the really great soldier, that the former's stability and his capacity for resistance had been rudely shaken. It was therefore imperative to launch a fresh attack as soon as possible.

This attack, arranged with the same care and forethought, was carried out on the 8th of August on one of the sides of the other pocket hollowed in the French front by the German advance of the previous 21st of March. The success gained was greater than ever. The French and English divisions literally swept the enemy before them, a whole German division failing to stand their ground.

Foch's impression that the German Army was becoming exhausted became more definite. The art of war consists above all in knowing when to seize an opportunity, and from that moment Foch felt that something had gone wrong with the German machinery. He therefore decided to redouble the force and number of his blows. He was now convinced, as he has often since told the writer of these lines, that the exhaustion of the German Army would rapidly increase and that the war

Y

might end that year. But he was almost the only person to hold this opinion.

His method, as distinguished from that of Ludendorff, and far more intelligent, stating the problem as it should be stated, consisted in awaiting the success not only of a single offensive, however encouraging the results of it might at first sight appear, but of a combination of attacks cleverly planned, and dovetailing into each other in such a way as to use up the enemy's reserves as quickly as possible.

It was to this that he applied all his energy and intellect. It was a question, after the immediate objectives had been attained by the attacks of the 18th of July and the 8th of August, to decide upon more distant objectives.

Two powerful offensives were arranged for—one in the direction of Mézières from south to north, and the other from west to east in the direction of Sarrebourg.

But it is also necessary, and this is not the least difficult part of the task, to know how to inspire all those who have to carry out such operations with confidence and the will to succeed; and it was as an inspirer that Foch proved unsurpassed. French, English, Americans, Belgians, Portuguese and Italians—he directed the whole heterogeneous mass with a firm hand.

As the results grew more and more encouraging, Foch, who was now certain of victory, ordered a general offensive on the part of all the Allies, a concentric advance in the direction of the Ardennes. As the enemy flinched more and more, it was important to turn his exhaustion to account and to increase the rapidity with which the attacks followed each other.

When one of his old comrades, who was in command of a group of armies, suggested to Foch after each one of these offensives : " Now we shall be able to take breath for a bit," the latter replied in his dry, affectionate way, " Certainly not, old boy, you haven't got it at all; there is no time to take breath, you must be up and off again."

And this is precisely what happened. From the beginning of October, Foch began to concern himself with the terms of the armistice for which he felt certain that Ludendorff would before long be begging. Knowing the close connection between political and military questions, he wrote to Clemenceau about the middle of the month, asking him to inform him immediately what the policy of France was going to be in connection with that all-important question—the left bank of the Rhine.

Unfortunately, however, Clemenceau, who was too deeply imbued with revolutionary doctrines, and jealously anxious to keep the military leaders in their place and not to relinquish to them a single iota of the prerogatives belonging to the civil Government, asked Foch to keep strictly to his task of commanding the armies.

" We are at war ! " This celebrated dictum of Clemenceau was all very well so long as peace was still far away, but was not quite so admirable when the end of the war was in sight. For the natural conclusion of war is peace, which is quite as difficult to arrange and conclude as the war itself, if not more so.

But the diplomatic, economic and financial preparation for peace was entirely lacking. Had it been arranged with care, political, economic, and financial, as well as military, clauses might have been inserted in the armistice, which was the seed from which the Peace Treaty was to spring.

Foch, thus forced by Clemenceau to keep strictly to the military side, became involved in a lively, though none the less courteous, struggle with the English Government and High Command, to insure that the conditions imposed upon Germany should be extremely severe, arranging not only for the evacuation of Belgium and France, including Alsace-Lorraine, with which the English wished to be content, but also for the occupation of the right bank of the Rhine and the bridgeheads.

Sir Douglas Haig, who was far less confident than Foch because, unlike the latter, he could not see things as a whole and did not realise what the real condition of the German armies was, alarmed, moreover, by the increasing exhaustion of his forces, was of opinion that Germany should not be driven to extremes by exaggerated demands.

But Foch won the day, and on the 11th of November, in the forest of Compiègne, the German delegates, who at first attempted to resist, were obliged to accept all the conditions demanded by the Allies.

The German Army was literally at the end of its resources. It was incapable, as its leaders were well aware, of warding off the fresh attacks prepared by the Allies, and especially the one that was to have been made in Lorraine in the direction of the Sarre.

Germany, after a prolonged resistance which had tried the material and moral resources of the country to the utmost, suddenly gave way. She was within an ace of utter collapse.

Behind the lines as well as at the front all capacity for resistance had been destroyed. A revolution broke out in Berlin, and the Kaiser and the Crown Prince, in terror of their lives, fled from General Headquarters and sought refuge in Holland.

The Armistice has been severely criticised. As the Peace only gave France the two things that were indispensable to her—reparations and security—on an extremely inadequate scale, it was the Armistice itself that was held to blame.

But an armistice is a temporary cessation of hostilities with a view of allowing the victor the opportunity of imposing his conditions on the vanquished; it is at the same time the preliminary to the treaty of peace. Thus it has, or rather it should have, a political as well as a military side.

From the military point of view, the only one with which Foch was concerned, the Armistice, by placing the Allies on the Rhine and, moreover, handing over to them the strong bridgeheads on the right bank, put them in a position to obtain from Germany, who had no possible means of resisting, absolutely everything they wanted.

In the event of the latter failing to acquiesce, they could in a few days, almost without striking a blow, occupy the greater part of her territory. Thus, in this respect, it fulfilled its main object.

A few more victories won by the Allies, a few tens or hundreds of thousands more prisoners, or thousands of guns taken, would in no way have bettered their position.

From the political and economic point of view, however, it is clear that the Armistice could and should have included certain conditions preliminary to the Treaty of Peace, arranging, for instance, for the immediate payment of a large war indemnity, which Germany at that moment was in a position to do, as well as contributions in kind over and above the locomotives and

324

trucks demanded of her, and perhaps also a special clause concerning the left bank of the Rhine.

BIBLIOGRAPHY.—*Histoire des Opérations*, by the History Section of the French General Staff; two volumes ready :
Vol. I (2nd part only ready : *La Manœuvre en Retraite et les Préliminaires de la Bataille de la Marne*, 24th of August to the 5th of September, 1914).
Vol. VII (1st part : *Les Offensives de Dégagement*, 8th of July 1918—21st of September 1918).
The German General Staff is compiling a *History of the Operations* which is in course of publication.
G. Hanotaux, *Histoire Illustrée de la Guerre de 1914.* General Palat, *La Guerre sur le Front Occidental* (1917). Ludendorff's *Memoirs* (1919). The *Memoirs* of Hindenburg (1920), of Conrad von Hœtzendorf (4 vols., 1922–3), of Liman von Sanders and von Morgen, and of Generals Dubail and Dubois, Admiral von Tirpitz and Erich von Falkenhayn. General A. von Cramon, *Quatre Ans au Quartier Général Austro-Hongrois* (1922). Jean Léry (Raymond Recouly), *La Bataille dans la Forêt d'Argonne* (1916). *Memoirs of the German Crown Prince* (1925). H. Corda, *La Guerre Mondiale.* V. Giraud, *Histoire de la Grande Guerre* (1918). General Buat, *Hindenburg et Ludendorf Stratèges* (1923). Raymond Recouly, *General Joffre and his Battles* (New York, 1016); *Foch le Vainqueur* (1918); *La Bataille de Foch* (1919). General Mangin, *Comment finit la Guerre* (1920). Joseph Bedier, *L'Effort Français* (1919). General Gallieni, *Mémoires* (1920). General Canonge, *La Bataille de la Marne* (1918). General von Bülow, *Mon Rapport sur la Bataille de la Marne* (1923). Von Hausen, *Souvenirs de la Campagne de la Marne* (1922). Von Kluck, *La Marche sur Paris* (1922). Reginald Kann, *Le Plan de Campagne Allemand de 1914 et son Exécution* (1923). Louis Madelin, *La Mêlée des Flandres* (1927). General Berthaut, *De la Marne à la Mer du Nord* (1920). Colonel Normand, *L'Evolution de la Fortification de Campagne en France et en Allemagne, 1914–18* (1921). Lieutenant-Colonel Pellegrin, *La Vie d'une Armée pendant la Guerre* (1922). Colonel Dutil, *Les Chars d'Assaut* (1919). Louis Gillet, *La Bataille de Verdun* (1920). Lieutenant-Colonel de Thomasson, *Les Préliminaires de Verdun* (1920). Henri Bordeaux, *Les Derniers Jours du Fort de Vaux* (1916); *Les Captifs Délivrés* (1917); *La Bataille devant Souville* (1920); *La Victoire de Verdun.* P. Heuzé, *La Voie Sacrée* (1919). De Pierrefeu, *L'Offensive du 6 Avril* (1918). Commandant de Civrieux, *L'Offensive de 1917* (1919). Painlevé, *Comment j'ai nommé Foch et Pétain* (1923). Louis Madelin, *La Bataille de France* (1920). De Pierrefeu, *La Deuxième Bataille de la Marne* (1920).

CHAPTER XXIII

THE WAR AND THE ALLIANCES

The Triple Entente *versus* the Central Empires. The entry of Italy into the war. Bulgaria and Greece. Roumania. The Russian Revolution. The Intervention of America.

THE war, which from the very first day of its outbreak had brought the most powerful nations of Europe into conflict, was bound to draw into its net most of the neighbouring countries whose vital interests were more or less affected by the struggle.

" In this war there are no neutrals."

This phrase, which was frequently repeated between 1914 and 1918, did not fall far short of the truth.

And indeed very few neutrals remained in Europe, and they were small states—Switzerland, Holland and the Scandinavian countries, and a nation like Spain, whose geographical position kept her out of the conflict.

And even the latter was on several occasions within an ac of joining in.

Each of these two groups tried from the very beginning to use every means in its power—promises occasionally mingled with threats, and pressure of all sorts, to raise fresh allies.

The Triple Entente *versus* the Central Empires. The Germans were the first to win a point— they succeeded in bringing Turkey over to their side.

German diplomacy displayed a far better knowledge of how to move the Young Turks than the Triple Entente, whose representatives in Constantinople were guilty of great weakness and made one mistake after another.

Germany, however, hastened to use every appropriate means for laying her hand on the little group of men who were guiding

326

the destinies of the country with a sledgehammer, and above all on the two leaders, the two adventurers, Enver and Talaat, high-handed and violent characters, full of energy and courage, who recoiled from nothing, not even crime, in order to gain their ends. From the moment that she could count upon them, Germany knew that the game was won.

Nevertheless, the Turkish Government, fully aware, in spite of all, of the vast risks entailed by a war against three such powerful countries as England, Russia and France, hesitated.

But, as frequently happens in human affairs, an incident which at first sight seemed to be of trifling importance made one side of the scale fall definitely in favour of Germany.

This was the arrival, at the beginning of the war, of the *Goeben* and the *Breslau*, two powerful German battle cruisers, in the Bosphorus.

The chasing of these two ships right through the Mediterranean, which was patrolled by strong French and English squadrons, their escape through the meshes of this net, which they should never have been allowed to get through, and their eventual arrival in the Dardanelles without having once been hit, constitutes one of the most dramatic episodes of the war. And it led to the most unforeseen results.

The energy, courage and intelligence of the German leaders, sailors and diplomats, the weakness of the English and French naval men, not to mention an element of luck which, as frequently happens, intervened on the side of the most audacious, explain the whole episode.

When once these two vessels were in the Bosphorus, where, in violation of every rule, they remained fully armed, there was only one means whereby the Entente could save the situation, and that was by striking a similar blow and, by fair means or foul, sending their ships through the Dardanelles.

Instead of speaking out plainly at Constantinople, and if necessary taking action, the Cabinets of London, Paris and St. Petersburg, badly informed by their local representatives, decided to go softly to work, a method which has never succeeded with the Turks.

The Entente made a similar mistake in the following year in the case of Bulgaria, with exactly the same result.

327

There was ample proof that the Turks—only a blind man would have failed to see it—had already decided to join Germany. Under the very noses of the English, French and Russian Ambassadors, who allowed themselves to be bamboozled and intimidated, they were making open preparations for intervention.

When everything was ready they threw off the mask (October 1914); the German cruisers went out and bombarded the Russian ports in the Black Sea, and Turkey came into the war against the Entente.

And thus at one blow the only practical means of communication between England, France and Russia was cut off. This was an event of the utmost gravity and exercised the greatest influence on the course of the war. Russia, who both materially and morally stood in such dire need of being sustained by her allies, was left isolated. The results of this very quickly became apparent.

In vain did the French and English, in a belated attempt to make good their mistake, try to force the Dardanelles. A naval action, undertaken with inadequate preparation, and unsupported by an expeditionary force, failed, and a military expedition on the part of the Franco-British troops met with a similar fate.

It was now the turn of the Entente to gain a point. In May 1915 it succeeded, after prolonged and laborious negotiations, in deciding Italy to intervene.

Entry of Italy into the War. The Italian Government had from the beginning of the war proclaimed the neutrality of their country; but this, as everybody knew, was merely a preliminary gesture. Whatever the issue of the war, if Italy did not take part in it, her position would have been extremely difficult.

A certain Italian statesman had once made use of the striking phrase " sacred egoism." Both the belligerents tried to exploit this egoism and draw Italy over to their own side. Germany sent her greatest diplomatist, Prince von Bülow, to Rome. His marriage with an Italian and his own tact made him feel himself in a position to influence the decisions that had to be made. But in Barrère, the representative of France, he met a formidable rival.

THE WAR AND THE ALLIANCES

Twofold negotiations took place between Italy and each of the two groups. Germany brought all her influence to bear upon Austria in order to induce her to meet, at her own expense, the Italian claims regarding the Trentino and Trieste.

The Viennese Government, who were always behindhand both in time and ideas, had to be urged on, and only decided to make the sacrifice with all sorts of stipulations and reservations.

The other side possessed considerable advantages in this respect, as they were in a position to offer Italy a tract of territory, which they could make all the larger since it did not belong to them.

In addition to this, invisible forces were at work in favour of the Entente and proved the determining factor. It was d'Annunzio, the prince of letters, who during those memorable days gave expression to the profoundest feelings of his country.

And thus Italy joined her destinies with those of England and France. Her army launched an offensive, which soon came to a standstill, but which to a certain extent compensated for the Russian defeat and the great retreat made by the Russian armies in Galicia.

Ferdinand, the ruler of Bulgaria, the most astute and scheming of men, naturally inclined to the side from which he thought he had most to gain. After long and careful

Bulgaria and Greece. watching and calculation, and weighing the *pros* and *cons*, he plumped for Germany and lost.

Weighty dynastic reasons, and possibly also financial considerations (it has been asserted, not without reason, that Ferdinand, who was always in need of money, had received a large sum from Germany), played a part in his decision, which was also influenced just as much, if not more, by the spectacle afforded by the weakness of the Entente, and the failure of its political and diplomatic action in the Balkans, first with regard to Turkey and then with regard to Greece.

In the latter country the mass of public opinion was openly in favour of the Entente, whilst the king, for dynastic reasons, inclined to the side of Germany.

France, England and Russia, the three " Protecting Powers " to whom Greece owed her existence, could adopt a firm and haughty attitude all the more easily because, being uncontested rulers of the sea, they held the country at their mercy. They had the right to insist upon the maintenance of a constitutional Government which Constantine was openly violating, behaving like a regular autocrat and king by Divine right, dismissing Venizelos and dissolving Parliament.

But they did nothing of the kind. For a long time, too long in fact, Constantine was able to make puppets of them with impunity. Lack of unity among the Allies, the influence of the English and Russian Courts exercised in favour of Constantine, the private interests of Italy, who did not regard altogether with favour the entry of Venizelist Greece into the war and the marked advantages she would thus gain in the basin of the Mediterranean—these were some of the reasons accounting for their policy.

Without the support of Greece, the Anglo-French expeditionary force in Salonica was placed in a very difficult position, and found it impossible to carry out its task.

It was necessary to wait until the spring of 1917, long after the massacre of the French sailors at Zappeion, for the Entente, at the instigation of France, to make up its mind at last to take action.

A French statesman, Jonnart, sometime Governor-General of Algeria, where for ten years he had conducted operations with the greatest success, carried out this extremely delicate and difficult task with consummate mastery.

In spite of inadequate instructions and the lack of unity among the Allies, and owing entirely to his own energy, determination and prudence, he insisted upon and succeeded in bringing about the abdication and departure of Constantine and the Crown Prince without striking a blow. From that moment Greece, freed from her trammels, openly ranged herself on the side of the Allies.

Here, more than in any other country, in addition to material reasons, the "invisible" forces were all working in favour of the Entente, and above all of France.

Roumania. Long diplomatic negotiations eventually secured to Roumania the satisfaction of her national aspirations in Transylvania, the Bukovina and the Banat, and in August 1916 the Roumanians came into the war.

330

Inadequately prepared from the military point of view, and badly supported by Russia, their intervention resulted in a defeat. Roumania was invaded by the Austro-German armies and Bucharest, the capital, was occupied.

Her system of government, her social structure and her economic organisation made it impossible for Russia to carry on war for any very great length of time. Ten years previously, the Russo-Japanese War, although it had been fought at the uttermost ends of Asia, had already shaken her to her foundations, and there was all the more reason that a war fought on her own territory should have a similar effect.

The Russian Revolution.

The Tsar, a well-meaning but incurably weak man, was entirely dominated by the Tsarina, a neurasthenic invalid, greedy of power, who abandoned herself more and more to the influence of an adventurer, a sort of wonder-working monk, a semi-illiterate moujik, named Rasputin. The Tsar was completely out of touch with his people, the governing classes, small in numbers, were impotent, the Grand Dukes, who might have intervened, as they had done in other days (the assassination of Paul I), were divided among themselves and, with the exception of Nicolas-Nicolaievitch, former generalissimo, who had been sent by the Tsar practically into exile on the Caucasus front, were, moreover, for the most part mediocrities.

Towards the end of 1916 and the beginning of 1917 the Tsar was displaying ever-increasing signs of weakness and subjection to the Tsarina, who, for her part, entirely dominated by Rasputin, was continually interfering in the Government and making and unmaking Ministers. Some of the Grand Dukes wanted to depose Nicholas II ; but, as is frequently the case in Russia, they went no further.

Matters continued to go from bad to worse, and confusion increased. Public opinion became more and more dissatisfied. The Ministry of the Interior was in the hands of a semi-lunatic, Protopopoff, who in spite of everything was kept in office by the Tsarina.

A somewhat violent strike, organised in St. Petersburg by the Socialist and revolutionary committees, developed in forty-eight hours with the greatest ease in the world into a regular revolution, when the regiments in garrison, one after the other, accumulating strength like a snowball, passed over to the side of the insurgents.

An active propaganda had for some time been carried on in these regiments consisting of thousands of men, but lacking in any proper cadre (the dearth of officers having reached an acute stage). The Tsar, who was at General Headquarters, was forced to abdicate. The revolution was triumphant. Who was to guide its destinies?

The Duma and Parliamentary circles endeavoured to undertake the task, but they did so timidly and without sufficient energy. It was certainly no easy matter, as there was no basis. And thus the lead and the power passed more and more into the hands of the Soviets, the elected committees of workmen and soldiers, where, as is always the case, the most advanced and most violent lay down the law to the moderates.

With lightning strides, disorder, confusion and anarchy invaded every department of life, the Government offices, the railways and very soon the army, those in the rear quickly contaminating the front-line troops. Within the space of a few months, Russia, as a well-organised and disciplined force, capable of playing a part in the struggle, had ceased to exist.

The Bolshevist *coup d'état* of October 1917, and the separate peace of Brest-Litowsk, put the finishing touch to the situation.

For the Allies this was the heaviest blow under which they ran the risk of succumbing. But fortunately just at this **The Intervention of America.** moment, America, provoked by the excesses committed by Germany in carrying on her submarine war, entered the conflict on their side. Her intervention soon to a large extent made up for the defection of Russia, and thanks to it the Entente was able to win the war.

The German Headquarters Staff, who had obliged the German Government eventually to declare war in 1914, had forced it to enter upon unrestricted submarine warfare, which had the inevitable result, in spite of all the caution and hesitation of President Wilson, of ranging the United States on the side of the Allies.

Admirals and generals brought all possible pressure to bear

upon the civilian leaders in order to convert them to the necessity for a submarine war, to be conducted without restrictions of any kind. At a council on the 9th of January, 1917, over which the Kaiser presided, the Chancellor, Bethmann-Hollweg, although he realised the manifold dangers to which this adventurous policy was likely to lead, ended by giving his consent to it. On the 31st of January a Note was addressed to the neutrals informing them that all maritime traffic was thenceforward forbidden within the limits of a wide zone embracing British, French and Italian waters.

America did not take long to retaliate. President Wilson, cut to the quick, convoked the two Chambers and the Supreme Court at the Capitol on the 3rd of February, and read to them the declaration that diplomatic relations had been broken off between the United States and Germany, and returned Count Bernstorff his papers.

As had been the case in 1914, the German leaders, as soon as they had struck their surprise blow, endeavoured by means of tortuous negotiations and all kinds of manœuvres to palliate the consequences. But President Wilson had now gone too far to stop. He convoked Congress for the 2nd of April, and declared war against Germany. And thus the United States came in full force to the help of the Allies at one of the most critical moments of the war, when their reserves, military, naval and financial, were becoming exhausted.

The material and moral consequences of this intervention were most important, and it might be said that at this juncture it proved one of the decisive factors in the war.

In France, England and Italy, the determination which was beginning to flag was immediately revived. With her soldiers, her navy, her mercantile marine, her supplies and her wealth, America provided the Allies, so to speak, with unlimited support. The latter now had the certainty that the longer the war dragged on the more the constantly renewed sources of supply from America would make their weight felt. Thus they could face the prolongation of hostilities without much fear. The Central Empires, whose fighting power was becoming exhausted, were obliged to attack and win quickly. The Allies, on the contrary, had plenty of time before them.

THE THIRD REPUBLIC

BIBLIOGRAPHY.—Austro-Hungarian Red Books on the negotiations with Roumania and Italy. Italian Green Book. Greek White Book. Raymond Recouly, *Les Heures Tragiques d'Avant-Guerre* (unpublished documents on the entry of Roumania into the war). Take Jonesco, *Souvenirs*. Venizelos, *Cinq Ans d'Histoire Grecque, 1912–17*. G. Deville, *L'Entente, la Grèce et la Bulgarie* (1919). B. Auerbach *L'Autriche et la Hongrie pendant la Guerre* (1925). Lémonon, *L'Italie d'Après-Guerre* (1922). A. Gorski, *La Pologne et la Guerre* (1922). Raymond Recouly, *Monsieur Jonnart en Grèce et l'Abdication de Constantin* (1918). Prince Sixte de Bourbon, *L'Offre de Paix séparée de l'Autriche* (1921). A. Demblin, *Czernin und die Sixtus-Affaire* (1920). G. Alphaud, *Les Etats-Unis contre l'Allemagne* (1917). President Wilson, *Messages and Speeches* (1919). Count Bernstorff, *My Three Years in America* (London, 1920). Ed. Delage, *Les Dessous Politiques de la Guerre Sous-Marine Allemande*. Admiral Scheer, *Mémoires*. Hindenburg's and Ludendorff's *Memoirs*. *Lettres de l'Impératrice à Tsar Nicolas II* (a work of the utmost importance for the understanding of events in Russia; the original text of the letters, written in English, has been published by the Soviet Government, with a Russian translation and explanatory notes in two volumes, Berlin, 1922 (French translation, 1924)). *Journal Intime de Nicolas II* (1925). *Lettres des Grands-Ducs à Nicolas II* (1926). Raymond Recouly, *Le Printemps Rouge* (1925). M. Paléologue, *La Russie des Tsars pendant la Guerre* (1922). Sir George Buchanan, *My Mission to Russia and other Diplomatic Memories* (London, 1923). Claude Anet, *La Révolution Russe* (2 vols., 1917–18). Dr. Lorris Melikoff, *La Révolution Russe et la Nouvelle République Transcaucasienne*. Pierre Gilliard, tutor to the Imperial family, *Le Tragique Destin de Nicolas II et sa Famille* (1921). Jacques Sadoul, *Notes sur la Révolution Bolchévique* (1919). Émile Vandervelde, *Après la Révolution Russe* (1918).

CHAPTER XXIV

THE PEACE TREATY

Difficulties of the negotiations. The Congress of Paris. The
" Five." The guarantees. The reparations.

AFTER a war lasting fifty-two months, during which not a
day passed without fighting, a war which was one of
the most murderous and ruinous in her whole history,
it was necessary for France to secure :

1. Reparation for the heavy damages she had incurred;

Difficulties of the Negotiations.   2. The certainty that for a long time, if not
for ever, she would not have to fear any further
aggression on the part of Germany.

Reparations and guarantees, these were the two essential
points in the claims she had to make.

Rarely have greater difficulties presented themselves to
French negotiators. The material damage caused by the war
reached such a colossal figure that it might well be questioned
whether Germany would even be in a position to make good the
whole amount. And although France was the chief victim, she
was very far from being the only one. The unity of the Allies,
which had been so difficult to secure even when hostilities were
at their height and fear of their common danger demanded it,
was to be far more difficult to maintain when the peril was past.

England, as soon as she saw Germany beaten and her dynasty
destroyed, faced with the twofold menace of revolution and
Bolshevism, inevitably returned to her traditional policy of not
allowing another nation, such as France, to occupy too
prominent a position in Europe in her stead. She was thus
instinctively inclined to use every effort in order to limit the
consequences of the Allied victory as far as possible.

The United States had played a leading part during the last
months of the war. The number of soldiers they sent with
unsparing hand from the other side of the Atlantic, and the

economic support which they gave unreservedly to the Allies, enabled the latter to secure victory far more quickly than they had hoped.   The important part the Americans had played gave them the right to intervene actively in the peace negotiations, and to put forward, if not to insist on, their own solutions.

President Wilson is an idealist and in some respects an ideologist in whom the professor speaks for and frequently dominates the statesman.   His knowledge of European problems is entirely culled from books and hearsay—by no means the best sources of knowledge.

His grand idea, which he had had time to mature, was to use the Treaty as a means for launching a colossal scheme of international rules and regulations which would make war impossible in the future.   This scheme consisted in the creation of a *League of Nations*, founded by the victorious Powers, which the neutrals were to join, and later on the vanquished also.

This was not a new idea, but had for long been haunting the minds of certain statesmen and philosophers.

In addition to the practical difficulties presented by a huge scheme of this kind, the very fact that he wanted to include it in a treaty, which in itself was already sufficiently complicated, since it was to create a new Europe, added yet another difficulty. President Wilson clung tenaciously to his plan.   And thus the creation of the League and the conclusion of peace had to proceed hand in hand.   The English, anxious to have Wilson on their side, supported his scheme from the beginning, demanding in exchange full satisfaction for their two claims—the destruction of the German fleet, together with the confiscation of her mercantile marine, and the handing over of her colonies.   These demands, which were in themselves enormous, more especially the last, were nevertheless accepted without any objection being raised.

This was due to the fact that the whole British nation and all the Dominions, which the Government had very wisely associated in its programme, were solidly behind it.   And President Wilson, being for his part certain of England's support in the realisation of his scheme, made no attempt at opposition.

It was in the interests of France to follow similar tactics, to support Wilson's pretensions, on condition that she also laid her cards on the table and made known her two main claims for reparation and guarantees.

But this was not the method adopted. Clemenceau, the man who was conducting the negotiations, was better qualified, both in mind, character and temperament, to conduct the war to a close than to discuss the terms of peace. He was a fighter, not a negotiator.

Among the statesmen of the Third Republic there is no more striking and vigorous personality. This " Red Radical " from the Vendée, who from the beginning of his life had hurled himself into the political fray, and at the age of twenty-five had been Mayor of Montmartre under the Commune, is a direct descendant of the men of the Revolution. A man who loves fighting and does not mind blows, his abrupt manner concealing a nature fundamentally good and full of human kindness, a believer in the idea of progress which he had learnt from the philosophers of the eighteenth century, the spiritual fathers of the Revolution, Clemenceau provided an admirable example of energy, determination and courage during the darkest hours of 1917 and 1918. When he took over the reins of power he instinctively felt that unless it was led with a strong hand, after the manner of the Jacobins, the country, exhausted by three years of hostilities, was in danger of succumbing. He stretched the national energies to breaking point ; and the gravest disasters, that of the Chemin des Dames, for instance, did not make him lose confidence for a single moment.

The fact that the war was won is due to Foch and to Clemenceau.

The enormous prestige he gained by the victory, and the immense services he had rendered, made him master of France. Whenever he opened his mouth, or laid down the law, no one could stand up against him, and, as a matter of fact, no one tried to do so.

There is a celebrated picture of the Congress of Berlin which in 1878 settled Balkan affairs after the Russo-Turkish War. **The Congress of Paris.** Reproductions of it are to be seen on the walls of all the Embassies and Chancelleries of Europe. In the centre is Prince Bismarck, acting as President with a mixture of brutal authority and good temper,

z

and beside him, his rival, the other tenor, the Russian Chancellor Gortchakoff, the English delegate Lord Beaconsfield, the French representative Waddington with his whiskers, relegated to the end of the table, and the Turk in national costume. Twenty people at most make up the picture, each one of them being placed in the right order demanded by the rules of etiquette and the regulations of the protocol.

Now in order to balance this harmonious group, supposing a painter had tried to reproduce the whole assembly collected for the Conference of Paris in 1919, instead of about twenty participants, several hundreds would have had to be included, and in addition to the hundreds of delegates there would have been several hundreds of journalists, crushed up against each other, listening, writing, drawing, discussing and criticising. Instead of the beautiful symmetry of the first picture there would have been a mere chaotic rabble.

In the number of the Powers represented and the importance of the interests at issue, this Congress far surpassed all those held in preceding centuries, even the Congress of Vienna, after the Napoleonic era.

The whole map of Europe had to be remade as the result of the collapse of three powerful empires—Germany, Austria-Hungary and Turkey. After Europe came Asia and the spoils of the Ottoman Empire, Syria, Palestine, Arabia, etc., and then Africa, with the German colonies, etc., etc. America, through the United States and Brazil, also played a part in the negotiations.

In a matter so vast and complicated, in which such huge and multifarious interests were involved, the choice of method assumed considerable importance.

The Conference spent the first weeks and even the first months deliberately avoiding the main issues. Like Parliament, to which it had a great resemblance, it might be seen flitting from one problem to another, leaving what it had on the stocks in order suddenly to attack a different question.

As the large number of delegates seemed to present an obstacle to the progress of the negotiations, the five great Powers, England, the United States, France, Italy and Japan, decided that the leaders of their delegations should meet together in order to decide the fundamental questions. They were the "Big Five," the five great countries, as the Anglo-Saxon **The "Five."** journalists, who had swooped down in hundreds, not to say thousands, upon the French capital, dubbed them. The representatives of the minor Powers, as might have been expected, did not fail to show their displeasure at this arrangement, which had grave inconveniences for France. For among the members of this Areopagus, Japan and America had no European interests, whilst England was more of a sea Power than a continental Power, less interested in European affairs than in those connected with her own empire. France had everything to gain by not leaving the minor European nations out in the cold, for her traditional policy had for centuries led her to rely upon them, more especially as most of these nations, Czecho-Slovakia, Poland, Roumania and Yugoslavia, owed their existence, their recovery or their aggrandisement in a large measure to her. It was therefore a mistake and a source of weakness for France to be deprived of their support.

Of the two great questions to be settled, that of guarantees was the most important.

During the course of the last hundred years, France had seen her territory invaded four times—in 1814, 1815, 1870 and 1914— **The Guarantees.** her richest provinces occupied by the invader, her capital captured or on the point of being captured. The last invasion and war had been particularly disastrous for her, owing to the unprecedented material damage and the terrible slaughter of her people, who are one of the least prolific in Europe.

Any further invasion or war within the space of ten, twenty or thirty years would run the risk of inflicting the final blow, so that her vital interest is concerned in preventing it at all costs, and if necessary sacrificing everything else to this object.

What is the best way of obtaining the security of which she stands in such pressing need? There are only two ways of warding off an enemy's blows—either his power of attack must be diminished, or one's own powers of resistance must be increased. The two methods may also be combined.

How was it possible to diminish the military power of Germany, who, in spite of her territorial losses, Alsace-Lorraine, Posen and Schleswig, nevertheless still possessed a population one-third as large again as that of France? Divide Germany up? That was not to be thought of. It is impossible to put the clock back, and there is no power in the world capable of forcing people of the same race and language, who for over half a century have been merged into a single State, to carry on a separate existence.

Would it be possible, on the other hand, to disarm her in an absolutely efficacious way? If it were a matter of temporary disarmament—yes. But if permanent disarmament were meant, common-sense and reason said—no. A great country like Germany, with strong military traditions, always succeeds, however great the efforts made to bind her, in raising an army commensurate with her means and her requirements. It is therefore only reasonable to expect strictly limited results from any measure of disarmament.

Thus the only alternative was for France to increase her defensive forces as much as possible, and a prerequisite of this was to possess a powerful, almost impregnable frontier—the Rhine. As long as this frontier is strongly held no attack need be feared from Germany. Moreover, it requires comparatively small forces to hold it, a good frontier being much easier to protect than a bad one.

This was the theory advanced by Marshal Foch in his three Memoranda, where with impressive precision and power, and an extraordinary wealth of arguments, he proves that all real safety for France lies here and here alone.

Foch, anxious not to go beyond his own domain, kept resolutely to the military side of the question—the Rhine barrier; but it was no very difficult matter to transfer his idea from the military to the political and economic sphere, and to contemplate the formation of some sort of autonomous Rhineland State under the control of the Allies. There was no lack of good reasons for such a step.

This was not the first time that the question of security had been raised at the end of an extremely long and costly war, when the victors were naturally anxious, after the heavy sacrifices they had made, to place their victory above all possibility of being assailed. In the eighteenth century the Low Countries had to take similar precautions against France, and after the Napoleonic wars England and Prussia tried to make any violation of the new frontiers by France an impossibility. In each of these cases the remedy was the same—the creation of a strong defensive barrier, which afforded a far better guarantee of peace than any diplomatic arrangements or scraps of paper. After 1815 political precautions added additional strength to the military measures, and Belgium, which was entirely the idea and creation of England, anxious not to see France spread in that direction, or to have a bloody war to wage in Flanders within ten or fifteen years, was formed.

The course that had been adopted in 1815 with regard to Belgium might have been tried in 1919 in the case of the Rhineland.

The French Government at first accepted the Marshal's proposal and endeavoured to have it adopted by the Allies. But it met with violent opposition on the part of the Americans, and above all the English, Lloyd George refusing under any consideration to consent to a permanent occupation of the Rhineland.

Many important circumstances combined to force France to pay attention to these objections. Nevertheless, on what was for her a vital question, the safeguarding of her frontiers, she could and should have used every possible effort to have her solution accepted. England, in her demands concerning the German fleet and colonies, had set the example, and from the very beginning had openly formulated her terms and had them accepted. France could have done likewise. But, precisely because the task was difficult, she should have played all her best cards, and relied upon Marshal Foch, whose prestige stood extremely high with the Allies, and on public opinion and the country as a whole. But she never made sufficient use of the means at her command. All too soon the representatives of France gave way and took a back seat. They allowed themselves to consent to England's suggestion that, instead of having the Rhine as a definite frontier, as Foch insisted, there should be a treaty guaranteeing the help of England and America in case of German aggression.

This meant dropping the substance for the shadow, and

abandoning a concrete reality for a diplomatic " promise " of which events were soon to prove the weakness.

For England, having adroitly made her guarantee depend upon the ratification of the treaty by America, everything now rested with the latter. But it is a well-known fact that American public opinion is instinctively opposed to all inter-ference (*entanglement*) in European affairs, a clause in the Constitution obliging the Government to obtain the ratification by two-thirds of the Senate, a majority extremely difficult and often impossible to secure, for any treaty signed with a foreign Power. Thus the French Government accepted with ill-founded confidence a cheque which stood in danger of never being honoured.

It was content with the signature of President Wilson when, according to the Constitution, the signature should have been endorsed by the Senate. If this were not done (and in matters of such great importance it is wise to expect the worst) the whole agreement would become null and void. And this is precisely what happened in the case of Wilson, who, in spite of every effort, did not succeed in getting the Senate to ratify either the treaty of guarantee or the agreement regarding the League of Nations. Thus the guarantee given by England automatically vanished into thin air, with the result that in the end France found she had received nothing in exchange for the important concession she had made.

The occupation of the Rhineland for fifteen years, with a withdrawal every five years, to a certain extent remedied this serious drawback. But fifteen years in the life of a people is not a very long period of time. Instead of a lasting solution, upon which France had every right to insist, she obtained only a temporary and precarious settlement.

A similar levity and absence of realism was shown with regard to reparations. To make Germany pay the maximum of which she was capable was only desirable and right.

Reparations. But in view of the colossal proportions of the bill presented by each of the belligerents, it stood to reason that the obligation could not be met in its entirety. Care had to be taken not to allow it to swell to exaggerated proportions, without regard to what was practicable, and also first and foremost to

THE PEACE TREATY

seek a practical and convenient method of obtaining the largest possible sum at the *earliest possible moment*.

France had been the battle-field for all the Allies, and although the terrible destruction carried out on her territory had for the most part, it is true, been the work of the enemy, a certain amount was due to the Allies themselves. This was an incontrovertible fact which she could use in demanding a formal right of priority for the restoration of the devastated regions. This claim, strong though it was, failed to be supported by the French delegates with all the vigour, precision and determination it warranted.

This was a grave mistake, the consequences of which were to weigh heavily on the finances of the nation. A wave of optimism, carelessness and *laisser-aller*, for which there were, however, sufficient psychological reasons in the sudden relaxation after an effort which had been unduly prolonged, spread over Europe as soon as the war was over. Instead of overcoming difficulties it was found simpler not to face them, and instead of determining once and for all, as common-sense demanded, the amount to be paid by Germany, while keeping the sum within reasonable limits, it was decided to leave it vague. The Allies appointed a Reparations Commission, one of the principal duties of which was to settle periodically the yearly amount to be disbursed by Germany. But it would be impossible to find any case of a debtor hastening to satisfy the claims of his creditor when the latter has been foolish enough not to inform him exactly what he owes him.

This initial mistake was followed by a second. The sum the Allies hoped to get from Germany was obviously too large, and beyond all bounds of possibility. The consequence might easily have been foreseen; Germany, riddled by Socialism, which, here as elsewhere, upset her Budget, increased her expenditure enormously without raising her receipts in proportion, so that year by year she saw the deficit grow larger and larger. Whereupon she quickly came to the conclusion that after all it would be more to her advantage to go bankrupt than to meet the heavy yearly payments expected by her conquerors.

Such as it was, with all its qualities and defects, the Treaty of Versailles and the supplementary treaties of Trianon, St. Germain and Reuilly made a new map of Europe.

France regained Alsace-Lorraine, where her armies made a triumphal entry on the day after the Armistice, and the enthusiasm of the people proved the depth and tenacity of their attachment to the mother-country. A special system was instituted in the Sarre, which, after a period of fifteen years, was to decide by means of a plebiscite whether it would become incorporated with France or Germany.

After suffering an eclipse of over a century, Poland was at last restored to life. She recovered all her territories which the neighbouring empires had cynically divided between themselves, and two of which had just collapsed.

Bohemia, which for centuries had been annexed to Austria, recovered her independence, with the addition of Slovakia, which was taken from the Magyars. Roumania, Yugoslavia and Italy received very considerable accretions of territory, chiefly at the expense of Austria-Hungary.

Thus the map of Europe was modified, not to say upset, far more drastically than it had been even after the Congress of Vienna some hundred years previously.

What was the value of these new structures raised in the place or at the expense of the old empires? Fears are frequently expressed regarding the solidity of certain among them, notably Poland and Czecho-Slovakia.

Nevertheless, both the Poles and the Czechs, to mention only these two peoples, possess all the requirements, and have the moral qualities as well as the material power, to develop into nations capable of living and growing. They are menaced by external dangers, Poland especially, who is placed in a dangerous geographical situation—hence her temporary eclipse—between Germany and Russia. But she is not the only one in this position.

It must also be borne in mind that the majority of the European nations, exhausted by a war lasting over four years, will not for a fairly long time be in a fit state to renew hostilities, even if they had the wish to do so. And this period can be turned to account by the young nations in order to settle down and develop.

If, on the other hand, the conquered are animated by the very natural desire to seek compensation for the consequences of their defeat, there is nothing to prevent the victors from devising means of defence against this spirit of revenge. But if they will only come to an agreement with each other (and the common danger threatening them is driving them in this direction) it will be possible for them to prevent any further act of aggression.

BIBLIOGRAPHY.—C. House, *What Really Happened at Paris : The Story of the Peace Conference* (1921). R. Lansing, *The Peace Negotiations* (1920). R. Stannard Baker, *Wilson and the World Settlement* (3 vols., abridged French translation, 1924). G. Clemenceau, *La France devant l'Allemagne*. H. W. Temperly, *A History of the Peace Conference of Paris* (6 vols., 1920). Léon Bourgeois, *Le Traité de Paix de Versailles* (1919). Louis Barthou, *Le Traité de Paix de Versailles* (1919) (Reports submitted to the Senate and the Chamber). G. Hanotaux, *Le Traité de Versailles du 28 Juin, 1919* (1919). Victor Bérard, *La Paix Française* (1919). F. Nitti, *La Paix* (1925). J. M. Keynes, *The Economic Consequences of the Peace* (1920); *A Revision of the Treaty : Being a Sequel to the Economic Consequences of the Peace* (1922).

CHAPTER XXV

MANNERS AND CHANGES IN THE LIFE OF THE NATION

The cost of living. Aviation. The appearance of Paris.

DURING the fifty years following the war of 1870, and especially during the last twenty-five, the extraordinary improvement in the means of transport, the motor-car and the aeroplane, together with electricity and the telephone, brought about a change in the conditions of life far greater than any that had taken place during the preceding two or three centuries.

The motor-car was one of the chief agents in this transformation. Although the railways had increased very considerably, in 1912 covering 31,875 miles as compared with 6000 in 1860, that is to say, more than five times as much ground, this increase had taken place gradually. The growth of motor transport, on the other hand, was accomplished far more quickly, and the changes introduced were more extensive and pronounced.

The railway had left certain distant regions untouched, towns and villages the appearance and daily life of which differed very little from what they had been a hundred years previously. But with the advent of the motor-car, owing to the network of roads with which France is so richly endowed, there is no longer any district, village or even hamlet, however remote, which has not been reached. The railway had led to the desertion of the roads and the inns scattered upon them, and they served only local needs. But suddenly the motor-car, as it were by a wave of a fairy wand, filled them once again with life and animation. The whole aspect of the countryside and its way of life have been completely changed by it.

Ever since its appearance during the last years of the nineteenth century, and the combination of an internal combustion

346

engine with pneumatic tyres, the number of vehicles has never ceased to grow.

The war interrupted this development, but no sooner was it over than it started again.

In 1913 there were 100,000 cars in France, double that number in 1920 and treble in 1922, in 1923 they reached the figure of 445,000, in 1924 578,000, and in 1925 720,000. Very soon there will be a million.

The United States, where there is hardly a family, however poor, that does not possess its car, shows the scope and direction of this development. By bringing the country districts into touch with the towns it is gradually modifying their relations with each other. The great centres where life is difficult, owing to the scarcity and costliness of accommodation and the increasing congestion in the streets, will tend to overflow into the neighbouring country districts and swell the suburbs to unwieldy proportions. The railway was one of the causes among many others of the depopulation of the countryside. It brought about the influx of a number of rural inhabitants into the urban centres. But it is possible that in a country like France, where the distances are not very great, the motor-car will have the opposite result, and bring back to the rural districts, and the provincial and small towns, if not to the villages, a part of the population that had left them. And thus to a certain extent it might remedy the disastrous depopulation of the countryside.

The migration of the village populations to the towns, especially to the largest towns, was taking place throughout the nineteenth century, and particularly from 1870 to the present day. It provided one of the reasons for the fall in population, and can be explained on various grounds, both material and moral. Not only did life remain hard, very hard in fact, in most of the country districts, where the comforts and amenities of existence had hardly improved at all for a hundred years, but life there seemed dismal and devoid of attraction to many of those, and especially the young people, who were able to compare it with life in the cities. Hence the disturbance of the equilibrium.

The lot of agricultural workers, labourers, farmers and small landowners, had made but little progress. The price of certain agricultural products, instead of rising, had, on the contrary, tended to go down, although the value of money had diminished.

Wheat, which in 1860 was worth a little over 32 francs per 100 kilogrammes, after going down to 19 francs in 1881, and 13 in 1895, stood at 15 fr. 50 cnts. in 1903. Butter, which was worth 2 fr. 90 cnts. the kilogramme in 1860, fetched no higher price in 1913. Wine, the price of which went up after the terrible epidemic of phylloxera, soon fell again. At one time in 1907 it was sold for less than 10 centimes the litre. This was one of the reasons for the grave disturbances in the South, where there were general conferences of the wine-growers, meetings, and strikes in Narbonne and Béziers, and a mutiny in one regiment, the 17th.

In this department, as in every other, the war was responsible for great changes. Agricultural produce now fetches a far higher price, and the prosperity and well-being of the rural populations have increased. Many villages now have electricity, the telephone and the cinema. The day is not far distant when every holder of a few acres will have his motor-car, and thus be able to visit the town whenever he wants, and to a large extent enjoy its advantages without having to put up with any of its inconveniences.

One of Balzac's characters round about 1830, when he wanted to treat himself to a succulent lunch, went to the best eating-house in the Palais Royal, chose an excellent bill of fare, and got off at the cost of 14 francs.

A few months before the war, in 1914, it was possible to get for this sum at the Café Anglais, which was still in existence, or at Larue's, a lunch which, if it was not succulent and made up of the rarest dishes, was at all events extremely good. This proves that, even in the capital, which owing to the influx of foreigners had become a sort of holiday haunt, prices had not materially increased during the course of the century. The same remark is even more true of the provinces.

The Cost of Living.

A student could live without over-much privation in the Quartier Latin for 150 francs a month. On 200 he could do himself well. He could obtain adequate board for 80 to 90 francs, and a room for 30 or 40. Certain agricultural products, as we have seen above, could be had for less than they had cost fifty years previously. This was the case with sugar and a great many imported articles—tea, coffee, etc.

When to-day one refers with a certain melancholy regret to the good old pre-war days, it is this ease and this cheapness of living that one chiefly has in mind, and they appear all the greater compared with the harsh conditions of the present day.

France, which was wonderfully well balanced, and where agriculture and industry played an equal part, afforded both the native and the visitor the means of leading a more agreeable existence than anywhere else at the smallest possible expense.

The war of 1870 and the Commune had only, so to speak, scratched the surface of her huge resources. As soon as peace was restored, the nation returned to work and to save, industry and thrift being its chief characteristics. Money and capital were plentiful, and when they were not used at home were largely invested abroad. They brought in a considerable revenue, which was added to the fund of wealth which had never ceased to grow.

What the motor-car has done for the inhabitants of a single country, aviation is accomplishing with regard to the various
Aviation. nations of the world. Here again the margin of progress is practically unlimited.

The aeroplane, of which the Wright Brothers were the pioneers, made its first appearance before the general public at the famous meeting of Rheims in the summer of 1908. These were wonderful, triumphant days. All of us who lived through them had the feeling that a tremendous step forward had been taken. At the gates of the wonderful city that Rheims was before the war, the spectators in their seats saw one, two, three, four, five, six aeroplanes rise from the ground at the end of the track, fly several times round the aerodrome and alight again as easily and gently as they had ascended. Man had conquered a new element, and the sphere of his victory has never ceased to grow.

THE THIRD REPUBLIC

The use of the aeroplane has increased with giant strides. There is a regular air service between the various capitals. From Paris, Casablanca can be reached in a day, which is three days shorter than the most rapid of the other means of transport. And this rapidity is continually increasing. Aviators, the majority of whom are Frenchmen, have accomplished prodigious non-stop flights of as much as 3750 miles or more— Paris to Omsk in the middle of Siberia; Paris to Karachi on the Persian Gulf. Flown over at such high speed, the world, which seemed so huge to our fathers, now suddenly appears to have shrunk to nothing. In hardly more than a week it would be possible to fly right round it.

Until the advent of the motor-car, in the first years of the century, the appearance of the Paris streets had changed very little. The horse-drawn vehicles, carts, cabs, omnibuses and private carriages allowed the pedestrian, even in the most crowded places, to cross the streets with ease and safety. The traffic moved to slow time. When the tramways made their first somewhat cautious appearance, many of them were horse-drawn and did not go any faster than the carriages. The underground railway, the Metropolitan, which for a long time remained under consideration, and which was made the butt of the music-hall comedian, as though it would never be carried out, was nevertheless built and the first lines opened to the public at the time of the Exhibition of 1900.

Those who did not know Paris at the end of the nineteenth century can have no idea of how delightful and easy it was to walk about there.

The motor-car quickly changed all that. By greatly increasing the speed of the traffic, it has almost swept the pedestrian off the streets. Crossing the road has become a problem fraught with considerable difficulty and danger. Fortunately Haussmann, who has been subjected to unjustifiable criticism, was in his day possessed of great foresight and vision. Thanks to the great arteries he built, it is still possible for the traffic to circulate in the principal avenues. But this will not be the case for long. The number of vehicles is continually increasing,

MANNERS AND CHANGES

and never ceases to do so, and it will accordingly soon become necessary either to widen the streets, which would be extremely expensive, or to take drastic measures, such as forbidding the use of horse-drawn vehicles, not allowing carriages to stop in the street, and abolishing the tramways, etc.

CHAPTER XXVI

THE PUBLIC MIND AND THE MARCH OF IDEAS

Political evolution. The new leaders. The Press. The trend
of philosophy. Taine and Renan. Bergson. Literature and
politics. The spread of French culture.

IF we examine the curve of political evolution since 1870, we
find a marked movement to the Left and in the direction
of the extremists. The war seemed to have upset and
disorganised the old parties and brought forward a new one in
their stead. But this was only apparently so. After a short
Political interval the movement started again. The
Evolution. absence of unity among the moderates, their lack
The New of political insight and the insufficient attention
Leaders. paid by them to the electoral campaigns, which
like all other battles can only be won after adequate preparation,
account for this change.

As this movement towards the parties of the Left became
defined, the quality and social standing of the deputies under-
went a corresponding modification. Some of the departments
in the West, where Conservative influence was still paramount,
elected aristocrats, chiefly large landowners. But almost
everywhere else, with but rare exceptions, these social classes,
which were still numerous during the years following 1870, came
to be disregarded more and more. It was almost exclusively
from the ranks of the bourgeoisie, and ever more from the
middle and lower sections among them, and in the case of the
Socialists from the people themselves, that parliamentary
representatives came to be chosen—the members of the liberal
professions, lawyers, doctors, professors and small country
landowners.

The lawyers formed a large majority. Their clients, and the
multifarious ramifications which through them they were able
to thrust out into their districts, their practice in speaking which

enabled them easily to take the lead at public meetings, all fitted them for the electoral campaign. The Chamber and Ministries resulting from this were largely composed of lawyers, who brought into the Government and into Parliament their own habits and methods and their professional outlook—that is, a facile and rapid grasp of a subject and a gift for exposition all too often combined with inadequate documentation, superficial views easily disguised under a torrent of words, and above all the inability to come to grips with reality and reach a conclusion, the lawyer being inclined to imagine that he has achieved his task as soon as he has finished pleading.

The newspapers, owing to the gigantic strides they had made, were destined to play an important part in the formation of the public mind. Nevertheless, their part is perhaps not quite so great as might at first sight be supposed.

Tho Pross.

The Press, which had been muzzled under the Empire, recovered full liberty of action immediately after the 4th of September. Newspapers were founded without let or hindrance. The editors, provided their directors approve, which is not always the case, write whatever they please; and only flagrant misdemeanours or libels bring them within the arm of the law. With the cheapening of paper and the invention of the rotary press, which allows of the printing of hundreds of thousands of copies in a few hours, newspapers with a huge circulation came into being—first of all the *Petit Journal*, then the *Petit Parisien*, *Le Matin*, *Le Journal*, etc. Owing to its wealth and the material power at its disposal, the journal which is a purveyor of news takes the precedence as far as circulation is concerned of the journal of *ideas*. Some of these papers have a daily circulation almost reaching the colossal figure of two million copies. Others stand at about one million. Editions such as these would have seemed incredible fifty years ago, as well as the low price at which they are sold—a halfpenny (which was the usual pre-war price, and out of that a certain amount was paid by the proprietors to the retail agents). How was it possible for that price to provide readers with six or eight pages, containing the most recent news, various articles, stories and one or two serials, etc.?

A A

Apparently these papers are sold at a loss. A newspaper is like a shopkeeper who sells for a halfpenny an article which costs him three-farthings. It is the advertisements alone that make up for this loss, the revenue from which increases with the growth in circulation. It is upon the advertisements that the whole concern depends, and the money derived from them, which in the old days was negligible, has become a power that rules everything. Suppress or reduce its sphere, and the paper would immediately become bankrupt. This essential factor has led to all manner of important results.

Obliged, on account of the advertisements, which are its only source of revenue, to print extremely large editions, the great newspaper is more and more condemned, if it does not wish to give offence to one or the other class of its wide public, to eliminate, especially in the sphere of politics, where susceptibilities are easily aroused, any definite expression of opinion or categoric verdict. It preserves a convenient neutrality which allows it to support, though without over-much zeal, the various Governments that succeed one another, however different and opposed to each other they may be. It abstains from taking sides in the party struggle, and when it is a matter of home or even of foreign policy, it states the facts without drawing any conclusions.

For similar reasons it replaces, in the daily bill of fare served up to its readers, the solid and substantial dishes by lighter articles of diet, pastries being given the preference over meat. Serious and well-documented articles give way on the first page to the description of various events dished up in the most attractive guise in order to whet the curiosity of the reader. The art of the journalist has become above all a matter of how to present his material, and, however varied this may be, the first page, and often the first two pages, of the newspapers that have a wide circulation are more or less identical. When one of them has been read the rest might at a pinch be dispensed with.

This abuse of political neutrality, this absence of standards and doctrines, has been pushed so far that it has ended in provoking a reaction, and those great papers, like the *Temps* and the *Journal des Débats*, to mention only two, that stand for definite ideas, have for this reason largely increased their circulation. New journals of this description, representing one side or the other, have come into being. Some of them achieved considerable success from the beginning, proving that they supplied a need.

As a result of this change it would not be correct to say that the Press as a whole, in spite of its extraordinary growth, its increase of power, and its material prosperity, holds a more important position with regard to the moulding and development of the public mind than it did at the beginning of the Third Republic. Indeed there would be no paradox in maintaining the opposite. In those days, when there were not so many papers and their circulation was much smaller, an article signed by a well-known name, and appearing at an opportune moment, had a notoriety and a scope which it would be hard to secure to-day.

The millions of readers of the great newspapers are like the spectators in the cinema, before whose eyes are unrolled all manner of the most diverse and incompatible scenes, one following on the heels of the other, and by the very rapidity of their sequence leaving no lasting impression on the mind. One of the masters of latter-day journalism, Adrien Hébrard, used to say : " The newspaper is a thing which is born in the morning and dies at night." And he would add with a cynical smile : " Sometimes it is dead by midday."

Similarly, the influence of individual journalists upon politics and the public mind has, on the whole, diminished rather than increased. And their material position, which in our society is becoming more and more the criterion of importance and standing, seems to be in process of decline, and is very far from having kept pace with the rise in the cost of living. But the journalist has this in common with men of letters, artists and some of the liberal professions.

It is impossible in these pages, for lack of space, to give even the most rapid sketch of the evolution of literature during the last fifty years. We must restrict ourselves, resolutely ignoring everything else, to pointing out the essential features connecting the development of ideas on the one hand and politics and public opinion on the other.

The Trend of Philosophy. Taine and Renan.

355

THE THIRD REPUBLIC

Just after 1870, Taine and Renan, who were at the height of their fame, were regarded as the two summits of French thought.

In both men the war, which they had not foreseen, caused a terrible upheaval, dissipating the clouds with one fell swoop, and revealing to their gaze a Germany as ferocious as she was strange. The country of scholars, philosophers and professors, their second intellectual home, suddenly appeared in her real light —the Prussian pointed helmet dominating and crushing everything else, or, rather, what was even more serious, the thinkers, philosophers and professors rendering willing and docile obedience to the pointed helmet.

In the case of Taine the disillusionment was profound and almost tragic. Everything in which he believed crashed before his very eyes. He was living in a vast cemetery in which his illusions lay scattered on the ground before him. Hence his feeling of distress. On the 7th of February, 1871, he wrote about the Germans to a friend of his, Émile Planat : " The war has brought to light the bad and ugly side of their nature, which had been covered by a veneer of civilisation. The Teutonic beast is brutal at heart, harsh, despotic and barbarous. . . . All this has been brought to light and fills one with horror."

His theories and visions had hidden from him the soul of Germany as Prussia, the " male organ of Germany," as it has aptly been termed, had been fashioning it for upwards of a century.

Renan had shown no better understanding. Nevertheless they were familiar with Germany, and Taine had visited it only a few weeks before the war.

Another who had also seen and suspected nothing was Flaubert. The year after Sadowa he wrote : " And now they are talking about war. But I do not believe it. With whom? Prussia? Prussia is not so foolish ! "

Flaubert was nothing but a man of letters, shut up in his ivory tower and refusing to become anything more. But Renan and Taine were philosophers and historians. The deception of which they had been the victims fell upon them like a hammer-stroke and stunned them for the moment. Taine for some weeks declared himself incapable of work, and he was obliged to make a supreme effort in order to continue his course at the Beaux-Arts. The war, the defeat, the Commune, and the disastrous effect they produced in him, determined the course of his future moral evolution, his judgment of history and politics as well as the exercise of his activities. His chief philosophic and literary works were written before the war. But now it was history that attracted him, recent history and its connection with politics. As that which exists to-day is, according to his theories, the direct and inevitable result of that which existed yesterday, how did nineteenth-century France develop out of the eighteenth century, how did the Revolution proceed from the *ancien régime*, and modern France from the Revolution?

Whilst he supported his young friend Boutmy with all his might, and helped him to found the School of Political Science, under the sway of similar preoccupations he harnessed himself, like a Benedictine, to his great work, *Les Origines de la France Contemporaine*. For days at a time he would shut himself up in the *Bibliothèque Nationale* and the *Archives*, turning over masses of old papers in his endeavour to find among them the hundred and one representative and typical little facts which explain and shed light upon the past. His great philosophic idea was the guiding line of his researches. It was entirely based upon Spinoza's famous phrase, " Man is not in the universe like an empire within an empire, but like a part within the whole." If the human animal was therefore only the result of natural forces—climate, environment and time—from which it was impossible for him, even in the smallest degree, to free himself, what were these forces, and how did they work? What results were they likely to produce?

Thus history became a vast structure, the arrangement of which was regulated by one general thought, and to which the multitudinous separate events, to which a vast documentation bears evidence, impart life and movement. First came the *ancien régime*, with all its apparent grandeur, its magnificent external façade, but also with all the weaknesses, all the imperfections of its internal mechanism, which grew worse from day to day, until at last the explosion occurred which blew everything up into the air. The Revolution proceeded from the *ancien régime* as surely as a river runs from its source; the forces directing it were blind, disorganised and chaotic. They loosed the bridle on the worst instincts of man, who then behaved like a " gorilla unchained." And behold, the Titan in whom the Revolution culminated, a kind of audacious *condottiere*, loving nothing so much as danger, living wholly and solely in the present and careless of the future, built up a new France in his own image, in which the college was but a preparation for the barracks, an over-centralised, dragooned country, made not to govern herself but to obey the command of a single man.

An atmosphere of bitterness and pessimism pervades the whole of this work. Everything in contemporary France must therefore be bad, and the whole edifice only fit to be rebuilt stone by stone. But who was to undertake the task of reconstruction ?

The anxieties and troubles of his day explain this pessimism to a large extent. No writer, however hidebound he might be, could altogether escape the preoccupations and worries which assailed him on every side. The agony of the terrible year darkened the colours on his palette. Taine, moreover, who was a great admirer of England, was always biassed in his judgment of France by a comparison with British history and politics.

Dark as was his outlook in dealing with his own country, as soon as he turned to her neighbour he saw everything through rose-coloured spectacles. In both cases his verdict was prejudiced. The love of the abstract and belief in a system fairly frequently distort the vision and falsify the judgment.

Nevertheless, his history remains, on account of the beauty of the whole and the animated profusion and vivacity of its detail, a magnificent work, the influence of which radiated far and wide. The praise and criticism with which it was met, the controversy and commotion to which it gave rise, awakened the curiosity of the public, even of the public at large, and turned their attention to the questions with which it dealt.

Renan also, whose illusions regarding Germany suffered a rude awakening, continued his *Origins of Christianity* after the war. The *Antichrist* dates from 1873, the *Gospels* from 1877, *Marcus Aurelius* from 1881. Between 1888 and 1894 he undertook the *History of the People of Israel*. The *Philosophic Dialogues* belong to 1876, and the *Philosophic Dramas* to 1878–86.

THE PUBLIC MIND

After 1870, in his *Réforme Intellectuale et Morale*, which in many respects seems to be a contradiction to the rest of his work, he recommended the reconstruction of France on the military and political, that is to say, the autocratic, model of Prussia, her victor. The brutal lesson of reality led him to throw some of his ideas overboard in this way. He returned to the writing of his great historical masterpiece, working steadily at it, adding stone to stone. From time to time he took a rest from this erudite occupation, of which the charm of his genius did not always succeed in softening the austerity. The love of ideas and of discussion for its own sake and for the mere pleasure such an exercise provides for the mind, and philosophic doubt, are poured forth in the *Dialogues* and the *Dramas*, where more than anywhere else the magic of his mind and the witchery of his style are apparent.

The Republicans and the anti-clerical party, without the slightest authority on his part, laid hold of him and used some of his conclusions in their struggle with the Church. In this way he exercised considerable influence on politics. What has been called the spirit of Renan, and his attitude of doubt, which occasionally is not very far removed from dilettantism, made themselves felt until almost the end of the century.

In the case of Taine, as in that of Renan, his beliefs and doctrines were but ill suited to the needs and the aspirations of a country anxious to resume her place in the front rank among the great nations of Europe and of the world, and to restore the power of France both from the material and the moral point of view. In many respects thought and action were in contradiction, and many, especially among the young, were tending to escape from the somewhat frigid circle in which their intellectual leaders had confined them.

And now Bergson, one of the great masters of contemporary thought, appeared and threw the whole issue open to discussion.

Bergson. His Doctrine. His first book, *Time and Free-will: an Essay on the Immediate Data of Consciousness* (1888), aroused lively interest, and through his courses of lectures at the Lycée Henri IV, the École Normale and the Collège de France, he exercised a very wide influence. A whole generation

359

of students, professors and writers has been deeply imbued with his ideas.

What is the quality at the base of this philosophy which adapts it far better than its predecessor to the spirit and tendencies of the new France? As happens in the case of every system which has attained a widespread popularity, arguments and conclusions are drawn from it in every domain, whether philosophical, intellectual or artistic, of which its author never dreamed.

In the beginning, a fact of experience and of internal observation, time, such as it has been defined by philosophers (hence the contradictions and conflicts to which they give rise), has no connection with actual duration, *the immediate fact of consciousness*, as it is perceived by us. In this duration, which is the only real duration, states of mind succeed each other uninterruptedly and are dovetailed into each other without any break of continuity. Their advance is like the flow of a river, the waters of which are in constant motion. This duration, as it is presented by internal observation, has no connection with time, as conceived by the philosophers, the latter, owing to the very fact that it can be measured, being really *nothing else than space*.

When one of us writes : "This moment seemed a hundred years to me," he merely gives expression in his own way to the fundamental and essential principle of Bergsonian doctrine. That minute which he has just lived can, on account of the intensity of his mental states and the rapidity with which they are unfolded, actually be longer than those which preceded or followed it. This amounts to saying that it cannot be measured by the movements of the minute-hand on the face of a watch.

The drowning man, who at the moment of losing consciousness sees again all the chief events of his life in a few moments, is not the victim of a mere illusion. Thus Dostoiewsky tells us that when, after the Decembrist plot, he was conducted to the execution ground and was expecting to be hanged in a few seconds, he was able in two or three minutes to recapitulate lengthy episodes in his life.

360

THE PUBLIC MIND

From this initial fact the most important deductions are made. If the problem of liberty, for instance, seems insoluble to philosophers, it is because they started on a false assumption by confusing the real duration of the soul with apparent duration. The latter, being but the external and frequently inaccurate projection of the former, does not seem to have escaped the rigorous determinism ruling everything belonging to the domain of extension. But this is by no means the case with the former.

In *Matter and Memory*, his second work, Bergson continues the development of his system, and discusses the great question of the connection between soul and body. *Creative Evolution*, which is the climax of his investigations, enlarges the problem and applies it to the universe as a whole, showing the relations between inanimate matter on the one hand and the creative principle of life on the other.

A style at once precise and clear, and at the same time possessed of marvellous facility, in which the most subtle shades always find exact expression and the thought is materialised in the most concrete and vivid forms, the outcome, as it were, of an uninterrupted flow of inspiration, greatly facilitated the spread of this doctrine. Only those who have attended the master's lectures can have any idea of the fervour and enthusiasm with which his teaching was received. The young men who listened to him might have said of him what Alcibiades said of Socrates : " When I hear him, the heart within me leaps higher than that of a corybant ! "

At first known only to his disciples, who spread and propagated them like a regular gospel, these Bergsonian ideas quickly reached the public at large. Suddenly they became the fashion, for even matters of the intellect do not escape this fate. In a day Bergson became a celebrity. The popularity of his doctrine marks, in the domain of ideas, a clear break between the generation which knew the war of 1870 and those who reached man's estate towards the end of the century. Taine and Renan had no more influence over them than Kant and Cousin and their academic successors.

In literature the days of naturalism as well as of Parnassian poetry are ended, for ever ended. The new generation requires less stereotyped and more animated and spontaneous forms of thought and art.

Literature and Politics. The most striking feature of the modern literary movement is the abundance and variety of its output. The circulation and cheapness of books has greatly increased both the number of readers and of writers. The profession of a man of letters, who lives by his pen, is becoming more and more common, and the war has only served to increase the need for reading and for producing books to be read.

Literature and politics have ever more and more points in common. When a great crisis, like the Dreyfus case, arouses the passions and shakes the soul of a nation, literary men, intellectuals and savants, take part in the battle.

If one examines the fifty years following the war of 1870 and tries to discern a few general tendencies, one finds that the literary movement as a whole followed more or less the curve of the philosophic movement, and the evolution of opinions and ideas.

After the naturalistic novel, of which the form was far too cut and dried, a strong reaction took place. The new generation enthusiastically burnt what their predecessors had adored. To those who reached man's estate shortly before the war, Zola already seemed terribly old-fashioned. A clear break had occurred similar in every way to that which, as we have already seen, took place in the domain of philosophic evolution when the ideas of Bergson supplanted those of Renan and Taine.

The revival of spiritualism and of religious feeling, the exaltation of moral forces, and the feeling of confidence in the power and destiny of France, of which there was a great outburst at the time of deep national trial during the war, proceed from the same causes.

The language and literature of France still continue to pervade the world. But they are met by rivals who become **The Spread of French Culture.** every day more numerous and more powerful. The supremacy they enjoyed in the eighteenth century is now contested, not because their capacity to spread has diminished, but merely because that of their rivals has increased.

362

THE PUBLIC MIND

The French-speaking countries, France, Belgium and Switzerland, have a population of barely fifty million inhabitants.

The English-speaking countries, America, England, the Colonies and the Far East, have a population of almost two hundred millions, that is to say, four times as great.

The German-speaking countries, Germany and Austria, and a part of Czecho-Slovakia and of Hungary, have over seventy millions.

Spanish, which is spoken in the whole of South America and Mexico, is the language of a larger number of people than French is.

Italian runs French very close.

Thus, if numbers alone are taken into account, France occupies only the fourth place.

At the same time it must be remembered—and this is a very important consideration—that among foreigners, and especially among the Latin nations, Spain and Italy, nearly every educated person speaks French, or at all events knows enough of the language to read French newspapers, reviews and books. And thus the intellectual influence of France is greatly increased, and she should see to it that it does not grow less, for it provides one of the principal elements of her moral prestige in the world. Throughout the East, France, during the last twenty-five years, has gained ground. The same applies to Latin America. Progress has been less obvious in the United States on account of the colossal difficulties with which the spread of the French language is met in a country made up of all kinds of races, and where the élite, the old governing classes, are swamped by the new arrivals.

CONCLUSION

FRANCE came out of the Great War with an increase of territory and an improved morale, having given to the world proof of her energy and powers of endurance. But the flower of her youth, one million five hundred thousand young men, not to mention the sick and the wounded, had been mown down on the field of battle. It was a terrible loss, the effects of which are likely to make themselves felt for a long time to come, if not for ever. The material damage she suffered was on a similar scale. Several years of hostilities, the unlimited expenditure which had to be met if the country was not to perish, the loss of a huge amount of capital invested abroad in Russia, Austria-Hungary and Turkey, etc., made a big hole in the wealth of the nation.

In order to raise all this money, which was spent without stint and often even wasted, it was necessary to have recourse to credit and to raise loans both at home and abroad. Thus the National Debt rose from year to year to terrifying dimensions. The foreign debts might, one would have thought, have been settled at the time of the peace treaty, by debiting them to the Allied account against Germany. But this was not done, and they became a fresh burden.

Weighed down beneath a load of indebtedness to her own and foreign countries, it was only natural that France should have shown herself somewhat exhausted by the burden. Four years of war, during which economic considerations had gone by the board, had got the State as well as individuals into bad habits which it was difficult to break when hostilities came to an end. The State, having lived for all that time on credit and loans, did not immediately abandon these practices. All the post-war Budgets showed a deficit. As Germany, on the other hand, who was not paying what she should have paid, the French State had to shoulder the task of restoring the devastated regions

364

CONCLUSION

in her stead. In addition to the regular Budget, therefore, another was drawn up, the amount of which was supposed to be recoverable, in which thousands of millions were swallowed up.

The deficit, the abuse of loans, which the more they increased in number the more difficult they became to raise, the growth in the use of paper money, were all causes contributing to the rapid depreciation of the franc. As is the case in every country where the currency is debased in this way, it was the middle . classes who were the greatest sufferers.

Thus a profound upheaval and transformation took place in the distribution of wealth, greater even than that which had followed the Revolution of 1789 and the sale of the national property. A little while ago, when a case came on in a country court in which a cheesemonger's assistant was suing his master, the president of the court asked the man, " What is your yearly salary ? " The latter, who was dressed in a blouse, answered, " Twenty thousand francs." At this the president exclaimed in surprise, " Then you earn a good deal more than I do."

This is a typical example showing the magnitude of the changes that have been brought about.

The financial and social crisis, moreover, was accompanied by a political crisis.

In order to secure the prosperity of the country and enable it to bear its terrible burdens, it was necessary to restore order in places where the war and post-war conditions had intro- duced disorder, that is to say, to reorganise the administration and institute a methodical system of taxation.

This was a formidable undertaking. The financial question alone was sufficient to make the bravest blanch. How was it possible, whilst securing for the State the funds necessary for the working of the services, to raise sufficient money to redeem the colossal national and foreign debt ?

For this task a strong Government was required, one that was certain of the morrow, endowed with continuity of vision, and free, when once it had conceived a vast and comprehensive programme, to carry it out at its leisure. But the parliamentary system as it is habitually worked in France makes a Government of this kind difficult, if not impossible.

Such a system is acceptable at ordinary times, when long years

365

of peace have created a superabundance of wealth in the country, when taxation is light and the Budget easily balanced.

But as soon as any violent crisis supervenes, the system no longer works. It has to be changed, *de facto* if not *de jure*. During the first part of the war Parliament was, so to speak, put under lock and key. The executive power in conjunction with the generalissimo was sole master and decided everything. But when this period was over, coalition Ministries were formed in order to impose a truce upon party strife.

As the post-war difficulties were just as great as those of the war itself, it was necessary to have recourse to more or less analogous measures.

But these obstacles, however great they may be, are not such that a well-balanced France, with all the wealth of her soil, the industry and hard work of her people, and her large and flourishing colonies, will not succeed in surmounting them.

A factor which makes the situation full of hope is to be found in the elasticity of the race which enables it, at the most critical moments, to recover and pull itself together when it is on the edge of the abyss. This is what has been termed the *miracle of France*, and it has shown itself at various times in her history.

If we wish to sum up the Third Republic as a whole, and its work both at home and abroad, the best way is to examine it during the period between the two wars, from the moment of its inception to the time when it reached its zenith.

The mistakes of which the Imperial Government had been guilty left its successor a terrible heritage—war, invasion and loss, and, moreover, an indemnity of five milliards, a huge sum for that period, the loss of two fair provinces, the Commune, which was the direct result of the war, in short a France very much impoverished both materially and morally.

Fifty years later this same country was able to bear without flinching for four years the most murderous war in her whole history, waged against an adversary far stronger than any of those—Charles V, Philip II, the House of Austria and England —with whom she had had to cross swords in the past.

Through her efforts in every domain, both military and economic, thanks to the skill of her leaders and the heroism of her soldiers, as well as to the alliances she had succeeded in

CONCLUSION

forming, she rose triumphant from this trial in which her very existence was at stake. A system which, starting from a signal defeat, results in a no less signal victory, cannot be so very bad.

This system has had at least this much in its favour—and it is a quality by which the power and virtue of all human achievement is measured—it was capable of lasting.

Compared with those which had preceded it after the Revolution, its superiority in this respect is indisputable. The First Empire lasted ten years (May 1804 to April 1814); the second eighteen; the Restoration (Louis XVIII and Charles X) fifteen; Louis Philippe, eighteen. The Third Republic is in its fifty-fifth year, and still seems hale and hearty.

In the period between the two wars it has (with the exception of the Commune, for which it would be unjust to hold it responsible) secured peace and prosperity. Even at the most critical moments, such as occurred at the time of the Boulanger episode, the Panama scandal and the Dreyfus case, law and order were never in danger. These crises seem trifles compared with the endless series of risings and strikes that took place under the July monarchy, for example. The Napoleonic Governments undoubtedly knew how to preserve order in the streets, but they only did so by the use of force, of which the inevitable counterpart is the destruction of public liberty.

But France, who loves liberty, could ill brook being deprived of it. It therefore became indispensable to provide her with a counter-irritant outside ; hence a whole series of wars which, in the long run, ended in catastrophe.

Thanks to this tranquillity and peace lasting almost half a century, the country, having free scope for her traditional qualities of work, industry and thrift, accumulated fresh wealth. When one speaks of the pleasure and ease of life towards the end of the Second Empire, it must also be confessed that this pleasure and ease were quite as great during the years that preceded the Great War. Comfort and well-being were more widespread. The growth of democracy, the advent of a new class of leaders, the slow and uninterrupted rise of new social strata took place without trouble or disorder. The system, which was supple and elastic, accommodated itself to this change.

367

Even the rise of Socialism (which is of the greatest importance) did not succeed in disturbing this equilibrium.

If we turn from France herself to her relation to the outside world, the results are even more remarkable. In 1870, the diplomacy of the Empire had left her without a single ally. Bismarck was able to plunder and despoil her as he pleased without anyone in Europe raising a finger.

In 1914, from the first hour of the conflict, England was by her side as well as Belgium. Italy, although she was a member of the Triple Alliance, immediately declared her neutrality, whilst awaiting an early opportunity for joining France. The same was the case with Roumania. The situation was completely reversed. It was Germany and not France who, from the diplomatic point of view, found herself in a very awkward position.

These alliances and friendships, of which France is the beneficiary, were the outcome of a reasonable and prudent foreign policy carried out for many years with a continuity of plan which many a monarchy might well envy the Republic. Take Jonesco, who, one of the most intelligent of modern statesmen, once described to us a curious interview he had, about the year 1900, with von Aerenthal, the Austrian Minister for Foreign Affairs. They were discussing European politics, and von Aerenthal said quite openly, " What has happened in France during the last twenty years has upset all my ideas on the subject of republican diplomacy. I had always believed, and I was not the only one to do so, that a Republic was incapable of having a foreign policy worthy of the name. But France is contradicting this idea in the most brilliant manner."

There was the preparation, formation and maintenance of the Russian alliance, which, in view of the radical opposition between the systems of Government of the two countries, seemed a *tour de force*, a veritable impossibility.

This was followed by the *Entente* with England, which also presented difficulties which seemed insurmountable. On every occasion during the course of French history, in the seventeenth and eighteenth centuries, when France, who was a great naval Power, had wanted to win a colonial empire, she had found England in her path. A conflict ensued in which the latter,

CONCLUSION

who was freer than France from continental entanglements, had inevitably gained the upper hand. Hence the loss of almost all the French colonies.

But the Third Republic conquered in every part of the globe, in Africa and in Asia, a vast empire, in comparison with which the colonial possessions of the preceding centuries were mere trifles. England, it is true, did not look kindly upon this achievement. But in spite of an instinctive antagonism, a rupture was avoided. France, who became badly entangled at Fashoda, had the wisdom to withdraw. A few years later, under the guidance of remarkable leaders, whom she had the good sense to maintain in power—Delcassé (for seven years Minister for Foreign Affairs), the two Cambons, and Barrère, she succeeded in coming to an understanding with her hereditary foe, and, without the sacrifice of any essential interests, reaching a settlement of all the colonial disputes.

This *Entente*, a unique event in French history, soon went beyond its original limits. It spread from the sphere of colonial to that of European politics. It laid the way for the companionship in arms of 1914.

The Third Republic in thus succeeding in the conquest for France of a vast and flourishing empire which embraced Tunisia and Morocco, the indispensable bastions of her ancient possessions in Algeria, West Africa and Equatorial Africa, Madagascar and Indo-China, which together contain a far larger population than the mother country, and that without embroiling itself, but quite the contrary, with countries like England, Italy and Spain, who might have taken umbrage at this aggrandisement, and without, on the other hand, sacrificing any of the requirements of its European policy, solved a problem and overcame a difficulty which the Governments of the *ancien régime* had been incapable of doing. Under the monarchy a just balance was never established between the European and the colonial policy of France, the latter being always deliberately sacrificed to the former.

The Republic has been reproached with having made inadequate military preparations in view of the conflict with Germany which, after the Agadir incident, must have seemed inevitable to every careful observer. This criticism is not altogether devoid of justification. The material preparations, especially those

B B

connected with the heavy artillery, certainly presented lamentable deficiencies. But it would be exaggerated and unjust to over-emphasise the importance of this. On the whole—and the results proved it—the army, as it had been prepared by the Government, showed itself entirely competent for its task.

The reproaches regarding the instability of the Government, with the various consequences this involved—bad administration, malversation of the public funds, etc., etc.—are better justified. At times of crisis these defects become glaring. But here, as elsewhere, the capacity for recovery almost always sees to it that the acuteness of the malady itself produces its own remedy. When the situation becomes desperate, the system, together with all the abuses it entails, is set aside for a certain length of time.

The system is no doubt capable of improvement. But as it was able, without overmuch inconvenience, to adapt itself to the difficulties of the war, why should it not succeed in overcoming those that arise after the war?

In certain respects it is extremely adaptable. And this is perhaps one of its chief merits. As in any case France has nothing else to put in its place, it is towards the realisation of these improvements that her citizens should strive with all the energy they possess.

INDEX

INDEX

cose attitude of, 267, 268, 269, 272;
strained relations with Roumania,
273; her ultimatum to Serbia, 278,
280, 281, 282, 283, 284, 296; urged
to meet Italy's demands, 329; 363,
364, 366
Austrian Empire, the, composition of,
240, 241
Aviation, 349, 350
Axar, 151
Aymes, Lieutenant, 153

Bachi-Bouzouks, 115
Bac Lé, 162
Bac-Ninh, 162
Baghirmi, 156, 158
Bahr-el-Ghazal, 157, 158
Balearic Isles, 138
Balkan Wars, 264, 265
Balkans, the, 119, 121; Austrian
intrigues in, 242; 243, 245, 246,
248, 249, 250, 262, 265, 266, 272;
England uninterested in, 292
Baltic Provinces, 234
Balzac, 348
Bamako, 145, 146
Banat, the, 241, 330
Bangkok, 164
Bapaume, 17
Bardo, Treaty of, 143, 144
Bardoux, 97
Barodet, election of, 52, 53
Barrère, Camille, 120, 225, 226, 328;
his Convention with Italy, 235;
247
Barrès, Maurice, 194
Barroua, 149
Barthou, Louis, 259, 260
Battenberg, Alexander of, 121; de-
position of, 244
Bavaria, 291
Bazaine, character of, 17; his parleys
with Bismarck, 18; trial of, 61–63
Beaconsfield, Lord, 142, 338
Beaune-la-Rolande, 16
Beaurepaire, Quesnay de, 19
Bedouins, the, 192
Béhanzin, King of Dahomey, 147, 149,
153
Beirut, case of consul-general in, 19;
167
Belfort, 16; returned to France, 26,
28
Belgians, King of the, and the Kaiser,
261

Belgium, 287; alleged French viola-
tion of, 291; violation of, by
Germany, 293, 294, 296; 301, 302,
307, 323; the creation of England,
341; 363, 368
Belgrade, 121, 242, 248, 250; Austrian
Minister leaves, 282
Bengowski, Count, proclaims himself
King of Madagascar, 166
Benin, Bight of, 147
Beni Ounif, 141
Benue, 150, 155
Berchtold, Count, 250, 272, 273, 276,
277
Bergeret, 38
Bergson, his works and doctrines,
359, 360, 361, 362
Berlin, Conference of, 146, 149
Berlin, Congress of, 110, 113, 116, 142,
240, 337
Berlin, meeting of the three Emperors
in, 110; 113, 119, 122, 142, 226;
panic in, 309; revolution in, 324
Berlin, Treaty of, 154
Berne, 226
Bernstorff, Count, 333
Bertrand, Louis, 138
Bethmann-Hollweg, his offer to Eng-
land, 287, 292; astonished at atti-
tude of England, 296; 333
Beys, the, of Tunisia, 141, 143
Béziers, 348
Bienvenu-Martin, 280
Binger, explores the Soudan, 147
Biskra, 139, 140
Bismarck, negotiates with Favre, 7, 8;
his Russian policy, 8, 9; his anxiety
to end the war, 10; his terms for
an armistice, 18; proclaims German
Empire, 19; and Thiers, 25, 26;
demands entry into Paris, 28; his
anxiety for French indemnity to be
paid, 51, 52; his *Kulturkampf*
against German Catholics, 67; aims
at Triple Alliance including Italy,
95; his psychology, 108; his policy
towards France, 110, 111; his conflict with Gortchakof, 113, 115; and
the Eastern Question, 116; and the
Triple Alliance, 117, 118; 121, 122;
his dismissal, 123; his colonial
policy, 135; commanded to release
Schnaebelé, 179; 224, 231, 238,
337, 368
Bizerte, 143

INDEX

INDEX

374

INDEX

INDEX

Faidherbe, 17; Governor of Senegal, 145, 146
Fallières, President, 214
Fashoda, 129; the, incident almost leads to war, 135; the French first to reach, 157; 221, 369
Faure, Félix, his sudden death, 204
Favre, Jules, announces capitulation of Sedan, 2; 3; negotiates with Bismarck, 7, 8
Ferdinand of Bulgaria, 121, 243, 244, 245; proclaimed Tsar, 245; 248, 266; joins Germany, 329
Fère-Champenoise, 308
Ferry, Jules, 3; at the Hôtel de Ville, 33; 87, 88, 89, 103; his educational reforms, 104, 105; his fall, 106; an empire builder, 134, 137, 171, 176; planned occupation of Tunisia, 141, 142; fall of his Ministry, 163; his unpopularity, 181; 225
Fez, 229, 230, 236
Figuig, Oasis of, 141
Finland, 238
Fismes, 310
Flanders, 317
Flatters, Colonel, murdered, 140
Flaubert, 356
Floquet, his Reform Bill, 185
Flourens, 4; leads the revolutionaries, 18, 33; death of, 38
Flourens, Foreign Minister, 178
Foch, his verdict on the war of 1870, 21, 23; his appreciation of Gambetta, 22; on the winning of battles, 26; on Bazaine, 63; 300, 304, 305, 308, 313, 315; Commander-in-Chief of Allied forces, 318; his character, 319; 320; takes the offensive, 321, 322; prepares for the Armistice, 323; 324, 337; demands the Rhine frontier, 340, 341
Fontane, Marius, 191
Foreign Legion, the, incident of the German deserters from, 236
Forgash, Count, advises war on Italy, 273
Formosa, 163, 168
Fortou, 71
Foureau–Lamy, mission, 140, 156
Fourneau, 155
Fournier, Frigate-Commander, 162
Fou-Tcheou, 163
France, Anatole, 241
Franceville, 154

Franchet d'Esperey, 304, 308
Francis I, 121, 245, 248
Francis-Joseph, Emperor of Austria, 118, 270, 273, 275, 276
Francis Salvator, Archduke, 275
Frankfort, Treaty of, 26, 108
Franz-Ferdinand, Archduke, 270; his morganatic marriage, 271, 272; murder of, 274, 275
Frederick, Prince, his opinion of his son, 224
Frederick II, 19
Freemasonry, 242
French Empire, the, 132
Freycinet, 97; description of, 98; his Ministry, 101; its weakness, 128; 176
Frohsdorf, description of, 47; 48
Fromentin, 139

Gabès, 143
Gabon, 129, 132, 153, 154, 155, 158
Gaiffier, Baron de, 295
Galicia, 241, 329
Gallieni, 134; in the Soudan, 146; in Madagascar, 169, 170; 263, 307
Gallifet, General, 204, 205; amuses Edward VII, 223
Gambetta, 3, 4, 6; a born leader, 10; his character and antecedents, 15; 20; admired by Foch, 22; 24, 26, 52; accuses Bazaine of treachery, 61; 68; a parliamentary strategist, 70; 75, 77, 80, 86, 87; proposes an income tax, 88; leader of Republican Party, 91; 92, 93; his moderation, 94; 98, 99; hated by Grévy, 100; President of the Chamber, 101; his Ministry, 106; 142, 176, 204, 206, 217; meets Edward VII, 222; 226
Gambia, 146
Garnier, Francis, 160; his death, 161
Genoyer, Lieutenant, 153
Gentil mission, 156
German Empire, proclamation of, 19
Germany, 7, 8; unification of, 9, 19; 10, 26, 51; her fear of isolation, 109; 110; her policy towards France, 111; intensive arming of, 112, 113; her desire for hegemony, 114; 117; forms Triple Alliance, 118; 119, 120, 121, 122, 124, 125; her cordial relations with Russia, 126; keeps the Cameroons, 155; 179, 221, 225; her policy in Morocco,

INDEX

230, 231, 234, 235, 236, 237, 262; 232, 238, 239, 252, 256; her armaments, 257, 258; 269, 280; her preconceived plan, 281; 282, 283; mobilisation of, 284, 285, 286; her offer to England, 287; her ultimatum to Russia, 288; declares war on Russia, 290; and on France, 291; her ultimatum to Belgium, 295; her central position, 299; her superiority in war material, 300; her plan of attack, 302; inaugurates submarine campaign, 317, 332, 333; collapse of, 324; wins Turkey to her side, 326; 338; bankruptcy of, 343; 363, 364, 368

Ghardaia, 139
Gibraltar, 234
Giesl, 282
Giffard, Pierre, 198
Giolitti, 267, 268
Gladstone, unfriendly to France, 8
Goeben, escape of the, 327
Gold Coast, 152
Goluchowski, Count, 241
Golz, von der, his tribute to Gambetta, 20
Goree, 132
Gortchakof, his jealousy of Bismarck, 110; his conflict with Bismarck, 113, 115; 338
Gouraud, Captain, 134, 150, 151
Government of National Defence, establishment of, 7
Grand Bassam, 145, 147
Grandmaison, Colonel de, 301
Grand Turk, the, 121
Gravelotte, 1
Greece, 248, 249, 329; joins the Allies, 330
Grévy, Albert, 193
Grévy, President, 53, 87; refuses to form Cabinet, 89; Republican candidate for Paris, 93; the Whiskered President, 100; 101, 106, 121, 176, 178, 179; his resignation, 181
Grey, Sir Edward, 237; his hesitation to enter the war, 283; 287, 291; his interviews with Paul Cambon, 292, 293; protests against violation of Belgium, 295
Guéchoff, 248, 249
Guesdists, 217
Guiana, 132
Guinea, 146, 147, 149, 151, 152

Guinea, Gulf of, 133
Guizot, his rivalry with Thiers, 25
Guliano, Marquis San, 267

Haifung, 161
Haig, Sir Douglas, 323
Hanoi, 161, 164
Hanotaux, 198
Harmand, Treaty of, 162
Harrach, Count, 274
Hébrard, Adrien, 176, 355
Heeringen, General von, 257
Henri, Colonel, his suicide, 203
Henry III, 32
Hentsch, Lieutenant-Colonel, responsible for German retreat from the Marne, 308
Hertz, Cornelius, 191, 192
Herzegovina, ceded to Austria, 116, 119; 240, 243, 245
Hindenburg, victorious at Tannenberg, 309
Hœtzendorff, General von, 273
Hoggar, 140
Hohenberg, Duchess of, wife of Franz-Ferdinand, 272; murder of, 274, 275
Holland, 324, 326
Holstein, Baron von, 231
Holy Alliance, the, 120
Hoskier, and the French loan to Russia, 122
Hourst, Lieutenant, 150
Hova, the, 166, 167, 169, 170
Hoyos, Count, 276
Hué, 162
Humber, Colonel, 148
Humbert, 134, 304
Humbert, King of Italy, 118
Hungary, 109, 110, 240, 338, 363, 364
Hung-Hoa, 162

India, 132, 134; cotton exports from, 152
Indian Ocean, 166
Indo-China, French expansion in, 160–166; 171, 263, 369
International African Society, 154
International Exhibition of 1889, 187
Ischl, 110
Ismail, his extravagance, 126; placed under European control, 127
Iswolsky, 237, 245, 249
Italians, in Tunisia, 145; defeated in Abyssinia, 157

INDEX

Italy, 9; unification of, 67; 95; and the Triple Alliance, 117, 118; and Abyssinia, 135; her interests in Tunis, 142; 226, 235; her Convention with France, 235; in Tripolitania, 247, 248; declares war against Turkey, 248; 267, 273; refuses to support Germany, 296, 297, 298; defeated at Caporetto, 316; joins the Allies, 328, 329; 333, 338, 368, 369
Ivory Coast, the, 145, 147, 149, 150, 151, 152, 155

Jacobins, the, 339
Jagow, his denial that Germany was mobilising, 286; 287
Japan, her war against Russia, 232, 233, 237; 298, 338, 339
Jaurès, a great Socialist leader, 217, 218; murdered, 289
Jena, Battle of, 306
Jerome, Prince, 102
Jesuits, the, dissolution of their Order, 105, 206
Jews, the, in Central Europe, 119; in Tunisia, 145; in Hungary, 241
Joalland–Meynier mission, 156
Joffre, 134, 149; urges Government to mobilise, 285, 288; appreciation of, 303, 304; 305, 307, 308; superseded, 312, 313, 315, 318
Jonnart, 134; in Algeria, 138, 330

Kabylie, 176; insurrection of, 136
Kairouan, 143, 144
Kaiser, the, William II, his landing at Tangier, 112, 179, 231, 252; 117; his accession, 123; his friendly relations with the Tsar, 126; his dislike of Edward VII, 223; meets the Tsar at Björkö, 238; 258, 261; decides for war, 261; tries to ingratiate himself with Franz-Ferdinand, 272; receives news of the Serajevo crime, 275; decides on war against Serbia, 276; 286, 295; appeals to the King of Italy, 297; flees to Holland, 324; 333
Kanem, 158
Kant, 361
Karachi, 350
Kautsky, 295
Kayes, 145, 152
Kelung, 163

Kerensky, 6
Ket, 143
Keta, 146
Khedive, the, 157
Khroumirs, the, rebellion of, 142, 143
Kiderlen-Waechter, 253, 254
Kinchassa, 160
Kitchener, defeats the Mahdi, 157; at Fashoda, 158
Kluck, von, his mistake in 1914, 20; his rapid advance, 306, 307; his retreat, 307, 308
Konakry, 147
Kong, 147, 150
Konopicht, 271; the conversations of, 272
Kordofan, 158
Kossovo, 273
Kronstadt, visit of French fleet to, 124
Ksourians, 139
Kulturkampf, Bismarck and his, against the German Catholics, 67
Kwangchow-wan, 165

Laborde, Jean, 166
Lachaux, defends Bazaine, 62
Ladmirault, 38
La Fosse-à-l'Eau, 305
Lancken, Baron, 255
Lancrenon, 156
Langson, 163
Languedoc, 136
Lanrezac, General, 302, 305
Lansdowne, Lord, 224, 237
Laos, 163; occupied by France, 164; 165
Larache, 227
Larba, the, 139
Largeau, Colonel, 156
Lawyers, in the Government, 352, 353
League of Nations, the, President Wilson's idea of, 336; 342
League of Patriots, 178, 184, 185
Leblois, 200
Le Bourget, 13
Lecomte, arrest of, 32; assassination of, 34
Lee, Sir Sidney, 223
Legitimists, the, 24, 45; a threat to peace, 66; represented by the clerical party, 67; their policy of despair, 70; support the Republicans, 71, 72, 77; responsible for the clerical agitation, 95; give their allegiance to Don Carlos, 102

378

INDEX

Le Myre de Villers, 167
Lenfant, 156
Lenin, 316
Leo XIII, Pope, 187, 209
Leopold II of Belgium, 154
Lesseps, Charles de, and the Panama scandal, 191, 194
Lesseps, Ferdinand de, and the Panama scandal, 189, 190, 191, 194
Liao-Yang, 233
Liberia, 146
Libreville, 153
Lichnowsky, Prince, 276, 287
Limon Bay, 189
Lloyd George, 224, 256; opposed to intervention, 291, 292; 341
Loeffler, 156
London, 225; Convention of, 158
Longwy, 16, 290
Lorraine, 8, 26, 258, 263, 305, 323, 324; returned to France, 340; triumphant entry of French into, 344
Loubet, President, 204, 209, 214
Louis XIV, 188
Louis XV, 166
Louis XVIII, 42, 367
Louis Philippe, his confidence in Thiers, 25; 32; his foolish obstinacy, 42; 43, 55, 244, 367
Low Countries, the, 340
Luang Prabang, 164
Ludendorff, 309; prepares to retreat, 313; his offensives, 317; 319; his mistakes, 320; 321, 322
Luxemburg, invaded by Germans, 290; 294, 296, 305
Lyautey, 134, 169, 170; in Morocco, 263, 264
Lyons, 78

Macedonia, 242; partition of, 248, 249; 265
Macine, 148
MacMahon, surrender of, 1, 9; made Commander-in-Chief, 38; 39; elected President, 53; above all a soldier, 55; refuses to see Chambord, 61, 65; 62, 71, 75, 80, 91; his temporising policy, 86; 89; appoints a Royalist Ministry, 90; his electoral campaign against the Radicals, 92, 93; his vacillations, 95, 96; resignation of, 99; 161
Madagascar, the French in, 166–170; 227, 263

Madrid, Conference of, 232
Mahdi, the, defeat of, 157
Majunga, 167, 168
Makoko, King, 154
Manchuria, 233
Manchurian war, 119
Mangin, 134, 157, 158, 304, 321
Marais de Saint-Gond, 308
Marchand, reaches Fashoda, 129; at Fashoda, 157, 158
Marche, Lieutenant, 153
Marne, the, Battle of, 304, 307, 308, 309, 310, 313, 315; retreat from, 305
Marrakesh, 235
Marsa, Treaty of, 144
Marseilles, 78, 86
Marx, Karl, 29
Massalit, Sultan of, 156
Matadi, 160
Mauchamp, Dr., 235
Maud'huy, 304
Maunoury, General, 305; his offensive, 307, 308
Mauritania, 151
Mauritius, 166
Mazarin, 32
Meaux, Vicomte de, 86
Meharists, the Corps of, 141
Mehemet Ali, 126
Meking, 160, 163, 164
Meknes, 236
Méline, 204
Mellinet, General, 3
Me-Nam, River, 164
Menelik, defeats Italians, 157
Menou, 31
Mercier, General, 168, 198
Messimy, Monsieur, 285, 288
Metz, 7; capitulation of, 17, 18; 20, 26, 178
Meuse, River, 302, 311
Mexico, 363
Mézières, 322
Michel, Louise, 183
Milanovitch, 248
Military service, three-years system of, restored in France, 259, 260
Millerand, 204, 212, 216, 217
Minduli, 160
Mingou, Lake, 140
Minot, Admiral, 167
Miquelon, 132
Miramar, 271
Mizon, Lieutenant, 150, 155

379

INDEX

Moll, 156

Moltke, von, 261; stops in his headquarters, 305, 308; 306

Monteil, Colonel, 149, 150, 155

Montenegro, 248, 249; declares war on Turkey, 250

Montenegro, King of, 250, 251

Morocco, 130, 132, 133, 136, 140, 141, 144, 151, 169, 171, 227; England's agreement with France concerning, 227; 228; a mediæval country, 229; 230, 231, 232, 234; French penetration in, 235, 236; 247; 252, 253, 255; agreement with Germany regarding, 256; organisation of the French protectorate in, 262, 263, 264; 369

Moscow, 234

Mossi, 147

Motor traffic, growth of, 346, 347

Moulay Hafid, Sultan of Morocco, 236; abdication of, 262

Moulay Hassan, Sultan of Morocco, 229

Moulay Idriss, 151

Moulay Ioussef, Sultan of Morocco, 262

Mukden, 233

Müller, Admiral, 275

Mungo Park, 148

Murat, 31

Murça, 138

Mussulmans in Tunisia, 145

Nancy, 194, 305

Nantes, 211

Napoleon Bonaparte, his memoir on the seizing of the guns, 31; severity of his rule, 42; 43, 300, 301; on the qualities of a great general, 303; 306

Napoleon III, a prisoner, 1; his blundering diplomacy, 9; a bad judge of men, 17; 25, 43, 63; and Cochin-China, 164

Naquet, Senator, 182, 183

Narbonne, 348

National Debt, the, 364

National Guard, seize the guns, 30

Négrier, General de, 163

New Caledonia, 132

Newfoundland, 227

New Hebrides, 227

Nicolas-Nicolaievitch, 331

Nicolas II, Tsar, signs constitutional manifesto, 234; meets the Kaiser at Björkö, 238; his weakness, 331; his abdication, 332

Niger, the, 133, 140, 145, 146, 147, 148, 149, 150, 151, 152, 155

Nigeria, 149, 150

Nigeria Company, 150

Nile, the, 126, 129, 155, 156, 157

Nivelle, appointed generalissimo, 313; 314

Nossi Bé, 167

Noyon, 313

Nuremberg, the bombs of, 291

Obrenovitch dynasty, 121

Oceania, 132

Ogowé, 153, 154

Omsk, 350

Oran, 138, 139, 140, 263

Orleanists, the, 24, 45, 46, 56; demand concessions of the Comte de Chambord, 56, 57

Orleans, recaptured and lost again, 16

Ouaghadougou, 147

Ouargla, 139; occupation of, 140

Ouidah, 147

Oujda, 171, 235, 236

Ouled Sidi Cheik, insurrection of the, 140

Pagny-sur-Moselle, 178

Painlevé, 201

Palestine, 338

Palikao, General de, announces capitulation of Sedan, 2

Panama scandal, 189–195; 236, 367

Paris, Comte de, his offer to become reconciled to the Comte de Chambord, 48; does not support MacMahon, 96; 177

Paris, the Congress of, 337, 338

Paris, the source of revolution, 5; siege of, 12 ff.; Prussians enter, 28; second siege of, 38; 78, 83, 86; Exhibition of 1878, 136; 248; changed appearance of, 350

Pas de Calais, 293

Patchich, 278

Patrimonio, Consul-General, 167

Paul I, Tsar, 331

Paulus, 177

Pechihli, 162, 163

Peking, 163

Pelletan, Camille, Naval Minister, 210

380

INDEX

INDEX

INDEX

INDEX

Date Due

MAR 1 8 '54		
MAR 2 4 '54		
APR 15		
APR 2 2 '57		
APR 10		
OCT 1 5 '65		
JAN 4		
MAR 2 5		
APR 3 '67		
DEC 2 3 1967		
NOV 2 3 197		
DEC 3 1972		
⊕		